What Educators Have to Say About Riane Eisler's *Tomorrow's Children: A Blueprint for Partnership Education in the 21st Century*

"At a time when advice to 'be realistic' is heard as a call to lower one's sights and lessen one's expectations, *Tomorrow's Children* shows us how utopian our futures could really be."

—Harry Brod
University of Northern Iowa

"A rich legacy and practical guidebook for creating relevant education for future generations. The partnership model is a catalyst for educational transformation, offering exceptional knowledge, skills, vision, and tools to create a better future."

—Angeles Arrien
cultural anthropologist and author of **The Four-Fold Way** *and* **Signs of Life**

"A rich historical and cross-cultural tapestry that will inform and delight teachers, parents, and all those active in building a better life for "tomorrow's children.""

—George Gerbner
professor of communications, Temple University

"A visionary guidebook for using education as the DNA of society to promote human survival in the new millennium. . . . Dr. Eisler articulates the partnership content, processes, and structures that are essential for the social transformation necessary for humans to survive and thrive in the future."

—Chuck Estin, Ph.D.
high school science teacher and educational consultant

"*Tomorrow's Children* is timely, inspirational, and a very valuable contribution for our children, our educators, and our planet."

—Sultana Parvanta, Ph.D.
director of the California Leadership Training Center
Communities In Schools, Inc.

"Timely and timeless—*Tomorrow's Children* brings Riane Eisler's powerful 'partnership' model to the classroom where it can inspire teachers now and benefit children for generations."

—Parker Page
President, Children's Television Resource & Education Center

"With *Tomorrow's Children*, Riane Eisler makes another huge contribution to human efforts to find a better way. . . . This book, and the thinking behind it . . . opens many new paths for everyone who wants to prepare our children to envision and create a more rewarding world for all of us."

—Nancy Gruver
co-director, New Moon Publishing
New Moon: The Magazine for Girls and Their Dreams

"Eisler's new work inspires, intrigues, and enthralls. Transformative, progressive, and practical, it's a great guide for educators interested in helping to change the direction of our planet."

—Joe Szwaja
teacher/counselor

"*Tomorrow's Children* is a wonderful guide for teachers and parents who are concerned about preparing young people to build a fairer society. . . . Because the book speaks directly to a variety of academic disciplines, teachers will easily be able to identify how it connects with the work they do day-to-day."

—Christine Sleeter, Ph.D.
professor of multicultural education,
California State University, Monterey Bay

"Riane Eisler's *Tomorrow's Children* puts the magic back into the biology and study of life and its evolution."

—Lyle Rudensey
high school teacher

"I recommend this book as a MUST for all educators, parents, and individuals who passionately believe in the possibility of a partnership society."

—Sr. Ruthmary Powers, H.M., Ph.D.
president, Sisters of the Humility of Mary

"*Tomorrow's Children* provides an inspirational, highly creative partnership model for educating ourselves and future citizens of the planet. . . . A book for the 21st century that reweaves history and culture into new partnership patterns."

—Carolyn Merchant
professor of environmental history, philosophy, and
ethics, University of California, Berkeley

Tomorrow's Children

Tomorrow's Children

Children

A Blueprint for Partnership Education in the 21st Century

Riane Eisler

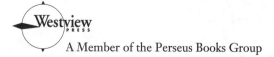

Westview
PRESS
A Member of the Perseus Books Group

Published in 2000 in the United States of America by Westview Press, 5500 Central Avenue, Boulder, Colorado 80301-2877, and in the United Kingdom by Westview Press, 12 Hid's Copse Road, Cumnor Hill, Oxford OX2 9JJ

Find us on the World Wide Web at www.westviewpress.com

Library of Congress Cataloging-in-Publication Data
Eisler, Riane Tennenhaus.
    Tomorrow's children : a blueprint for partnership education in the 21st century / Riane Eisler.
        p.   cm.
    Includes bibliographical references (p.) and index.
    ISBN 0-8133-9040-0
    1. Education, Humanistic—United States.   2. Critical pedagogy—
United States.   3. Affective education—United States.
4. Educational change—United States.   I. Title.
LC1023.E57   2000
370.11'5—dc21   99-41892
                                                                                                                        CIP

Design by Heather Hutchison

The paper used in this publication meets the requirements of the American National Standard for Permanence of Paper for Printed Library Materials Z39.48-1984.

10   9   8   7   6   5   4   3   2

To my children and grandchildren

Contents

ADDITIONAL RESOURCES

Foreword

Nel Noddings

Lee L. Jacks Professor of Child Education,
Stanford University

In *Tomorrow's Children*, Riane Eisler has given us a picture of how education might function in the 21st century. She argues persuasively that the adoption of a *partnership model* in both schools and the larger society is essential for human life to flourish. For too long, a *dominator model* has controlled most of the world's societies and, although it has been accompanied by a vast growth in technology, it has also induced violence, exploitation, and the denigration or neglect of a huge proportion of the population. Both partnership and dominator models recognize difference but, whereas the partnership model cherishes difference and actively works to form relationships that enrich individual lives and strengthen communities, the dominator model construes difference in terms of superiority and inferiority. Students need to understand how both models operate, but schools must adopt the partnership model.

Eisler recommends sweeping changes in both content and process. Drawing effectively on her highly successful earlier book, *The Chalice and the Blade*, she provides a wealth of material for a fully human study of history and science—a study that includes women's traditions as well as men's. She wants children to know that the partnership model has actually existed in some societies and that these societies exhibited a high level of cultural sophistication: advanced technologies, art, commerce, religion, and diplomacy. They were marked by peace and human flourishing. The dominator attitude is, thus, not necessary for progress and, indeed, it may endanger our survival. The *agon* of the Greeks must give way to the harmony of the Minoans. Struggle, conquest, and destruction must be supplanted by cooperation, mutual aid, and respect for creation.

Eisler would have children study both models, and she is careful to point out that pure models of either type have not existed. Teachers can help students to identify elements of the two models in the cultures they study and to analyze their effects on both individual lives and entire societies. Has our own society invested too heavily in the implements of destruction? Does it sufficiently value creation and the preservation of natural environments? Does it encourage both self-actualization and collective responsibility for the maintenance of communities? Students should find evidence to support their answers to such vital questions.

Eisler and I agree that schools should give children opportunities to study things that really matter. Not only should they learn about their own bodies and sexuality in positive terms, but they should also learn about love and commitment, about spirituality, and about self-regulation and life-planning. In my own work, I have recommended teaching themes of care: caring for self, for intimate others, for global others and strangers, for non-human life and the environment, for the human-made world and its incredible artifacts, and for ideas. Time spent in helping students to learn about matters of central importance to human flourishing should enhance the study of human life in all its fullness; they should not be set up as the point of life or used to distract students from what really matters to their own growth and happiness. *Tomorrow's Children* shows convincingly that large and important bodies of knowledge can be mastered as children tackle topics that matter in developing satisfying and useful lives.

The work that Riane Eisler sets out for educators is both fascinating and challenging. Like her, I see such a project as eminently reasonable and practical in a world that is learning to appreciate partnership, but I do not see many signs that education is encouraging this appreciation. The dominator model is not weakening in schools. Everywhere we hear more demands for control, standardization, and keener competition. When other-regarding comments are made, they are often cast in terms of granting others fair opportunities to compete in the well-established dominator model. Although it is clearly impossible, many policymakers seem to want everyone to have a fair chance at beating everyone else in a competition for the good life construed materially. When the contributions of Others are acknowledged, they are identified as contributions to the dominator model; challenges to it are, for the most part, omitted. When change is recommended, it is often described as "systemic," but that does not mean a change from dominator to partnership education. It means, to the contrary, a thorough overhaul directed at more control from top to bottom to preserve the highly competitive model already in place.

Countering this backward movement will not be easy. But *Tomorrow's Children* is an important book precisely because it provides a vision and some of the practical tools we need to meet this challenge. In that sense, it is a call to action, to preserve, to retain hope. As Emily Dickinson wrote, "Hope is the thing with feathers/That perches in the human soul." With Eisler, I hope that the vision she has put forward here can be realized. With her, I believe that human happiness, if not survival itself, depends on it.

Prologue

Education for the 21st Century

What will the world be like for tomorrow's children? When I look at my little two-year-old granddaughter's face, bright with wide-eyed curiosity and joyful expectation of love and life, I see wonderful possibilities. But when I look at the challenges she and her generation will inherit, I see that these possibilities will not be realized unless today's and tomorrow's children learn to live in more environmentally conscious, equitable, and peaceful ways.[1]

Today, young people often feel powerless to change the course of their lives, much less the course of the world around them. Many become immersed in the me-firstism and overmaterialism that permeates much of our mass culture, futilely seeking meaning and belonging in the latest fad or commercial offering. Some bury their pain and anger in drugs, gangs, and other destructive activities, unconscious and seemingly uncaring of the effect their actions have on themselves and others. A number become violent, under the thrall of hate-mongering or religious fanaticism, or simply because our video games, television, ads, and movies make violence seen normal and even fun. And the vast majority, including the young people who expect to get a decent job or go on to college to pursue a professional career, fail to see how what we do with our lives is both affected by, and affects, our cultural beliefs and social institutions.

There are many factors that contribute to all this. But there is one factor that can play a major role in providing young people with the understandings and skills to both live good lives and create a more sustainable, less violent, more equitable future: education.

For over two centuries, educational reformers such as Johann Pestalozzi, Maria Montessori, John Dewey, and Paolo Freire have called for an education that prepares us for democracy rather than authoritarianism and fosters ethical and caring relations.[2] Building on the work of these and other germinal educational thinkers, *Tomorrow's Children* proposes an expanded approach to educational reform that can help young people meet the unprecedented challenges of a world in which technology can either destroy us or free us to actualize our unique human capacities for creativity and caring.

I call this approach partnership education. It is an education to help children not only better navigate through our difficult times but also create a future orienting more to what in my study of cultural evolution I have identified as a partnership rather than dominator model.[3]

We are all familiar with these two models from our own lives. We know the pain, fear, and tension of relations based on domination and submission, on coercion and accommodation, of jockeying for control, of trying to manipulate and cajole when we are unable to express our real feelings and needs, of the miserable, awkward tug of war for that illusory moment of power rather than powerlessness, of our unfulfilled yearning for caring and mutuality, of all the misery, suffering, and lost lives and potentials that come from these kinds of relations. Most of us have also, at least intermittently, experienced another way of being, one where we feel safe and seen for who we truly are, where our essential humanity and that of others shines through, perhaps only for a little while, lifting our hearts and spirits, enfolding us in a sense that the world can after all be right, that we are valued and valuable.

But the partnership and dominator models not only describe individual relationships. As I will detail, they describe systems of belief and social structures that either nurture and support—or inhibit and undermine—equitable, democratic, nonviolent, and caring relations. Without an understanding of these configurations—and the kind of education that creates and replicates each—we unwittingly reinforce structures and beliefs that maintain the inequitable, undemocratic, violent, and uncaring relations which breed pathologies that afflict and distort the human spirit and are today decimating our natural habitat.

Once we understand the cultural, social, and personal configurations of the partnership and dominator models, we can more effectively develop the educational methods, materials, and institutions that foster a less violent, more equitable, democratic, and sustainable future. We can also more effectively sort out what in existing educational approaches we want to retain and strengthen or leave behind.

The partnership framework outlined in this book offers the basic design for a new integrated primary and secondary education for the 21st century. This framework draws from my research over three decades, from my own teaching experiences, and from the work of educators at many levels.

Partnership education has three core interconnected components: partnership *process*, partnership *content*, and partnership *structure*.

Partnership process is about *how* we learn and teach. It applies the guiding template of the partnership model to educational *methods* and *techniques*. Are each child's intelligences and capabilities treated as unique gifts to be nurtured and developed? Do students have a real stake in their education so that their innate enthusiasm for learning is not dampened? Do teachers act primarily as lesson-dispensers and controllers, or as mentors and facilitators? Is caring an integral part of teaching and learning? Are young people learning the teamwork needed for the postindustrial economy or must they continuously compete with each other? Are students offered the opportunity for both self-directed learning and peer teaching? In short, is educating children merely a matter of filling an "empty vessel," or are students and teachers partners in the adventure of learning?

Partnership content is *what* we learn and teach. It is the *educational curriculum*. Does the curriculum not only effectively teach students basic skills such as the three R's of reading, writing, and arithmetic but also model the life-skills they need to be competent and caring citizens, workers, parents, and community members? Are we telling young people to be responsible, kind, and nonviolent at the same time that the curriculum content celebrates male violence and conveys environmentally unsustainable and socially irresponsible messages? Does it present science in holistic, relevant ways? Does what is taught as important knowledge and truth include—not just as an add-on but as integral to what is learned—both the female and male halves of humanity as well as children of various races and ethnicities? Does it teach young people the difference between the partnership and dominator models as two basic human possibilities and the feasibility of creating a partnership way of life? Or, both overtly and covertly, is this presented as unrealistic in "the real world"? Does what young people are learning about "human nature" limit or expand human possibilities? In short, what view of ourselves, our world, and our roles and responsibilities in it are children taking away from their schooling?

Partnership structure is about *where* learning and teaching take place: what kind of *learning environment* we construct if we follow the partnership model. Is the structure of a school, classroom, and/or home school one of top-down authoritarian rankings, or is it a more democratic one? If it were diagrammed as an organizational chart, would decisions flow only from the top down and accountability only from the bottom up, or would there be interactive feedback loops? Are management structures flexible, so that leadership is encouraged at all organizational levels? Are there ways of involving parents and other community members? Do students, teachers, and other staff participate in school decisionmaking and rule setting? In short, is the learning environment organized in terms of hierarchies of domination ultimately backed up by fear, or is it a combination of horizontal linkings and hierarchies of actualization where power is used not to disempower others but, rather, to empower them?

As we will see, teachers all over the world are already working with some of these elements of partnership education. Good resources are available for moving toward both partnership process and structure. There are also good supplementary materials for teaching science in more holistic ways, for bringing information about women and various cultures into our schools, and for engendering greater consciousness about social and economic equity and our natural environment.

But still lacking, and urgently needed, is an integrated partnership curriculum that will not only help today's and tomorrow's children build healthy bodies, psyches, families, businesses, governments, and communities but also give them a clearer understanding of our human potential, our place in history, our relationship to nature, and our responsibility to future generations.

What I am interested in is systemic or long-term educational change. Certainly schools need the best new technologies if they are to prepare children for the future. But schools also need to help students look at the environmental, social, and economic challenges that they face in the 21st century from a partnership perspective.

The curriculum proposed in this book will make it possible for young people to more clearly understand our past, present, and the possibilities for our future. It integrates the practical and the theoretical and the sciences and the humanities. It brings science to life by placing it in the larger context of both the history of our planet and our species and our day-to-day lives. Because the social construction of the roles and relations of the female and male halves of humanity is central to either a partnership or dominator social configuration, unlike the traditional male-centered curricula, partnership education is gender-balanced. It integrates the history, needs, problems, and aspirations of *both* halves of humanity into what is taught as important knowledge and truth. Because in the partnership model difference is *not* automatically equated with inferiority or superiority, partnership education is multicultural. It offers a pluralistic perspective that includes peoples of all races and a variety of backgrounds, as well as the real-life drama of the animals and plants of the Earth we share. Since partnership education offers a systemic approach, environmental education is not an add-on but an integral part of the curriculum.

Through partnership education, young people will learn the dramatic story of our human adventure on this Earth against the backdrop of the need and prospects for a major cultural transformation. They will begin to see school as a place of exploration, a place to share feelings and ideas, an exciting community of educators, students, and parents working together to ensure that each child is recognized and valued, that the human spirit will be nurtured and grow. Above all, partnership education will help young people form visions of what *can* be and acquire the understandings and skills to make these visions come true.

The materials that follow offer resources for restructuring primary and secondary education that can be immediately put to use by teachers, parents, and students in public schools, in private schools, and in home schooling. These resources are also designed to be useful in universities and colleges, not only in education departments that offer teacher and school counselor education, but in all departments interested in teaching that more adequately addresses current needs and problems. *Tomorrow's Children* can further be useful for community-based study and action groups, both those with a direct interest in education and those concerned with personal development and positive social and environmental action.

In sum, although the focus of *Tomorrow's Children* is on primary and secondary education, it is for all who want to explore new frontiers and become more active co-creators of our future.

I want to close these brief opening remarks with an invitation. I want to invite not only parents, students, primary- and secondary-school teachers, university professors, and other educators, but also all those working for a better future, to become active partners in developing partnership education from the early years on. I want to invite you to use the materials offered in this book in your own teaching and learning as well as to develop replicable materials for others. These can be lesson plans or entire units to be incorporated into existing classes. They can be whole new courses, like those being developed through the Center for Partnership Studies in collaboration with a number of schools and universities for distribution through the Center website, bookstores, and other avenues.[4] They can even be curricula for an entire school. The goal is to gradually put together new partnership curricula for kindergarten to 12th grade and beyond.

Some of what I am proposing will create controversy. But without controversy there is no possibility for real change.

If enough of us are committed to personal and collective transformation—if together we keep moving forward, as Marian Wright Edelman wrote, "putting one foot ahead of the other, basking in the beauty of our children, in the chance to serve and engage in a struggle for a purpose higher than ourselves"[5]—we will succeed in laying the educational foundations for a safer, more livable, more loving world for tomorrow's children and generations still to come.

Riane Eisler

Acknowledgments

Many people have contributed to this book. Nel Noddings not only made invaluable suggestions but wrote her beautiful, much appreciated Foreword. Barbara Ardinger, Maj Britt Eagle, Chuck Estin, Lethea Erz, Bill Gladstone, Ruthmarie Hoffman, Del Jones, Rob Koegel, Raz M.J., Parker Page, Ruthmary Powers, Christine Sleeter, Joe Szwaja, and Gail Young reviewed the entire manuscript and made excellent contributions. George Gerbner, Marty Kirschner, Joshua Hornick, Sheila Mannix, Sharon Thomas, and Adrienne Zihlman, who read portions, were also extremely helpful. Herb Martin and Terri Wheeler contributed multicultural materials, and Patricia Cane and Steve Shafarman contributed materials for the discussion of somatic (bodily) learning.

John Mason's wonderful art and evocative graphs, photos, line drawings, and cartoons, together with Betty LaDuke's and Jane Evershed's splendid art and other images, have greatly enlivened the contents.

Many educational institutions and conferences—ranging from the Heartland Area Educational Agency, Montessori International, the Ross School, the University of California, Yale University, and the European Educational House International to Prescott College, the California Institute of Integral Studies, the Wilfrid Laurier University, the Mediterranean Women's Studies Institute, the United Nations University for Peace, and the University of Costa Rica—provided me the opportunity to explore the development of some of the ideas in this book over a period of ten years.

My editor at Westview Press, Catherine Murphy, provided invaluable help in honing these ideas for the final manuscript. I also want to thank Lisa Wigutoff, Christine Arden, Meegan Finnegan, Dave Tobey, and all the others at Westview Press who have worked on this book for their able assistance. My agent Ellen Levine and her associate Louise Quayle were, as always, not only supportive but indispensable.

My special thanks go to the Fetzer Foundation, especially Tom Callanan, who graciously offered me a grant to complete *Tomorrow's Children*, and Amy Milligan, who helped shepherd it through, as well as to

Wendy Grace, Michael Henry Honack, and Marion and Allan Hunt-Badiner, who, as members of the Board of the Center for Partnership Studies, supported this work.

Hannah Liebmann provided invaluable assistance at all stages of the writing and editing. Connie Fishman and Heather Peet not only transcribed many drafts but made useful suggestions. Karen Davis-Brown, Debra Lynne Edwards Skene, Leah Gowron, and Hyon Chu Yi helped with both the references and final revisions. I also received essential help from our local reference librarians, including Victor Bausch, Rosy Brewer, Diana Brown, Janet Cubbage, Lani Fremier, Doug Holtzman, Arlene Hess, Joe Johnson, Bridget McConnell, Steve Parker, Margaret Pelikan, Janis Rodman, and Halina Szczesiak.

David Loye, my partner in life, was, as always, a great in-house resource for discussing the ideas that led to *Tomorrow's Children*. And my children and grandchildren provided much of the inspiration for writing it.

R. E.

Part One

Partnership Education:
The Basics

Reconstructing Education
Basic Building Blocks

Wʜᴇɴ I ᴡᴀꜱ ʟɪᴛᴛʟᴇ, I loved to play with building blocks. I loved the freedom of, block by block, constructing rooms, houses, towers, and castles—worlds where I could let my imagination roam.

I would like the reader of this book to also use the ideas in it as building blocks that can imaginatively be put together in a variety of contexts, grade levels, or classes into a new way of structuring education from early childhood onward.

Each chapter is a building block by itself. Each chapter contains miniature building blocks for bringing the partnership model into different aspects of education.

I want to begin by briefly outlining the basic differences between what I have called the partnership and dominator models, how I came to see them, and why I so passionately want to bring the partnership model into education.

The journey of exploration that led to my discovery of the configurations I named the partnership and dominator models is rooted in my childhood. I needed answers to questions many of us have asked: questions about human society and human possibilities.

These questions had a particular immediacy for me as a refugee child from Nazi Austria. I saw my father brutalized by Gestapo men and dragged away. I also saw my mother stand up to these men, demanding that they let my father go, risking her life, shouting that what they were doing was wrong. And I saw that, miraculously, my father was returned to us, and we were able to escape my native Vienna.

In my child's mind, I tried to make sense of all this. As time went on, I began to ask questions. Why are people cruel? Why do they hurt and kill one another? If this is really just human nature, as we are often told, why isn't everyone like that? Why are some people caring and peaceful? What pushes us in one direction or the other? And what can we do to affect this?

My formal research began many years later, after a stint as a social scientist at the Rand Corporation's Systems Development Division, after law school, after marriage and two children, and after the omnivorous consumption of information from a huge range of fields—from sociology, anthropology, history, psychology, and systems science to archeology, mythology, literature, evolutionary studies, and the arts.

A Journey of Discovery

Gradually, as if watching the pieces of a jigsaw puzzle coming together, I began to glimpse patterns, connections. I was by now drawing from a very large database. I was looking at the whole of human history, including prehistory. I was looking at both the so-called public sphere of economics and politics and the private sphere of intimate parent-child and gender relations. I was deliberately including data about both halves of humanity: both women and men.

What I found is that underneath the many differences in societies throughout human history—differences in geographical locations, time periods, religions, economics, politics, levels of technological development—are two basic possibilities for structuring our relations with one another and our natural environment. There were no terms available for describing this discovery, so I had to coin new ones.[1] Yet I did not want to use terms that were arcane; I wanted terms that would immediately convey some sense of the two contrasting social configurations I was seeing.

The four core elements of one of these configurations are an authoritarian top-down social and family structure, rigid male-dominance, a high level of fear and built-in violence and abuse (from child and wife beating to chronic warfare), and a system of beliefs, stories, and values that make this kind of structure seem normal and right. Since rankings of domination—man over woman, race over race, religion over religion, nation over nation, man over nature—define this way of structuring relations, I called it the *dominator model.*

At the other end of the spectrum were societies orienting to a very different configuration. The four core elements of this configuration are a more democratic and egalitarian family and social structure, gender equity, a low level of institutionalized violence and abuse (as there is no need for fear and force to maintain rigid rankings of domination), and a system of beliefs, stories, and values that supports and validates this kind of structure as normal and right. After much pondering, I chose the term *partnership model* to describe this template for structuring relations.

My first book deriving from this research was *The Chalice and the Blade: Our History, Our Future*. It traced the cultural evolution of Western societies from prehistory to the present in terms of the underlying tension between these two basic alternatives for organizing how we think and live. It also outlined the new macrohistorical analysis I call *cultural transformation theory*, which proposes that shifts from one model to the other are possible in times of extreme social and technological disequilibrium; that there is strong evidence of such a shift during our prehistory; and that in our time of massive technological and social dislocation another fundamental shift is possible—to a world orienting more to partnership than domination.

My findings show that we have the power to create for ourselves the reality we yearn for. Indeed, sensing the partnership possibilities for our lives and our children's future, many of us are today questioning assumptions that were once considered unquestionable. We are rejecting the inevitability of war, injustice, and the course that decimates, pollutes, and destroys our natural habitat in the name of the once-hallowed "conquest of nature." We are learning that the war of the sexes is also not inevitable, that women and men can live and love in partnership. We are searching for a morality and spirituality that no longer direct us to an afterlife for better things or instill in us fear of angry deities, but recognize the divine in that which makes us fully human: our great capacity to love and to create.

Because many of us are today searching for paths that can take us and today's and tomorrow's children into a future guided by partnership rather than domination, I was invited to many places to speak about my work. I lectured at universities, wrote for many publications, and was asked to do educational consulting for schools.

More and more, I began to think of systemic educational change. When I had taught university classes, I had experimented with what I now saw were partnership methods. I had also given a great deal of thought to how the structure of schools does not encourage partnership in their top-down administrative hierarchies, and that many grading methods encourage the formation of dominator mindsets. Most jarring, however, were the conclusions I reached about what the curriculum content, much of the old educational canon, was actually instilling in the minds of students as knowledge and truth.

I began to think of writing this book. I have been writing it for five years. I write it with a tremendous sense of urgency, because in our time of mounting environmental, economic, and political crises, all the world's children are at risk. At the same time, I see in our children the hope for the future.

Nurturing Children's Humanity

At the core of every child is an intact human. Children have an enormous capacity for love, joy, creativity, and caring. Children have a voracious curiosity, a hunger for understanding and meaning. Children also have an acute inborn sense of fairness and unfairness. Above all, children yearn for love and validation and, given half a chance, are able to give them bountifully in return.

In today's world of lightning-speed technological, economic, and social flux, the development of these capacities is more crucial than ever before. Children need to understand and appreciate our natural habitat, our Mother Earth. They need to develop their innate capacity for love and friendship, for caring and caretaking, for creativity, for sensitivity to their own real needs and those of others.

In a time when the mass media are children's first teachers about the larger world, when children in the United States spend more time watching television than in any other activity, children also need to understand that much of what they see in television shows, films, and video games is counterfeit. They need to understand that violence only begets violence and solves nothing, that obtaining material goods, while necessary for living, is not a worthy end in itself no matter how many commercial messages to the contrary. They need to know that suffering is real, that hurting people has terrible, often life-long, consequences no matter how many cartoons and video games make mayhem and brutality seem normal, exciting, and even funny. They need to learn to distinguish between being hyped up and feeling real joy, between frantic fun and real pleasure, between healthy questioning and indifference or cynicism.

If today's children are to find faith that is grounded in reality, they need a new vision of human nature and our place in the unfolding drama of life on this Earth. If they are to retain their essential humanity, they need to hold fast to their dreams, rather than give in to the cynicism and

At the core of every child is an intact human.
CREDIT: *David Loye.*

me-firstism that is today often considered "cool." They need all this for themselves, but they also need it for their children, lest they raise another generation X, a generation struggling in this uncertain time to find identity and purpose and all too often becoming lost.

One of the greatest and most urgent challenges facing today's children relates to how they will nurture and educate tomorrow's children. Therein lies the real hope for our world.

I passionately believe that if we give a substantial number of today's children the nurturance and education that enable them to live and work in the equitable, nonviolent, gender-fair, environmentally conscious, caring, and creative ways that characterize partnership rather than dominator relations, they will be able to make enough changes in beliefs and institutions to support this way of relating in all spheres of life. They will also be able to give their children the nurturance and education that make the difference between realizing, or stunting, our great human potentials.

Early childhood care and education are critical, as psychologists have long known. But now this information comes to us with lightning-bolt force from neuroscience. When a baby is born, the brain continues to develop and grow. In the process, it produces trillions of synapses or connections between neurons. But then the brain strengthens those connections or synapses that are used, and eliminates those that are seldom or never used. We now know that the emotional and cognitive patterns established through this process are radically different depending on how supportive and nurturing or deprived and abusive the child's human and physical environment is. This environment largely determines such critical matters as whether or not we are venturesome and creative, whether we can work with peers or only take orders from above, and whether or not we are able to resolve conflicts nonviolently—matters of key importance for how we meet life's challenges, as well as for the postindustrial information economy.

The kind of childcare—material, emotional, and mental—a child receives, particularly during the first three years of life, will lay neural pathways that will largely determine both our mental capacities and our habitual emotional repertoire. Positive childhood caretaking that relies substantially on praise, loving touch, affection, and avoidance of violence or threats releases the chemicals dopamine and serotonin into particular areas of the brain, promoting emotional stability and mental health. (An excellent resource for parents and teachers is Rob Reiner's video *I Am Your Child: The First Years Last Forever*.)[2]

By contrast, if children are subjected to negative, uncaring, fear-, shame-, and threat-based treatment or other aversive experiences such as violence or sexual violation, they develop responses appropriate for this kind of dominator environment. They become tyrannical, abusive and aggressive or withdrawn and chronically depressed, defensive, hypervigilant, and numb to their own pain as well as to that of others. Often these children lack the capacity for aggressive impulse control and long-term planning. Neuroscientists have found that regions of the brain's cortex and its limbic system (responsible for emotions, including attachment) are 20 to 30 percent smaller in abused children than in normal children, and that many children exposed to chronic and unpredictable stress suffer deficits in their ability to learn.[3]

In short, caring and nurturing childcare has a direct influence not only on children's emotional development but also on their mental development, on their capacity to learn both in school and throughout their lives.

Most parents love their children. But what makes the difference is the expression of that love through loving touch, holding, talking, smiling, singing, and warmly responding to the child's needs and cries by providing comfort, food, warmth, and a sense of safety and self-worth.[4] This kind of childcare can be learned, as can an understanding of the stages of child development, of what babies and children are capable or incapable of comprehending and doing, and of the harm sometimes done to children through "traditional" punishment-based childrearing.

Hence the pivotal importance of teaching partnership childcare and parenting based on praise, loving touch, rewards, and lack of threat. For optimal results, in addition to parenting classes for adults, the teaching of this kind of parenting and childcare should start early in our schools, as it would in a partnership curriculum. This will ensure that people learn about it while they are still young and more receptive.

But it is all of education, not only early childhood education and education for parenting, that has to be reexamined and reframed so as to provide children, teenagers, and, later, adults the mental and emotional wherewithal to live good lives and create a good society. If we change our educational system today, we will help tomorrow's children flourish. If we prepare today's children to meet the unprecedented challenges they face, if we help them begin to lay the foundations for a partnership rather than a dominator world, then tomorrow's children will have the potential to create a new era of human evolution.

The Partnership and Dominator Possibilities

Our biological repertoire offers many possibilities: violence and nonviolence, indifference and empathy, caring and cruelty, creativity and destructiveness. Which of these possibilities we actualize largely depends on social contexts and cues—on what we experience and what we learn to believe is normal, necessary, or appropriate.

Through partnership education, young people can experience partnership relations with their teachers and their peers. They can find in their teachers what Alice Miller called "helping witnesses" when in need.[5] They can learn to have greater self-awareness and greater awareness of others and our natural habitat. They can be encouraged to ask questions about the narratives they are taught, to seek meaning and purpose in life, and to make healthy and informed life choices.

At the core of partnership education is learning, both intellectually and experientially, that the partnership and dominator models are two underlying alternatives for human relations. Relations based on fear, violence, and domination are a possibility. However, what distinguishes us as a species is not our cruelty and violence but our enormous capacity for caring and creativity. Constructing relations and institutions that more

FIGURE 1.1   Paradigm Shift
A new perspective changes how we see the world.
CREDIT: *John Mason.*

closely approximate the partnership model helps us actualize these capacities.

Partnership education helps students look beyond conventional social categories, such as capitalism versus communism, right versus left, religious versus secular, and even industrial versus preindustrial or postindustrial. They can instead begin to focus on *relationships*—and on the underlying question of what kinds of beliefs and social structures support or inhibit relations of violence or nonviolence, democracy or authoritarianism, justice or injustice, caring or cruelty, environmental sustainability or collapse (see Figure 1.1).

Through partnership education, young people can learn to use what I have called the *partnership-dominator continuum* as an analytical lens to look at our present and past (see Figure 1.2). They will see that the degree to which a society, organization, or family orients to one or the other of these alternatives profoundly affects our lives, for better or for worse. They will be better able to decide what in our culture and society we want to leave behind and what we need to strengthen. And they will understand that, even though no society will be a utopia where there is never any violence or injustice, these do not have to be idealized or built into the social and cultural fabric.

Obviously there has already been considerable movement toward the partnership model. If there had not been, we could not be discussing fundamental educational changes today without risking severe consequences, even death—as was the case for such free thought and speech not so long ago during the European Middle Ages, and is still the case in some world

FIGURE 1.2 The Partnership-Dominator Continuum: Core Configurations

Partnership Model	→	*Dominator Model*
Egalitarian structure with hierarchies of actualization		Authoritarian structure with hierarchies of domination
Equal valuing of females and males		Ranking of males over females
Institutionalization of mutual honoring, respect, and peaceful conflict resolution		Institutionalization of fear, violence, and abuse
High social investment in stereotypically "feminine"[a] traits and activities, such as empathy, caring, nonviolence, and caretaking		High social investment in stereotypically "masculine"[a] traits and activities, such as the control and conquest of people and nature
Myth and stories honoring and sacralizing partnership		Myths and stories honoring and sacralizing domination

SOURCE: Reprinted from Riane Eisler, *Redefining Destiny* (work in progress).
[a] "Feminine" and "masculine" refer to stereotypes that we inherited from more rigid dominator times, and not to any qualities inherent in women and men.

regions today. However, powerful dominator elements remain in our society. And some of these dominator elements are reflected in, and perpetuated by, our education.

Although we do not usually think of education in this way, what has been passed from generation to generation as knowledge and truth derives from earlier times. This is important, since otherwise we would, as the expression goes, constantly have to reinvent the wheel, and much that is valuable would be lost. But it also poses problems.

To begin with, during much of recorded Western history[6] prior to the last several hundred years, most institutions, including schools, were designed to support authoritarian, inequitable, rigidly male-dominant, and chronically violent social structures. That is, they were designed to support the core configuration of the dominator model. Although this kind of education was appropriate for autocratic kingdoms, empires, and feudal fiefdoms that were constantly at war, it is not appropriate for a democratic and more peaceful society. Nonetheless, much in the present curricula still reflects this legacy.

Many of our teaching methods also stem from much more authoritarian, inequitable, male-dominated, and violent times. Like childrearing methods based on mottoes such as "spare the rod and spoil the child," these teaching methods were designed to prepare people to accept their place in rigid hierarchies of domination and unquestioningly obey orders from above, whether from their teachers in school, supervisors at work, or rulers in government. These educational methods often model uncaring, even violent, behaviors, teaching children that violence and abuse by those who hold power is normal and right. They heavily rely on negative motivations, such as fear, guilt, and shame. They force children to focus primarily on unempathic competition (as is still done by grading on the curve) rather than empathic cooperation (as in team projects). And in significant ways, they suppress inquisitiveness.

Again, all this was appropriate for the autocratic monarchies, empires, and feudal fiefdoms that preceded more democratic societies. It was appropriate for industrial assembly lines structured to conform to the dominator model, where workers were forced to be mere cogs in the industrial machine and to strictly follow orders without question. But it is decidedly *not* appropriate for a democratic society.

Nor is it appropriate for a world facing unprecedented environmental problems. A dominator mindset focused on control gives the illusion that we can arbitrarily control nature, promoting the short-sighted "technology will fix everything and clean up every mess we make" worldview that is leading to ever-increasing despoilation of our finite resources, mounting pollution, and the threat of unforeseen and potentially disastrous ecological consequences. Partnership education can prepare young people to more realistically address environmental issues and use new technologies in responsible and appropriate ways, focusing on long-term consequences, not just quick fixes. It will teach them to think in holistic or systemic terms—that is, in terms of relationships, including our relationship to Mother Earth.

Partnership education also better prepares young people for the new information- and service-oriented postindustrial economy. Here, as organizational development and management consultants emphasize, inquisitiveness and innovativeness, flexibility and creativity, teamwork, and more stereotypically "feminine" nurturant or facilitative management styles get the best results.[7] Whether they reside in women or men, these are all qualities and behaviors appropriate for partnership rather than dominator relations. Indeed, when we talk of stereotypically feminine or masculine traits or behaviors, we are always talking about stereotypes that are our legacy from more dominator-oriented times, and not about anything inherent in women or men.

By providing the partnership-dominator continuum as an analytical lens for examining all aspects of life and society, partnership education can help students develop a capacity that is essential in our age of information overload: the capacity to recognize patterns or configurations in what otherwise seems a jumble of disconnected, equally weighted data bits. This in turn can lead to an awareness of how social structures, policies, and laws affect our day-to-day lives, strengthening young people's ability to make sounder personal, economic, and political decisions.

By facilitating a new understanding of the dynamics of social change, partnership education can also help students distinguish between surface and transformational change. This makes it possible for them to see that our time of cultural and technological ferment offers an opportunity for changes in basic assumptions and patterns of behavior—and that we can play an active role in this process. All this will engage them in learning not as a chore to be avoided but as an adventure to be enjoyed.

Partnership Process

How can we build the foundations for partnership education? How can we bring the joy of learning, of exploring new possibilities, into our classrooms? What are the basic building blocks?

As I outlined in the Prologue, there are three cornerstones for partnership education. These are partnership *process*, partnership *content*, and partnership *structure:* how we teach, what we teach, and what kinds of educational structures we build.

A primary aim of partnership education is to show, not only intellectually but also experientially, that partnership relations are possible. Hence partnership process, or *how* we teach and learn, is an essential part of education.

Child-centered education, the cooperative learning movement, and other progressive educational movements are already laying the groundwork for partnership educational process. Focusing primarily on how we teach rather than on what we teach, these movements promote learning experiences in which teachers facilitate rather than control, students learn to work together, and each child is treated with empathy and caring.

Partnership process is an integrated teaching style or pedagogy that honors students as whole individuals with diverse learning styles. It focuses not only on cognitive or intellectual learning but also on affective or emotional learning. It recognizes the additional dimensions of somatic or bodily learning and of conative learning—the cultivation of *conation*, or the will to act. It recognizes what Howard Gardner calls "multiple intelligences" and what Rob Koegel calls "partnership intelligence." It cultivates less linear, more intuitive, contextualized, and holistic ways of learning through what Mary Belenky, Blythe Clinchy, Nancy Goldberger, and Jill Tarule call "connected teaching" in their book *Women's Ways of Knowing*.[8]

Partnership process models partnership relations in day-to-day settings, showing children that their voices will be heard, their ideas respected, and their emotional needs understood. It helps counter the limitations and dysfunctions that, as psychiatrist Alice Miller and others document, are still often replicated under the guise of sound childrearing and teaching. It helps heal the psychic wounds of children at risk. By providing caring intervention shown by many studies to make the difference between a life lost to self and society and one that is productive and creative[9]—partnership process promotes not only learning and personal growth but also the shift to a less violent, more equitable and caring society.

As many teachers know, children learn better in an environment conducive to mutual caring and respect rather than punishments and controls, to open-mindedness rather than closed-mindedness, to empowerment rather than disempowerment.[10] As teachers also know, creating this kind of learning environment requires recognizing that we all carry attitudes and behaviors that get in the way. This does not mean we should hold ourselves or others to impossible standards of perfection, much less blame or shame ourselves and others. We are all in this together, trying to help children learn to resolve conflicts nonviolently, work together in teams while still valuing each individual, and treat others, including their teachers, with consideration and respect.

Studies on various aspects of partnership educational process—for example, child-centered learning and cooperative or collaborative learning—support the conclusion that partnership process can help achieve these goals. Researchers such as David W. Johnson, Spencer Kagan, and Robert Slavin note that when students are effectively helped to work together to accomplish shared goals, they learn both the teamwork and personal accountability needed for the postmodern workplace.[11] Researchers at the California Developmental Studies Center found that when schools become "caring communities" there are positive outcomes for both students and teachers, such as more personal motivation, nonviolent conflict resolution, and altruistic behaviors.[12]

There are many studies on the advantages of small schools and self-directed learning that also contain data supporting the conclusion that partnership process brings about good results. As Robert Gladden noted in "The Small School Movement: A Review of the Literature," these studies show that it is not just small size but also "the quality of relationships that existed among students, teachers, and administrators" that made the difference.[13] Or as a student attending an alternative small public school in New York wrote, "I feel better about school because I am learning what I want to learn. I feel more like a person. At my previous high school, they treated us like smart monkeys. Learning was not seen as being for ourselves or controlled by ourselves. We were ushered from class to class. There was no room for anything else."[14]

Some of the data on the advantages of partnership education are qualitative rather than quantitative, but qualitative studies are today gaining wider recognition and currency. Howard Gardner's work on multiple intelligences further supports the need to treat children as whole persons—yet another component of partnership process.[15]

Other works deal with different aspects of partnership education. For example, *In Search of Understanding* by Jacqueline G. Brooks and Martin G. Brooks and Michael Strong's *The Habit of Thought* also show the advantages of a more dialogic or Socratic partnership approach, as opposed to what Paolo Freire called "banking education" in which teachers just deposit lessons into children's minds.[16]

In addition, there is a huge body of literature from the organizational development and management field showing the advantages of both partnership process and structure for what is today sometimes referred to as "the learning organization."[17] Well-known works are those of David Bohm and Peter Senge from MIT. William Isaacs, who developed the method he calls Dialogos, has shown the advantage of partnership process in business.[18] And Alfie Kohn has written on the problems of focusing solely on competition and extrinsic rewards and punishments. His work, too, is consistent with some aspects of the partnership model.[19]

Successful uses of partnership teaching processes are reported in other publications, ranging from journals such as *Holistic Education, Democracy and Education, Cooperative Learning, Connections, Paths of Learning, Montessori Leadership,* and *Rethinking Schools* to books such as Nancy Schniedewind and Ellen Davidson's *Open Minds to Equality,*[20] Jeanne Gibbs's *Tribes: A New Way of Learning Together,*[21] and *Restructuring for Caring and Effective Education* by Richard Vila and his colleagues.[22]

Teachers who use partnership process can engage young peoples' natural curiosity, stretch their minds, and help them experientially understand democracy not only in governments and elections but in all spheres of life. Partnership teaching helps young people learn through acceptance and understanding, through rules that instill respect rather than fear, venturesomeness rather than rote obedience. Partnership teaching also relies on nonverbal experiences through art and music, drama and poetry, contact with nature, and, above all, play—whether the actual play of younger children or the conceptual play of more mature minds exploring the rich possibilities in ourselves and our world.

This kind of learning helps young people think for themselves and trust their own observations and experiences, fosters responsibility in the classroom, and encourages students to practice caring and ethical behaviors. By cultivating personal and social creativity, it inspires and empowers them to deal with personal, social, and ecological problems in more constructive, creative ways.[23]

This is not to say that teaching that fosters these capacities in children will solve all their problems, particularly of young people who live in circumstances of desperate poverty, alienation, and violence. But making a child feel seen and cared for can make a big difference, particularly at this time, when so many young people feel helpless and hopeless.[24]

Partnership Content

That so much attention is beginning to be given to partnership educational process is important. But it is not enough. Transforming *how* we teach without also transforming *what* we teach—without equal attention to curriculum content—is like trying to fly with only one wing. We may be able to get off the ground a little, but we will never be able to sustain flight, much less soar. It is like teaching children to play a beautiful instrument without paying attention to whether we provide them with melodious or discordant music to play.

Transforming curriculum content is basic to transforming education. The curriculum we teach is the food we offer children's minds: food for thought and, from there, action. It is the wherewithal out of which young people will form their views of our world and their place in it. If we focus only on partnership process, we provide an education that at best gives children conflicting messages, creating mental and emotional confusion through process-content mismatch. Most critically, we fail to provide them with cognitive maps that will help them construct a better future.

Partnership process and partnership content are the two complementary halves of partnership education in action. They are inextricably interconnected. Recognizing this, *Tomorrow's Children* addresses both. It also deals with the need for building partnership educational structures that will support, rather than impede, both partnership process and content. But because there are already many guidelines for transforming how we teach as well as for building more participatory rather than top-down educational structures,[25] the materials that follow focus primarily on *what* we teach: on the basic building blocks for a new partnership curriculum.

Today, a battle over curriculum content—a battle that will decisively affect the future—is already in full gear. On one side are those who see the solution to our problems as a return to the "traditional curriculum." Among them are those who advocate an end to the constitutional separation of church and state and a return to what they call "Christian values"—a term that, in this context, is often misinterpreted to mean rejection of scientific theories that do not fit with their views, as well as reimposition of more rigid controls and severe punishments, including corporal punishment in schools. On the other side are those who argue that changing times require changes in what children are taught about "reality," and that some aspects of the traditional curriculum have never served children well. There are many strands here, ranging from those who want to modify particular portions of the existing curriculum to those with an overarching transformative vision. But in practice, these efforts have resulted primarily in add-ons ranging from black history month and women's history month to education for emotional and environmental literacy and education for nonviolent conflict resolution.

These are all important contributions. But education for the 21st century requires more than add-ons. As important as they are, add-ons are like patches on an old, worn-out fabric. They only remedy a few symptoms, rather than solving the underlying problems.

Critical pedagogy, multicultural pedagogy, feminist pedagogy, education organized around themes of care, and other newer approaches to education highlight that we need to reexamine and redefine what we mean by *education*. As Nel Noddings writes, "All children must learn to care for other human beings, and all must find an ultimate concern in some center of care: care for self, for intimate others, for associates and acquaintances, for distant others, for animals, for plants, and the physical environment, for objects and instruments, and for ideas." But she also notes that "today the curriculum is organized almost entirely around the last center, ideas." And even this "is so poorly put together that important ideas are often swamped," given the emphasis on so-called facts and a very limited set of skills.[26]

What this calls for is a new curriculum design that provides an integrated framework for curriculum transformation.[27] This does *not* mean that we should discard everything we have been using. But, as we will see in the chapters that follow, it does mean that we need to start from the ground up and, out of both old and new elements, construct a curriculum that can meet the needs and challenges of our time.

Psychological research certainly supports the conclusion that what children learn, what they internalize from narratives and stories, profoundly affects their attitudes, values, and behaviors. Indeed, one of the basic tenets of Sigmund Freud, Karl Jung, Alfred Adler, Karen Horney, and other founders of the field was that how we view ourselves and others is rooted in how we are taught to perceive ourselves and the world.[28]

More recently, research on the effects of television violence on attitudes and behaviors, not only children's but adults', shows how cultural narratives mold attitudes and behaviors. For example, the studies done by George Gerbner and others at the Annenberg School of Communication and by David Loye and Rod Gorney at UCLA flatly contradict the assertion by some mass media executives that their programs do not influence attitudes and behavior, that somehow only purchasing choices and behaviors are affected by television.[29]

There is also a large body of literature on the power of cultural narratives from anthropology, sociology, social psychology, the study of myth, and other disciplines.[30] The work of scholars such as Milton Rokeach and Joan Rockwell shows that our values are largely formed through cultural narratives transmitted from generation to generation—and can be changed through new narratives. Rockwell's analysis of how the ancient Greeks used theater to instill dominator values is particularly illuminating when we apply it to contemporary entertainment.[31] And Milton Rokeach's work is instructive in that it demonstrates that values can be changed through the introduction of narratives that cause conflict between ostensible or consciously held values such as democracy and equality and latent or unconsciously held values such as biases against people of different races or social groups.[32] My own research on ancient myths shows that with the shift to a dominator model of organization there also occurred a massive transformation of both religious and secular myths; for example, in both *The Chalice and the Blade* and *Sacred Pleasure* I trace the transformation of images and narratives showing women in positions of power to images and narratives in which they are subordinate to men.[33]

Other studies specifically focusing on education have examined the effect of narratives about gender and race on student attitudes, perceptions, and behaviors. Most of these studies date from the 1960s and 1970s, when funding was available for them, and most deal only with single interventions or, at best, interventions of just a few weeks' or months' duration. But, strikingly, many of these interventions were found to have some positive effects—indicating that a curriculum informed by gender balance and multiculturalism could indeed have lasting results.[34] For instance, when a group of eight- to eleven-year-old students studied a semester unit on Africa, they developed more positive attitudes toward African-Americans than did a control group who were not exposed to this curriculum. When the students were tested eight weeks later, the experimental group still scored lower in prejudice.[35]

As James Banks writes in "Multicultural Education: Its Effects on Students' Racial and Gender Role Attitudes," interventions appear "to be most successful with young children, particularly preschoolers and kindergartners."[36] Consider, for example, a 1979 investigation of toy choices and game preferences of nursery school, kindergarten, and first-grade children. Before they saw a film showing a model choosing non-gender-stereotyped toys, the children displayed high levels of gender stereotyping in their choices. After viewing the film, the students in the experimental groups made fewer such choices. But the older children and the boys still made more stereotyped choices than the younger children and the girls.

Picture books can also influence the kinds of toys children choose. After children were presented with books containing characters who selected either stereotypical or nonstereotypical toys, the children who were read the nonstereotypical book chose less stereotyped toys themselves.[37]

In sum, although there have as yet been no studies specifically addressing the question of what kinds of attitudes and behaviors are fostered by an integrated partnership curriculum, a considerable body of literature supports the conclusion that partnership narratives can foster partnership attitudes and behaviors.

Moreover, data on educational outcomes from a school that has consciously used partnership education, the Nova High School in Seattle, support the conclusion that the *whole-systems* approach of partnership education has excellent results. Nova has not only ranked first among the Seattle area's high schools in educational climate surveys; it can also boast that a high percentage of its graduates have the academic accomplishments to get into prestigious universities. These young people (of mixed racial and ethnic origins, many from poor families, and some even from homeless families) also tend to have more awareness, sensitivity, and a greater sense of human possibilities—as teachers at Nova will attest and as I observed firsthand during a recent visit to this school (which is one of the Center for Partnership Studies' pilot partnership education development sites).

Partnership Structure

The Nova School exemplifies the beneficial results of partnership process and content. It also demonstrates that the best results come from an approach that integrates partnership process, content, and structure.

At Nova, the primary governing body that makes school policy and rules is open to both students and faculty. At this school, students play a key role in formulating and enforcing school rules. This practice not only encourages responsibility; it also offers hands-on experience in democratic process and leadership.

As noted earlier, the core elements of partnership structure are a democratic and egalitarian rather than top-down authoritarian organizational structure, gender balance rather than male dominance, and, in contrast to the dominator-model requirement of a high level of built-in abuse and violence, emphasis on nonviolent and mutually caring and respectful relations. When educational institutions follow this template, their structure models partnership relations and supports both partnership process and content.

In schools that orient primarily to the dominator model, it is extremely difficult for students and teachers to experience democracy in action. Nor can they move toward their optimal functioning. This has been demonstrated in the business world by organization development and management research for decades.[38] Accordingly, many successful corporations have been gradually dismantling top-down hierarchies in a process I call *debureaucratization.*

The same principle applies to educational institutions. However, a partnership structure does not mean a completely horizontal organization. There is a distinction between *hierarchies of domination* and *hierarchies of actualization.* Hierarchies of domination are imposed and maintained by fear. They are held in place by the power that is idealized, and even sanctified, in societies that orient primarily to the dominator model: the power to inflict pain, to hurt and kill. By contrast, hierarchies of actualization are primarily based not on power *over*, but on power *to* (creative power, the power to help and to nurture others) as well as power *with* (the collective power to accomplish things together, as in what is today called teamwork). In hierarchies of actualization, accountability flows not only from the bottom up but also from the top down. That is, accountability flows in both directions.

In other words, educational structures orienting to the partnership model are not unstructured or laissez-faire; they still have administrators, managers, leaders, and other positions where responsibility for particular tasks and functions is assigned.[39] However, the leaders and managers inspire rather than coerce. They empower rather than disempower, making it possible for the organization to access and utilize the knowledge and skills of all its members.

Having said this, I want to add that partnership structures are not equivalent to consensus structures, although in certain situations the latter can be appropriate. Yet the consensus mechanism can actually lead to domination by individuals with unmet needs for attention. Although there is great emphasis on real participatory democracy in partnership structures, following interactive discussions the individual or team responsible for making something happen can proceed to see that it does.

Partnership school structures facilitate cooperation among different individuals and groups. But once again—and this, too, is a critical point— partnership as an organizing template is not equivalent to cooperating or working together. People also work together in societies, institutions, or organizations orienting closely to the dominator model—for example, to attack other nations, to persecute minorities, or in cut-throat competition designed to put competitors out of business.

This is not to say that there is no competition or conflict in the partnership model of relations. But in the partnership model, conflict is used not to select winners and losers, or who dominates and who is dominated, but rather to creatively arrive at solutions that go beyond compromise to a higher ideal. And competition is directed toward striving for excellence and using the achievements of the other person or group as a spur or incentive to the attainment of one's own highest potentials.

In partnership school structures, young people have responsibilities for determining some of the school rules, and for seeing that they are honored. This promotes habit patterns needed to function optimally in the postindustrial information economy, where taking responsibility, flexibility, and creativity are essential. More immediately, it contributes to a mutually respectful, undisrupted, and, of course, nonviolent school environment. Despite the assumption that adolescents naturally rebel, we may find that when students feel that they are heard and cared for and have a stake in the functioning of their school, they are less likely to do so—as in this kind of structure rebelling would be rebelling against rules in which they themselves have had a significant input.

Partnership school structures also require a much higher teacher-student ratio, not only through reduced class sizes but through innovations such as team teaching. This, in turn, requires far greater fiscal and social support for our schools. Although much good teaching goes on, it does so despite the fact that our schools are understaffed and underfunded.

(See Figure 1.3 for specific examples of the partnership-dominator continuum in educational process, content, and structure.)

Schools as Communities of Learning

To create the kind of education children need, our social and economic policies cannot continue to shortchange education. We must give much greater social recognition to the value of teachers, both through better pay and through increased funding for continuing teacher development, education, and support. Teachers need more time for thoughtful preparation and assessments, for curriculum development with other professionals, and for training when new developments in education occur.

We need to pay more attention to how children can develop their unique individual potentials rather than merely focusing on standardized test scores. We need to strengthen and build on the various elements of partnership process and content already being used in many schools. And rather than dismantling our public school system, as some propose, we

FIGURE 1.3 Examples of the Partnership-Dominator Continuum in Educational Process, Content, and Structure

The Partnership Model *Values and Supports*	*The Dominator Model* *Values and Supports*
Teacher and student knowledge and experience are valued	Teacher is the sole source of information and knowledge
Learning and teaching are integrated and multidisciplinary	Learning and teaching are artificially fragmented and compartmentalized
Curriculm, leadership, and decisionmaking are gender balanced	Curriculum is male-centered; leadership and decisionmaking are male-controlled
Multicultural reality of human experience is valued and tapped as source of learning	One culture's worldview is the measure with which others are analyzed and evaluated
Social and physical sciences emphasize our interconnection with other people and nature	Social and physical sciences emphasize the conquest of people and nature
Mutual responsibility, empathy, and caring are highlighted and modeled	Relations based on control, manipulation, and one-upmanship are highlighted and modeled

SOURCE: Reprinted from Riane Eisler, *Redefining Destiny* (work in progress).

should debureaucratize our schools, not only making them smaller but restructuring them to more closely approximate partnership rather than dominator organizations.

Are teachers, school counselors, and other staff treated with respect by administrators? Are partnerships formed to make decisions about policy? Are students involved in this process? Are opportunities created for parent participation? Are there referral systems for parents to access social agencies and other community resources? Are there counseling and educational opportunities for parents and other caretakers that will benefit children and further their development (for example, workshops for parenting education where mothers and fathers can share challenges and appropriate solutions)? Are social agencies and other community resources enlisted to support teachers in their growing responsibilities to help children develop not only intellectually but emotionally, to ensure that basic needs such as good nutrition and health care are met, and that each child's unique talents are developed? Are efforts made to bring education into the community to meet community needs?

Much greater attention to the interactive relationship between schools and both their communities and the natural environment is needed if our schools are to support and model partnership relations. I would like to see a parent resources center at each school, and social services housed in at least some of the schools in every community. I would like to see some classrooms in buildings within the community itself, rather than tucked away from community life. I would like to see small schools, none with more than 350 students and, where possible, even fewer. These are part of my vision for schools as communities of learning where every child can grow and flourish.

As Sheila Mannix and Mark Harris write, what is urgently needed is a school "that can be an effective antidote to the stress of the street and the hurt of the home, a haven of safety, orderly learning, and personal growth, the school as the guarantor of a child's right to protection, education, and love."[40] Because schools are increasingly in a position of having to meet these needs, but not equipped to do so, Mannix and Harris call for social investments that will make it possible for schools to become "the social hub of the community, a mechanism with which society can reach out to families in trouble and ensure that help is provided."[41]

This may sound like a tall order, but it is part of the vision of the partnership school of the future: a vision to plan and work for. It is, I believe, a vision that can gradually be realized as schools are transformed through partnership education. But it requires that society at large recognize our responsibility to all children.

We must have the courage to open our eyes to the needs, suffering, and hopes of children worldwide, to question prescribed conventions, and to become the architects of a partnership future for generations to come through an enlightened, empathic global public education. Adapted for different regions and cultures, partnership education can be a blueprint for refocusing, reframing, and redesigning education to help all children realize their full humanity and preserve our natural habitat.

Transforming education is an ambitious goal. It will undoubtedly be criticized, opposed, or dismissed as impossible by some. But by exploring, taking creative risks, and holding fast to our partnership principles and vision, we can make partnership education a reality. This is not only necessary, but doable—if we join together and, step by step, lay the foundations for the education that can make the 21st century a bridge into the better future for which we all yearn.

BOX 1.1 Suggestions for How to Use This Book

When I read a book, I often have a conversation with the author. Sometimes I am passionately in agreement, sometimes I disagree, sometimes I have questions. I underline, attach note tags, and write comments in the margins—from "Yes!" or "No way" to thoughts that come to me prompted by the content.

I invite you to have a similar dialogue with this book.

I would also like to suggest that in your teaching and in your conversations about partnership education with students, colleagues, administrators, parents, and others, you consider using a dialogic approach.

By dialogic approach I do not mean just a discussion. This term describes a way of thinking, talking, and interacting that allows for the free flow of information among two or more people in a way that facilitates the surfacing of taken-for-granted assumptions. Dialogic communication is integral to partnership process, as it makes it possible, at least for the moment, to consider different ways of looking at the world.

For example, instead of asking students to repeat information to you, consider asking questions that do not have yes or no "right" answers but, instead, provoke thought. Some questions proposed by partnership educator Jim Knight are: What does this make you think of? How do you feel about this? How do you see this working? What is another way of looking at this? What would prevent you from doing this?

(continues)

BOX 1.1 *(continued)*

Using this approach, you can create more open space for conversations. The fear of giving a wrong answer is displaced by the pleasure of exploring new ideas and possibilities. When clashing views surface, these can be acknowledged and explored.

Sometimes it is important to probe deeper by acknowledging issues that make us feel uncomfortable. I have found this approach particularly useful in talking about gender. After some initial discomfort, people generally enjoy the process of freely exploring different perspectives that stimulate each other's thinking.

One of the challenges this book presents is the paradox of needing to communicate new perspectives to people who are caught up in a paradigm that makes it difficult, if not impossible, to see them. This dilemma is inherent in sharing knowledge about the partnership model with people who deny its reality because they accept the assumption that "human nature" is suited only for a dominator way of relating.

In fact, we have all been exposed to narratives that, at best, present a partnership mode of relating as peripheral. And many of the conventional curricula still convey dominator assumptions, with only an uneasy sprinkling of partnership ones.

I have therefore in this book focused on alternative partnership-supporting narratives. Although I would like to see these alternatives given adequate prominence, I do not wish to imply that the materials in this book should totally displace the materials found in many texts that support the dominator paradigm. My aim is to make it possible for students, teachers, and others to engage in dialogic conversation, using the partnership and dominator models as analytical tools.

As many of us have experienced in our own lives, when taken-for-granted assumptions are made visible we can choose to accept, reject, or modify them. Choice is central to partnership. Partners are always free to choose to agree or disagree. This has enormous implications for how knowledge is shared, since without the opportunity to exercise choice there can be no critical thinking.

As new data and new perspectives arise, our paradigms, or ways of looking at ourselves and the world, need to be reexamined. This can effectively be done by using a dialogic method, which makes it possible for us to explore and construct knowledge together, opening the door for our intellectual, emotional, and spiritual growth.

Refocusing and Reframing Education

The Basic Design

CHILDREN ARE BEING GIVEN a false picture of what it means to be human. We tell them to be good and kind, nonviolent and giving. But on all sides they see media images and hear and read stories that portray us as bad, cruel, violent, and selfish.

In the mass media, the focus of both action entertainment and news is on hurting and killing. Talk shows capitalize on human suffering. Situation comedies make insensitivity, rudeness, and cruelty seem funny. Even children's cartoons incessantly present violence as not only exciting and funny, but also without real consequences.

Our media also communicate massive cynicism. As portrayed in news, talk shows, and many "hip" entertainment programs, nobody believes in anything—to quote the columnist Leonard Pitts, "not the nihilistic rapper with the hard streets rep, not the bad-boy athlete with the big-bucks contract, not even the politician with the aw-shucks smile and the gleam of sincerity in his eye."[1] Contemptuous terms such as *do-gooder* and *bleeding-heart* dismiss empathy and progressive activism as wimpy and foolish. The phrase *nanny state* has become a term of derision to express contempt for caring as not only inappropriate for government officials, but as unmanly.

Media political coverage is far less about issues than about who won and who lost, or, as Deborah Tannen puts it in her book *The Argument Culture*, about "who's up and who's down." In short, much of our public discourse is framed in terms of a dominator model of relations—with a tough and angry ideal of masculinity, as Tannen notes, the ideal norm.[2] Even much of today's talk about morality is angry and vitriolic, focusing on persecuting and punishing rather than on the age-old "golden rule" central to genuine morality: Do unto others as you would have them do unto you.

All this holds up a distorted mirror of themselves to children. And rather than correcting this false image of what it means to be human, many of the narratives in our school and Sunday school curricula actually reinforce it.

Although teachers in early grades try to impart the values of sharing, caring, honesty, and nonviolence, this message is largely offset not only by popular entertainment but by nursery rhymes and fairy tales full of cruelty, trickery, and violence. Later on, it is further contradicted by much in the school curriculum. The way history is taught emphasizes battles and wars—in other words, violence. Classics such as Homer's *Iliad* and Shakespeare's kings trilogy romanticize "heroic violence" and present a worldview in which rulers and warriors are the only noteworthy protagonists. Scientific stories tell children that we are the puppets of "selfish genes" ruthlessly competing on the evolutionary stage. And religious stories teach children that we are a species irretrievably flawed by "original sin." Small wonder that so many children and adults are plagued by conflicting messages and learn to compartmentalize what they hold as knowledge and truth.

Even worse, this kind of education produces people susceptible to domination and control. If we are inherently violent, bad, and selfish, obviously we need to be strictly controlled by punishments and fear of punishments.

Narratives that provide a negative picture about "human nature" are central to dominator mythology. They are, however, totally inappropriate if young people are to learn to live in the democratic, peaceful, equitable, and Earth-honoring ways needed if today's and tomorrow's children are to have a better future—perhaps even a future at all.

How can we ensure that during the formative years of childhood and adolescence education reflects back to young people a less distorted, less negative, more accurate picture of what it means to be human? What can we do so that this picture includes all children—that it integrates the history, needs, problems, and aspirations of both the female and male halves of humanity, and that, to borrow Emily Style's words,[3] it both reflects our own experiences and provides a window through which to see those of people of different races and ethnic origins? How can we reframe education so that what we teach and how we teach are structured around what Nel Noddings calls competences of caring—for self, for intimate others, for global others, and for the natural world?[4] How can we refocus education in ways that will more effectively help young people avert the crises that threaten their future? What do they need so they can instead move toward a 21st century where all children can develop their enormous human potentials?

Partnership education addresses these urgent questions from a new perspective, with three main goals in mind:

- The first goal is to help children grow into healthy, caring, competent, self-realized adults.
- The second goal is to help them develop the knowledge and skills that will see them through this time of environmental, economic, and social upheavals.
- The third goal is to equip young people to create for themselves and future generations a sustainable future of greater personal, social, economic, and environmental responsibility and caring—a world in which human beings and our natural habitat are truly valued and chronic violence and injustice are no longer seen as "just the way things are."

Partnership and Dominator Values

Like many of us, I am heartbroken when I pick up the newspaper and read yet another headline about children brutalizing and killing other children. I am often shocked by the barbarically cruel video games, essentially training tools for mayhem and murder, I see boys playing with, as well as by other aspects of our mass culture that desensitize and deaden empathy. I am also concerned about the media-induced fixation of many children on ever more material acquisitions.

There are many factors contributing to these and other contemporary problems. But clearly our educational system is not teaching children sound values.

It is not enough for parents and teachers to preach to children about sound values such as kindness and sensitivity rather than cruelty and insensitivity, democracy and equality rather than tyranny and inequality, and environmental responsibility rather than irresponsibility. *What counts is what our homes and schools model, and what the school curriculum itself communicates about values.*

Some people will undoubtedly argue that it is just up to parents, not schools, to teach children values. But all schools teach values, whether they do so explicitly or implicitly, by inclusion or by omission. All educational curricula are based on certain assumptions about social relations: about what was, what is, and what can be. The issue therefore is not whether schools should teach values but what kinds of values schools teach.

Children are born curious, hungry to learn, to satisfy their need for meaning and fulfillment, to realize their enormous potentials for creativity and caring. Much of what children internalize as knowledge and truth is spontaneously formed through their interactions with the living world around them. Young children in particular learn from what their parents, teachers, and other caregivers model. Hence partnership process—the interaction of student and teacher in caring and respectful ways that deepen rather than dampen our human capacity for empathy—is of critical importance. So also is partnership structure: a learning environment that both models and supports respectful and caring interactions, a school to which parents and other members of the community can turn for information and support, which is in turn supported by the entire community.

But a great deal of what children learn about the world and their place in it comes from the narratives transmitted to them as knowledge and truth in schools and through the larger culture. In fact, studies have shown that what children learn in their schools and their larger cultural environment can even override what children see in their immediate environment. Consider, for example, the little girl described in Eleanor Maccoby and Carol Nagy Jacklin's *The Psychology of Sex Differences*, who asserted that only boys can be doctors—even though her own mother was a physician.[5]

As children get older and their cognitive faculties become more developed, the need for partnership educational content becomes even more important.[6] At this point, when they become more aware of themselves and the larger world around them, when they begin to consciously think about what is right or wrong, normal or abnormal, important or unimportant, young people need narratives that help them develop pro-human and environmentally sensitive values.

This is particularly crucial today, since so much in both our popular and traditional culture contradicts these values, or at best conveys conflicting and confusing messages about values, standards, and morality. Young people are often given the false impression that our only choices are either repressive controls or a total lack of any standards, ethics, or morals. Indeed, this second view is today propagated not only in much of popular culture but in some intellectual circles, as in the extremes of libertarianism and academic cultural relativism.

A curriculum that teaches young people to recognize the contrasting configurations of the partnership model and the dominator model makes it possible to sort through conflicting messages and cut through much of the contemporary confusion about values. It makes clear that the issue is not either returning to dominator controls or rebelling against all standards, but developing and applying standards appropriate for partnership relations in our families, schools, workplaces, communities, and the world at large.

I believe that we are all responsible for the choices we make. But to make sound choices, we need to understand our alternatives. And one of the most important functions of education is to help young people see the full range of their alternatives, both individually and socially.

A curriculum informed by the partnership model makes it possible to see that dominator relations are not inevitable, that there are viable partnership alternatives. It offers young people a larger perspective on both their day-to-day lives and on the world at large—showing that the tension between the partnership and dominator models as two basic human possibilities has punctuated all of human history.

To illustrate, by learning to use the partnership-dominator continuum as an analytical lens in the study of history, students can contrast economic inventions such as slavery and serfdom, which came out of ancient societies that oriented closely to the dominator model (and thus placed no value on freedom for "inferior" groups), with more partnership-oriented economic inventions such as trade guilds and labor unions, which were developed as workers began to challenge traditions of economic domination. They can contrast the ancient Roman business motto *caveat emptor* ("buyer beware") with product warnings that were the result of organized action by consumer protection groups that place higher value on ethics and human well-being than on freedom for businesses to sell what they see fit without consideration for these matters. They can then see how profoundly values are influenced by social structures, and how sound values in turn can motivate people to change unsound institutions and practices.

Students can also see how laws can enforce either dominator or partnership values. For example, because no value was given to freedom and equality for women in the European Middle Ages, laws deprived women of both freedom and equality, and even permitted husbands to beat wives—a practice still legally condoned in some rigidly male-dominated countries such as Iran and Afghanistan. They can contrast these kinds of laws with laws making it possible for women to own and control property, vote, run for office, and receive some measure of protection from domestic violence—and learn that these laws supporting freedom and equality for women were enacted as a response to women's persistent organized efforts.

They can contrast solar power (a noncentralized technology potentially available for all, once the investment in developing affordable and efficient solar delivery is made) with nuclear power (which, besides being dangerous to our safety and health, requires centralized operation and control). And they can explore what kind of social and economic system—one orienting more to partnership or domination—would accord funding priority (and thus value) to the development of solar or nuclear power as an energy source.

In short, a partnership curriculum can help young people learn values appropriate for sustainable and humane ways of living. It can help them develop standards based on environmental and social responsibility and respect for human rights—and to make choices guided by these standards. It can also help them acquire the competences they need to live by partnership ethical and moral standards through role models that highlight our enormous human potential to learn, to grow, to create, and to relate to one another in mutually supporting and caring ways.

Partnership and Dominator Structures

When Sharon Thomas introduced the concept of partnership to her fourth-grade class, she started with games that communicate a different perspective from the dominator one of life being a struggle between winners and losers. She found that collaborative games such as "frozen beanbag" (where you "freeze" if a beanbag you put on your head falls off, and can go on playing only if another person puts it back on your head) became popular, fun activities.[7]

When Urban Paul Thatcher Edlefsen was introduced to the concept of partnership in his high school American Government and Economics class, he lucidly expressed the changes this brought to his worldview in a paper worthy of a graduate university student. Called "President Clinton's State of the Union Address: A Partnership Analysis," it emphasized the need to find solutions for violence and other contemporary problems through "bottom-up, grass-roots means, and through the redefinition of men, women, heroes, and government."[8]

Other students and teachers have also found that the pattern recognition skills learned by using the analytical templates of the partnership and dominator models transfer to all their studies—and their lives. As students learn to look at the world from this new perspective, they develop their critical faculties. They become interested in matters that earlier seemed distant and abstract. And they begin to see recurrent patterns.

However, as in the story of the blind men and the elephant, these patterns are only visible once we look at a larger picture that takes into account the whole of our lives (both the so-called public and private spheres) and the whole of humanity (both its female and male halves). The blind man who felt the elephant's trunk described it as a leathery snake, the one who felt its leg described it as a solid tube or tower, and so forth. But none of the blind men was able to describe the animal's total configuration. In the same way, studying human society by focusing on only one area—psychology on personal relations, economics on economic relations, political science on political relations, and so forth—and at only one historical period at a time is like looking out of a window that only overlooks a small portion of a landscape. And if our view is still further narrowed by looking at only one-half of humanity—as is true of almost all traditional studies, which are aptly called "the study of man"—we can never see more than half the picture.

By looking at the whole picture, we can see that societies that at first glance seem very different—a tribal society like the Masai of 19th-century Africa, an industrial society like 20th-century Nazi Germany or Stalin's Soviet Union, and a religious society like Khomeini's Iran or the European Middle Ages—actually have the same core configuration. They are all characterized by authoritarian rule based on fear of pain in both the family and the tribe or state, rigid male dominance,[9] and a high degree of socially condoned violence, ranging from child and wife beating to brutal scapegoating and warfare. We can also see that, transcending differences in time, location, and other conventionally studied categories,

societies orienting primarily to the partnership model have a very different core structure. As illustrated by contemporary Scandinavian nations,
tribal societies such as the Tiduray,[10] and prehistoric societies such as Minoan Crete, this core configuration consists of a more democratic and equitable family and social organization, a more equal partnership between
women and men, and the absence of a structural requirement for idealizing or building violence into the social system, as it is not required to im-
pose or maintain rigid rankings of domination. Moreover, rather than
systems of belief, myths, and values that make a dominator configuration
seem normal and even moral, the ideological systems of these societies—
including the narratives that define what is "human nature"—present a
partnership social structure as not only desirable but possible. (For a listing of the core configurations of the partnership-dominator continuum,
see Figure 1.2 in the previous chapter.).

It is vitally important that students understand these connections in
light of today's call by some Christian fundamentalists for a return to
"traditional family values." In fact, what are being advocated under the
guise of Christianity are authoritarian, male-dominated, and punitive
family relations—even though there is nothing in the teachings of Jesus
to support this type of family structure.[11] Habits of thinking and feeling
(and thus beliefs and values) that are unconsciously developed through
our family experiences provide basic mental and emotional blueprints for
what kinds of relationships we consider possible, normal, and moral. This
is why authoritarian societies have historically supported authoritarian
families whereas democratic families are foundational to democratic societies. The slogan of the United Nations Year of the Family, for example,
described the family as the smallest democracy at the heart of democratic
society.

The tragedy, and irony, is that dominator socialization—and with this,
the unconscious valuing of undemocratic, abusive, and even violent relations as not only normal but moral—has been unwittingly passed on from
generation to generation. Psychologist have found that children who are
dependent on especially abusive adults tend to replicate these behaviors
with their children, as they have been taught to associate love with coercion
and abuse. Many of these children also learn to use such psychological defense mechanisms as denial and the deflection of repressed pain and anger
onto those perceived as weak. Sometimes these are directed against themselves, particularly in the case of women, who are made to feel that anger is
a male prerogative. Usually they are directed against others through the

bullying, scapegoating, and other forms of emotional and physical violence characteristic of the properly socialized dominator psyche.

What we find in dominator systems is the institutionalization of trauma—whether through the pain of physical and/or emotional abuse, through humiliating and painful rituals of male initiation, or through the creation of artificial scarcity of both material and emotional sustenance in all areas of life.[12] This is how rigid hierarchies of domination are maintained. In short, the conditions that cause pain and anger are built into dominator systems. (See the "Maintaining Domination" sidebar in Chapter 4.)

The degree to which a society or period orients to the dominator or partnership configuration has profound implications for all aspects of our lives. For example, the concept of "human rights"—which is fundamental to the partnership model—was not known during the Middle Ages. This is *not* coincidental. Although intermittent attempts were made to inject partnership elements (such as the veneration of Mary as the compassionate mother of God or the courtly love and chivalry codes of the troubadours and their female counterparts, the trobaritzes), the Middle Ages oriented closely to the interactive, mutually reinforcing configuration of the authoritarian, male-dominated, and highly violent social organization characteristic of the dominator model.

It is important for teachers to emphasize that no family, society, or organization orients exclusively to a partnership or dominator configuration. As noted in Chapter 1, what we are dealing with is a *continuum*, a matter of degree. For instance, societies orienting closely to the dominator model always co-opt (absorb, distort, and exploit) partnership elements, as these elements (for example, love) are necessary if we are to survive. Moreover, we are not dealing with simple causes and effects, but with mutually interactive and reinforcing elements that maintain a system's basic character.

Through a curriculum informed by partnership education, teachers can help students look at the whole range of human relations, from intimate to international, and discuss their interconnections and interactive psychosocial dynamics. This more holistic or systemic approach helps young people develop both cognitive (intellectual) intelligence and emotional (affective) intelligence. Most important, it enables them to better navigate through our difficult times and to better understand, and begin to lay, the structural foundations for a world where both other humans and Mother Nature are truly valued. (See the "Shifting to Partnership" sidebar in Chapter 4.)

Partnership and Dominator Narratives

An important element of partnership education involves helping young people more critically evaluate narratives that make the dominator model seem inevitable, desirable, and even moral. Postmodern scholarship highlights the importance of narratives or stories in how we come to perceive what we call reality. Although the term *story* is often associated with fiction, in fact almost everything we learn is through stories. Whether they are religious or secular, whether we learn them from our parents, our schools, or the mass media, the stories we are taught largely shape how we view our world and how we live in it.

Partnership education can help young people become more aware of how stories and images shape our mental maps and, through these, our world. As we will see, the curriculum design I am proposing offers two different kinds of narratives about our world and our place in it, showing how knowledge—and with this, what is considered natural, important, and valuable—is constructed differently from a partnership or dominator perspective. In other words, partnership education offers both some of the conventional narratives that present dominator relations as normal, even inevitable, and alternative narratives that help young people explore other alternatives.

For example, in the natural sciences, partnership narratives emphasize what scientists are increasingly documenting: the interconnection of all forms of life. Such narratives lead to a greater awareness of the web of life that is our environment—which has largely been ignored in the traditional curriculum—and thus to a greater understanding, and valuing, of activities and policies that promote environmental sustainability. Organically flowing from this approach is the new partnership ethic for human and ecological relations urgently needed in our time.

I have personally seen how excited children become when they learn that we are partners on this planet with trees and plants. When I gave my seven-year-old friend Karen the Rainforest Action Network's *Kid's Action Guide* to illustrate this point, and she found out that we cannot survive without the oxygen given off by trees and plants, she was both amazed and concerned. "That's neat," she said, quickly adding, "But we better take good care of plants and trees, so they will want to be our friends."[13]

Most educators today agree that students need a better grounding in science. But although some progress has been made toward a stronger science curriculum, all too often it fails to adequately reflect scientific discoveries about our universe and our species that do not conform to a dominator model of relations. This severely handicaps young people, as if we learn primarily about our limitations, and if these are presented to us as inevitable, either as religious truth or scientific fact, why even bother to try to change anything for the better?

For example, the narratives still taught in many schools and universities tell us that Darwin's scientific theories show that "natural selection," "random variation," and later ideas such as "kinship selection" and "parental investment" are the only principles in evolution. Actually, as we will see, Darwin did *not* share this view, noting that, particularly as we move to human evolution, other dynamics, including the evolution of what he called the "moral sense," come into play.[14] Or, as Frans deWaal writes in *Good Natured: The Origins of Right and Wrong in Humans and Other Animals*, "the desire for a *modus vivendi* fair to everyone may be regarded as an evolutionary outgrowth of the need to get along and cooperate."[15]

But the story that emphasizes violence, predation, and randomness persists, making repression, inequity, and violence appear natural and normal. Through partnership narratives, teachers can help students understand that, although such a system is a human possibility, it is not "just human nature." They can offer them scientific narratives that focus not only on competition but also, following the new evolutionary scholarship, on cooperation. As we will see, these include information about seldom-noted evolutionary developments such as the biochemicals known as neuropeptides that, by the grace of evolution, reward our species with sensations of great pleasure not only when we are cared for but also when we care for others. This fascinating scientific discovery is as yet not highlighted either in our schools or in most popular scientific writings. Much has been made of the discovery that emotional states are created by the release in the body of biochemicals called endorphins. But the emphasis is still mainly on those biochemicals that induce negative emotions, such as fear and aggressive impulses.[16]

The approach I propose offers a narrative that is not only grounded in science but also supportive of spiritual values. It does not leave young people with the sense that life is devoid of meaning or that we humans are inherently violent and selfish. This approach takes us past the contemporary debate between creationists and scientists. Drawing from empirical evidence that our human strivings for love, beauty, and justice are just as rooted in evolution as our capacity for violence and aggression, it can be a bridge between science and authentic spirituality and morality. (See the "Meaningful Evolution" sidebar in Chapter 3.)

A partnership curriculum makes it possible to see that many assumptions about our past, present, and potential future have been projections of dominator mindsets. For example, by looking at not only history but also prehistory, young people will see that familiar images conveyed by cartoons of our early ancestors as brutal cavemen dragging women around by their hair are completely absent from early prehistoric art. On the contrary, images that honor the giving and nurturing, rather than the taking, of life play a central role in Stone Age art.

Looking at our more recent past from this new perspective, young people will also see that there is far more to history than wars, dates of battles, and who won or lost in struggles for political control. They will be able to see the last three hundred years in a new, and more hopeful, light. By focusing on the efforts of women and men worldwide to construct a more equitable, democratic, gender-fair, environmentally sustainable, and nonviolent world, teachers can help young people see that these efforts are not disconnected, that they are part of the movement to shift from dominator to partnership societies worldwide. They will also see that, despite all the talk of the failure of liberalism, feminism, and other progressive modern social movements, organized social action has made major contributions to human welfare.

Students can look at how not so long ago in the United States child labor was legally condoned and fifteen-hour workdays were commonplace. They can see how at the turn of the 20th century women were still barred from universities and how just a few decades ago blacks had to sit in the back of buses and domestic violence was rarely prosecuted. They can also consider how these and other harmful practices were changed by the determined actions of a small—and, at the time, highly unpopular—minority.

By focusing on the movement toward a partnership society, teachers can help students comprehend the enormous difference these gains continue to make in our lives—and to better understand how they were made. This makes it possible to relate history to daily concerns, to what kinds of relations we have with friends, parents, teachers, employees, and public officials—as well as with our natural habitat. It also makes it possible to see that nonviolent tactics have brought about important social changes.

For example, in the United States women won the right to vote, despite enormous opposition, when courageous women such as Elizabeth

Cady Stanton and Alice Paul gained support through demonstrations, hunger strikes, and extensive political lobbying. In India, Gandhi used the same methods in his successful struggle for independence from British colonial rule. And, again, in the United States, women and men such as Frederick Douglass, Emma Goldman, Martin Luther King, Rosa Parks, Cesar Chavez, Dolores Huerta, Rachel Carson, and David Brower have peacefully worked for civil rights for blacks, workers' rights for all Americans, and environmental sustainability.

Studying the lives of women and men who played an active part in these progressive movements will provide inspiring role models for tomorrow's children. Understanding that progress has been made over the last three hundred years despite enormous resistance and periodic setbacks, young people will see that they, too, can make a difference.

This leads to something of critical importance: that the shape of our future will be profoundly affected by what is, or is not, included in the school curriculum. As Jane Martin shows in *Schoolhome: Rethinking Schools for Changing Families*,[17] including certain kinds of information in the curriculum—and not including other kinds of information—effectively teaches children what is, and is not, valuable. Such decisions also largely determine what children come to believe is important or unimportant, possible or impossible, good or bad, normal or abnormal.

Partnership and Dominator Priorities

As noted earlier, the partnership curriculum is gender-balanced. This is essential if all children are to be valued—and if all children are to learn more pro-human and environmentally sensitive values.

Following dominator educational traditions, most existing textbooks still focus primarily on the male half of humanity: on what men did and thought. We need only look at our texts on literature, art, history, and philosophy to see how our education still omits a huge part of the human story. Studies show that an education that minimizes the role and contribution of women has negative effects on girls' sense of self-worth and severely limits the realization of their potentials.[18] But it also has negative effects on boys, and on the whole of our social system, as this kind of education distorts our entire system of values in significant and highly destructive ways.

Some people, like a human rights luminary with whom I discussed discrimination against women some years ago, still argue that gender issues should take a back seat to more important issues—matters, as he put it, of life and death. But valuing the male half of humanity more than the female half is all too often a matter of life and death. In some world regions, it means that female children get not only less education but less health care and even food—literally condemning girl children to death. (See also Figure 2.1.)

It is hard to believe that parents would so treat their own children. But that they do is starkly borne out by the statistics. According to United Nations reports, in 1991 the yearly ratio of deaths per thousand children ages two to five in Pakistan was 54.4 for girls versus 36.9 for boys. In Thailand, it was 26.8 versus 17.3. In Syria, it was 14.6 versus 9.3.[19] As my Pakistani friend Abida Khanum told me, when a boy was born the women sang songs of celebration, but when a girl was born they mourned.

The very fact that many of us see nothing strange about calling any issue that affects the 51 percent of Americans who are female "just a women's issue"—even though we would think it peculiar to call issues that affect the 49 percent of Americans who are male "just a men's issue"—indicates how profoundly we have been influenced by this hidden system of gender valuations and priorities.

Whether gender roles and relations are socially constructed in accordance with the dominator or partnership model directly impacts not only our entire system of values but every aspect of society. It affects whether families are egalitarian and democratic or authoritarian and violent. It affects whether activities stereotypically associated with women, such as caring for children and maintaining a clean and healthy physical environment, are, or are not, given government policy priority, and hence funding.[20]

Through a partnership curriculum, teachers can help students see how learning to accept the ranking of half of humanity over the other as normal and right provides a mental map for all rankings of domination—whether race over race, religion over religion, or nation over nation. They can help students see that we need to give greater value to traits such as empathy and nonviolence that are still stereotypically associated with women—whether they are found in women or men. In short, they can impart values that are appropriate not only for a truly democratic society but also for a more equitable and less violent world.

To this end, there are many materials about women in the chapters that follow. Some people may even feel that there is too much emphasis on women. However, despite efforts since the late 1960s to include women in the curriculum, studies show that there is still a long way to go. In their examination of forty-seven U.S. textbooks for grades one through eight published

FIGURE 2.1
Women's Work

During the United Nations Decade for Women, as noted in the State of the World's Women Report *(United Nations, 1985), "for the first time in history the eyes of the world were focussed on that half of the population who, by virtue of an accident of birth, perform two-thirds of the world's work, receive one-tenth of its income, and own less than one-hundredth of its property."*
CREDIT: *Wendy Hoile.*

between 1980 and 1988, Christine Sleeter and Carl Grant found that males, or more specifically white males, were still predominant. Not only that, women in these textbooks are still incidental to the main storyline. As Sleeter and Grant write, "One gains little sense of the history or culture of women, and learns very little about sexism or current issues involving gender."[21]

Today teachers are still faced with an overwhelmingly male-based curriculum in which women and anything associated with them is deemed unimportant. If we are to change this, our curriculum needs to recognize what should have been obvious all along. This is the fact that women and men are the two halves of humanity and hence that what we teach young people about what it means to be a woman or a man basically teaches them what it means to be human.

The way in which the roles and relations of men and women are socially constructed differs in partnership- and dominator-oriented societies. For example, the popular belief that testosterone inevitably makes men violent is not borne out by research. In fact, studies show that the issue is not hormonal arousal, but rather the combination of hormonal arousal and social cues—and that men with low testosterone have actually been found to become *less* violent when their testosterone levels are increased.[22] Many men are today beginning to challenge a definition of fathering once primarily associated with a disciplinarian/provider role to include the nurturing once only associated with mothering[23]—just as many women are beginning to break into the once aptly termed "men's world" of government, business, and the more lucrative professions.

In other words, there is strong movement toward the more flexible gender roles and equitable relations appropriate for a more peaceful and caring society. But there is also strong resistance. A gender-balanced partnership education can reduce this resistance—and help us move toward a future when all children are valued and essential human activities such as caring for children and maintaining a clean and healthy environment are accorded the importance they merit.

Partnership and Dominator Relations

Partnership educational narratives integrate materials on peoples of all races and many cultures, not only in the United States but worldwide. They also include materials on other people who are "different," people who are blind, deaf, or otherwise physically or developmentally challenged, highlighting not only their problems but also their enormous achievements and courage. (For example, Helen Keller was blind and deaf, yet, through the caring of her teacher Annie Sullivan, became an inspiring public figure; and actor Christopher Reeves, after suffering a paralyzing accident, became a spokesperson for the physically challenged.) By clearing up stereotypes and misinformation, these kinds of material can help students see through scapegoating and become more empathic (see Figure 2.2).

Again, despite changes in textbooks since the 1960s to make them more pluralistic, as Sleeter and Grant found in their study of reading, science, mathematics, and social studies textbooks, even where more diversity was incorporated, it has often been in a fragmented, superficial fashion, as a mere add-on to the "important" material dealing with white Anglo-Saxon males. They found that most of these books contain little about contemporary race relations, poverty, discrimination, and other issues that profoundly affect the lives of a large number of nonwhite chil-

FIGURE 2.2   "Many Voices, One Vision"

Partnership education integrates materials on people of all races and cultures.
CREDIT: *"Many Voices, One Vision," by Jane Evershed.*

dren. In readers, the story lines generally centered on whites; and even when blacks, Native Americans, Hispanics, or Asians were included in pictures, they were often involved in mundane activities, such as writing a letter or drinking a glass of juice, rather than in meaningful pursuits. And although the textbooks dealt with problems such as slavery or the Great Depression that existed in the past, they rarely dealt with current social problems—giving the young readers a false impression about life today.[24]

Children whose identity is not valued or recognized in the school curriculum suffer in many ways from their exclusion—as evidenced by the much higher dropout rates among black, Hispanic, and Native American students and the much higher suicide-attempt rates among gay and lesbian students. For example, a study by Gary Remafede of the University of Minnesota (based on a statewide adolescent health survey) reports that suicide attempts by boys who identified themselves as gay or bisexual occurred at a rate of 28.1 percent, compared to 4.2 percent for heterosexual males. The rate for girls who identified themselves as lesbian or bisexual was 20.5 percent, compared to 14.5 percent for heterosexual girls. (Curiously, the news story mentions only in passing the shocking statistic that this suicide-attempt rate of 14.5 percent for heterosexual girls is four times higher than that for heterosexual boys.)[25]

As we will see in the chapters that follow, through partnership educational narratives teachers can integrate multicultural materials into all areas of study. Students need texts and other materials that reflect the reality of life experienced by children who are marginalized in U.S. culture. Indeed, in this age when technologies of communication and transportation, as well as destruction, have radically shrunk our world, a pluralistic/multicultural partnership curriculum is essential for all children.

Partnership narratives can promote more equitable relations between different races and ethnic groups in schools, neighborhoods, and the planet. They provide a clearer understanding of the global realities of poverty, including the fact that, worldwide, peoples of color, women, and children are the vast majority of the hungry and poor. They document the need to narrow the gap between haves and have-nots for the sake of all children, reveal cultural and structural obstacles blocking this goal, and highlight action for positive change.

Partnership educational narratives not only include the often-ignored wisdom of women and men of many cultures, they also include materials from ancient traditions from all world regions—many of them orienting more to the partnership model. This makes it possible to look to cultures that have retained a closer relationship to Mother Earth for what we today call environmental consciousness. For instance, many of the indigenous peoples of the Americas still view the Earth as sacred, and have rites and rituals that honor our interconnection with nature. This connectedness is an important aspect of the partnership worldview—one that, as we will see, is the common heritage of many world cultures from a time before the dominator model became the norm.

In short, through a pluralistic partnership curriculum, teachers can help young people find common ground with one another, rather than, as some people fear, promoting dissension and enmity. By providing the partnership and dominator models as analytical tools, teachers can help students sort what in their own and other cultures promotes equitable and caring versus inequitable and uncaring relations. This helps students see that just as we need to work to change the dominator aspects of our own culture, we need to support those women and men within other cultures who are working for these ends.

By applying these human rights standards—which are one of the foundations for partnership morality—to all cultures, students will not fall into the old trap of thinking that we are superior. Nor will they fall into the more recent trap of a cultural relativism, whereby any and every practice is justified on the grounds that it is a cultural or religious tradition. Rather, they will see that the issue is the degree to which any culture—our own or another—orients to the dominator model or the partnership model. This helps children learn the real meaning of one of the core values of democracy: that we are all responsible for making ours a better society and a better world. It also makes learning more relevant to our day-to-day lives, to how we act in our families, workplaces, and communities.

The Partnership Curriculum Loom and Learning Tapestry

When I think about education, I think of the interweaving of many different strands into a continually growing and changing tapestry of learning. I am using this image of a tapestry being woven on a loom as the metaphor for partnership curriculum planning.

Looms are the framework on which threads are interwoven into designs. Every educational curriculum is woven on a loom or conceptual framework consisting of the basic philosophical assumptions about our world and our place in it that the curriculum both explicitly and implicitly communicates.

The loom or framework holding partnership education together is a worldview that emphasizes our human possibilities rather than our limitations, showing that it is possible—and essential at this time in history—to structure relations in ways that help us actualize, rather than inhibit, our great human potentials for creativity and caring. This is the worldview expressed by *cultural transformation theory*, which identifies the partnership and dominator models as two underlying possibilities for social organization. Hence cultural transformation theory is integral to the partnership curriculum loom.

Cultural transformation theory provides a new perspective on our past, present, and the possibilities for our future as a larger frame for education. It traces the tension between the partnership and dominator models as two pulls or attractors from the earliest human societies to our time. It charts thousands of years during prehistory when there is evidence that the cultural mainstream was less violent and more equitable—an era orienting more to the partnership model[26]—before there was a shift to a social organization orienting primarily to the dominator model in all major centers of civilization.[27] Cultural transformation theory also maps recorded history from this perspective, showing that it has been punctuated by movement toward partnership, countered by dominator resistance and periodic regressions. Focusing on the last three centuries—a period of great disequilibrium due to rapid technological change—it proposes that the currents and crosscurrents of our time can best be understood in terms of movement toward another fundamental shift: this time, from a dominator to a partnership model. It further proposes that we today stand at an evolutionary crossroads when completing the shift to a partnership model can take us past the danger of breakdown to an evolutionary breakthrough.

In short, cultural transformation theory proposes that the underlying struggle for our future is not between the conventional polarities of right and left, religion and secularism, or capitalism and communism. Rather, it is between a mounting grassroots partnership resurgence that transcends these classifications and the entrenched, often unconscious, dominator resistance to it.

In proposing that the evolution of self and society are inextricably interconnected, cultural transformation theory provides a framework for identifying and analyzing dominator narratives embedded in traditional curricula. It suggests new narratives that expand our consciousness. It also suggests questions that need to be asked, programs that need to be developed, and personal practices and social innovations that can help us accelerate the shift to a world orienting primarily to partnership rather than domination.

As illustrated in Figure 2.3, the learning tapestry woven on the partnership curriculum loom consists of three main bundles or strands of educational threads.

The Vertical Threads

The vertical threads provide the basic story line for a new set of narratives about our world and our place in it. They take us from the beginning of our universe to a point where we fit into the evolutionary picture. As detailed in Chapters 3 and 4, and as illustrated in Figure 2.3, they tell a story that continues into our own time: the extraordinary saga of cosmic, planetary, biological, and cultural evolution. They culminate in two possible futures: evolutionary breakdown or breakthrough.

47

EXAMPLES:

Ethics

Computer Literacy

Physical Education

Current Events

Social Sciences

Art and Music

History

Life Sciences

Math

Reading and Writing

Cosmic and Planetary Evolution · Biological Evolution · Cultural Evolution · Prehistory Gathering/Hunting · Agrarian Revolution · History Industrial Revolution · Nuclear, Electronic, and Biochemical Revolutions · The Partnership or Dominator Future

FIGURE 2.3 The Partnership Curriculum Loom and Learning Tapestry

The vertical and horizontal threads are delineated as shown. Not shown are the cross-stitchings, which represent (1) the partnership and dominator models, (2) partnership values and ethical/moral standards, (3) partnership literacies and competences, (4) gender balance, (5) pluralism/multiculturalism, and (6) partnership process.

CREDIT: *John Mason.*

These chronological threads give students the grounding many of us lack today: a clear sense of our world and our place in it, which we need to function optimally—psychologically, socially, technologically, and ecologically. They dispel many misconceptions about nature and our own human nature; highlight the relationship between values and social structures; engender environmental responsibility; and integrate seemingly disparate areas of study, contextualizing science in a larger story. By showing that ours is a contingent universe in which at every turn there are different possibilities and choices, they inspire constructive action.

The Horizontal Threads

The horizontal threads provide both the old and new tools of mind that children need. As we will see in Chapter 5, one bundle of horizontal threads represents established fields, such as math, reading and writing, science, social studies, art, physical education, and music, as well as fields that are now entering the curriculum, such as computer literacy. The second bundle, discussed in Chapter 6, consists of immediate and long-term needs, interests, aspirations, hopes, and concerns of students, thus helping us prioritize what is more, or less, important in education for the 21st century.

Like a design that suddenly begins to come to life in the weaving of a tapestry, these topics acquire new meaning when interwoven with the vertical chronological threads. What then comes together is relevant to our day-to-day lives and to our choices for the future (see Figure 2.4).

The Cross-Stitchings

Cross-stitchings hold a tapestry together and bring its patterns to life. Six sets of cross-stitchings integrate and enrich partnership education.

The first set consists of the *partnership and dominator models* as tools to develop pattern recognition skills. Through an understanding of the core configurations of these two different possibilities for relations, we can see connections between what otherwise seem disconnected bits of information. We deepen our understanding of the relationship between values and social structures. And we see that the shape of our future depends on whether we succeed in shifting further toward the partnership model.

The second set of cross-stitchings are *partnership values and ethical/moral standards:* guidelines for day-to-day life in our families, workplaces, and

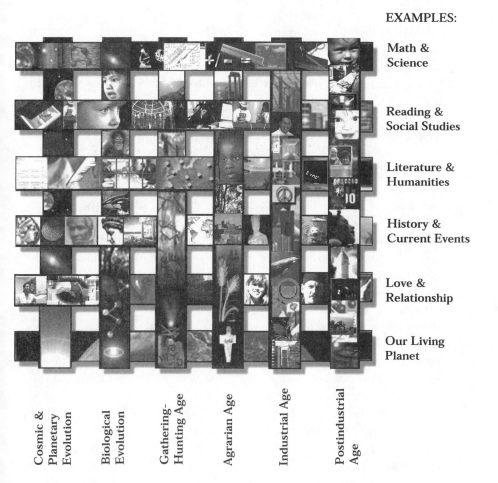

EXAMPLES:

Math &
Science

Reading &
Social Studies

Literature &
Humanities

History &
Current Events

Love &
Relationship

Our Living
Planet

Cosmic &
Planetary
Evolution

Biological
Evolution

Gathering-
Hunting Age

Agrarian Age

Industrial Age

Postindustrial
Age

FIGURE 2.4   The Partnership Curriculum Loom and Tapestry: A Cross-Section
CREDIT: *John Mason.*

communities, and for how we treat our Mother Earth. This set also includes education for the moral and ethical leadership required to construct a more equitable, peaceful, and creative rather than destructive 21st century.

The third, and closely related, set of cross-stitchings consists of basic *partnership literacies and competences*, ranging from emotional, parenting, and systems competence to political, spiritual, and leadership competence. These competences help young people develop the pro-human values, environmental sensitivities, and life-skills we need to more fully realize our personal and social potentials. The materials that follow contain many examples of how these can be taught—for example, teaching what I have called "Caring for Life" (self, others, and nature) discussed in the section on Self-Regulation and Life Planning in Chapter 6.

The fourth set of cross-stitchings consists of materials that ensure *gender-balance:* that equal value is given to both the female and male halves of humanity in what is taught. Gender-balanced education not only profoundly alters what children learn as valuable knowledge and truth; it also makes them aware that they have the potential for a wide range of traits and behaviors, not just those we have been taught to associate with our basic identity as women or men. It encourages young people to recognize the value, in both women and men, of traits and activities stereotypically considered "masculine" (such as assertiveness) and "feminine" (such as the caring and caretaking work without which none of us would survive), and to see that the association of domination and violence with "real" masculinity is not inevitable.

The fifth set of cross-stitchings consists of materials that make for a *pluralistic/multicultural curriculum* that values diversity in both humans and nature. Rather than providing environmental education as an add-on, these materials integrate it into the entire curriculum. Rather than diminishing the contribution of European influences, they enrich our understanding of European cultures by showing the similarities between some of their early partnership roots and those found in other cultural traditions. Pluralistic education is key to the future of children from otherwise marginalized nonwhite, non-European groups. It is also critical to the future of us all in our age of globalization, when we need to understand many world cultures and learn to live in partnership with one another and our Mother Earth.

The sixth set of cross-stitchings represents *partnership process:* a way of teaching that models and supports partnership relations, honors diverse learning styles, and makes each child feel seen and cared for. This approach integrates emotional and intellectual learning, recognizes what Howard Gardner called multiple intelligences, promotes teamwork, and lends itself well to self-directed learning.

The Partnership Curriculum Loom and Learning Tapestry is a useful guide to this book. It is also a useful tool for teachers, home-schooling parents, and others who want to develop partnership curricula, teaching methods, and learning environments. Another useful tool is the chart titled "Six Keys to Partnership Education" in the sidebar at the end of this chapter.

Weaving the Future: Partnership Schools

The overall design of the Partnership Curriculum Loom and Learning Tapestry encourages systemic or holistic thinking. It provides a biological and social matrix for understanding children's capacity to learn, grow, and create. It offers teachers a structure to use in incorporating the materials that follow, as well as for reexamining the curriculum they currently use through the analytical lens of the partnership-dominator continuum.

In the pages that follow you will find many resources that you can weave together to put partnership education into action. The "Weaving the Future: Partnership Schools" project of the Center for Partnership Studies (CPS) is already using some of these materials in collaboration with schools, universities, and other organizations to develop and disseminate curriculum content, learning processes, and educational structures that reflect partnership attitudes, values, and skills.

For example, at the School in Rose Valley (Pennsylvania), CPS is assisting the development, testing, and evaluation of curricula for younger students that integrate service learning and simultaneously help children think critically about the partnership and dominator models. With *New Moon*, the Minnesota-based award-winning magazine for girls edited by girls ages eight to fourteen, CPS brings together girls on the culturally diverse *New Moon* editorial board to write stories on partnership themes for children of various ages. At the Nova High School in Seattle, Washington (a public charter school with a multicultural student body), CPS is working with teachers, students, and recent graduates in developing, testing, and evaluating new biology and cultural history curricula.

Of particular interest for teachers and home-schooling parents is that, in collaboration with the University of Kansas Center for Research and

Learning (a leader in continuing teacher education), CPS offers teacher professional development workshops in various U.S. regions. These short workshops can be taken for continuing education credit. Longer workshops for "training of trainers" are being planned to accelerate replication of partnership education nationally and internationally. In addition, plans are under way at California State University, Monterey Bay, for a Master's program for educators who want to incorporate the partnership model in their classrooms.

These project sites are developing components for an integrated partnership education, blending content (what we learn and teach), process (how we learn and teach), and structure (where we learn and teach). Some of these materials will be available, and periodically updated, through the CPS website at <www.partnershipway.org>. Where appropriate, they will also be available through educational publishers, bookstores, and other channels of distribution.

I am delighted that even in advance of the publication of this book there is so much interest in using it to begin reweaving the present educational tapestry and help children learn to live more fulfilling, productive, and caring lives. Again, this does not mean that all the problems young people face, particularly young people living in poverty and daily violence, can be solved by partnership education. But by stimulating children's enormous curiosity, offering them new and inspiring stories, supporting them and encouraging them to help each other (for example, through team assignments and peer teaching), and facilitating their use of partnership education to meet real-life needs, become involved in their communities, maintain a clean and healthy environment, and put themselves in the place of those in need, partnership education will be a powerful force for transforming our communities and our world.

This cultivation of empathy—and the life-skills to put empathy into action—is one of the core goals of partnership education. It is an ambitious goal, and will not be easy to accomplish in a world that still orients heavily to the dominator model. But there is evidence that movement in this direction is already under way.

As seen in progressive corporations today, the partnership leader or manager is not a cop or controller who gives orders that must be obeyed, but someone who inspires productivity and empathically facilitates creative teamwork. In progressive schools, teachers inspire and facilitate learning and creativity, modeling caring and empathic behaviors. A critical difference between the dominator and partnership models lies in the distinction between authoritarian families, which model inequality and replicate the kind of unempathic childrearing required to mold a dominator psyche, and democratic families that model empathy, caring, and equality, instilling democratic values on an experiential day-to-day level. There is today strong movement toward not only more equality between adults in households but also more empathic childcare.

Empathy, caring, and equality are, of course, what great religious teachers such as Jesus preached. Partnership education can build on these basic, universally recognized values. It can help young people escape the cynicism and nihilism of our time, not through the old dominator morality of punishment and coercion but through the partnership morality of caring and empathy.

The universality and persistence of partnership values as ideals, even in the face of all that militates against their expression, says something important about our human species—and about the possibilities of a fundamental cultural transformation in a time when the kind of breakdowns that could come with the end of the modern industrial era could bring a virtual avalanche of multiple systems failures. Many of us realize that unless we prepare today's and tomorrow's children to live together more equitably and peacefully, they may have no future in our age of biological and nuclear weapons. We also realize that if we do not leave behind our once-hallowed "conquest of nature," we endanger not only the future of other species with whom we share our planet but also the future of our own human species.[28]

If, unlike the ancient story of how the Emperor Nero fiddled while Rome burned, teachers, parents, and all of us who care about the future of today's and tomorrow's children join together, all this can be averted. If through partnership education we nurture the wonderful range of human capacities now largely ignored in schools—particularly our human capacities for caring and creativity—we will help lay the foundations for a partnership world.

SIX KEYS TO PARTNERSHIP EDUCATION

The six keys that follow are useful for opening minds to new ways of thinking, feeling, and acting. Teachers, parents, community activists, and other educational innovators can return to this box, as well as to Figures 2.3 and 2.4, as they develop lesson plans and curriculum modules for partnership education.

Tools

In our rapidly changing world, we need new tools for thinking and acting. The partnership and dominator models are tools for more clearly understanding our world as it is—and how it can be if we more fully develop our personal and social potentials. The partnership-dominator continuum is an analytical lens that reveals patterns in what otherwise seems random and disconnected, helping us sort the information overload of our postmodern age. A related set of tools are partnership competences, ranging from emotional and parenting competence to scientific, environmental, and spiritual competence. Partnership education also offers the teaching tool of partnership process, which complements partnership content. It models partnership in action, helping to create a democratic, stimulating, and nurturing learning environment: a partnership structure where all students are valued and teachers, other staff, and students can relate in mutually respectful and caring ways.

Values

Partnership education provides guidelines for living on this Earth in less destructive, more peaceful, equitable, and sustainable ways. Much in our culture focuses on acquiring material possessions rather than on living rich and meaningful lives. It presents violence as not only inevitable but manly. And it often gives the false impression that our only choice is between regressing to more authoritarian and less equitable ways of living or a total lack of standards. Rather than conditioning young people to live rudderless lives or to rely on external controls and fear of punishments, partnership education teaches young people values such as empathy and responsibility, showing that our actions have consequences. It empowers young people to think for themselves, develop standards for ethical and moral life choices, be better citizens, create more caring families and communities, preserve our natural habitat, and live more emotionally and spiritually satisfying lives.

Structures

To prepare young people to meet the challenges of the 21st century, partnership education grounds learning in an understanding of social, economic, and political structures. This makes it possible for students to see that neither personal choices nor social policies occur in a vacuum—that they are largely shaped by the constraints or opportunities of these structures. It highlights how partnership or dominator structures provide incentives and disincentives for different kinds of decisions and behaviors. It shows how all aspects of our lives—from our intimate relations to our relations with our natural habitat—are influenced by the degree to which social arrangements orient to either a partnership or dominator model. But it also highlights that we in turn can influence these social arrangements. It shows that social, economic, and political structures are human inventions—and hence can be changed to creatively meet the challenges of the 21st century.

Science

A core component of education today is scientific information about our universe and our place and responsibilities in it. Partnership education explores the mysteries probed by science against the backdrop of a story that spans billions of years, from the first stars and planets to the appearance on Earth of our unique human species. It highlights new scientific findings about human evolution, such as the great human capacity for pleasure from caring behaviors and the critical importance of the early years of a child's home and cultural environment. By highlighting our interconnection with our Mother Earth, partnership education fosters ecological consciousness. It also shows that technological developments guided by a partnership ethos can be beneficial rather than destructive, and that at this critical juncture in the history of our planet we humans must be conscious co-creators of our future—for our own sake and for that of generations still to come.

Integration

In the ever more complex, technologically interconnected, postindustrial world, young people need a new integrated approach to learning. Partnership education offers a systemic approach that weaves together materials from different subject areas, showing how they interrelate. It integrates cognitive and experiential learning, melds the theoretical and the practical, desegregates multicultural materials, and balances information about both the female and male halves of humanity. It validates the experiences of girls and boys of varying races and backgrounds. Grounded in a clearer understanding of both ancient and modern history, it offers a larger perspective on our human adventure. It both personalizes and universalizes what is taught as important knowledge and truth, helping young people envision a more equitable and peaceful world where the wonder of humanity and the richness of nature can be truly valued.

Inspiration

Children need education that inspires them to be the best they can be. Much in our mass media presents a world of constant conflict, cruelty, and pain—whether in the news stories that get headlines or in the endless "entertainment" depicting violence and abuse as "fun." Partnership education counters this false picture of what is possible and desirable for human relations. It shows that, despite massive resistance and periodic regressions, there has during the last three hundred years been movement toward partnership rather than dominator relations in families, workplace, and governments. It highlights the inspiring stories of courageous women and men of all races and ethnic origins who have braved ridicule, censure, and violence to bring us greater freedom and equality. It shows that all of us can, through both individual and group action, through both consciousness and service, continue to strengthen this forward movement—and find real meaning and purpose in our lives.

Part Two

Reweaving the Educational Tapestry: The Vertical and Horizontal Threads

Beginnings

From the Stars to Us

WHAT IS THE MEANING of our journey on this Earth? What about us connects us with, and distinguishes us from, the rest of nature? Are there patterns in the movement of the stars, sun, and moon across the sky and in our own movement through life? What are our ethical and moral responsibilities as human beings? What impels us to wonder about such things?

Since time immemorial, humans have sought answers to these kinds of questions through religion, philosophy, and the empirical method of investigation we call science. But science is usually taught in bits and pieces disconnected from one another and from questions that engage the intellect and imagination to probe the mysteries of our universe and the meaning of our lives.

There is a more effective and exciting way of teaching science. An integrative framework for learning more than just a series of unconnected, constantly changing, exponentially increasing "scientific facts" engages children's imagination and helps them become interested in science as an exploration of the mysteries of the universe.

This approach offers young people a panoramic view of the creative sweep of evolution. It reveals the general evolutionary movement toward ever greater variability, complexity of structure, integration of function, and flexibility of behavior. It also makes it possible to see our lives as part of a still-unfolding drama—not a predetermined sequence, but a process in which at every turn there were, and are, different possible outcomes.

As many science teachers recognize, an integrative framework is particularly important at this time when there is so much turmoil and change. It helps students look for larger patterns and connections rather than merely memorize masses of data, to ask meaningful questions, and to explore basic matters such as the history and possibilities of our universe, of life, and of our own species.

Most important, as Maria Montessori observed, it helps awaken in children a sense of awe and wonder at the mystery and grandeur of our universe and, with this, a larger sense of meaning and purpose. It stimulates questions such as "What am I? What is our task in this wonderful universe? Do we merely live here for ourselves, or is there something more for us to do?"[1] As Brian Swimme writes in *The Universe Is a Green Dragon*, "We will discover our larger role only by reinventing the human as a dimension of the emergent universe."[2]

The Unfolding Drama

There are, of course, those who still consider any talk of evolution to be heresy. In a strange replay of the Scopes trial of the 1920s (where a biology teacher was tried for the "crime" of teaching evolution), there is again today pressure from some fundamentalist religious groups to force teaching of the biblical creation story in public schools. At the same time, one of the world's most powerful religious leaders, Pope John Paul II, recently stated that belief in evolution and religious faith are not inconsistent. Rather than denouncing scientific findings about evolution (as a seventeenth-century pope did with Galileo's findings), he spoke approvingly of Darwin's theory of evolution as "more than a hypothesis" and as not inconsistent with belief in a Creator.[3]

The approach I propose leaves open the question of whether there is creative intelligence in evolution. It leaves the door open for the question everyone must ultimately answer for themselves: whether or not this evolutionary process originates from what we call the divine.

But it also shows that what we call the divine incorporates many of our own highest potentials—our great potential for creativity and caring, and our strong striving for justice, beauty, and love. This and similar matters of values, norms, and beliefs constitute the ideal we seek to move toward as a species and as individuals.

In other words, this approach does not negate a spiritual dimension in evolution. On the contrary, it shows that the emergence of spirituality— of our human yearning for oneness with other living beings and with what we call the divine—is part of the evolution of consciousness. Most important, it shows that through a clearer understanding of how our human alternatives are shaped by both our biological and cultural evolution, we can create the conditions that support, rather than impede, our powerful human striving for beauty, justice, and love (see "Meaningful Evolution" sidebar).

This leads to an important point I alluded to earlier. When I speak of biological evolution, it is not only in the sense biologists use the term in trying to explain how a particular species developed or evolved. It is in the much larger sense of the history of life on our planet. It is from a systems perspective, following the tradition of systems scientists from many fields—for example, Humberto Maturana, Paul MacLean, Vilmos Csanyi, and Elisabet Sahtouris from biology; Adrienne Zihlman from paleoanthropology; Fritjof Capra from physics; Nancy Tanner from anthropology; Ervin Laszlo from philosophy; and David Loye and Allan Combs from psychology.[4] It does *not* mean teaching only the theories of "natural selection" and "random variation." As Darwin himself stated, these are only part of a much larger story. Particularly at the human level, the evolution of the moral sense, love, our ability to reason and learn, and education generally, are more important factors.[5]

Taught from this larger perspective, geological, biological, and cultural evolution provides an overview of the development of our cosmos, our planet, and life on this Earth—including the emergence of human consciousness and the possibility of becoming conscious co-creators of our future.

The vertical threads of the partnership learning tapestry follow the general sequence of this story. They begin with cosmic, planetary, and biological evolution. They then continue with cultural evolution: with human prehistory and history. But, again, this is from a new perspective—one that makes visible the underlying tension between the partnership and dominator models as two basic human possibilities, and the consequences that flow from each.

Within this larger narrative—or rather narratives—are a myriad of smaller ones. How material is presented will depend on the maturation of the students' capacities.

For instance, World Wide Web sites, such as the *National Geographic* and the *Scientific American*, provide interesting resources for various age levels on the diversity of life on this planet. Grade-school children can be invited to study other species by beginning with an adventure story: the story of Darwin's journey to the Galapagos Islands and his explorations of South America. For young children, there can be stories about how different species relate (some of which follow), coupled with field trips for first-hand observations of animals in children's zoos. Some of the visuals in this book—for example, on the seahorses—can also be used with young children.

In middle school and high school, young people can be made aware of the extraordinary fact that there are in nature mathematical patterns or ratios that repeat themselves in seemingly totally unconnected natural bodies and phenomena—from the spirals of hurricanes, sea waves, galaxies, DNA, seashells, seahorses, ram's horns, and pine cones to the fingers of human hands, arms, legs, and feet, even the reproduction rates of rabbits. The mathematical ratio of one radius to the next larger is always .618 or *phi*, and of a larger to a smaller, it is 1.618. These patterns, already discovered by early Egyptian and Greek scientist-philosophers such as Pythagoras, who called them the "golden ratio" or "golden spiral," are also found in numbers. Leonardo Fibonacci showed this in his famous series of Fibonacci numbers (1, 1, 2, 3, 5, 8, 13, 21, 34, 55, 89, 144, etc.). When added together, the ratios of these adjacent pairs moves toward the golden ratios; for example, if you add 2 and its adjacent number 3, you get 5; when you add 3 and 5, you get 8, and so on. In all these the ratio is .618. Fibonacci described his series as representing a natural growth progression, related to the Greek *phi* or creative order of the universe, the *logos* (the root of *logarithmic*).[6] Students can perhaps relate this to one of the themes in the movie *Contact*, where the only way the message from the aliens could be deciphered was through the "universal language of mathematics" in which they communicated.

Studying the natural sciences in this larger frame highlights the interconnection of all life—providing a sound footing for the environmental ethic we urgently need in this time of mounting environmental problems caused by the irresponsible use of advanced technology in service of the conquest and domination of nature. It arouses girls' and boys' interest in science early on, and paves the way for a clearer understanding of how science and technology are guided by cultural values, and how these values differ, depending on the degree to which a society orients to the partnership or dominator model.

In this chapter, we will look at cosmic, planetary, and biological evolution. In the chapter that follows, we will go on to look at cultural evolution, and at how, with the emergence of our species, evolution takes a dramatic new turn as it enters the new phase we may call the age of human co-evolution.

The Emergence and Evolution of the Universe

The story of the evolution of the universe is the first major vertical curriculum thread on the partnership learning tapestry. As the astrophysicist Eric Chaisson writes in his book *The Life Era*,[7] scientists have been piecing together this remarkable story by "studying the galaxies that light up the far away and the long ago."[8]

Many centuries ago, scientists discovered that the Earth is not flat and that neither the Earth nor the sun is the center of the universe, as had been believed by Aristotle and maintained by medieval Church doctrine. Today we know much more. We know that our galaxy of stars, in which our sun is only one star, is just one of many other galaxies, huge structures of matter spanning on average 100,000 light years across.[9]

Over the past half-century, using powerful new technologies, scientists have been able to study the most minuscule subatomic particles and look at distant stars in the farthest vistas of space. They have found out that since the universe began, about 15 billion years ago, it has been constantly changing. Our Milky Way galaxy emerged only 5 billion years ago, after the universe had been expanding and developing for 10 billion years.[10] It took another billion years until the first living cell on our planet Earth emerged, about 4 billion years ago.[11]

Scientists have also found that ours is what they call a contingent universe, where at every stage there are different possible outcomes. That is, ours is a universe of uncertainties as well as probabilities. As quantum mechanics shows, rather than being predetermined, different possibilities arise at every stage. We know, for example, to a very high degree of probability that the sun will "rise" tomorrow. However, the unexpected can happen; for example, tornadoes can strike and stock markets can crash without warning.

This fascinating saga of the evolution of our universe, our planet, and life on this Earth can—in as simplified a form as needed, depending on the grade level—introduce children to such subjects as astronomy, geology, and physics. Teachers can engage children in this story through a variety of old and new approaches. They can invite students to create visual images of the birth of our planetary system or images of the evolution of

FIGURE 3.1   "Tree"

Imagine the emergence of the first tree.
CREDIT: *"Tree," by John Mason.*

Earth in its earliest stage of lava and rocks, long before the first appearance of life. Teachers can bring different kinds of rocks to class and ask students to imagine what the Earth looked like before there was vegetation or any other form of life (see Figure 3.1).

Teachers can also tell stories about some of the scientists who have played an important role in the exploration of the Earth and the heavens, including women and nonwhite people, who are rarely noted in most textbooks on the subject.

Teachers could begin by asking students to draw a picture of an astronomer. This is a good way of making visible certain common assumptions for later discussion. How is the astronomer depicted in the students' drawings? What gender is represented? What race or ethnicity?[12]

Typically, children think of astronomers—and most scientists—as European-American men wearing glasses and labcoats. Most children will not see themselves in the image they have drawn because they are of a different sex or ethnic background. Some may not want to become like this person, who resembles what they think of as a "nerd."

This image of scientists works to the disadvantage of most children. Because they cannot identify with it, they do not see themselves entering the professions that will in the 21st century not only be highly paid but also will determine many of the policies that shape everyone's future.

To counter such stereotypes, students can learn about a woman who lived 1,600 years ago and was considered the most eminent intellectual of her time. This is the story of Hypatia, the legendary philosopher and scientist of ancient Alexandria. This remarkable woman wrote many books that perished when the great library of Alexandria, one of the last repositories of ancient wisdom and knowledge, was burnt down. But Bishop Cyril of Alexandria (later canonized as Saint Cyril) condemned her to death for the "crime" of teaching "pagan" knowledge and presuming, against God's commandments, to teach men. As a result of his orders (the equivalent of what Muslim fanatics today call a *fatwa*, or command to kill a sinner or infidel), Hypatia died a terrible and much too early death. She was murdered in the name of religion by Christian fanatics in 391, cut to pieces with razor-sharp oyster shells, on her way to the Academy of Alexandria.[13]

Students can also learn about Sofie Brahe, who lived and worked more than one thousand years later. At a time when women were effectively barred from entry into scientific professions, Brahe managed to learn astronomy. Defying convention, she often worked with her brother, the well-known astronomer Tycho Brahe (1546–1601). In their legendary castle-observatory on an island near Copenhagen, the Uraniborg, they etched the sky, painstakingly remapping the positions of a thousand stars.[14] Maria Kunitz (1610–1664) also broke with the convention that excluded women from scientific pursuits. She was a mathematician and astronomer who set herself to the task of simplifying the monumental, but complex, planetary tables developed by the famous astronomer Johannes Kepler. When she published her more accessible tables in her book *Urania Propitia* (1650), the notion of a woman writing a book on mathematical science was so novel that few people believed it was her own work. In later editions, in fact, a preface had to be added in which her husband asserted that he had taken no part in the effort.[15]

Students can also learn about Hispanic and black scientists—for example, the Cuban scientist Carlos Finlay (1833–1915), who identified the mosquito as a carrier of the deadly yellow-fever germ. His work and the resulting control of the mosquito population helped to contain the spread of yellow fever. Another example is the American astronomer Benjamin

Banneker, whose story can also inspire children who might otherwise have no role models for becoming interested in astronomy. Banneker was a black man who was taught to read and write by his grandmother, an indentured servant who bought her freedom and that of Banneker's African grandfather, Banaka. Each day, when the farm work was done, Banneker used his reading and writing skills to educate himself in literature, history, and mathematics. At the age of twenty-two, he amazed his neighbors by building a striking clock with only a borrowed pocket watch as a model. Banneker did not begin studying astronomy and surveying until he was fifty years old, when he taught himself how to calculate the positions of the planets and to predict the dates of lunar and solar eclipses using borrowed astronomy books and instruments. Then, after thousands of calculations, he created astronomical data tables setting times and sky locations for the sun, moon, and planets on each day of the year. In 1790, Banneker became the astronomer for the surveying team that helped draw the plans for building Washington, D.C. When in 1804 Banneker sent his astronomical tables to Thomas Jefferson, Jefferson was so impressed that he sent the manuscript to the French Academy of Sciences. These tables were later distributed internationally by the anti-slavery movement as "proof that the powers of the mind are disconnected with colour of the skin."[16]

After learning stories about female, Hispanic, African-American, and other scientists who do not fit the conventional stereotype, children can again be asked to draw pictures of astronomers and scientists. Chances are that these will now be much more varied and inclusive than before.

Another way to enlarge and deepen students' perceptions of scientists and science is to introduce materials about premodern cultures that extensively investigated the heavens long before the advent of modern science. For example, more than 5,000 years ago the ancient Egyptians aligned their pyramids with particular stellar bodies. And approximately 3,000 years ago the Neolithic peoples who built Stonehenge and Avebury aligned circles of immense stones to the movements of the sun and moon. They focused particularly on the winter solstice, the shortest day of the year—a day on which, according to the ancients' belief, the sun was reborn every year. The implication, as archeologist Marija Gimbutas notes, is that the ancient human interest in astronomy—a field that was already extremely sophisticated thousands of years ago in cultures whose knowledge has since been forgotten—was connected with religious beliefs and rituals focusing on the regeneration of life.[17]

This ancient connection of astronomical investigations with religious myths and rituals recently came to light through the investigations by French ethnologists of a contemporary African tribe. In studying the Dogon of Mali, they found that Dogon mythology and cosmology reveal an astonishingly sophisticated knowledge of astronomy, centering on Sirius, the brightest star in the sky. Some theorists have contended that the Dogon acquired this astronomical knowledge from European visitors. But given how deeply rooted this astronomy is in Dogon mythology, it seems more likely that it was developed in Africa by the ancestors of the Dogon themselves.[18]

Students can be asked to imagine why the Dogon were so interested in the movements of the stars. They can also be invited to make up their own stories (or, in later grades, to do research about) why constellations in our solar system might have been given such fanciful names as the Big Dipper, Scorpius, Ursa Minor (Little Bear), Taurus, and Sagittarius.

Teachers could begin with something as simple as asking children to look at the stars in the sky and inviting them to share their own observations. They can also encourage students to pursue the study of scientific explorations by stimulating their imaginations with stories of astronauts, including Sally Ride, Rhea Seddon, and Ellen Ochoa, who have explored the uncharted territory of outer space.

Using this story-telling approach, teachers can illuminate the study of cosmic and planetary evolution, astronomy, and physics in the context of the thrill of exploration, both physical and mental.

The Emergence and Evolution of Life

Scientists have recently discovered that the first emergence of life on our planet can be traced back even earlier than was thought, to approximately 4 billion years ago.[19] This shift from inanimate to animate matter is one of the great mysteries of the universe. We do not know why this happened, but we do know that once life appeared it continued to reinvent itself.

The first molecules, or combinations of cells, arose relatively soon thereafter. But the first vertebrates, complex life forms with a skeletal structure to hold together huge numbers of cells, only emerged approximately 500 million years ago.[20] The first mammals emerged only 250 million years ago.[21] The genus *homo* emerged between 5 and 2 million years ago.[22] Our species, *homo sapiens sapiens*, which coexisted with the earlier Neanderthals for some time, emerged only about 100,000 years ago.[23]

This fascinating story of the evolution of life on our Earth is the second major vertical curriculum thread, following the earlier inanimate era of our planet. It is an evolutionary thread that takes us on an extraordinary journey: from the simplest one-celled organisms to ever more complex crawling, flying, and, most recently, walking and talking life forms. And today, human minds and hands—and the extension of these capacities through ever more complex technologies—are literally co-creating our planet with the processes of nature.

This second chronological thread, the history of life on our planet, runs through the entire curriculum from kindergarten to twelfth grade. It introduces students—in as simplified a form as needed, depending on the grade—to subjects such as chemistry and biology. These subjects, too, can effectively be contextualized in a story: the amazing story of the enormously varied shapes, sizes, and forms that life takes on our wondrous planet.

This story brings the natural sciences to life. It also encourages children to appreciate the wonder and awe of our natural habitat and the many creatures who share it with us.

By emphasizing diversity, teachers can help students understand that, contrary to what they are still often told, no particular human behavior is "natural" just because it also can be found in some other related species. For example, that some species of apes, such as savanna baboons, are male-dominant does not justify an argument for a male-dominated human society. As we will see, there are enormous differences in the behavior patterns and social organization of different species, including different species of apes. Most important, in our use of language, huge behavioral repertoire, and variability of social organizations, our human species is different from the vast majority of animals on Earth.

This is a more balanced perspective on biological evolution than the view offered by neo-Darwinian theories that focus primarily on a competitive struggle for genetic survival. It is different from evolutionary theories about how and why particular species spring up and/or change. And it is different from sociobiological popularizations that make it seem that humans are innately flawed and violent, and that this is something we share with all primates—an impression often given by television specials on evolution.

Students need information that enables them to watch such programs more critically. Partnership education provides this kind of information. Even more important, it offers students a wider standpoint that includes two different views, or stories, of biological—including human—evolution: one told from the perspective of the dominator model and the other told from a larger perspective that includes, and often highlights, the partnership model.

The first story, drawing primarily from the neo-Darwinist and sociobiological writings that are found in many textbooks, focuses on natural selection. Generally, the picture we get from these and other sources is that ours is a species driven by selfishness and "natural" violence to ruthlessly compete with one another. This view is reinforced by nature films endlessly focusing on predatory killer animals, with snippets of neo-Darwinian evolution theory in the background as a "reminder" that violence is natural to us because of our descent from animals. In discussing this dominator view with students, teachers in the higher grades may wish to use excerpts from the books of Richard Dawkins, who made this view come to life by portraying evolution as "a blind watchmaker" and ours as a species driven by "selfish genes." Other theorists, such as David Barash and Michael Ghiselin, further asserted that the only thing in evolution pushing us to become morally better, or to develop a sense of right and wrong, is our innate selfishness.[24]

Teachers can invite students to critically examine the assumptions on which this perspective is based. Then they can introduce students to quotations from Darwin himself, such as his statement that natural selection is *not* the only principle operating in biological evolution—that particularly when we come to human evolution, other factors, such as the evolution of what he called the "moral sense," come into play.[25] A fact long overlooked is that in *The Descent of Man* Darwin identifies "conscience" as the "supreme judge and monitor" for our species.[26] In addition, he specifically tells us that "the moral qualities are advanced, either directly or indirectly, much more through the effects of habit, the reasoning powers, instruction, religion, etc., than through natural selection."[27] Teachers can also help students reexamine, and critique, the "nature red-in-tooth-and-claw" evolutionary focus by assigning excerpts from books such as *Not in Our Genes* [28] and *Cooperation*.[29]

After this critique, students can go on to look at a different story about the evolution of life and of our own species. This story recognizes that there is in evolution a food chain, that there are predators and prey, that species compete for evolutionary niches, and that this is part of the reality of life on this Earth. But it also recognizes that there is—and has been almost from the beginning—another side to evolution. This is the element of cooperation and caring that Darwin recognized as the biological root of our moral sense. It is an element that we see in species ranging from ants and bats to geese and beavers. And it is an element that in some species—such as dogs, dolphins, and humans—manifests itself in what we would call empathy with and compassion for other species. (See Boxes 3.1 and 3.2 for relevant readings.)

An important contributor to this second perspective on evolution, emphasizing caring bonds between mothers and infants beginning already with the emergence of mammals, is the paleoanthropologist Adrienne Zihlman. In contrast to the male-centered "man the hunter" view of early hominid and human evolution in which women are invisible except in occasional references to male sexual competition for females and maternal care for infants, Zihlman emphasizes the role of "woman the gatherer," pointing to the important, though neglected, paleoanthropological finding that hominids and early humans relied far more on plants than on meat for subsistence.[35] Also in contrast to "man the hunter" speculations that male bonding to facilitate killing animals for food was central to the formation of the first social units, Zihlman (as well as other scholars such as Nancy Tanner[36] and Sally Linton Slocum[37]) focus on the important role in evolution of mother-infant bonds. They propose that these constitute not only "the foundation for social bonds with other individuals later in life" but also (as we will see in this chapter) the basis for the development of that most important human capacity: the ability to communicate through language that is at the core of our complex social networks.[38]

Paul MacLean takes a similar position. Based on extensive brain research, he proposes that the development of language came out of the caring relationship between mother and child and that social intelligence evolved largely through play.[39] Neurobiologists Humberto Maturana and Francisco Varela also emphasize that language is rooted in caring behaviors;[40] and in his introduction to *El Caliz y la Espada* (the Spanish edition of *The Chalice and the Blade*), Maturana introduces the concept of the biology of love, which he has since developed further in *Origins of Humanness in the Biology of Love*, written with the psychologist Gerda Verden-Zöller.[41]

A significant, and fascinating, aspect of the evolution of love as intrinsic to human biology is the fact that we humans derive intense pleasure

---

BOX 3.1   Readings on Evolution

This dual side of evolution is recognized not only by Darwin but also by later scientists such as Peter Kropotkin in *Mutual Aid* and Ashley Montagu in *The Nature of Human Aggression*.[30] It is also a theme in the works of numerous contemporary biologists, neurologists, and anthropologists, such as Lynn Margulis in her theory of symbiogenesis;[31] Mae-Wan Ho in her theory that the organism participates in evolution through a network driven more by linking than by brutal struggle;[32] Glynn Isaac in his hypothesis that food-sharing favored the development of language, social reciprocity, and the intellect;[33] and Ralph Holloway in his theory that language originated in a basically cooperative rather than aggressive social matrix.[34]

---

from love—not only from receiving it but from giving it. Scientists are today finding that our bodies are equipped with the capacity to release powerful chemicals when we engage in caring and caretaking behaviors—chemicals that reward these activities by making us feel good.

These chemicals, known as neuropeptides, provide us with sensations ranging from the euphoria or high of "falling in love," to the enormous joy that parents and other adults often experience when caring for babies, to the serene contentment reported by people in long-term loving relationships. A good resource here is my book *Sacred Pleasure*, which suggests that in looking at the history of life we need to focus more on these biological rewards for loving behaviors—as they represent the development of what, in the normative sense of the word, are more evolved ways of living on this Earth.

Another important resource is David Loye's *Darwin's Lost Theory of Love*. Loye, a psychologist and evolution theorist, details how love, cooperation, and our evolutionary "nudge" toward moral sensitivity evolved over millions of years. Particularly useful for comparing popular neo-Darwinist and sociobiological accounts with more complex evolutionary theories is Loye's documentation of Darwin's view of morality as rooted in biological evolution.[42] Loye identifies two halves to Darwin's theory of evolution: (1) a foundation, articulated in *Origin of Species*, that focuses on natural selection and random variation, and (2) a superstructure, articulated in Darwin's notebooks and *Descent of Man*, consisting of love, moral sensitivity, reasoning, and other factors that became primary at the human level.[43]

The primatologist Frans deWaal, too, departs from some of the standard sociobiological views in arguing that we humans are basically good-natured rather than bad-natured. Although deWaal also notes unempathic, cruel, and violent behavior in monkeys and apes, his focus is on empathy, caring, and the drive for peaceful relations as important evolutionary developments that are observable in nonhuman species. He argues in his book *Good Natured* that the roots of morality can be found in other primates as well as in species such as elephants and dolphins.[44]

The work of psychiatrists and psychologists such as Abraham Maslow, Roberto Assagioli, Kasimierz Dabrowski, Robert Ornstein, and Allan Combs adds other dimensions to this second story about the evolution of "human nature." These works are not to be confused with some of the writings in the field that calls itself evolutionary psychology, as these have tended to remain squarely within the more dominator-oriented worldview of most sociobiologists, focusing primarily on what Maslow calls "defense" or survival needs. By contrast, Assagioli and Dabrowski are primarily interested in what Maslow calls "growth" or self-actualizing needs, such as the need to love and be loved and the need to work for some higher goal. In contrast to Freud's emphasis on the unconscious, Assagioli focuses on what he calls the "superconscious" as the source of our higher aspirations and our moral drives. Dabrowski writes of the distinction between the authentic and inauthentic self, and of the human drive to become attuned to our higher nature, which he considers our human authenticity. Maslow's work, which became the basis for humanistic psychology and the later human potential movement, focuses on the drive of what he called the self-actualizing personality to move toward altruism as an integral part of self-actualization.[45] Drawing on Eastern as well as Western evolutionary thinking, Ornstein and Combs focus on the evolution of consciousness.[46]

This important psychological and humanistic dimension in the study of human evolution provides insights that are not available in most of the literature by biologists, who usually have no background in social science. In addition, as we will see, social psychology and sociology provide a third dimension that must be included in the study of human evolution. It is here that the two social configurations characteristic of the dominator and partnership models play a major role.[47]

A More Balanced View of Evolution

Looking at human evolution from this more multidisciplinary perspective offers us a more balanced view (see Box 3.3). In dealing with our own species, it makes it possible to see beyond selfishness as the only evolutionary motivation (countering the sociobiological theory of selfish genes). This larger perspective recognizes that we humans have a vast repertoire of emotions and behaviors—including cruelty and caring, violence and nonviolence, and hate and love. But it emphasizes those traits that most distinguish humans from other species—our enormous capacity for creativity and caring, as well as our enormous capacity for learning—which means that most of our behaviors are shaped by cultural rather than biological evolution.

The early roots of our caring behaviors can be observed in other species. Indeed, the evolution of love and the evolution of empathy are two fascinating, interconnected themes that become apparent once we look at the history of life on our planet from this more balanced perspective (see "Evolution of Love and Empathy" sidebar). What we are learning today about the cooperative behaviors of elephants, dolphins, and whales—also intelligent species with complex systems of communication—is of particular interest here. A good resource for teachers is *When Elephants Weep: The Emotional Lives of Animals* by Jeffrey Moussaieff Masson and Susan McCarthy,[48] which contains many stories about animals and their caring and empathic behaviors.

Beginning in lower grades, teachers can tell stories about the mutual aid and altruism shown by many species. For example, geese in flight will often support an injured or exhausted bird, helping it continue its long migratory journey. Bats not only share food with one another but care for the elderly and infirm and often adopt orphan bats and care for them.

Maternal love is an extremely powerful force among many species of mammals and birds. Mothers have been known to risk and even sacrifice their own lives to protect their young; a giraffe mother, for example, stood by her calf when a lion attacked, kicking it with her forelegs whenever it came close.[49] Cats have been known to jump into water to rescue their kittens.[50] In the publicized case of "Scarlett," an alley cat kept running into a burning building until she had rescued her four-week old litter, despite terrible, almost fatal, burns. (Scarlett, who fully recovered from her burns and was adopted, now has her own website called "Scar-

Dogs are noted for their empathy, as many children will attest.
CREDIT: *David Loye.*

lett's Web," which students can visit to learn more about her heroic story.)[51]

Paternal care is also vividly apparent in some species. For example, when a cotton-topped marmoset at the Jersey Zoo gave birth to the usual marmoset twins, the father took them, washed them, and carried them with him everywhere he went, often with one on each hip, only returning them to the mother to suckle. Marmoset males in the wild have also been observed to assist at the birth and to be very protective of the young. In the case of lionheaded marmosets, males have been seen mashing fruit in their fingers for the babies when they begin to wean.[52]

The males of still other primate species—for example, owl monkeys—carry their babies, play with them, and share food with them.[53] Direct paternal care is also seen in many species of birds. For example, kiwi bird fathers incubate the eggs and raise the chicks without help from the mother.[54] Contrary to the Freudian paradigm of murderous rivalry between fathers and sons, which has sometimes been claimed to represent the state of nature, father zebras remain on good terms with their grown sons and have been observed mourning the death of their young.[55]

In some species, the care and protection of the young has been observed to involve the whole group. Explorer Peter Freuchen reported that, when a wolf cub got caught in a trap set in a cairn of stones over a food cache, the adult wolves in the pack overturned many of the large stones and scraped the frozen earth around the trap in an effort to free the cub.[56] Elephants have frequently been observed to form a circle to protect their young. And bonds of affection between elephants are so strong that elephants often return to "elephant cemeteries" to touch the bones of their dead.[57] Elephant rescue stories also abound. In one case, when a baby elephant fell into a drinking hole and was being sucked down in the mud, the whole herd mobilized and, at the risk of their own safety, worked successfully to free the calf.

Caring bonds between mates and among family and friends are common as well. According to naturalist George Steller, when the crew of a ship killed a female sea cow, the male returned to the body for two consecutive days. When Kiko, a dolphin in a marine park in Hawaii, suddenly died, her companion Hoku refused to eat, swimming circles slowly with his eyes clenched shut, clearly grieving.[58] And, as noted, the caring of elephants for one another has been widely documented. Cynthia Moss, who spent years observing elephants in the wild, touchingly described their grief when one of their group dies. Baby elephants whose mothers have been killed by poachers illegally hunting elephants, a practice that is increasing, become so despondent that, despite efforts to comfort and care for them, most die of broken hearts.[59]

In some cases, caring extends across species boundaries. Dogs are legendary for their devotion to humans, even forfeiting their lives to save them. Schools of dolphins have been known to attack sharks to save humans. In 1996, a West African gorilla named Binti-Jua (Swahili for "daughter of sunshine") made headlines worldwide when a three-year-old boy fell into the gorilla enclosure at the Brookfield Zoo near Chicago and lay there unconscious. Seven-year-old Binti, with her own baby on her back, cradled the boy's limp body in her arms, rocked him softly, and kept the other gorillas (including the male silverback) at bay. She then carried him to an entrance door where the paramedics and zoo staff were waiting.[60] This kind of behavior—caring for not only an unrelated individual but for another species—is still another way in which theories that survival and/or passing on one's genes are the only driving forces in evolution are contradicted when we actually observe animal behavior from the more balanced perspective I propose.

As for the notion that dominant males get to mate more than others, this too is a myth that is today being disproved. As primatologist Barbara Smuts notes, the female savannah baboons she observed often mated not with the dominant males, but with the males with whom they had formed friendships. In other words, rather than choosing the biggest and most aggressive male (presumably, as some sociobiologists tell us, because he has "superior genes"), they preferred males they did not fear.[61] Indeed, far from trying to get mates by showing dominance, many animals go to great lengths to avoid frightening the females they are wooing. For example, a courting male mountain goat lowers his back to look smaller, keeps his horns back, and takes small steps. Male brown bears slouch, flatten their ears, and act playful.[62]

As we will see later in this chapter as well as in Chapter 5, among our close primate relatives, the bonobos (or pygmy chimpanzees, as they are also called, although they are no smaller than common chimpanzees), bonds based on sharing—particularly the sharing of sexual pleasure— are more important than hierarchies of domination. Indeed, this is one reason that bonobos in the wild have not been observed in violent engagements with other groups. An example reminiscent of the 1960s slogan "Make love, not war" was reported by a primatologist who witnessed two groups of bonobos meeting in the forest. He observed how tension was diffused through a female's initiation of a sexual liaison.[63]

Learning about what primatologists are today discovering about the varying lives of apes and monkeys in the wild can engage the interest of children of all ages in biological diversity. Children are also interested in stories about people who have spent their lives studying animals in their natural habitats. Here again teachers have an opportunity to include women, providing role models of scientists for girls.

Indeed, some of the most prominent observers of animal behavior in the last several decades have been women. These include not only the legendary Jane Goodall, who continues to study common chimpanzees, but also scientists such as Barbara Smuts and Shirley Strum, who have studied baboons; Dian Fossey, who, as depicted in the film *Gorillas in the Mist*, lost her life protecting the troop of gorillas she was living with from poachers; and Cynthia Moss, who has spent many years with African elephant herds and movingly describes the emotional bonds between these extraordinary creatures, who are today, like the bonobo chimpanzees and many other species, irresponsibly being killed.

BOX 3.2   More Readings on Evolution

In addition to the materials mentioned earlier, teachers in the higher grades can use as a handout an excerpt from chapter 9 of my book *Sacred Pleasure*. This excerpt describes the evolution of love as a major, though still largely neglected, evolutionary development—one that needs to be emphasized in teaching about human evolution. (The same topic is discussed further in the "Love and Being Human" sidebar at the end of this chapter.) Another resource that can be used as a handout is the article by brain researcher Paul MacLean titled "Women: A More Balanced Brain?"[64] in which he discusses the evolution of caring as well as the bilateral brain characteristic of human females and how it relates to qualities such as empathy. A third resource is the article by Sharon Begley titled "How to Build a Baby's Brain,"[65] which summarizes information about the importance of early childhood years in shaping human emotions, intelligence, and behavior. It highlights findings from neuroscience showing that the human brain's neural pathways are largely put in place during the critical first years of a child's life—in other words, that many of our traits and behaviors depend on the kind of childrearing we are given. Another good resource here is the video *I Am Your Child: The First Years Last Forever*, narrated by Rob Reiner and produced by the Reiner Foundation.

For an overview of evolution, from the Precambrian Era to the emergence of *homo sapiens*, I especially recommend Adrienne Zihlman's *The Human Evolution Coloring Book* to teachers. Though a coloring book, it is designed not for children but, rather, for college and possibly high school students, who, by coloring line-drawing illustrations, can effectively understand and learn complex information. This book is of particular value for a number of reasons, including its gender-balanced approach and its inclusion of bonobo chimpanzees. A visual excerpt from it is included in Appendix A.[66]

Humans and Other Primates

Since we humans are primates, works that deal with human evolution often give special attention to our primate relatives: monkeys and apes. But once again, rather than using particular species to claim that we humans are naturally inclined to be violent and male-dominant, as many of these accounts do, the more balanced account I am proposing highlights the variability of primate behaviors and social organization.

As Linda Marie Fedigan notes in her book *Primate Paradigms: Sex Roles and Social Bonds*,[67] in many sociobiological accounts the savannah baboon, a species characterized by rigid hierarchies of domination in which males are approximately twice the size of females, has been presented as the prototype for our primate ancestors. By contrast, I am in this account proposing a multilinear rather than unilinear model for primate (including human) evolution: one in which the analytical lenses of the dominator and partnership models are useful tools.[68] This account gives special attention to our species' two closest primate relatives: the common chimpanzees and the so-called pygmy chimpanzees or bonobos.

The DNA of bonobos (pygmy chimpanzees) and that of common chimpanzees (who are actually no larger) is basically the same; moreover, it is not very different from that of our own species. However, observations of both these species in the wild indicate that there are marked differences between the behaviors and social organizations of bonobos and common chimps. As we will see in the section on life sciences in Chapter 5, the bonobos orient much more to the partnership model than do the common chimps.

This shows that primates can—and in the case of the bonobo chimpanzees, do—rely more on bonds based on pleasure and the sharing of benefits than on rankings based on fear and force. It contradicts the notion that a social organization orienting primarily to the dominator model is inevitable in primates, or that it is rooted in "selfish genes." To convey this point more clearly, teachers can use as a handout the article "The Bonobos' Peaceable Kingdom" by primatologist Takayoshi Kano,[69] along with the excerpts on bonobos from *Sacred Pleasure*.

As we have seen, learning more about how these and many other animals form caring and cohesive communities is an important component in the study of biological evolution. Zoology and animal ethology then become not dry technical topics but the stories of other sentient beings with whom we share our planet.

One of the most interesting chapters in this more balanced account of biological evolution is the story of the emergence of our own human species. There are two theories about human evolution: one placing our origins in Africa, the other arguing for multiregional origins. There is also a great deal of controversy about time scales, sequences, and such critical matters as the evolution of that most distinctive of human capacities—our ability to communicate, and think, using complex systems of language. Some scientists argue that language goes back over a million years, while others argue that it is as recent as the Upper Paleolithic, or just 35,000 years ago.[70]

As noted earlier, much of what is still being written about the story of human evolution follows the so-called neo-Darwinian trajectory, as well as the old male-centered view that "man the hunter" was its main protagonist. Indeed, most of the scientists in this field have been men, although there are some notable exceptions, such as Mary Leakey, who found the first early human fossil in East Africa in 1959,[71] and Adrienne Zihlman, who has proposed that the bonobo chimpanzee is the most likely prototype for the "missing link" between hominids and earlier primates, and who has also helped to develop a theory about the origins of human tools in which women play an important role.[72]

Zihlman is among a growing number of scientists—most of them women in fields ranging from physical anthropology and biology to cultural anthropology, psychology, and sociology—who, over the last thirty years, have been developing a more gender-balanced narrative of early human evolution. As Zihlman notes, this has been an uphill struggle. No sooner are earlier male-centered accounts of human evolution contradicted by new evidence than new theories are put forward to again render women invisible, or at best portray them as "handmaidens to men"— squarely placing men, and with them an emphasis on aggression and competition, at the center of our human adventure.[73] Not only that, these male-centered theories—which invariably portray male dominance as natural—continue to be replicated in the vast majority of textbooks, as well as in visual representations of human evolution. Typical are museum dioramas where a male stands tall in the foreground while a group of females sit in the background, or where a male towers over a smaller crouching female, as in the dioramas of Neanderthals and *homo sapiens* at the American Museum of Natural History. (For a survey of such scenes in books, see Diane Gifford-Gonzales, "You Can Hide, But You Can't Run: Representations of Women's Work in Illustrations of Paleolithic Life," in which the author speaks of one classic pattern for depicting women sitting on or working with animal skins as the faceless "drudge-on-the-hide."[74]

By developing more balanced, and accurate, narratives in which women, and not just men, play a major role in innovating and making hominid and human evolution happen, women scientists are making significant contributions to our understanding of how we became human. These contributions not only take into account new findings that do not fit with the old "man the hunter" narratives; they also present a view of our human emergence in which more stereotypically "feminine" human characteristics, such as nurturance and nonviolence, are highlighted—whether they reside in women or men.

For example, as noted earlier, Zihlman goes beyond earlier accounts about what distinguishes our species: our upright posture, which free our hands for tool use, and our large brains, which give us our great capacity to learn, making possible our immense behavioral flexibility. Like other theorists, such as Glynn Isaacs, Nancy Tanner, Ralph Holloway, Paul MacLean, and Humberto Maturana, she emphasizes the role of communication and caring in human evolution. The theory she developed together with Nancy Tanner also emphasizes our enormous human capacity for creativity. Indeed, Tanner and Zihlman propose that, to some degree, we humans have been co-creators of our own biological evolution—and that females played a key part in this process.

As Tanner writes in *Becoming Human*, not only is it more than likely that females developed and used some of the earliest tools, such as slings and other means of carrying infants, baskets to carry gathered plants, and possibly also tools to dig for tubers and roots, but it is very likely that these tools, in turn, affected our evolution. "Tools for gathering meant mothers could collect more food for offspring who, then, could be supported longer before becoming independent"[75]—a longer period of dependency being a salient characteristic of our species. It was this creativity that made it possible for children to have a longer period in which to "learn social and technological traditions."[76] This was a key development in human evolution, as it also led to the much greater role of culture in shaping our behavior as compared to that of other species.[77]

One could even speculate that as we increasingly relied not on teeth but on the use of tools and cooking methods to soften food, the huge molars characteristic of most other primates became less necessary, leaving more cranial room for larger brains. As many scientists have noted, it is our larger relative brain size—averaging 1,350 cubic centimeters (a quantum leap from even our first hominid ancestors, who attained a brain size of 450 cubic centimeters)—that characterizes our human emergence.[78] One could further speculate that this reduction in molar size also left more room for the voice boxes required for the complex verbalizations of human language—leading to the much greater capacity for communication and symbolization that made possible the complex social, technological, and artistic development that we call human culture.

Indeed, as Paul MacLean argues, it is highly probable that the most unique and important of human tools, our highly complex language, originated from the mother-child bond—in other words, from the bond of caring and love between mother and child.[79] Moreover, as Humberto Maturana and Gerda Verden-Zöller emphasize in writing about what Maturana calls the biology of love, one of the most important developments in our evolution was this human capacity for love.[80]

Without this human capacity for love, our species could not survive. It is only through the caring motivated by love that human babies, who are helpless for a prolonged period of time, not only survive but continue to develop their brains after birth. (Again, see "Evolution of Love and Empathy" sidebar.)

This approach to the study of human evolution makes it possible for young people to refocus from selfishness and violence as the main themes in our evolution to caring and creativity as equally, and in some ways more important, themes. It also makes it possible for them to see that our primary and most meaningful identity is as human beings, regardless of gender, race, religion, or nationality. This reminder of our essential oneness as a species is a particularly pressing lesson in a time of mounting worldwide regression toward in-group versus out-group scapegoating and violence.

At the same time, this approach encourages young people to appreciate, and respect, other life forms and our Mother Earth, thus better equipping them to deal responsibly with the environmental challenges we all face. It also highlights the critical importance of human cultural and technological evolution—the subject of the chapter that follows.

BRIDGING THE GAP BETWEEN
SCIENCE AND SPIRITUALITY:
MEANINGFUL EVOLUTION

Is evolution, and thus life on this Earth, devoid of meaning—to borrow Shakespeare's poignant words, a tale "full of sound and fury, signifying nothing"? Some people believe that the only argument for a larger meaning comes from religious traditions. But science too can provide us with this argument.

I have chosen the phrase *meaningful evolution* to describe a view of evolution in which we can find a larger sense of purpose. This view differs sharply from fundamentalist religious interpretations that totally ignore scientific findings, such as empirical evidence that life on our planet is not 5,000 years old but billions of years old. But it also differs from many so-called neo-Darwinian theories that, as evolution theorist David Loye points out in his book *Darwin's Lost Theory of Love*, ignore what Darwin himself emphasized: that factors other than random variation and natural selection—for example, what he called "the moral sense" and "mutual aid" or caring cooperation—come into play at the human level of evolution. It is an approach that draws from an emerging body of scientific findings pointing to the evolutionary roots of caring for others and caring for what happens to future generations. It highlights that what we do in this lifetime is meaningful because it advances the evolution of our species and fulfills our responsibilities to this planet.

In short, the approach I call meaningful evolution provides a third alternative: an alternative to both creationism and theories of evolution that leave us with the sense that randomness and selfishness are the governing principles of evolution. It offers a bridge between the core partnership values of religion and the empirical findings of science.

Meaningful evolution transcends the conventional polarity between spirituality and science, grounding spirituality in evolution. It identifies for us as a species a meaningful relationship to life and the wonder of the universe. It takes into account key evolutionary developments such as the evolution of consciousness, creativity, and love. By offering a more inclusive story of evolution—one that does not ignore the fact that love and creativity are just as grounded in evolution as violence and destructiveness—it also supports what I have called spiritual courage: putting love into action, even when it means going against established dominator norms.[81]

Young people are empowered to be the best they can be when they know that our strivings for love, beauty, and justice—what for centuries have been called the highest ideals that drive civilization ahead—are part of human biology, rooted in evolution. Whether or not they are given a formal religious context, these strivings constitute the core of a partnership spirituality that recognizes a larger mission for us in life and imbues us with a sense of awe and wonder at the majesty of the universe.

When young people understand that these strivings are at the core of our humanity, they can imbue their lives with greater meaning. Most important, they can more consciously and caringly participate in the great adventure of the evolution of life on our planet.

THE EVOLUTION OF LOVE AND EMPATHY

Two seldom-noted evolutionary developments that warrant special notice are the evolution of love and the evolution of empathy. Empathy is integral to love. And love brings with it empathy. These interconnected developments have played a key role in human evolution.

How did these trends begin?

Empathy and love have ancient evolutionary roots. They originated with parental care of the young, which, in turn, became much more developed with the emergence of mammals, since all mammalian young require parental care to survive.

What happens with mammals?

Unlike most reptiles, baby mammals, like baby birds, cannot simply walk (or fly) off and survive on their own when they are born. Both require food, protection from predators, and guidance in learning survival skills. But among mammals the bond between mother and infant is closer because mammals gestate in their mothers' wombs and survive only by nursing— that is, by suckling their mothers' milk (hence the term *mammal*).

Some reptiles display a degree of parental caring. For example, crocodiles protect the eggs they lay as well as the baby crocodiles that emerge from them. However, other reptiles, such as lizards, lay their eggs and then leave them to hatch on their own. Moreover, the young of reptile species such as the rainbow lizard must hide in the deep underbrush after they hatch if they are to avoid being eaten by their parents.

The evolutionary movement from reptiles to birds and mammals was in significant respects a movement toward more caring and empathy. Like all trends in evolution, this was not linear. But it was a discernible trend, since to motivate parental care all mammals and birds need some degree of what we call love, and with it empathy (or feeling with another being).

In most mammalian species, this caring is evident in maternal behavior. For example, a documentary on cheetahs shows how a cheetah mother allowed her daughter (whom she recognized through her distinctive call) and her daughter's three malnourished cubs to eat from her kill, while she herself ate nothing—a behavior we might call altruism. Even beyond this, among many species of birds and mammals mothers have been known to sacrifice their own lives to protect their young.

In some species, this empathic caring goes beyond maternal to paternal caring. Examples include kiwi birds, marmosets, owl monkeys, and tamarin monkeys. Among elephants, empathic caring is extended to other members of the herd; when danger threatens, adults form a protective circle around the young. Caring sometimes extends to other species, as illustrated by dolphins and dogs who have saved human lives. And it is clearly visible in our species, not only in maternal and paternal love, but in altruistic behavior toward strangers. Dramatic examples are the people who risked, and sometimes lost, their own lives and the lives of their entire family to help Jews in Nazi Europe. (This behavior brings into question the sociobiological contention that altruism is really only a matter of kin helping kin as a way of ensuring that related genes will be passed on, since the Nazis made it clear that, as punishment, the whole family would be killed if any single member helped Jews.)

What happens with humans?

Human babies require an extended period of care and protection, far more than any other species. Thus the evolution of love and empathy had to advance still further with the emergence of our own species, since to sustain care for such a long period, and to the degree needed by human infants, necessitated a more fully developed and sustained capacity to love.

This long period of care is critical for the child's development. Human babies do not have fully developed brains when they are born. If they did, they would not be able to fit through the birth canal. So the human brain must instead continue to develop outside the mother's womb after the baby is born, particularly during the first year, but also for many years after.

Findings from neuroscience show that many of the brain's neural pathways are in critical respects laid *after* birth. *This means that, for humans, nurture is just as critical as nature, if not more so.*

Neuroscientists are today dramatically verifying that for a child's brain to properly develop, intellectually as well as emotionally, a high quality of empathy and caring are needed. We know that if babies are given empathic attention and stimulation from birth onward, they thrive both emotionally and intellectually. We also know that when babies are neglected and abused—that is, when they do not receive empathic love—they fail to develop their potentials. Not only that, they move into an emotional and behavioral mode responsive to, and replicative of, the dominator model—in a sense, an adaptation to an unsafe, abusive, violent environment.

As Dr. Bruce Perry of the Baylor College of Medicine puts it, these early experiences literally provide the organizing framework for the brain of a child. Or as Dr. Linda Mayes of the Yale Child Study Center notes, traumatic experiences in childhood change the structure of the brain.

Perry reports that the regions of the cortex and limbic system responsible for emotions, including attachment, are in the brains of severely abused children 20 to 30 percent smaller than in normal children. In adults who were abused as children the memory-making hippocampus is smaller than in nonabused adults. High cortisol levels associated with trauma during the vulnerable years of zero to three also increase activity in the brain structures involved in vigilance and arousal. As Perry notes, this leads to problems in attention regulation and self-control as well as to deficits in the ability to learn. It also changes the most basic behaviors—from how people eat (traumatized individuals tend to ingest more fat) to how they relate to others and themselves (traumatized children and adults tend either to act out aggression against others—including their own children—or to unconsciously turn it against themselves).[82] In short, both the individual child, and later adult, as well as society at large pay a high price if families, schools, and other social institutions fail to provide empathic caring.

Viewed from the perspective of the partnership and dominator models as two basic cultural possibilities, the partnership model—which supports and rewards caring and caretaking and is structured primarily around linkings based on the exchange of mutual benefits as well as hierarchies of actualization rather than domination[83]—is more in tune with the trend in evolution toward love and empathy.

But at this point we move from biological to cultural evolution. We see the need for a society that highly values and rewards caring and caretaking by both women and men. We also see that this is urgently needed if we are to survive in our age of powerful technologies of instant destruction, and advance evolution by actualizing our great human potentials for caring and creativity.

As we have seen, evolution is not predetermined. As scientists today emphasize, it is a contingent process—one that at this point in our evolution is largely contingent or dependent on what kind of family, social, economic, and cultural system we humans fashion.

LOVE AND BEING HUMAN

The impetus for the evolution of love was the need to motivate parents and/or other group members to nurture and protect babies. But, as we can already see in baby elephants and apes, who seem to die of a broken heart when their mothers die, the need to be loved—as distinguished from just being physically provided for—in the course of evolution became a survival need of human babies and infants. We see this most heartwrenchingly among human babies in orphanages, many of whom develop enormous emotional and learning difficulties, and sometimes even die, when their physical needs are attended to by people with no real emotional or empathic attachment to them.

This is a mysterious aspect of the evolution of love. It raises the question of why these babies could not thrive, or even survive, with rote care. How and why did this powerful need for being loved emerge?

We do not know the answer to these questions. But we do know that this human yearning for caring connection—the yearning of both young and old for love—is built into our species. It is one of our most basic human drives. It is so basic that the deprivation of empathic love—an early environment where what love we get is linked with insensitivity, neglect, coercion, abuse, and/or violence—has been shown to severely damage, even cripple, our development.

For this reason we humans need a partnership rather than dominator social organization to realize our evolutionary potentials. But there is still another, closely related reason: the fact that, as noted earlier, by the grace of evolution, we are provided with chemical rewards of pleasure not only when we are loved but when we love; not only when we are touched with caring but when we touch another with caring; nor only when we are cared for but when we care for others. In other words, there is in our human biology a push toward love through chemicals that make us feel good both when we receive love and when we give love—whether to a child, a lover, a friend, a pet, our sister and brother humans, or our beautiful Earth.

Not only that, people who have supportive and caring relations have been shown to recover more readily from illnesses and accidents. Likewise, people who empathically care for others, such as those who do volunteer work, tend to be healthier and live longer.

There is clearly some degree of empathy and love in societies that orient primarily to the dominator model—as there must be for human survival. But a rigid dominator social organization requires the suppression or, at best, compartmentalization of empathy; otherwise, rankings of domination and submission backed up by fear and force could not be maintained.

Dominator childrearing and education habituate children—in extreme cases, through the shaping of the neural pathways of their developing brains—to the psychological and often physical abuse required to function in rigid hierarchies of domination. Children chronically subjected to threats and aggression tend to become more vigilant, defensive, and aggressive, and to numb themselves so as to not feel their pain. All of these responses are ways of surviving in a hostile environment and, thus, could be said to be adaptive in rigid dominator contexts.[84] But they also lead to the unconscious replication, from generation to generation, of precisely the kinds of behaviors that make people feel bad and hold back their development. Moreover, they often make it extremely difficult for people with this kind of background to believe that there is an alternative to dominating or being dominated.[85]

Nonetheless, change is possible—and has actually been escalating for several centuries. Despite enormous resistance, there has been a strong movement worldwide to shift from authoritarian, male-dominated, violent families and nations to more democratic, gender-fair, and nonviolent families and nations.

At this point in our cultural evolution, when the rapid change from industrial to postindustrial society is destabilizing many entrenched beliefs and institutions, we have the opportunity to bring our cultural evolution more in line with the evolutionary thrust in our species toward our highest human potentials—including our powerful need and capacity for love. In fact, we humans have from the beginning been unconscious co-creators of our evolution. Both our culture and much of our physical environment are human creations. But to take advantage of the tremendous opportunity offered by our unsettled time, we have to become *conscious* co-creators of a partnership future.[86]

First, we need a clear understanding of the partnership and dominator models. *Second*, we need to identify the most effective interventions that, through changes in beliefs and behaviors, can interrupt the replication of the dominator elements of our culture.[87] (See "Shifting to Partnership" sidebar in Chapter 4.) *Third*, we need to develop new social and economic inventions that promote partnership relations. These ultimately are the aims of partnership education.

Our Human Adventure

Patterns and Possibilities

Scientists tell us that we are latecomers on Earth. We are such recent arrivals that if we think of the history of our planet as a twenty-four-hour day, we do not come into the picture until just before midnight.

But now the fate of our Earth is in our hands. The emergence of our species marked the beginning of a new era in planetary evolution: the age of human co-creation. Using our capacity to imagine changes, coupled with our capacity to make and use tools, we have radically altered our natural habitat. Today our technologies are so powerful that they rival the forces of nature. The ideas, values, and practices that guide these technologies will largely determine our future and that of other life forms on our planet. This is why it is essential that young people gain a clearer understanding of our cultural possibilities.

Partnership education exposes young people to two accounts of human cultural possibilities. It gives them the opportunity to think about two different pictures of what it means to be human, to evaluate the evidence for each, and to reach their own conclusions.

One account is the version still taught in most schools and universities. It is a story of random events with little meaning, of human inventiveness and achievement punctuated by constant wars, oppression, and bloodshed, by never-ending battles between men, tribes, and nations for domination and control. This is the familiar story of the rise and seemingly inevitable fall of civilizations that leave behind them monuments built by the rulers: a history written by conquerors in which women, children, and men of "lower classes" and "inferior races" play only minor roles. This story tells us that ours is a deeply flawed species—one that, despite its great capacities and aspirations, cannot live in equity and peace.

The other story widens the analytical lens to reveal a much larger picture: one that encompasses the whole of our history, including prehistory; the whole of humanity, both its female and male halves; and the whole of our lives, both the so-called public sphere and the private sphere of "ordinary" people's everyday lives. This story recognizes the dominator aspects of our past and present. But it focuses on the possibility of a more peaceful and equitable way of living. It highlights the underlying patterns characteristic of societies or periods orienting primarily to the partnership or dominator model, offering grounded hope and inspiration for creating a sustainable and humane future.

Being acquainted with the two stories of biological evolution sketched in the last chapter, students will already be aware that much of what we are still taught about animals in schools, universities, or through television and other mass media focuses primarily on aggression, violence, and domination—even though new studies show that many theories about animals need to be reexamined. To review this topic, students can be reminded how one television program after another leads viewers to believe that in many species—olive baboons, for example—the more high-ranking and aggressive a male is, the more likely females are to mate with him. In observing olive baboons in the wild, however, primatologists such as Shirley Strum have found that the most high-ranking and aggressive males were actually the least likely to mate. Not only that, such males also lost out when special foods were found, apparently because they had fewer friends willing to share with them.[1]

Students can be asked to quickly review some of the materials from Chapter 3. A good resource here is the book review titled "Myths of Gender," by paleoanthropologist Adrienne Zihlman, in which the author discusses both the old and new approaches to primate mating behaviors.[2]

Teachers can then proceed to tell the two different stories about our cultural evolution outlined in the pages that follow: one presenting the dominator model as the only human possibility and the other showing there is the partnership alternative.

Two Views of Our Cultural Origins

Much of what we are exposed to leads us to believe that what distinguishes our species is its "superior" capacity for violence and aggression.

This is illustrated by Stanley Kubrick's film *2001: A Space Odyssey* (based on Arthur C. Clark's novel) in a dramatic scene that shows the discovery of tools beginning with the realization by an ape-like creature that a large bone can be used as a weapon to kill another member of his species.

Students can be invited to discuss how this scene mirrors theories that the development of a dominator society and the development of human society are one and the same. They can observe how this message is all around us, in many subtle and not so subtle ways.

The "innocent" cartoon of a brutal caveman carrying a large club in one hand and with the other dragging a woman around by her hair (a cartoon we think nothing of showing to children) communicates the same message. In a few "amusing" strokes it tells us that from time immemorial men have equated sex with violence and that women have been passive sex objects—in other words, that the linking of sex with male dominance and violence is just "human nature."

Scholars from many disciplines tell us a different story of our cultural origins. In this story, the invention of tools does not begin with the discovery that we can use bones, stones, or sticks to kill one another. It begins much earlier, with the use of sticks and stones to dig up roots (which chimpanzees do), and continues with the fashioning of ways to carry food other than with bare hands (rudimentary vegetable slings and baskets) and of mortars and other tools to soften foods. In short, it focuses on tools that support, rather than take, life.[3]

In this story, the evolution of hominid, and then human, culture also follows more than one path. We have alternatives. We can organize relations in ways that reward violence and domination. Or, as some of our earliest art suggests, we can recognize our essential interconnection with one another and the rest of the living world. We can construct social relations based primarily on hierarchies of domination backed up by fear—and, ultimately, force. Or we can construct hierarchies of actualization, in which power is used not to control others but to enable others to realize their highest human potentials. When this happens, all in the society benefit.

Students can look at the differences between the partnership and dominator models and between hierarchies of domination and hierarchies of actualization through simple examples from their experiences in daily life both inside and outside their schools.[4] In higher grades, students can analyze the benefits of enabling others to realize their highest potentials (actualization) versus the crippling effects of controlling others (domination).

Teachers can begin with material on the familiar old theories of cultural and technological evolution that propose a progression of linear upward cultural and technological stages from "savagery" or "barbarism" to "civilization" with no distinction between societies that orient primarily to the partnership or dominator model. They can give examples of how, in fact, technologies have been invented and then lost (as in the European Dark Ages), and how "civilized societies" even in recent times (such as the Nazis' Third Reich and Milosevic's Yugoslavia), have been savage and barbaric—in other words, how these theories do not conform with reality.

Students can then be invited to take a fresh look at our human adventure on this Earth from the perspective of the underlying tension between the partnership and dominator models as two different possibilities. This can be done by introducing students to some of the materials in the sections that follow. These materials show that there is more than one possibility for organizing human relations. They provide a more hopeful view of what could lie ahead, by showing that, in times and places orienting primarily to a partnership model, people's lives are better—regardless of the level of technological development.

A useful resource is the material for high school classes developed by Maj Britt Eagle and Robin Andrea, included in Appendix A. Another useful resource is Box 4.1.

The reexamination of earlier cultures and myths in terms of their location on the partnership-dominator continuum can be an important ingredient in the multicultural education we need today to help reduce the tensions, and all too often violence, in our schools and nations stemming from racial and ethnic prejudices. One of the most effective ways of helping young people find common ground with different racial and ethnic groups is through an exploration of myths from cultures in Europe, Asia, Africa, North and South America, and Australia that still retain traces of more partnership-oriented ways of living. Most children will be fascinated by this exploration.

As teachers introduce the materials that follow, they can invite students to look at the present-day conflict between those who still view early human cultural evolution solely through a dominator lens and those who point to evidence of earlier cultures that oriented more to partnership. In higher grades, students can discuss this topic in the context of what historian of science Thomas Kuhn calls conflicts between old and new scientific paradigms. As Kuhn documents in *The Structure of Scientific*

BOX 4.1   Cultural Transformation Theory

In higher grades, students can be exposed to the more sophisticated analysis provided by *cultural transformation theory*. This approach takes into account not just one but two evolutionary movements, focusing on the interaction between them.

One movement consists of the shifts from one major technological phase to another. These are the familiar technological phases brought about by fundamental technological breakthroughs: the agrarian revolution, the industrial revolution, and the nuclear, electronic, and biochemical revolutions of our time.

The second movement is not technological, but social and cultural. It consists of shifts between periods orienting primarily to the partnership or dominator model.

By looking at the interactions of these two movements, students can see how the development and use of technological breakthroughs are profoundly affected by the degree to which a period or society orients primarily to the partnership or dominator model. For instance, as discussed later in this chapter, metals were used by the more partnership-oriented Neolithic peoples of prehistoric Europe primarily for tools, jewelry and other ornaments, and ritual objects. But the more dominator-oriented Indo-European invaders who later overran Europe applied metal smelting technology primarily to the making of weapons.

The interaction of these two movements throughout our cultural evolution—on the one hand, of technological phase-changes and consequent changes in modes of production, and, on the other, periods of partnership or dominator resurgence and consequent changes in technological priorities—is outlined in "Riane Eisler, Dominator and Partnership Shifts" in *Macrohistory and Macrohistorians: Perspectives on Individual, Social and Civilizational Change*, a book that also describes the theories of well-known figures such as Vico, Hegel, Marx, Weber, Spengler, and Toynbee.[5]

Revolutions,[6] many such battles have been waged in science when new evidence accumulated that did not fit old theories or interpretations. And, particularly when there was a perceived threat to existing power structures, the resistance to new interpretations has been strong—as in Galileo's near-fatal disagreement with the Church.

Students can then be invited to explore the question of how the older and newer interpretations of prehistory—that long span of cultural evolution for which we have no deciphered written records—support two different perspectives on human nature.

Although many teachers will be able to use what follows only to supplement existing curricula, this is an important first step. It makes it possible for students to see patterns in what otherwise seems inexplicable and overwhelming. It also sheds light on how much of what has been taught us about human history, despite its veneer of objectivity, is actually racist and sexist. Most important, it encourages students to discover how human choices, whether conscious or unconscious, play a major part in what kind of future we have—and even in whether we have a future at all.

The Old Stone Age

Culture (the beliefs and behaviors transmitted through learning from generation to generation) and technology (the fashioning of tools) have ancient roots among mammals, particularly primates. But it is among humans that culture and technology assume critical importance.

The early members of the human family, the so-called hominids, go back millions of years to Africa. Human culture and technology also have deep roots in Africa, as it was there that species after species of hominids sprang up.

Our own species, *homo sapiens sapiens*, appeared only about 120,000 years ago. But we, too, stem from Africa and, according to DNA studies, have even earlier ancestors there.

A team of scientists studying maternally inherited DNA believe they have traced back all present-day humans to a female who lived in Africa between 140,000 and 280,000 years ago. Although biologists point out that she was in no sense the only ancestral mother of all humans, since there were other females reproducing at that time, these DNA studies indicate that she was the only one among them who had female descendants who survived in all succeeding generations. Scientists are therefore calling her "Eve," our common mother.[7]

There are also early hominid finds in Asia. According to Professor Jiao Tianlong of the Institute of Archeology of the Chinese Academy of Social Sciences, archeological data indicate that, as early as 1,800,000 years ago, hominids already inhabited the area we now call China. These data do not indicate what kind of culture theirs was.[8] But Professor Jiao Tianlong suggests that, like the later gathering/hunting peoples of the European Paleolithic, they consisted of small groups, varying from area to area, who went through changes with the passage of time. He also believes it is reasonable to infer that "there must have been equality and mutual aid between the members, who struggled together against immense odds in order to subsist."[9]

This is not to say that violence was absent in these earlier societies. The point is that many earlier interpretations supporting assumptions about the inevitability of chronic warfare, male-dominance, and human relations based on fear and force are not congruent with the available evidence.[10]

Indeed, if we look at the most thoroughly excavated Stone Age sites, those of the European Upper Paleolithic, the popular pictures of primitive club-carrying Stone Age cavemen have no basis. These finds are more suggestive of a partnership-oriented way of life than of a dominator-oriented one. They are certainly *not* consistent with the conventional interpretation of this period as "the story of man the hunter/warrior."

For example, students can look at the "wrong-way arrows" depicted in Figure 4.1 and see how this view has colored and distorted the interpretation of Stone Age finds. This ancient carving had puzzled scholars because what they perceived were four arrows going the wrong way, missing the bison head engraved next to them. It took a newcomer to archeology, Alexander Marshack, to point out that, viewed from outside the prevailing paradigm, these objects can be recognized for what they are: engravings of vegetation with branches going the *right* way.[11]

Students can also be invited to discuss a major theme of Stone Age cave art: the life-giving and sustaining aspect of nature. In this 30,000-year-old art, still mainly known for its beautiful depictions of animals, are numerous female figures. Notable among these are the broad-hipped, sometimes pregnant, so-called Venus figurines that were earlier interpreted as ancient counterparts of Playboy centerfolds or as idols for "fertility cults." Scholars are increasingly recognizing these female figures as symbols of the regenerative powers of nature. As the archaeologist James Mellaart notes, they seem to be early precursors of the female deities associated with nature's abundance and creativity found in later agrarian and Bronze Age civilizations.[12]

One such figure may be the oldest piece of art ever found. This is a carved object excavated in Israel at the site of Berekhat Ram in the Golan Heights: a grooved pebble that "bore some characteristics of a female body," with "incised grooves delimiting the head and arms."[13] This site is

FIGURE 4.1   Wrong-Way Arrows

"Wrong-way arrows" are shown in this sketch of a carving of an antelope on a piece of bone dating back to 20,000 B.C.E.
CREDIT: The Partnership Way: New Tools for Living and Learning, *by Riane Eisler and David Loye. Line drawing from the original: Jeff Helwig.*

estimated to be approximately 230,000 years old—that is, almost 200,000 years older than the European Paleolithic sites. But, astonishingly, the figure found at Berekhat Ram bears a striking resemblance to the so-called Venus of Willendorf found in a European cave dating back approximately 30,000 years. (See Figure 4.2.)

In other world regions, there have as yet been no excavations of early female figurines. But there are finds of early human settlements. For example, human remains found at Lewisville, Texas, have been carbon-dated at 38,000 years old. And sites in the Sandia Mountains near Albuquerque, New Mexico, have been carbon-dated to 27,000 to 17,000 years ago.[14] As we will see in the pages that follow, also contrary to popular stereotypes, the people in these settlements developed highly sophisticated cultures.

The First Farmers

The agricultural revolution ushered in a major technological phase-change: from a gathering/hunting economy to a primarily farming economy. This technological phase began approximately 10,000 years ago in some world regions, marking the onset of what scholars call the Neolithic or New Stone Age. Actually these terms are misleading, since we now know that in the later part of this period, sometimes called the Chalcolithic or Copper Age, metals were already being smelted and used for tools, jewelry, and ritual objects.

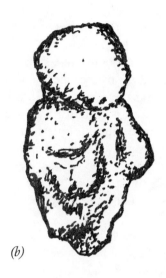

(b)

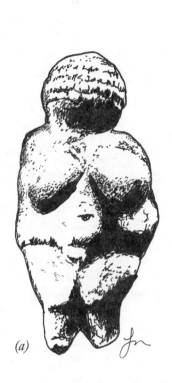

(a)

FIGURE 4.2   Venus Figures

(a) European Stone Age figurine known as Venus of Willendorf, approximately 30,000 years old. CREDIT: John Mason. (b) Middle Eastern figurine found in Berekhat Ram, Israel, approximately 230,000 years old. CREDIT: John Mason.

The Neolithic brought with it the earliest cradles of civilization, which are now known to date back approximately 8,500 years in Europe and the Middle East. This is much earlier than had been thought before new scientific methods such as radiocarbon dating prompted a reassessment of Neolithic time scales. But it is not only the time scales, but the interpretations of Neolithic finds that are beginning to change.[15]

The older interpretation of the Neolithic, still taught in many places, is that the invention of agriculture ushered in male dominance, chronic warfare, and the rule by rich and powerful male elites over slaves, women, and "common people." This story is inconsistent with claims that male dominance and chronic warfare were there from the beginning of human evolution—that they are in our genes, and that hormones such as testosterone make men inevitably violent.

However, both these stories are consistent in their underlying message: They "explain" the "inevitability" of a dominator social organization.

Just as there is no solid basis for the theory that a dominator social organization is genetically based, the theory that the technological shift from gathering/hunting to farming brought the shift to the dominator model is not well grounded. It was already challenged in the 19th century, when archaeology was in its infancy. At that time, a number of scholars began to write of what they termed "matriarchies" rather than "patriarchies"—and the battle over our cultural origins that continues to our day began.

Scholars such as Edward Westermarck argued that there never was nor could be anything other than families and societies ruled by men—that patriarchy is the only possible human form.[16] Other scholars, including J. J. Bachofen and Lewis Henry Morgan, and, later, Friedrich Engels and Alexander Rustow, argued that not only did the evidence from both archaeology and myth point to earlier societies that were matriarchies, but that these societies were guided by more stereotypically feminine and egalitarian values.[17] Still others agreed that matriarchies once existed but claimed that these societies were cruelly ruled by women, imputing to them the origin of barbarous practices such as human sacrifice. For example, James Frazer asserted that later stories such as that of a "king of the wood" who to assume that position had to pluck a branch of a certain tree associated with the Roman goddess Diana and then slay his predecessor "must have been handed down from a time beyond the memory of man, when Italy was still in a far ruder state."[18] This interpretation, which Frazer buttressed with analogies from 19th-century tribal societies where a chieftain or king was slain when he was no longer vigorous—societies that were, however, hardly matriarchies but rather rigidly male-dominated[19]—conformed to the 19th-century view of cultural history as a linear upward progression from barbarism to civilization, a view that still prevails in some quarters today.

Some scholars still assert that practices such as ritual sacrifice prevailed in primitive societies ruled by women.[20] In fact, there is no solid evidence that ritual sacrifice was customary in pre-patriarchal cultures. Nor is there evidence to support the position that these earlier societies were matriarchies or simply the reverse side of patriarchies—in other words, societies where women ruled and subjugated men.

Rather, excavations such as those by James Mellaart in the Turkish site of Catal Huyuk and by Marija Gimbutas in the Balkans and Greece, as well as the analysis of Neolithic burial practices in various regions around the Mediterranean by British archaeologist Lucy Goodison, indicate that for thousands of years Neolithic cultures appear to have oriented more to what I have called a *gylanic* model. (*Gylanic* is a gender-specific term for the partnership model that I coined as the alternative to both patriarchy and matriarchy.)[21]

In her book *The Civilization of the Goddess: The World of Old Europe*, Gimbutas examines the way of life, religion, and social structure of the peoples who inhabited Europe from the 7th to the 3rd millennia B.C.E.[22]—that is, from about 9,000 to about 5,000 years ago. She also looks at the later civilization of Minoan Crete, which flourished until 3,500 years ago.[23] She writes:

> The difficulty with the term *matriarchy* in 20th century anthropological scholarship is that it is assumed to represent a complete mirror image of patriarchy or androcracy—that is to say, a hierarchical structure with women ruling by force in the place of men. This is far from the reality of Old Europe. Indeed, we do not find in Old Europe, nor in all of the Old World, a system of autocratic rule by women with an equivalent suppression of men. Rather, we find a structure in which the sexes are more or less on equal footing, a society that could be termed a *gylany*. This is a term coined by Riane Eisler (from *gyne*, referring to woman, and *andros*, man, linked by the letter *l* for *lyen*, to resolve, or *lyo*, to set free). Gylany implies that the sexes are "linked" rather than hierarchically "ranked."[24]

Gimbutas also notes that "it is a gross misunderstanding to imagine warfare as endemic to the human condition." She writes: "widespread fighting and fortification-building have indeed been the way of life for most of our direct ancestors from the Bronze Age up until now. However, this was not the case in the Paleolithic and Neolithic. There are no depictions of arms (weapons used against other humans) in Paleolithic cave paintings, nor are there remains of weapons used by man against man during the Neolithic of Old Europe." Among "some hundred and fifty paintings that survived at Catal Huyuk," she continues, "there is not one depicting a scene of conflict or fighting, or of war or torture."[25]

This does not mean that these were violence-free societies in which all was ideal. This is a point I want to emphasize again and again. There are indications of some violence in early Neolithic societies. But they are not extensive. As R. Brian Ferguson points out, violence and war leave recoverable traces in both art and other archaeological remains.[26] The fact that such traces are rare during this period is significant.

Many influential theories simply project back to earlier times what has been observed in later history. As Ferguson notes, to build theories of prehistoric violence on the premise that "absence of evidence is not evidence of absence" is unsound.[27] What the absence of evidence of chronic violence actually indicates is that, while not utopian or ideal, these were societies organized differently from what came later.

Based on hundreds of excavations, Gimbutas notes that the settlements of Old Europe were "chosen for their convenient setting, good water and soil, and availability of animal pastures, and not for their defensive positions." They are occasionally "encircled by ditches but seldom by palisades or stone retaining walls." In fact, "earthen ramparts and other defensive structures occur only in later Neolithic and Copper Age settlements when measures were taken to protect villages from an influx of human intruders"—specifically, toward the end of the 5th and during the 4th millennium B.C.E.[28]

The overall social structure of this early European civilization was also different from the Indo-European cultures that followed. "There is no evidence in all of Old Europe of a patriarchal chieftainate of the Indo-European type," Gimbutas reports. "There are no male royal tombs and no residences in magarons on hill forts. The burial rites and settlement patterns reflect a matrilineal structure, whereas the distribution of wealth in graves speaks for an economic egalitarianism."[29]

In other words, human relations, including those between the female and male halves of humanity, appear to have followed a more egalitarian pattern. Although the principal depiction of deity in human form appears to have been female (namely, the Goddess of whom Gimbutas writes),[30] reflecting a matrifocal or mother-centered social organization, this depiction, as Gimbutas emphasizes, does not indicate a matriarchy.

The way that these ancient, more partnership-oriented societies conceptualized power appears to have been very different from the way that we have been taught to see it. Here the powers that govern the universe were not represented as a male deity whose symbols of authority are a thunderbolt (like Jehovah or Wotan) or a weapon (like Zeus or Thor). Their conception of power focused on the power to give, sustain, and nurture life. Symbolized since remote antiquity by the female figure

known in later history as the Great Goddess—from whose womb all life
ensues and to whose womb it returns at death, like the cycles of vegetation, to be reborn again—the highest power was imaged not as "power
over" (domination, conquest, and control) but as "power *to*" (life-giving
and life-nurturing). While death was an important part of this cycle, the
emphasis was on birth and rebirth. Moreover, one of the central myths of
this earlier, more nature-based religion was the sacred marriage between
a female and male deity. In other words, here both the male and female
principles were viewed as part of both nature and the sacred.[31]

The same picture Gimbutas describes in Old Europe is revealed by
archeological findings in China. Extensive excavations, carried out by the
Institute of Archeology of the Chinese Academy of Sciences at the site of
Banpo on the outskirts of Xi'an City since 1994, have unearthed substantial prehistoric remains that provide a vital new chapter in Chinese prehistory. The archaeologist Shi Xingbang, director of the Banpo excavations, believes that "the Banpo settlement was the dwelling place of a
matrilineal gens community"[32] According to Professor Jiao Tianlong,
"the whole settlement displayed strong cohesion, and emphasized collec-
tivism and equality."[33]

As Professor Min Jiayin notes, these relationships, including egalitarian relationships between women and men, survived in some Neolithic
farming Chinese communities well into historic times. Examples include
the Naxi people in the Yongning region. Here, families were female-
centered, and they practiced a form of marriage, called Ah Xiao, in which
love prevailed over economic considerations.[34]

In sum, one of the most important and interesting aspects of the new
information about our prehistory is that cultures in very different world
regions share an early partnership heritage (see Figure 4.3). This common heritage is a unifying theme for peoples worldwide. As it becomes
better known, it can help different racial and ethnic groups find common
ground. It can also help women and men end "the war of the sexes"—
showing that a partnership between equals is a viable alternative.

The Metamorphosis of Myth—and Reality

Stories about female deities with great power and importance, as well as
about functioning partnerships between priestesses and priests, are found
in all world regions—from Ireland to Iran, from China to Mexico.

(a)

FIGURE 4.3   European and Japanese Goddesses with Spiral Motifs

Cultures from very different world regions share an early partnership heritage, as demonstrated by this comparison of figurines from (a) Europe and (b) Japan.

CREDIT: *John Mason.*

(b)

In European Celtic tradition, dating from roughly 4000 b.c.e. to a zenith at about 500 b.c.e.,[35] we find figures such as the Great Piast,[36] who is pictured as a giant horned sea snake and appears to be a Goddess/ Creator. Although Celtic culture exhibited a strong dominator overlay, reflecting a mix of Indo-European invaders and the indigenous European population, these are clues to earlier, more partnership-oriented traditions. From the other end of the world, in Australian aboriginal legend, there are also stories about a great serpent, the Rainbow Serpent. This creature, sometimes associated with the uterus of a "Great Mother," is also related to the sun, which, in some Australian aboriginal myths, is a feminine symbol represented as a diffused, warming, nourishing agent of plant growth and life.[37]

These Australian myths originated in gathering/hunting societies, but the theme of the sun as feminine is also found in agrarian civilizations. For example, the ancient Egyptian Goddess Hathor, associated with the rise of the life-giving waters of the Nile, was associated with the sun and, like the Rainbow Serpent, had a masculine component as well, symbolized by her horns.[38]

Female deities are also in many world traditions associated with important inventions that most texts still credit solely to men. In Mesopotamia, the Goddess Ninlil was revered for providing her people with an understanding of planting and harvesting methods. The official scribe of the Sumerian heaven was a woman, and the Sumerian Goddess Nidaba—honored as the one who initially invented clay tablets and the art of writing—appeared in that position earlier than any of the male deities who replaced her. Similarly, in India, the Goddess Sarasvati was honored as the inventor of the original alphabet.[39]

When we find basic human inventions—from farming to writing— credited to female deities, the implication is that women most probably played a key part in their development. The attribution of so much power to female deities, including the power to create the world and humanity, also suggests a time when women occupied positions of leadership in their communities. And the fact that we find these powerful female deities in ancient stories of every world region suggests that women's leadership was once widespread.

We find clues to this earlier period in the traditions of many indigenous North American tribes. As Paula Gunn Allen writes in *The Sacred Hoop: Recovering the Feminine in American Indian Traditions*, many Indian myths revolve around powerful female figures.[40] Serpent Woman is one.

Corn Woman is another. Earth Woman is another. Still another is Grandmother of the Corn. As Allen writes, "Her variety and multiplicity testified to her complexity: she is the true creatrix for she is thought itself, from which all else is born. . . . She is also the spirit that forms right balance, right harmony, and these in turn order all relationships in conformity with her law."[41]

In the Hopi account, the Creatrix is called Hard Beings Woman. She is "of the earth, although she lives in the worlds above, where she empowers the moon and stars, and she has solidity and hardness as her major aspects. Like Thought Woman, she does not give birth to creation or human beings, but breathes life into male and female effigies that become the parents of the Hopi."[42] Similarly, central to Keres Pueblo theology is a Creatrix called She Who Thinks, who is the supreme spirit, both mother and father to all people and to all creatures.[43]

Although, as Allen notes, the conquest of Native American people by Europeans radically changed their social structures, stories like these provide clues to an earlier time when many tribes in North America were still organized more along partnership lines. Allen calls these gynocratic structures. She writes that "in gynocratic tribal systems, egalitarianism, personal autonomy, and communal harmony were highly valued, rendering the good of the individual and the good of the society mutually reinforcing rather than divisive. Tribal societies found a way to institutionalize both values, providing a coherent, harmonized, supportive social system that nurtured and protected, and was enriched by, individual life and creativity."[44]

From China, too, we have myths about a time when the yin or feminine principle was not yet subservient to the yang or male principle. This is a time that the Chinese sage Lao Tsu, who dates to about 2,600 years ago, describes as peaceful and just. Likewise, one of the earliest known European writers, the Greek poet Hesiod, who lived approximately 2,800 years ago, tells us that there was once a "golden race" who lived in peaceful ease before a "lesser race" brought with them Ares, the Greek god of war.

These stories were undoubtedly greatly idealized folk memories of earlier times. Nonetheless, they tell us that, although the early agricultural era was not a violence-free utopian period, it oriented more to a partnership model than to a dominator one. Moreover, the Neolithic was a period during which many of the technologies on which civilization is based were developed and refined.[45]

Toward the end of the Neolithic period, however, we begin to see evidence of a fundamental social and cultural shift. In the Americas, even before the European conquests, there are indications of incursions from warlike tribes during a time of great drought. For example, a drought in the western part of the American continent is documented by dendrochronology as having occurred between approximately 1275 and 1290. There is evidence of raiders who came down from the north and destroyed or took over earlier Mogollan and Anasazi communities—highly developed cultures that scholars believe represent a Golden Age of American Prehistory. (The Anasazi later regrouped as the Hopi and Zuñi Pueblo Indians.)[46]

In Europe and Asia Minor, this shift from a partnership to dominator orientation began much earlier, approximately 5,500 years ago. At that point, in the words of British archaeologist James Mellaart, severe signs of stress appeared. There were natural disasters and severe climate changes. And here, too, there were invasions by nomadic herders, who brought with them a dominator social organization.[47]

In the area archeologist Marija Gimbutas calls Old Europe (the Balkans and Northern Greece) we now, for the first time, find evidence of large stores of weapons. Often these were found in a new type of burial: "chieftain graves." Horses, women, and children were often sacrificed and placed in these graves to accompany their masters into the afterworld.

Scholars at the Chinese Academy of Social Sciences in Beijing have also traced this shift from more peaceful and egalitarian societies in which female deities seem to have played leading roles to a later time when Chinese society oriented more to the dominator model.[48] For example, in "Myth and Reality: The Projection of Gender Relations in Prehistoric China," Professor Cai Junsheng writes: "NuWa is the most important mythological female figure handed down from the prehistoric age. NuWa was long considered by the Chinese as the creator/creatrix of the world. However, a careful examination of Chinese myths shows how, at the same time that the social structure changed to a patriarchal one, NuWa lost her power until finally there are myths where she dies."[49]

Because of the transformation of myths during the shift to a dominator society—or as Professor Cai Junsheng puts it, "due to the elimination and misinterpretation of information during the subsequent long period of patriarchal society"—available data have to be carefully analyzed.[50] However, as he also notes, such an analysis provides clues to a massive cultural shift.

In Africa, too, the female status in sacred mythology seems to have followed the pattern found in other world regions, where female mythological figures start out as the Creatrix, then become a wife or mother of a male god, first in an equal role and then in a subservient role, are next demoted to nondivine status, and finally are demonized as witches or monsters. African goddesses can be found which run the gamut of these roles. The South African Ma is the "Goddess of Creation"; Mebeli of the Congo is the "Supreme Being"; Haine is the Tanzanian Moon Goddess whose husband is Ishoye (the sun); Dugbo of Sierra Leone is an Earth Goddess, responsible for all plants and trees. There are also La-hkima Oqla of Morocco, a female "jenn" who inhabits a river and rules over other evil spirits, and Yalode of Benin who causes foot infections. Watamaraka of South Africa is the "Goddess of Evil," said to have given birth to all the demons.[51]

Today all these female mythic representations are found side by side. But if we do a little detective work, we can trace their origins and situate them in a sequence from Creatrix to subservience to conversion to a male deity or to a demonic witch or monster. For example, in the iconography of old Europe, the figure that Gimbutas calls the Snake Goddess plays a prominent role, probably because the snake was viewed as one of the manifestations of the power of regeneration, since snakes shed and renew their skins (see Figure 4.4). But in later Greek mythology, we find the story of the monstrous Medusa, a terrible female with hair of coiled snakes. Significantly, she has been stripped of the power to give life, but retains the power to take life, as she is said to turn men to stone. Similarly, the Hindu Kali is noted for her bloodthirsty cruelty. Yet there are also remnants in Hindu mythology of the female power to give life, splintered off into a number of deities, including Parvati. Along a somewhat different trajectory, the early Greek Mother Goddess Demeter is first turned into Saint Demetra through Christian remything and finally masculinized as Saint Demetrius. Following still another trajectory, female deities such as Athena in Greek mythology and Ishtar in Middle Eastern mythology become goddesses of war and human sacrifice—reflecting the shift to a more violent, hierarchic, and male-dominated social structure.

Myths about bloodthirsty female deities sometimes go along with myths demonizing earlier cultures—a time-tested strategy used by conquerors to justify their killing and/or subjugation of other peoples. For example, when Christians were fed to lions by the Romans in their amphitheaters, there were stories that Christians practiced human sacri-

(a)

(b)

FIGURE 4.4 Demonizing the Goddess

(a) Minoan Snake Goddess.
CREDIT: The Partnership Way: New Tools for Living and Learning, *by Riane Eisler and David Loye. Line drawing from the original: John Mason.*
(b) Medusa.
CREDIT: *John Mason.*

fice—as "proven" by the Christian Eucharist service in which the death and resurrection of Jesus was, and still is, commemorated by symbolically eating his body and drinking his blood. To justify the killing of Jews, similar stories were circulated as late as the 20th century, accusing them of killing and eating Christian babies. In much the same way, the myth that pre-patriarchal cultures practiced human sacrifice has been used to demonize them, when in reality it is only after the shift to the dominator model that we begin to see clear indications of human sacrifice as a cultural custom.

In the Indo-European "chieftain graves," dead men were accompanied by sacrificed women, as well as by sacrificed horses, weapons, and other material possessions. In the lavish graves of Egyptian royalty, slaves were interred. Among the Aztecs, human sacrifice was a central religious rite. We can read of this practice in the Bible, a document written long after the shift to a dominator social structure. And there are indications that, at least among the ruling classes, human sacrifice was practiced by the ancient Carthaginians in relation to a female deity called Tanit.[52]

But the old view of a steady upward movement from barbarism and cruelty, from primitive practices such as ritual sacrifice and constant intertribal warfare to civilization and progress, persists to this day. It persists despite the barbarities of "civilized" societies such as Nazi Germany. It persists despite evidence that history is hardly a linear process—that even technological evolution is marked by regressions, such as the Greek and Christian Dark Ages. It persists despite the fact that Neolithic finds, thought at one time to suggest human sacrifice, are frequently shown to have been secondary burials—a ritual now known to have been prevalent at that time, and one still practiced in some places today.[53] And it does not abate despite the fact that there are no pictorial representations or other images of human sacrifice until *after* the shift to a dominator form of social organization of "strong-man" rule.[54]

The time lines for this shift vary from region to region. But almost invariably it is accompanied by a major technological shift. The emphasis is increasingly on more effective technologies that destroy life: armaments that maim and kill people and destroy both natural and human-made resources. Such armaments—along with greater inequality, violence, and the ranking of men (and traits stereotypically associated with "masculinity") over women (and traits stereotypically linked with "femininity")—are characteristic of a dominator social organization that, as we still see today, diverts energy and resources that could otherwise be used to care for human needs.

From Prehistory to History

In some regions, what scholars call "recorded history"—that is, the time from which written records have been deciphered—began about 5,000 years ago. This period is exemplified by the Bronze Age civilizations we read about in our Western history textbooks: the Sumerian, Babylonian, and Egyptian civilizations. These are hybrid civilizations that already oriented primarily to the dominator model, although partnership elements can still be found.

In one of his last books (which used my cultural transformation theory as its framework), the Sumerologist Samuel Noah Kramer wrote of a shift in Sumerian society to strong-man rule, when rule of the *lugul* (literally translated as "big man") began to emerge in response to a more warlike environment.[55] However, many Sumerian writings—notably the Hymns of Inanna, the Sumerian Goddess of Love and Procreation—show that for some time women were still not viewed as male property and marriage still took an egalitarian form.[56]

Though rarely studied—or even mentioned in most textbooks—the most interesting Western Bronze Age culture is the Minoan civilization that flourished on the Mediterranean island of Crete. Deciphered writings from this civilization are not yet available, but it has been extensively excavated since the early part of the 20th century. Its discovery was called an archeological bombshell, as scholars had no idea of the existence of this technologically advanced civilization that lasted until approximately 3,400 years ago. Here we find the first paved roads in Europe, the first viaducts, a sanitation system that we would today call modern (it included indoor plumbing), and a generally high standard of living.

Yet, sharply contradicting the theory still taught in universities that greater technological, and thus social, complexity inevitably brings with it a dominator social organization, Minoan civilization preserved many of the elements of the earlier, more partnership-oriented Neolithic societies. Unlike the other "high civilizations" of that time, there are here no massive differences between rulers and ruled. Here women still had high status. And here trade, rather than conquest, brought prosperity.

One remarkable feature of Minoan society, distinguishing it from other ancient high civilizations, is that there seems to have been a rather equitable sharing of wealth. "The standard of living—even of peasants—seems to have been high," reports Greek archaeologist Nikolas Platon, who excavated Crete for more than fifty years. "None of the homes found so far have suggested very poor living conditions."[57]

Another remarkable feature of Minoan civilization is that no statues or reliefs of royal rulers or any grandiose scenes of battle or of hunting have been found. Although the Minoans had finely crafted daggers and other weapons, which they undoubtedly used to defend their merchant fleets, this absence of art idealizing domination and violence reflected what Platon terms "an exceptionally peace-loving people" who lived in generally unfortified settlements.[58]

The Minoans were a highly creative culture. Their art has been described as "the most inspired in the ancient world,"[59] and their crafts were exquisite. As we will see in the next chapter, the difference between civilizations orienting more to the partnership model than to the dominator model is reflected in their art.[60]

As anthropologist Ruby Rohrlich-Leavitt writes, Minoan women are "the central subjects, the most frequently portrayed in the arts and crafts." And "they are shown mainly in the public sphere."[61] In keeping with the partnership configuration, stereotypically feminine values appear to have had social governance in Minoan Crete. According to Platon, "here all of life was pervaded by an ardent faith in the goddess Nature, the source of all creation and harmony."[62] So, although Minoan civilization was not ideal or utopian, it continued to incorporate many elements of the earlier, more partnership-oriented Neolithic societies.

Also of particular interest in relation to what we today call "ecological consciousness" is the celebration of nature in Minoan art. This veneration of nature is encoded in the worship of a Mother Goddess, today still remembered in the phrase "Mother Earth" (see Figure 4.5).

The veneration of the life-giving and -enhancing powers of nature incarnated in female form (found in the early Neolithic in most world regions) continued in many places well into the Bronze Age. However, as mentioned earlier, the character of this deity increasingly reflected the new dominator order in an uneasy mix of earlier and later elements.

In India, we still find traces of the Dravidian tradition of the Indus Valley. This civilization was indigenous to India before Indo-European invaders brought with them their warlike culture, caste system, and male-dominated order. These Indo-Europeans (or Aryans, as they are called in India) were of the same linguistic and cultural stock as the invaders who, millennia earlier, overran Europe. They, too, came from the Central Asian steppes and deserts, conquering India during the period of approximately 1800 to 1700 B.C.E. They are described by Veronica Ions as "light-skinned, hard-drinking folk, whose mastery of horses and chariots

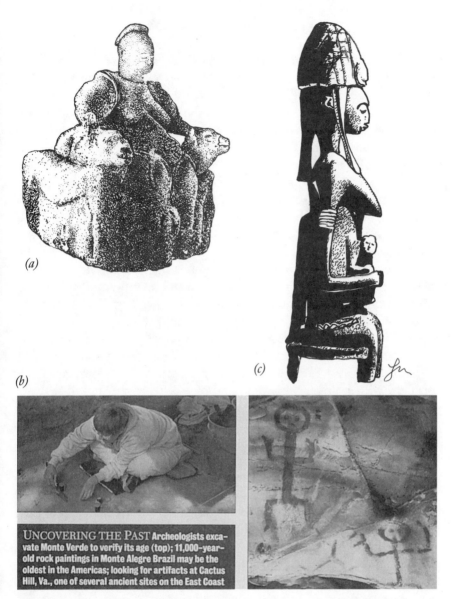

(a)

(b)

(c)

UNCOVERING THE PAST Archeologists excavate Monte Verde to verify its age (top); 11,000-year-old rock paintings in Monte Alegre Brazil may be the oldest in the Americas; looking for artifacts at Cactus Hill, Va., one of several ancient sites on the East Coast

FIGURE 4.5   Mother Goddesses

(a) Depicted here is the Catal Huyuk Goddess giving birth. CREDIT: The Partnership Way: New Tools for Living and Learning, *by Riane Eisler and David Loye. Line drawing from the original: John Mason. (b) This 11,000-year-old rock painting of birthgiving, from Monte Alegre, Brazil, is one of the oldest works of art in the Americas.* CREDIT: Newsweek, *April 26, 1999, p. 53. (c) Known as Maleeoo in the Ivory Coast, Ala in Nigeria, and Moussou Koroni Koundye in Mali, this Creatrix figure representing nature, humans, and culture is venerated as She who gives birth to all.* CREDIT: *John Mason.*

and whose use of swords brought them swift victory over the Dravidians, whom they accordingly despised as 'Dasyus,' or dark-skinned."[63] The Aryans brought with them their own religion, which included the storm god Indra, who in Hindu mythology is shown slaying or subduing older deities. Still, we find traces of Dravidian traditions in the Hindu Vedas. But although these holy books contain some partnership elements, they portray female deities as consorts of more powerful male gods and demand that worshipers humble themselves and obsequiously praise deities in their prayers. We also see evidence of this shift in Indian art. For example, a female deity such as Shakti is sometimes depicted as being only a fraction of the size of her husband Shiva, even though we are told that they balance each other's power.

These contradictions are clues to a conflict of cultures. Older elements have been retained, but in an altered form that met the requirements of the new rigidly hierarchic, male supremacist, and violent dominator order.

In Europe, too, there are mythical clues to this shift. Even though Hesiod's work already reflected the ancient Greek's denigration and subordination of women, as noted earlier, he wrote of a "golden race" who lived in "peaceful ease" until it was replaced by a "lesser race" that brought with it Ares, the Greek god of war—a story Hesiod said was handed down from his mother. Similarly, in Irish legend the invasion of the Celts with their iron weapons is reflected in a mythology that speaks of fairy-folk or Tuatha de Danaan—people of the Goddess Dana—having been sickened or destroyed by the touch of iron. Yet, as noted earlier, the warlike Celts also assimilated some of the earlier Irish traditions. They continued to worship the Earth in female form "as a mother, defender, and provider."[64] The status of Celtic women was higher than that of their Roman and Greek contemporaries. Even though Celtic men already exercised control over their wives and daughters, sometimes in brutal ways, women sometimes continued to wield political power, as illustrated by the famous story of Boudicia, an already fiercely warlike Celtic queen who led a rebellion against the Romans.[65]

There are clues to an earlier more partnership-oriented time in Aztec mythology, as documented by the anthropologist June Nash. Drawing from such primary sources as the four surviving codices of the Aztecs as well as the writings of three 16th-century Spaniards, Nash writes that the "history of the Aztecs provides an example of the transformation from a kinship-based society with a minimum of status differentiation to a class-structured empire." Of particular interest in relation to the contrast between the partnership and dominator core configurations is the fact that Nash specifically writes of "the interrelationship between male specialization in warfare, predatory conquest, a state bureaucracy based on patrilineal nobility supported by an ideology of male dominance, and the differential access to its benefits between men and women."[66]

The Aztecs left their homeland in Aztlan about the year 820 and migrated to the central plateau where Mexico City is now located, but where at that time the civilization of the Toltecs flourished. Some three hundred years after they left Aztlan, as they came close to the capital of the Toltec Empire, a confrontation took place between the god Huitzilopochtli and his sister the goddess Malinalzoch. This confrontation, as Nash writes, "reveals something of the changing structure of authority in this wandering tribe."

Huitzilopochtli accused his sister of being a sorceress who used her supernatural power over animals to control the tribe and urged his men to "show by the valor of arms and their courage" that they could conquer the Toltec people. In some versions of the myth, Malinalzoch was killed by the warriors and her son stayed with those Aztecs who did not wish to go on with Huitzilopochtli's group. In other versions, she lived on and formed a community on the site where the confrontation took place. In any event, we see in this myth a break from lines of authority that included women, as well as a direct appeal to force of arms and valor (which later became the basis for the Aztec climb to power). This points to the beginning of a shift in Aztec culture to a rigid dominator society: one that became extremely warlike, male dominated, and autocratically ruled by kings and priests who constantly demanded human sacrifices, whether in battles or religious rites.

By the time of Itzcoaltl's reign (1429–1440), Aztec mythology had apparently been rewritten again, reflecting the further consolidation of power in the hands of warlike rulers, and justifying the Aztec's predatory conquests and sacrifices. However, as Nash notes, there is also evidence of resistance, particularly in the outer regions of the empire.

For example, in one of the provinces in the Tonoc area, a "cult of the Goddess of Heavens" that forbade human sacrifice was still found. And despite their loss of position in state and imperial iconography, female deities associated with crops and rains survived in various domestic and local pantheons.

As Nash writes, in a period of less than three centuries "Aztec social structure was transformed." Reflected in the subordination of female deities, a male-dominated society emerged. Women still played important roles, but they were denied positions of power in what was now a rigidly hierarchic society characterized by strong-man rule and a high degree of built-in social violence, including not only wars of conquest but also ritual sacrifice of conquered peoples.

Ironically, as Nash also notes, it was because of this society's dominator character that in the final days of the Spanish siege of Tenochtitlan its rulers could not mobilize the populace to the defense of the city. Nor could they draw support throughout the empire. Indeed, some of the conquered people became the allies of the Spaniards—who in their turn imposed their own version of a brutal dominator state.[67]

Nash's work illustrates what Marija Gimbutas called "archeomythology" (see Box 4.2). This is a method of inquiry in which scholars not only look at the physical evidence from excavations but also consider mythological evidence, including changes in symbols and the roles of deities (female and male) during various periods, and investigate how these mythological changes were reflected in social structures.

Successful use of this method requires careful analysis of the available data. As Professor Cai Junsheng has noted, during periods of shift from partnership to domination, myths are often radically transformed and earlier myths are gradually lost. Using this systemic approach is much like a detective searching for clues. Students in higher grades can be invited to use it to examine cultures throughout the world, utilizing the partnership and dominator templates in quest of our common partnership heritage.

This mythological detective work can be an exciting adventure for both girls and boys. When Rosie Martin's 11th-grade art teacher showed her class pictures of the Neolithic Snake Goddess—depicting the snake (which periodically sheds and regrows its skin) as a benevolent symbol of the regenerative powers of nature—Rosie realized that the association of women with snakes was not always negative. Following the journey of the Snake Goddess through time, the class saw how this female archetype came to be known as the monstrous Greek Medusa, who turns men to stone—becoming a symbol of the power to destroy rather than create. They also observed how this association of female power with a destructive threat to men lingers in our time—as in the movie *The Clash of the Titans*, where the Greek hero Perseus decapitates a still demonic, but now powerless, Medusa. Both girls and boys could now look at these archetypes from a more critical perspective, aware that they reflect dominator rather than partnership constructions of masculinity and femininity.

BOX 4.2   Archeomythology in the Classroom

Students can be invited to look at African myths about female deities, as well as at myths such as those from Dahomey, where the supreme deity of the Fon, NaNa Buluku, is at the same time both male and female.[68] They can also explore ancient myths through books such as *The Woman's Companion to Mythology*, edited by Carolyne Larrington,[69] and Barbara Walker's *The Women's Encyclopedia of Myths and Secrets*, and look for threads that lead to themes that are still generally ignored in the study of both history and prehistory.

Another venue for student activities (and peer teaching) is the Internet, where sites have been posted by women (and men) who are today exploring this ancient heritage. Two interesting possibilities are <http://member.aol.com/ATOYA/ GODDESS/html> and <http://www. gg.caltech.edu/~maeve/relax4.html>. Another is <www.goddess2000. org>, featuring the Goddess 2000 Project's outpouring of Goddess art from twenty-seven countries. The site <http://www.voiceofwomen. com/omi.html> is maintained by an African-American woman who speaks of how, while visiting traditional elders in Nigeria in the summer of 1984, she became determined to help preserve the ancient knowledge of the Yoruba people. Of particular interest to her were stories about female deities, or "Orisas," such as Yemoja (goddess of the sea and water buffalo), Osun (goddess of the rivers), and Oya (goddess of the winds, tornadoes, lightning, and buffalo women), as well as folktales about how women played an important part in Yoruba tradition.

The Hidden Patterns of History

The underlying tension between the partnership and dominator models can be traced throughout recorded history. In all world regions, we find societies that, while already primarily orienting to the dominator model, retain important partnership elements. A notable example, familiar to students in European and classical history courses, is the civilization of ancient Greece.

Most curriculum materials give the impression that European civilization began with classical Greece. But the Greeks were descendants of the Indo-European Mycenaeans, who borrowed much of their civilization from the Minoan civilization they conquered. As cultural historian Jacquetta Hawkes writes in *Dawn of the Gods: Minoan and Mycenaean Origins of Greece*, "by the time the earliest barbarian forebears of the Greeks had begun to thrust down into mainland Greece, the Cretans were already well advanced in creating their Minoan culture and making their island the first outpost of civilization in Europe."[70]

As she also notes, the art and architecture of the technologically advanced Minoan civilization provided much of the foundation for later Greek art and architecture. The Minoan religion, centering on the worship of a female deity or Goddess, also influenced the Greeks, who adopted many Minoan deities into their later Olympian pantheon—although, following the pattern we looked at earlier, they were already subservient to Zeus, the violent Greek thunder-god.

Most high school texts on Athenian society also fail to bring out the fact that this "democracy" excluded the vast majority of the population: the half of Athens that was composed of women plus the women and men who made up the large Athenian slave population. Nor is there any discussion of the indications in Greek plays such as Aristophanes' *Lysistrata* that ancient Athens witnessed a social phenomenon akin to our modern women's anti-war movement.[71] In a curriculum informed by partnership education, these fascinating matters, so relevant to our own American history, *are* addressed—as ancient Greece would be examined in terms of the conflict between lingering partnership elements and the later dominator overlay.[72]

Homer, for example, is much more interesting when read from this perspective. Homer's warrior heroes reflect the Indo-European emphasis on violence. But, reflecting the lingering high status of women in Mycenaean culture, we still find many powerful female figures in Homer's *Odyssey:* the mighty queen-sorceress Circe, the nymph Calypso who rules the island of Ogygia, the seductive Sirens, the princess Nausicaa and her mother Queen Arete. (This last figure Homer describes as worshipped by "all the folk, who look upon her as a goddess.")

We read a great deal about philosophers such as Socrates and statesmen such as Pericles. But rarely are we informed that Socrates' teacher was a woman, Diotema, a priestess of Mantinea. Or that Pericles' companion was a philosopher from Miletus named Aspasia. (I should add that when Aspasia is mentioned at all, she is often referred to as a *hetaera*, a Greek word referring to women in Athenian society who played multiple roles as sexual objects, entertainers, musicians, and/or intellectual companions for men, since "respectable" women were rarely given an education and were confined to women's quarters much like those found in fundamentalist Muslim societies today. However, as Professor Mario Montuori notes in his book on Socrates, the characterization of Aspasia as a *hetaera* has no factual basis.)[73]

Only occasionally do we read about a Greek woman such as the poet Sappho, fragments of whose poetry have survived. There is, for example, the passage where she lovingly writes that the sight of her child is more beautiful and moving than the launching of a thousand warships. But by and large the conventional curriculum still focuses on men—still further obscuring the significant fact that Greek civilization was an uneasy blend of partnership and dominator elements.

The study of ancient Rome in the conventional curriculum also fails to make any distinction between partnership and dominator elements during various phases of Roman civilization. As with the study of classical Greece, most reading assignments are by and about men—for example, the writings of Julius Caesar that I had to memorize in Latin when I was a child. Moreover, these documents frequently focus on the politics of domination: on who wins over whom, usually through "heroic" violence. Consider Plutarch's biographies, for instance. In fact, reading Plutarch is an amazing experience because he so idealizes in men the qualities that make it possible for them to cause pain to others. There is absolutely nothing in these famous biographies about caring, much less love.

Yet in less-read writings from some periods in Roman history we do find the subject of love. In some elegies written by Ovid and Catullus during the 1st century B.C.E., women play important parts. We even find heroines who view love as a partnership or "bond of shared trust" between equals. These works indicate that during this period both women and men struggled to find more partnership-oriented ways of relating. Nonetheless, they contain may instances of sexism and misogynism, or woman-hating—reflecting the conflict between partnership and dominator elements in Roman civilization.[74]

Partnership education highlights such matters. It also gives greater visibility even in what has conventionally been taught as Roman history to the important role of women—although most of the women in question were primarily, so to speak, working in the employ of men. For example, Fulvia, one of Mark Anthony's wives, led an army for his cause during his absence in Egypt. The Emperor Claudius's grandmother, Livia, played a major part in maintaining the imperial power of her husband and son. And Claudius's wife, Agrippina, is said to have poisoned him so that her son by a prior marriage, Nero, could become emperor.

Partnership education also highlights the fact that, despite the restrictions they faced, some women maintained an independent identity. A case in point is Cleopatra, who ruled Egypt from the time she was a teenager. (Unfortunately, most books about the life of Cleopatra contain more fiction than fact. Or, like the extensive material about Cleopatra in Plutarch, they focus on her relationship with two well-known Romans: Julius Caesar and Mark Anthony.) As scholars today search through long-ignored records, it is possible that they will uncover information about more women who, in their own right, made significant cultural contributions in ancient Rome. Students can search the World Wide Web and other sources for recent research on this issue.

Looking at recorded history from the perspective of the tension between the partnership and dominator models as underlying possibilities for social organization, students will also find intermittent periods of partnership resurgence. During the 1st century, the assumption that human relations have to be ordered into rankings of domination and submission (as Aristotle had claimed was natural for relations between male masters and both slaves and women) was challenged. This occurred in Rome itself, as well as in outlying parts of the Roman Empire such as Palestine. Here a young Jew named Jesus began preaching a partnership morality: the elevation of stereotypically "feminine" values such as compassion, empathy, and nonviolence to social and personal governance.

Of particular interest in terms of its partnership configuration is the fact that women held leadership positions in early Christianity. This is to some extent reflected in the official Christian scriptures. A reexamination of the New Testament reveals that women played an important role in the early Christian movement (which was considered a subversive movement in its time). For instance, we read that meetings were often held in the homes of women (usually widows, who, compared to wives, were more independent of male control). Consider Romans 16:7, where we find Paul respectfully greeting a woman apostle named Junia, whom he describes as senior to himself in the movement. He also mentions other women who play pivotal roles in early Christianity.

The most interesting sources of information about women's key roles, however, are the Gnostic Gospels. These "lost books"—which were buried by Gnostic Christians to avoid their destruction by the men who after Jesus's death used the story of his death and resurrection to build their "orthodox Church"—indicate that Mary Magdalene played a major part in early Christian history. These documents (some predating the Gospels in the New Testament) were discovered during the 20th century hidden in a cave in Nag Hammadi, an outlying province of upper Egypt. In them, Mary Magdalene is not dismissed as a prostitute but, rather, described as Jesus's "favorite disciple." Not only that, we learn that she was the only one with the courage to challenge Peter for trying to establish his Church as another religious hierarchy of the type Jesus preached against.[75]

Indeed, by the 4th century, following the Church's alliance with the Roman emperor Constantine, the Church had become an authoritarian and rigidly male-dominant institution that habitually used violence against competing "heretic" Christian sects. Whereas the partnership core of Jesus's teachings remained part of official doctrine, and was practiced by many nuns and priests, the Church itself again began to look like the kind of religious hierarchy Jesus had denounced. Moreover, while in the early days of the Christian movement its adherents were violently persecuted by Roman authorities who saw Christianity as a threat to their power, throughout medieval Christian history the Church used violence to maintain its power—through its Crusades, Inquisition, and witch burnings.[76]

It is important for students to look at the history that followed the rise of early Christianity in the Middle East and Europe in terms of this underlying tension between the partnership and dominator models. It is also important for them to understand what the European Middle Ages were really like, because there is today so much misguided nostalgia for this "age of faith."

According to some people, this was a time when a religious rather than scientific worldview made for a better, less violent, more orderly and moral life. In actuality, the Middle Ages were a *very* violent time. With a few exceptions, the medieval period was also a time of repressive state and church control. Control notwithstanding, it was far from being orderly. On the contrary, these centuries were one long series of battles between feudal lords and/or kings and popes trying to enlarge their real-estate holdings.

Shortly after the Middle Ages, but still during this preindustrial span of history, Western Europe began its conquest and colonization of other world regions—a conquest and colonization in which the Church actively collaborated. These often brutal conquests and colonizations of dark-skinned peoples, which profoundly influenced cultures in Africa, Asia, Australia, and the Americas, were expressions of the dominator elements of European culture. But it is important to remember that there were also in Western European culture partnership elements, and periods of partnership resurgence.

A fascinating example occurred in the south of France during the 11th and 12th centuries, before the Church launched the Albigensian Crusade—the only crusade launched not against Jews or Muslims but against other Christians. This period saw the rise of the troubadours and their far less known female counterparts, the trobaritzes.

These poets were inspired by some of the poetry brought back by Crusaders captivated by the erotic poetry of Muslim mystics, who, like the Sufis in our day, celebrated the divine using the language of erotic love. (It is important to point out that, while Europe was still mired in the Dark Ages, an Islamic renaissance of arts and sciences occurred, and in centers of learning such as Alexandria in Egypt, a cosmopolitan culture flourished that combined Jewish, Islamic, and Greek culture.) What the troubadours brought to life were some of these influences, particularly the mystical traditions of Islamic Sufism, Jewish Cabbalism, and Christian Esotericism, along with traces of the more female-honoring cultures we looked at earlier.

Examining this period from a more gender-balanced perspective, we can see that times of partnership resurgence are characteristically periods when women, and values stereotypically associated with women, gain some measure of ascendancy. This is illustrated by the role Eleanor of Aquitaine, together with her daughters Alix and Marie, played in bringing to birth the more gentle or "effeminate" culture of the troubadours and trobaritzes.

In most history books, all we learn about Eleanor of Aquitaine is that she was the wife and mother of kings. This inaccurate and incomplete portrayal of this remarkable woman is of little help to girls and boys who need to learn that, even in face of severe constraints, women have been leaders and have made important contributions in their own right. Reading about Eleanor of Aquitaine in books such as Marion Meade's *Eleanor of Aquitaine: A Biography* (which could be excerpted and/or adapted for high school students), we discover what enormous determination she had and how she overcame many obstacles. Moreover, Eleanor of Aquitane made contributions to history that, in many ways, are more significant than those of the kings to whom she was mother and wife, since it was in her court and the courts of her daughters that the subculture of the troubadours and trobaritzes flourished.

This subculture had a significant, and positive, influence on the course of Western civilization. It is from the troubadours (as detailed in *Sacred Pleasure*) that we have inherited the term *gentleman*. This ideal for men, though at best selectively applied, given the constraints of medieval social structure, was a sharp departure from the dominator model of "real masculinity" associated with the male as warrior (that is, with a "superior" capacity to inflict pain on others).

The troubadours were also instrumental in popularizing the veneration of Mary, Mother of God (see Figure 4.6). This homage was at first vehemently resisted by Church authorities, who may have perceived it as a way of keeping alive earlier Goddess-worship traditions as well as of elevating the status of women. But in the end, the Church itself took over, and many of the most beautiful cathedrals of Europe, including Chartes and Notre Dame de Paris, are dedicated to "Our Lady."

The poetry of the troubadours—and trobaritzes—was a major cultural contribution in itself. Even though we rarely read about these female poets in writings about that period, their verses are fascinating in terms of what they say about the qualities they valued in a man—qualities that many women still value today. They wrote that their lovers should be frank and humble, courteous with everyone, and noble, loving, and discreet, and that they should not pick fights with any man.

During the Renaissance—a period that saw the ascendancy of humanistic values—women also played important, though still rarely recognized, roles. An example is Christine de Pisan, who wrote *La Cite des Dames* (or *City of Women*), a protofeminist work. Although this book employed many of the gender stereotypes perceived as immutable at the time (in the early 15th century), it stands as a passionate defense against the vilification, trivialization, and derogation of women. The Renaissance also saw the rise of women who achieved political importance—for example, Caterina Sforza, a strange blend of Amazon warrior, tolerant ruler, and woman of the world. (For tongue-in-cheek short biographies of Medieval and Renaissance women, including Sforza, see Vicki Leon's *Uppity Women of Medieval Times*.[77]) Though rarely included in art histories, important women artists also emerged during the Renaissance. An example is Sofonisba Anguissola, an Italian Renaissance painter whose portraits were so alive that the king of Spain (one of the great patrons of the arts) invited her to be a royal portraitist in his court. Once again, it is only thanks to feminist scholars that we have rediscovered this role model for girls with artistic ambitions. (For a beautiful book on this painter, see *Sofonisba Anguissola* by art historian Ilya Sandra Perlingieri.)[78]

The Renaissance can best be understood in terms of a heightening tension between the partnership and dominator models. In many respects it was a time of partnership resurgence—for example, in the challenge to women's subservience to men, the Renaissance ideal of equal education

(a)

(b)

FIGURE 4.6   Mary and Kuan Yin

(a) Over time, the Great Goddess was transformed into Mary, mother of God.
CREDIT: The Partnership Way: New Tools for Living and Learning, *by Riane Eisler and David Loye. Line drawing from the original: John Mason.*
(b) Kuan Yin is the Chinese Goddess of Compassion who protects women and grants children to those who want them.
CREDIT: *John Mason.*

FIGURE 4.7   Witch Burning

This drawing is of a medieval woodcut, dating back to 1555 A.D., that depicts the burning of three witches.

CREDIT: The Partnership Way: New Tools for Living and Learning, *by Riane Eisler and David Loye. Line drawing from the original: Jeff Helwig.*

for women, the ascendancy of more stereotypically "feminine" values, and the emphasis on "effete" arts. But the movement toward partnership was countered by strong dominator resistance.

Christian inquisitors continued their reign of terror against "heretics" and Jews, whose property, when they were expelled or murdered, was confiscated by the Spanish rulers. The witch hunts continued, resulting in the torture and death of at least 100,000 women—a huge percentage of the European population at the time (see Figure 4.7).[79] In the process, by exterminating the women healers or wise women/midwives who had since remote antiquity passed down herbal and other means of contraception from generation to generation, as John M. Riddle writes in his book *Eve's Herbs: A History of Contraception and Abortion in the West*, the Church also ensured that this knowledge was lost.[80]

The Renaissance also witnessed the enactment of regressive new laws such as the reintroduction of primogeniture (whereby firstborn sons inherit the bulk of a family's property). Like the witch hunts that terrorized European women (leaving some villages without any women at all), primogeniture countered any challenge to male dominance, making it even more difficult for women to achieve economic, and thus personal, independence.

The Industrial or Modern Age

This point-counterpoint of partnership resurgence and dominator resistance and backlash became even more intense in the next major period of European history—in large part due to the great dislocations entailed in a second major technological phase-change: the shift from the agrarian to the industrial age.

The last three hundred years of European and North American history are the most extensively studied in schools in the United States. This period is generally known as the industrial or machine era, even though industrialization came much later in many world regions. China, Japan, and India opened to industrialization only during the late 19th century, and there are indigenous societies in Africa, Asia, the Americas, Australia, and other world regions that, although affected by industrialization, are still primarily agrarian.

In Europe and North America the increased use of machines actually started before the 18th-century Enlightenment. However, it was only after the Enlightenment that industrialization began to go into high gear. The last three hundred years have therefore been a time of great technological and social disequilibrium.

Largely due to this disequilibrium—which brought with it inventions such as the printing press and the greater literacy needed for industrial work—these years also ushered in one organized social movement after another that frontally challenged traditions of domination. For, although this is still seldom noted in conventional history texts and classes, as new technologies destabilized established institutional forms there were opportunities to challenge systems of belief and social structures that had once been thought immutable.

As we will see on the section on U.S. history in Chapter 5, the European Enlightenment was influenced by partnership elements in American Indian cultures. For example, Rousseau's writings on the "noble savage" were influenced by the fact that some Native American societies were less hierarchic and authoritarian than the European societies of the time.

But despite this, European colonial policy continued to be guided by a dominator ethos of conquest and domination, as American Indians were slaughtered and enslaved and African women and men were imported for enslavement in both North and South American colonies. In short, although organized challenges to entrenched traditions of domination are a major, though far too little noted, theme in modern history, dominator elements also abound.

Indeed, if we look at this period from the perspective of the underlying tension between the dominator and partnership models as underlying human possibilities, we see a mounting partnership thrust countered every inch of the way by dominator resistance and periodic regressions.

Certainly the Enlightenment was a period in which we begin to see a massive questioning of entrenched patterns of domination. The so-called rights-of-man movement of the late 17th and early 18th centuries eventually led to both the American and French Revolutions and to a gradual shift from monarchies to republics. Paralleling the challenge to the supposedly divinely ordained right of kings to rule was the feminist movement of the 18th and 19th centuries, which challenged the supposedly divinely ordained right by men to rule over women and children in the "castles" of their homes, bringing about a gradual shift to less autocratic and male-dominated families.

It was also during this period that we begin to see the rise of a sizable middle class, challenging the old "nobility," including the slaveholding landed ruling classes in the American South. Concomitant with the shift from authoritarian monarchies to more democratic republics, and from authoritarian families to more democratic ones, was the beginning of a movement against slavery, culminating in an organized movement for the emancipation of black slaves.

During both the 19th and 20th centuries there were movements to shift from the colonization and exploitation of indigenous peoples to their independence from foreign rule, as well as global movements challenging economic exploitation and injustice. The rise of organized labor and socialism was followed by the toppling of feudal monarchies and war lords by communist revolutions in Russia, China, and other countries. In the United States, meanwhile, there was a gradual shift from unregulated robber-baron capitalism to government regulations, including anti-monopoly laws and economic safety nets such as Social Security and unemployment insurance. There was the 19th-century feminist movement demanding equal education and suffrage for women and the organized movement by blacks for the vote, followed by the 20th-century civil rights and women's liberation and women's rights movements. There was the 19th-century pacifist movement followed by the 20th-century peace movement, expressing the first fully organized rejection of war as a means of resolving international conflicts. And there was the 20th-century family planning movement, which was key to women's emancipation, greater opportunities for children, and the alleviation of poverty.

In basic respects, however, the dominator system remained firmly entrenched. Colonialism and the killing and exploitation of darker-skinned peoples continued the tradition of conquest and domination on a global scale. Periodic backlashes also occurred. For example, Jim Crow laws were passed after the abolition of slavery, anti-union violence was frequent during the first half of the 20th century, and anti-feminist agitation continued—ranging from resistance to higher education and the vote for women in the 19th century to the defeat of the Equal Rights Amendment and renewed opposition to reproductive rights for women in the 20th century.

The 20th century also witnessed massive dominator regressions. In Europe, for example, we saw Hitler's Germany (from the early 1930s to the mid-1940s) and Stalin's Soviet Union (from the 1920s to the 1950s), in which the ideals of a more just society were co-opted into a "dictatorship of the proletariat," creating still another version of a brutal dominator model. And even after Western colonial regimes were overthrown in Africa and Asia, authoritarian dictatorships by local elites rose up over their own people, resulting in renewed repression and exploitation.

This modern industrial age also brought the use of ever more advanced technologies to more effectively exploit, dominate, and kill. (For a discussion of the influence of a dominator orientation on industrial technologies, see my chapter in *Macrohistory and Macrohistorians*.[81]) Moreover, it was during the industrial age that high technology began to be harnessed to further "man's conquest of nature"—wreaking ever more environmental damage.

The Postmodern Age

Postmodern is a term that began to gain currency toward the end of the 20th century. It describes the period ushered in by nuclear/electronic/biochemical technological revolutions, which are even more fundamentally destabilizing existing structures and beliefs. Now the mix of the dominator model and advanced technology becomes increasingly unsustainable. The blade is the nuclear bomb and/or biological warfare and terrorism. Ever more advanced technologies in the service of a dominator ethos threaten our natural habitat, as well as that of most species with whom we share our planet.

This period brings further challenges to traditions of domination. It brings a strong environmental movement—millions of people coming together to challenge "man's conquest of nature." It also brings a strengthening of the family-planning movement as integral to environmental sustainability, an expanding movement against the domination and exploitation of indigenous peoples, a growing challenge by peoples in the "developing world" against domination by the "developed world," and thousands of grassroots organizations all over the world working toward political democracy, nonviolent ways of living, and economic, racial, and gender equity.[82]

Significantly, the postmodern age brings a much more organized challenge to traditions of domination and violence in intimate relations. Child abuse, rape, and wife-beating are increasingly prosecuted in some world regions. A global women's rights movement frontally challenges the domination of half of humanity by the other half, gaining impetus from the unprecedented United Nations conferences (1975–1995) that brought women from all world regions together around such pivotal issues as violence against women, equal legal rights and economic opportunities, and reproductive freedom.

However, precisely because the movement toward partnership is intensifying and deepening—for the first time focusing on the foundational "private" sphere of human relations where we first learn and continually practice either partnership or domination—the resistance to change is stiffening. There is continued, and in some places increasing, violence against women and children. Some of the statistical increase is due to the fact that this violence was formerly unreported, as it was not prosecuted and, instead, often blamed on the victims. But since violence is what ultimately maintains dominator relations, as women's and children's human rights are asserted, violence against them has also increased to literally beat them back into submission. In some countries, this violence is perpetrated by government officials; for example, in Afghanistan, Algeria, Pakistan, Bangladesh, and Iran, the stoning to death of women for any act perceived as countering male sexual and personal control—even a young woman exposing her ankles—is again being justified on "moral" grounds.[83]

There is also, under the guise of economic globalization, a worldwide recentralization of economic power. Under pressure from major economic players, governments are cutting social services and shredding economic safety-nets—resulting in "economic restructuring" that is particularly hurtful to women and children throughout the world. In the developing world, this restructuring is enriching dominator elites through a shift from production of food and goods for local consumption to production of food and goods for export. At the same time, it is contributing to the impoverishment of Third World people, who no longer produce what they need and are ever more dependent on jobs in urban centers. Concurrently, well-paying jobs in postindustrial economies are shrinking, creating increased competition for low-paying jobs (generally without benefits) and displacing blue-collar, pink-collar, and middle-management workers through automation or corporate downsizing. From the former Soviet Union to Asia, Africa, and Latin America, many regions are being forced into a replay of the robber-baron days of early capitalism, complete with sweatshops, forced child labor, rampant political corruption, and organized crime.[84] In short, there is a widening gap between haves and have-nots both within countries and between them.

There is also burgeoning population growth. The world's population, which has doubled in the last forty years—in only a few decades reaching more than 5 billion people, the vast majority of whom live in the poorest world regions—is projected to double again by the middle of the 21st century, exacerbating hunger, violence, and other causes of human suffering, and straining the world's natural resources. This unsustainable population growth is largely due to dominator systems dynamics—to the continued denial of reproductive freedom to women (and the loss of gains already made) and to the often violent efforts to deny women access to life options other than procreation.

There is also growing scapegoating of women (particularly single mothers living in poverty) and minorities, sometimes in the name of religious fundamentalism. Terrorism is on the rise, even in once supposedly impregnable nations such as the United States, sometimes perpetrated by its own citizens. "Ethnic cleansings" have ravaged Bosnia and Kosovo. Resurgent genocidal warfare has wreaked havoc in Rwanda and Zaire. And all the while, in the name of entertainment, the mass media obsessively focuses on violence—constantly emphasizing the infliction of pain and suffering that are mainstays of dominator politics and economics.

In sum, the outcome of the tension between the partnership and dominator models as two basic human possibilities is far from settled.

Two Possible Futures

We are now at what scientists call a bifurcation point, where there are two very different scenarios for our future.

One scenario is *dominator systems breakdown:* the unsustainable future of high technology guided by the dominator model (see "Maintaining Domination" sidebar). This is a future of nuclear bombs, biological warfare, and ever more sophisticated terrorism. It is a future where high technology in service of the domination of nature despoils and pollutes our natural habitat.

In the name of religious fundamentalism, new theocratic regimes replay the violence, scapegoating, and absolute control over women that characterized the worst aspects of the Middle Ages. Unrestrained by international regulations, megacorporations control more and more economic resources and governments. Although the nation-state becomes increasingly obsolete, it still serves as an instrument whereby dominator elites maintain political and economic control—not just over women and marginalized groups but over the population as a whole. The socially essential "women's work" of caring and caretaking is still so devalued that childcare workers continue to be paid less than parking lot attendants, and caring for children in homes is not even classified as work—further contributing to an ever widening gap between haves and have-nots.[85]

This is a future where advanced technologies will be used not to free our human potentials but to more effectively control and dominate. Ultimately, it is a future of environmental, nuclear, or biological holocaust.

The other scenario is *breakthrough to partnership:* the sustainable future of a world primarily orienting to the partnership model (see "Shifting to Partnership" sidebar). This is a future in which advanced technologies are developed and used in ways that promote environmental balance and the realization of our species' great untapped potentials.

International regulations ensure corporate accountability to workers, communities, and our natural habitat. New economic institutions and rules recognize the value of the work of caring and caretaking, and discourage violence, exploitation, and the despoilation of nature.[86]

Although nation-states also continue to break down in this world, genocidal ethnic civil wars are avoided because diversity is valued and our shared partnership heritage binds cultures together. Although there is still some violence, it is not built into the system as a means of maintaining rankings of domination. Although there is still conflict, as is inevitable in human relations, young people have the tools to resolve it in creative ways.

Women and men are equal partners in both the "private" or family sphere and the "public" or outside sphere. And children are valued and nurtured not only by their biological parents but by the entire community—which recognizes that children are our most precious resource.

This partnership world is a world governed by standards of human rights and responsibilities, a world where the only hunger is the human hunger for learning and creative expression, where the basic needs for food, shelter, and education can be met by all. It is a world where our human adventure unfolds in creative and caring ways, where the human spirit can flourish. To move toward this world, however, requires fundamental changes, including changes in our education that make it possible for today's and tomorrow's children to see that we *can* create a more equitable, peaceful, and sustainable future—once we acquire the knowledge and skills to do so.[87]

MAINTAINING DOMINATION

How do people learn to unconsciously collaborate in maintaining rankings of domination, despite their great human toll? Although many dynamics are involved, as discussed in other works,[88] four are of particular importance.

First, if, in childhood, love is linked with domination and coercion, with emotional or physical abuse, with the infliction and suffering of pain, taking away domination and submission may unconsciously seem equivalent to taking away love.[89] If this association is chronic, it produces a mindset in which one can think of human relations only in terms of obeying the orders of superiors (being dominated) or giving orders (dominating) and/or rebelling and taking over (becoming the dominator). Hence, this early linking of love—of the caring and caretaking we humans depend on to survive when we are small—with domination and submission is one of the most effective mechanisms underlying dominator systems maintenance.

The mere thought that there is a partnership alternative—that we can have relations based primarily on mutuality, caring, and empathy—causes profound unease among people who in early childhood were forced to internalize this mindset. They associate love with domination and submission on an unconscious, probably even neural, level. Therefore, people socialized in rigid dominator families and schools tend to vehemently resist change, insisting that rankings of domination and submission are just human nature.

A second mechanism through which people are psychologically molded so that they unwittingly replicate a system that causes them and others a great deal of pain is the internalization, from early childhood on, of a mental map in which the subordination of one half of humanity to the other is normal. The notion that one half of humanity (the female "other") is put on this earth only to serve the male half as a "helpmate," and that (as in the stories of Pandora and Eve) woman is to blame for all of "man's" troubles, provides a psychic template for dominator-dominated human relations. Once in place, this template can easily be generalized to other out-groups—races, religions, classes, and cultures—who are then also viewed as inferior and/or dangerous.

A third mechanism of dominator systems maintenance is the fact that the dominator model, by its nature, continually creates artificial scarcity—not only material scarcity but love scarcity, since empathic and loving impulses must constantly be suppressed, or at least severely limited, if this system is to be replicated. Given its devastating wars, massive expenditures for armaments, misdistribution of resources to those on top with only a "trickling down" to the rest, denial to women of means of limiting pregnancy (resulting in increased population growth), and destructive "conquest of nature" technologies, the dominator system is ultimately extremely inefficient. But it is this very economic inefficiency that keeps the system in place, as scarcity is the soil out of which dominator systems have historically developed and continue to reinvent themselves.

Fourth, dominator societies have historically maintained themselves through myths that liken society's authority figures to punitive parents. These myths, which we are taught from childhood on, are our cultural legacy from earlier times that oriented far more closely to the dominator model. We still find these myths today worldwide, of angry and punitive deities constantly punishing humanity for being evil—just like children in rigid dominator families are constantly told that they are being punished because they are bad. And just as children in rigid dominator families learn to suppress and deny their pain and anger against the adults who inflict it, in these religious myths there is also a total denial that capricious, cruel, violent divine acts are in any way blameworthy. On the contrary, these acts are idealized as the will of the gods, and if any blame is assigned, it is against those who have disobeyed divine commands. For, as in rigid dominator families, even when these deities are depicted as loving, theirs is a love that is conditional on absolute obedience.

Becoming aware of these dynamics can be uncomfortable, even painful. It is therefore important to discuss them in ways that make it possible for us to freely voice our reactions and express our feelings. If we use this dialogic approach, we can, at least for the moment, put aside entrenched assumptions, and explore other alternatives.

SHIFTING TO PARTNERSHIP

During the last several centuries, along with the challenge to entrenched traditions of political and economic domination, the domination of women by men has been challenged and parenting has begun to move away from "spare the rod and spoil the child" as sound pedagogy. But every progressive movement has been, and continues to be, fiercely resisted, and there have been powerful backlashes.

Many people feel disheartened, fearing that, as we are often told, the progressive social movements have failed. However, from the perspective of cultural transformation theory, dominator regressions are part of a dynamic process where backlashes against movement toward partnership reconstruct, in both old and new forms, the kinds of social structures, beliefs, and behaviors that support and strengthen dominator elements in our culture.

It is instructive that—whether in Europe under Hitler and Stalin, or in the Mideast under Khomeini and the Taliban—periods of regressions have been times when there is a push to force women back into their "traditional roles" in male-dominated families where children are severely punished for any failure to obey orders, no matter how arbitrary or unjust. We are today experiencing such a regressive movement in many world regions, including the United States. Although far from the genocide of a Hitler or Stalin, here so-called religious fundamentalist leaders fan fear and hate, advocate a move back to more authoritarian and male-dominated families and schools, and support public policies in which there is always enough government funding for armies and prisons (defense, coercion, and punishment), but not for caring for children or the elderly (empathic caregiving).

How can we avoid these backlashes? My research shows that they will continue unless we take advantage of the dislocations of the shift from an industrial to a postindustrial economy to build the foundations on which a less violent, more equitable, and more humane system of relations can rest. These foundations consist of five major interconnected areas: partnership childcare, partnership gender relations, partnership economics, partnership spirituality, and, overarching all these, partnership formal and informal education.[90]

I have identified three key interventions for accelerating the movement toward partnership. The first is the formation of national and international alliances to work for an end to violence against children and women. The second is a concerted global campaign for gender equity, encompassing issues ranging from raising the status, rights, and opportunities of women to increasing the availability of community-supported family planning. The third is the development of new economic rules and institutions that recognize and reward the socially essential work of caregiving.[91]

On the grassroots level worldwide, there is already strong movement in these directions, as illustrated by two examples that I am personally involved in. One, which I co-founded with the Nobel Peace Prize Laureate Betty Williams, is the Spiritual Alliance to Stop Intimate Violence (SAIV). The goal of SAIV is to gather support from both well-known and grass-roots spiritual leaders to take a strong stand against intimate or domestic violence—the violence against children and women that is not only the most prevalent human rights violation on our globe but the most basic betrayal of trust. The second example is the Alliance for a Caring

Economy (ACE), which I founded to promote policies and practices that recognize and adequately reward the essential work of caregiving—from paid parental leave and state-supported benefits for childcare workers to other "caring economic inventions" still to be developed. (See the Center for Partnership Studies website at <www.partnershipway.org>.)

Clearly, we still have a long way to go if we are to strengthen and consolidate the movement toward a more equitable and peaceful way of life. But if we actively support the three interventions described above, we can begin to replace the imbalanced foundations on which dominator systems have been rebuilt during periods of backlash, and instead lay the foundations on which a better future can be built.

This is not an easy undertaking. But our culture and much of our physical environment have been human creations. As we become conscious co-creators of our cultural evolution, we *can* complete the shift to a partnership future.

From Counting to Current Events

Making the Three R's Meaningful

I REMEMBER WHEN I DISCOVERED that there were women who had written important philosophical works. It was a revelation—and a validation. I was particularly moved by the feminist philosopher Charlotte Perkins Gilman, who observed that "until we see what we are, we cannot take steps to become what we should be."[1]

I believe that offering a more realistic, and hopeful, picture of who we are and can be is one of the key tasks of education, and that the vertical curriculum threads outlined in the last chapters do exactly this. They situate our lives in a wondrous drama that begins with the emergence of our universe, our planet, and life itself, continues with the appearance on the evolutionary horizon of our human species, moves on to our creation of cultures and technologies, and shows that we can become conscious co-creators of both our individual and social future.

Within this epic drama are many stories, some of which we touched on in the last two chapters. In this chapter, we will see how stories relating to various aspects of our human adventure on this Earth can be incorporated into existing curricula by interweaving them with the horizontal threads of the partnership learning tapestry. These horizontal threads are of two types.

The first bundle consists of established and emerging fields of study. Examples of established units of study are the three R's (reading, writing, and arithmetic), the physical sciences, the life sciences, the social sciences, the humanities, art, music, and physical education. More recently, newer units of study, such as courses in computer literacy, have begun to emerge as part of the established U.S. curriculum.

The second bundle consists of issues of immediate interest to students. These include relationships, sexuality, television and other mass media, and morality.

Like all aspects of the partnership learning tapestry—and like all aspects of our lives—these two types of horizontal threads are intertwined and often overlap. Moreover, as teachers know, learning takes place on many levels: through cognition (the intellect), affect (the emotions), conation (the will), and—because everything involves somatic processes—soma (the body).

Partnership education cultivates cognition, or thinking. It engages children's minds by stimulating their natural curiosity. In fact, when children's curiosity is stimulated, they have such a good time learning that they don't even realize this is what they are doing. But if learning is to be effective and lasting, young people's emotions must also be engaged. It is this combination of affect and cognition with somatic, or bodily, learning (helping to ground learning in experience) that leads to conation or the will to act—which is, after all, the aim of education.

The materials that follow illustrate how teachers can bring all these elements into the classroom in courses ranging from the life sciences, math, and literature to art, history, and current events. I have prefaced each section with a list of themes that connect the subject to the vertical threads.

In this chapter, we will look at how interweaving themes from the vertical curriculum threads into established classes makes for a more meaningful and colorful learning tapestry. We will use examples I have already touched on as well as new ones. Then, in the next chapter, we will focus on areas of immediate student interest, and on how these offer opportunities to look at ourselves and our world through the analytical lens of the partnership-dominator continuum.

Throughout these two chapters we will continue to see how using the lens of the partnership-dominator continuum can help students sort information, learn positive values and behaviors, and prepare for active participation in the creation of their future. Since a key feature of partnership education is that it is gender-balanced and multicultural, these two chapters also continue to integrate materials on women, ethnic minorities, and other disempowered groups as important aspects of a more holistic curriculum. In addition, they show how teachers can integrate various ways of learning, making school more interesting and relevant.

The Life Sciences

All life forms are interconnected.

Cooperation is a major theme in evolution.

Learning about species for whom partnership is the primary model for relations, such as the bonobo chimpanzees, can help dispel myths about "human nature."

Using the analytical lens of the partnership-dominator continuum facilitates intellectual, emotional, and action-oriented learning.

A holistic (multicultural and gender-balanced) approach facilitates habits of critical thinking, including the understanding that perceptions and interpretations of reality are affected by social contexts.

Interweaving the chronological sequence leading to the evolution of our human species (described in Chapter 3) into life science classes makes it possible to engage children's interest in science through stories. Doing so is particularly important today since education for the 21st century must include a sound grounding in science. It also helps students better understand the world of nature. At a time of increasing urbanization, and the resulting disconnection of humans from nature, this understanding, too, is extremely important.

In lower grades, learning about the life sciences can be facilitated by stories about life forms with whom we share our natural habitat (again, see Chapter 3). As they already do in some schools, children can bring their pets to class or enjoy interactive experiences with baby animals at children's zoos. Both activities have the advantage of grounding knowledge in experience, thus combining mental or cognitive learning with affective or emotional learning.

By high school and college, students are ready to learn about the latest scientific findings. For instance, in as simplified a form as necessary, students can learn about studies showing that when we humans engage in caring behavior, we are rewarded by pleasure through the action of neuropeptides and other chemicals.[2] Talking about these studies brings up feelings, not just thoughts, making it possible both to stimulate thinking and to engage emotions.

By studying the life sciences in an evolutionary context, students can become aware that we live in symbiotic relationship with plants, trees, and many other living organisms that make it possible for us to survive. They can also become aware of earlier cultural traditions in which the Earth was considered part of the sacred—anticipating what we today call *environmental consciousness*. The knowledge that these traditions, still preserved by some tribal societies, are our lost human heritage, once shared by cultures in all world regions, reinforces the understanding that today we, too, must honor nature and work together to maintain a clean and healthy habitat (see Box 5.1).

I want to touch again on ways teachers can help young people more critically examine the misconceptions spread by popularizations of sociobiological theories that make it seem that because certain traits and behaviors are found in animals, they are therefore "natural" for humans. Although PBS documentaries on animals often focus primarily on predatory behaviors—on animals stalking, killing, and eating other animals—these behaviors, as primatologist Frans deWaal writes, occupy only a small percentage of time in the lives of even the most aggressive species. DeWaal recounts how during the 1970s, when funding floodgates for research on aggression were thrown open, he embarked on a study on aggressive behavior in long-tailed macaques, a species with a reputation for great belligerence. He waited many hours with a tape recorder and video equipment to record fights in a captive group of these monkeys. "What struck me most while sitting and waiting," he reports, "was how rarely these monkeys fought. . . . I calculated that they devoted less than five percent to this activity. Most of the time they played, groomed, slept in large huddles, or were otherwise peacefully occupied."[5]

But in the televised nature programs watched by millions of children and adults, there is hardly ever a focus of cooperative behaviors. This is all the more misleading since cooperation is a major theme in evolution. In fact, it is central to the survival of many species, ranging from acorn woodpeckers, wolves, and elephants to as unlikely a species as bats, who share food and try to take care of those who cannot do so themselves. (Among the handful of nature programs that *do* focus on cooperative behaviors is "Primetime Primates," a 1996 PBS documentary starring Alan Alda and featuring the work of de Waal on cooperation and peacemaking among primates.)

Television documentaries also tend to present dominator gender stereotypes and relations as inevitable. Some documentaries even claim as scientific fact that male supremacy is "wired" into our genes. To counter

BOX 5.1   Partnership-Oriented Perspectives

In higher grade levels, students can study the partnership-oriented perspectives of scholars such as Adrienne Zihlman, Nancy Tanner, Humberto Maturana, David Loye, and Allan Combs mentioned in Chapters 3 and 4. See the sources listed there, as well as the excerpt from *Sacred Pleasure* and the excerpt from David Loye's *Darwin's Lost Theory of Love* cited at the end of this book. Additional information can be obtained from *Sacred Pleasure* (chs. 2 and 9), as well as from Evelyn Fox Keller's *Reflections on Gender and Science*[3] and Linda Jean Shepherd's *Lifting the Veil: The Feminine Face of Science*,[4] which explore what science and scientists might be like if they were working more from an ethos expressive of feelings and morality.

this misinformation, students need an opportunity to learn about the enormous, and fascinating, variability of mating behaviors among different species.

A delightful example of a species with partnership rather than dominator mating behaviors is the seahorse. Every time these beautiful little creatures mate, they do a little "dance" of touch and intertwinement. And after the female deposits her eggs in the male's pouch, so he can fertilize them, he carries the eggs for twenty-one days, until (after a prolonged "labor") they are born out of his pouch (see Figure 5.1).

Emperor penguins also share birthing. As shown in the National Geographic documentary "Emperors of Ice," fathers sit on the eggs laid by the mothers through the coldest winter months, sometimes losing their lives in the process. Finally, the mothers return and the parents are reunited in a touching rush.

Also contradicting many popular assumptions about animal mating, as we glimpsed earlier, are the bonobo chimpanzees. These fascinating primates, who are sometimes called pygmy chimpanzees even though they are actually no smaller than common chimpanzees, have begun to be intensively studied only in recent years. Hence, little information on them is available in most primary and secondary texts. (An important exception is Adrienne Zihlman's *The Human Evolution Coloring Book*,[6] a resource for learning complex biological information through visuals that has been successfully used in high school and university courses.)

FIGURE 5.1　Seahorses Mating

Seahorses are today threatened by a legal global trade. They are killed for traditional Chinese medicines, aphrodisiacs, curios, and food. Twenty million are killed each year. This may lead to the extinction of this extraordinary, beautiful, nurturing little creature.
CREDIT: *Garbo Chang.*

In many ways, bonobo chimpanzees prefigure more of what we find in humans than do any other primates. They have what primatologists call a more gracile or slender build, longer legs that stretch while walking, and a smaller head, smaller ears, a thinner neck, a more open face, and thinner eyebrow ridges than most other apes. Of particular interest is the fact that—like humans but unlike most other species—bonobos have sex not just for reproduction but purely for pleasure and, beyond this, for pleasure-bonding.

Indeed, this sharing of pleasure through the sharing of food as well as through sexual relations is a striking aspect of bonobo social organization. Just as striking is that even though their social organization is not violence-free, it is held together, to a far greater degree than among common chimps, by the exchange of mutual benefits characteristic of partnership relations. To maintain social cohesion and order, this species, so closely related to us, relies primarily on the sharing of pleasure—and not

---

BOX 5.2   Bonobos and Common Chimps

For materials on the bonobo chimpanzees, see the article from *Nature* by the primatologist Takayoshi Kano, who has studied these apes in the wild in the forests of Zaire. See also Adrienne Zihlman's "Myths of Gender," *Nature* 364 (August 12, 1993), as well as *Sacred Pleasure* (ch. 2). For more information on the common chimpanzees, see the National Geographic video titled *The Legend and Life of Jane Goodall.*

---

on the fear of pain (or violence) required to maintain rigid rankings of domination.

Equally striking is that, even though males are not dominated by females, in bonobo society females—particularly older females—wield a great deal of power. Moreover, it is through the association of females in groups that bonobo females seem to have avoided the kind of predatory sexual behavior that has been observed among common chimps, whereby males force sexual relations on females (see Box 5.2).

The study of the bonobo chimpanzees—who together with the common chimpanzees are our closest primate relatives—is extremely useful for learning about the evolution of human sexuality. It helps us understand that human sexuality, as somewhat foreshadowed by the bonobos, is *not* what is "animal" about us—that, in fact, human sexuality is different from that of most animals. (For materials on this topic, see *Sacred Pleasure*, chs. 2 and 14.)

Learning about the bonobo chimpanzees also offers students an opportunity to hone their skills in using the partnership and dominator models as cognitive tools. For example, by using these models as analytical lenses, students can compare the ways in which common chimps and bonobo chimpanzees relate. This examination will reveal that, although the common chimpanzees do not have a rigid dominator social organization, the bonobo chimpanzees orient more closely to the partnership model. In fact, we see here core elements of the partnership configuration. Bonobo chimpanzees are not male dominated. They engage in more food-sharing (an egalitarian behavior) than common chimpanzees. And, as noted in Chapter 3, even though theirs is not a completely violence-free society, they successfully use the pleasure bonding of sex as a means of diffusing tension and avoiding explosions of violence, both among individuals and between different groups.

Students can be invited, while studying the importance of sexual bonding in bonobo social organization, to think about why we have been taught to giggle in embarrassment when the topic is sex (which gives pleasure), whereas we are taught not to be embarrassed when we talk about violence (which causes pain). How does this relate to the desensitization to pain appropriate for unempathic relations? Why should talking about sexual pleasure embarrass us? Why are we not embarrassed when talking about behaviors that cause physical or emotional pain—even about sadism? Will this continue to be so as we move further toward the partnership model?

Exposure of children (and adults) to information about the bonobo chimpanzees—how they look, how we see in them expressions that seem to foreshadow our own human emotions (such as the attachment of a child to its mother)—will also elicit strong feelings of empathy. It can help young people develop empathy for other life forms—and thus an ecological consciousness. It also raises ethical questions, such as whether we should imprison bonobo chimpanzees in zoos (their behavior changes when in captivity) and use them for medical experiments.

Helping students develop empathy for other species is particularly important for the fate of the three species just mentioned: seahorses, emperor penguins, and bonobo chimpanzees, who are threatened with extinction. It is also a matter of life and death for elephants, who are today mercilessly hunted for their ivory tusks. Once we learn about these species, it is difficult not to want to do something to preserve them on this planet—for their sake, and for our own—because how they relate in the wild tells us so much about the extraordinary richness of possibilities for life on our Earth.

This takes us to our own human species and to the third component of integrated learning: conation, or the will to act. Effective education requires not only the cultivation of our great human capacity to think and feel; it also requires cultivation of our capacity to act. Life science classes can help students see that we are all interconnected—with one another and with our natural habitat—and that we are all adversely affected when we act only out of selfishness and greed. When we do so, we rend not only the fabric of our communities but the fabric of life itself. By destroying the biodiversity of our planet we not only destroy other life forms; we also harm ourselves and future generations.

Students in life science classes will be interested in knowing about businesspeople who are working hard at changing the way businesses operate, making them more environmentally and socially responsible.[7] But they also need to understand that to change the behaviors of enough people in this world, we need to change the larger social and economic system.

Here again, an understanding of the dynamics of the partnership and dominator models is useful, as it makes it possible to see how actions are shaped by economic opportunities and constraints. For example, people tend to go into denial when their livelihoods are at stake, denying until the last possible minute that what they are doing is harmful. This point was dramatically demonstrated in 1966 during the congressional hearings on the cigarette industry. There are, of course, whistle-blowers. But at present, the system does not reward or even protect them. What is needed are new economic rules that discourage environmentally destructive behaviors, rather than, as is still often the case, rewarding them.

A good resource here is my book *Redefining Destiny*, particularly the chapters on social, economic, political, and environmental literacy. The Video Project, which distributes videos for a safe and sustainable world suitable for kindergarten through twelfth grade,[8] and The Alliance for a Caring Economy, which focuses on changing economic rules,[9] are additional sources of materials.

The study of the natural sciences also offers an opportunity to help young people understand how scientific knowledge is culturally constructed. Specifically, when the curriculum includes a gendered perspective (see Box 5.3), students can begin to see that, along with the virtual exclusion of women from scientific fields, Western scientific methodology and theory have largely excluded anything considered feminine—such as empathic (involved) rather than objective (detached) observation.

The greater entry of women into science has begun to change the exclusion of approaches stereotypically considered feminine from scientific methodology. For example, Barbara McClintock's work in plant genetics, for which she won a Nobel prize in 1983, used the approach described by Evelyn Fox Keller as "feeling for the organism."[16] The work of animal ethnologists such as Jane Goodall, Dian Fossey, and Cynthia Moss has revolutionized their fields by likewise combining a more empathic approach with painstaking observation.

Scientists of both genders are beginning to shift toward a blend of intuitive/empathic and objective methods, which in turn are vastly enriching

---

BOX 5.3   A Gendered Perspective on Science

Good sources on this gendered perspective are David Noble, *A World Without Women: The Christian Clerical Culture of Western Science;*[10] Margaret Wertheim, *Pythagoras' Trousers: God, Physics, and the Gender Wars;*[11] Ruth Bleier, ed., *Feminist Approaches to Science;*[12] Linda Jean Shepherd, *Lifting the Veil: The Feminine Face of Science;*[13] and Evelyn Fox Keller, *Reflections on Gender and Science.*[14] For information on the related topic of multicultural science teaching, see *Keepers of the Earth* by Michael J. Caduto and Joseph Bruchac.[15]

---

science. For example, as scientists begin to move toward this more balanced style of observation, basing theories on observations that include not only precise quantitative measures but also value-laden qualitative descriptions, physicists are beginning to accept, and thus observe, ambiguity in nature.[17] Perhaps most famous here is the finding that light is neither purely matter (particles) nor energy (waves), but a combination of both. Scientists using this more holistic approach are also coming up with important technological applications, such as the development of computers that are able to base decisions on generalizations rather than on binary measurements. These "fuzzy logic" computers can, for example, slow down air conditioning gradually as a room cools, rather than merely turning it on or off, thus saving a great deal of energy. Revealingly, the phrase "fuzzy logic" was used in the past to denigrate women's thinking processes.[18]

Teaching science from a multicultural perspective is yet another way to help students understand the social construction of knowledge. As James A. Banks writes,

The main goals of presenting different kinds of knowledge are to help students understand how knowledge is constructed and how it reflects the social context in which it is created, and to enable them to develop the understandings and skills needed to become knowledge builders themselves. An important goal of multicultural education is to transform the school curriculum so that students not only learn the knowledge that has been constructed by others, but learn how to critically analyze the knowledge they master and how to construct their own interpretations of the past, present, and future.[19]

In short, the study of natural science offers an opportunity to help young people understand that, like literature, art, philosophy, and other human enterprises, science and technology reflect their cultural context. To illustrate, students can look at the indications that the more partnership-oriented Minoans used their considerable technological knowledge to ensure a high living standard for all, and that even though they had weapons, there is no evidence of a major investment in weaponry or in fortifications. This emphasis on life-enhancing rather than life-destroying technologies also seems to have been the norm in much of the European Neolithic before the Indo-European invasions brought with them a dominator orientation. The Indo-Europeans, on the other hand, focused their technological investment on weapons. Huge piles of weapons have been found in their chieftains' tombs, at the same time that, with the advance of the Indo-Europeans into Old Europe, crafts such as pottery and the arts went into decline. There are also indications that, at the time of European contact, some of the native people of North America made a greater investment in science and technology to support life (native medicines and pharmaceuticals were well in advance of those of the Europeans) than in weaponry. Certainly the science of ecology, the study of the interactions between living things and their environments, circles back to many ancient wisdoms found in the spiritual traditions of American Indian stories, which, time and again, emphasize the interconnectedness of life on our Earth.

Math

People from many cultures all over the world have been working with numbers since prehistoric times.
Women played an important part in the development of numbers.
Mathematics can serve as a tool for building a partnership society.

Mathematics is a field of particular importance in our high-technology age. To increase student motivation to learn math beginning in the earliest years, and to help with math anxiety (which later makes it harder for them in scientific and technological fields), math can be taught in more contextualized ways.

One way to make math more interesting is to show its multicultural connections (see Box 5.4). Instead of beginning the story of mathematics

> **BOX 5.4   Teaching Math from a Multicultural Perspective**
>
> Two excellent sources for teaching mathematics from a multicultural per-spective are *Multiculturalism in Mathematics, Science, and Technology*[20] and *Math Across Cultures*.[21] The latter features income mathematics and Madagascar solitaire, and provides examples of mathematics patterns in the basket-weaving designs of various tribal cultures. Additional sources in this area are Claudia Zaslavsky's *Tic-Tac-Toe and Other Three-in-a-Row Games: From Ancient Egypt to the Modern Computer*,[22] Zaslavsky's "Bringing the World into the Math Class,"[23] Muriel Feelings's *Moja Means One: Swahili Counting Book*,[24] and *Multicultural Mathematics: Teaching Mathematics from a Global Perspective* by D. Nelson, G. Joseph, and J. Williams.[25]

with the Greeks, as has been traditional, these materials help students see that mathematics is not solely a product of Western thinking; that, on the contrary, mathematical concepts have been developed and used by most world cultures. For instance, the symbols in our numbering system are sometimes called Arabic numbers because they were invented by Arab cultures, and the abacus, invented in China, was an ancient precursor of modern adding machines. In addition, most cultures have developed cal-endars, and, as we saw in Chapter 4, many cultures from all over the world have used mathematics for often complex astronomical calcula-tions.

As Christine Sleeter writes, "Teaching mathematics multiculturally counters ethnocentrism and helps all children understand mathematics better by encouraging them to compare mathematic systems that humans have created throughout history for different purposes. . . . Ethnomathe-matics engages students in the kind of practical problem solving through which ordinary people worldwide have built mathematical knowledge." This is an important aspect of teaching mathematics, since, as Sleeter notes, "children come to school with everyday practical knowledge of mathematics, and teachers can build on this foundation."[26]

This observation leads to a second important aspect of successfully en-gaging all children in learning math: introducing into math instruction an emotional, rather than just mental, dimension. One way this can be done is by relating the study of mathematics to our day-to-day lives. For exam-ple, we use numbers to make household budgets.

We also need to understand business and corporate finances, as well as government budgets—all of which directly affect our lives. By learning that a government's budget is basically a set of priorities in which high numbers are assigned to high priorities and low, or no, numbers are assigned to matters that legislators do not consider priorities, students can become more informed about political decisions. They can better evaluate policies such as subsidizing the growth of tobacco while cutting the funding for children born to low-income families.

This knowledge, in turn, can lead to greater citizen attention to substantive political and economic issues. For example, we need some grasp of statistics to better understand, and change, economic inequities. Numbers are the hard-core facts in the disheartening picture of poverty.

Consider the following U.S. government statistics. In 1989, 1 percent of the U.S. population held 48 percent of U.S. wealth, whereas 80 percent held only 6 percent—and this gap has been widening, rather than narrowing, during the 1990s.[27] Although the media emphasized a 1.2 percent median (midpoint or average) household income rise in 1996, in fact what the U.S. Census Bureau figures showed was that the 20 percent of the population at the lowest income level made 1.8 percent *less* than they did in the prior year whereas the wealthiest 20 percent of the population saw their incomes rise by 2.2 percent.[28]

Studying math—and thereby learning to focus on numbers as an important aspect of human culture and life—can help students become more observant when reading news stories or listening to the news on television when economic figures are discussed. They can then put together *qualitative* information, such as accounts of the suffering and struggles of impoverished people, with *quantitative* information, such as statistics on poverty and the amount of money that politicians allocate to funding different programs.

In short, discussing mathematics in a real-life context can motivate children to study math as a means of making quantitative and qualitative sense of their world. It can also motivate them to become involved in working for a more equitable, partnership-oriented world (see Box 5.5).

Another way to stimulate and deepen students' interest in math is to pose the questions of *why* and *how* we humans developed numbers. The art of the Upper Paleolithic offers an interesting entry point for these questions. Here we find ancient time-sequenced markings that, as Alexander Marshack notes, show a sophisticated (even what we would call scientific, or at least empirically based) understanding of the cycles of na-

---

BOX 5.5   Mathematics in a Real-Life Context

Some good sources are Holly Sklar, "Imagine a Country";[29] Gregory Mantsios, "Class in America: Myths and Realities";[30] the newsletter *Too Much*;[31] Paul Kivel and Ellen Creighton, "Making the Peace: Violence Prevention as Social Justice";[32] Holly Sklar, *Chaos or Community: Seeking Solutions, Not Scapegoats, for Bad Economics*,[33] M. Frankenstein, *Relearning Mathematics: A Different Third R—Radical Maths*; and Nancy Folbre, *The New Field Guide to the U.S. Economy*.[34] The section on social, economic, and political literacy in my book *Redefining Destiny* is another good resource, as is Jeff Gates' *The Ownership Solution*.[35] (See also the further discussion of social and economic priorities in the section on current events below.)

---

ture. Not only that, these markings provide important clues to why our ancestors first devised numbers.

Numbers, like words, are mental tools. Developing the symbols we call numbers, and learning to count, made it possible for our ancestors to chart the units of time we call days and months. Keeping track of time enabled them to more accurately predict when the ice of winter would melt and spring would come. This need to predict the seasons could be one reason our forebears developed numbering systems. Such knowledge would have been of utmost importance in a gathering/hunting economy dependent on expectations of new sources of food from the rebirth of vegetation every spring.

Another possible reason numbers were invented is that the numbered sequences we call counting would have enabled women to predict when their menstrual bleeding would start again. This origin of numbering systems is suggested by a remarkable nude female figure carved 30,000 years ago at the mouth of a cave in the south of France where ancient rites were probably held. This figure, known as the Venus of Laussel, holds a crescent moon with thirteen notches in one of her hands while the other points to her pubic triangle (see Figure 5.2). Thirteen is the number of yearly lunar months, which were undoubtedly the first cycles of time charted by our ancestors, since the waning and waxing of the moon is a clearly observable phenomenon. But thirteen is also the number of menstrual cycles that would normally occur in a year, cycles that, in nature, coincide with the cycles of the moon—a pattern particularly evident in

FIGURE 5.2   Venus of Laussel

Shown here is an early image of the Goddess found carved on a rock from Paleolithic times.
CREDIT: The Partnership Way: New Tools for Living and Learning, *by Riane Eisler and David Loye. Line drawing from the original: Jeff Helwig.*

tribal societies without artificial sources of light such as gas or electricity (which would otherwise tend to somewhat affect menstrual patterns). Indeed, there are indications that the tracking by women of their menstrual cycles during the Stone Age may have been connected with attempts at fertility regulation, given that women tend to ovulate close to the full moon (when they are thus more likely to conceive) whereas infertile times are associated with the other part of the lunar cycle.[36]

Looking at numbers from a partnership perspective in which women are more than just male helpmates helps dispel the notion communicated by much in existing curricula that women had no role in the creation of human culture and technology. It is of interest in this connection that female deities in many ancient spiritual traditions—for example, the Egyptian Hathor and the Indian Sarasvati—were said to have invented both numbers and the alphabet. There are also, as we saw in Chapter 4, myths crediting women with the invention of one of the most important human technologies: agriculture. This would indicate the ancient recognition that these were cultural contributions made by women—something that children need to know.

Knowledge of women's capacities and achievements in fields with which they are not usually associated in the conventional curriculum is extremely important for girls. Girls need role models of women who managed to infiltrate and excel in scientific fields where a knowledge of higher mathematics is essential. In addition to some of the examples noted in Chapter 3, a well-known case in point is Marie Curie, the only scientist ever to win two Nobel Prizes in the same field (one for her discovery of radium—the first known material capable of emitting light and heat with no appreciable transformation—and her subsequent development of the concept of radioactivity, which ushered in the atomic age). Less well known are women such as the German-Jewish physicist Lise Meitner, who was fleeing the Nazis when her theory of atomic fission was utilized for weapons research—an enterprise with which she never wanted to be identified. There is also Rosalyn Yalow, who in 1977 won the Nobel Prize in medicine for her invention of the medical tool called radioimmunoassay, which brought about a revolution in medical research by making it possible to measure minute substances in the body, using radioactive particles as tracers.[37] The accomplishments of these women are all the more remarkable considering that only a century ago women were still being denied higher education. Even today—although girls are excellent in math and score even higher than boys in the lower grades—they are derailed from studying higher math by gender stereotypes and, all too often, by teachers and counselors as well (see Box 5.6).

This derailing of girls from pursuing the study of higher math, however, is due not only to counseling and conventional role models that exclude women from the category of "important" mathematicians and scientists; it also happens because the way that math has conventionally been taught in higher grades divorces it from any personal or philosophical context, meaning, and relevance. As demonstrated in works such as Jean Baker Miller's *Toward a New Psychology of Women*, Carol Gilligan's *In a Different Voice*, and David McClelland's *Power: The Inner Experience*, stereotypical gender socialization teaches girls to be more concerned about contexts or relationships, whereas boys are pointed more toward abstraction and detachment.[41] For this reason, math needs to be taught in ways that contextualize math within day-to-day life.

Without proper training in mathematics, girls will be unprepared to study physics, chemistry, biology, and other sciences, and women will be

BOX 5.6   Effects of Gender Stereotypes

Good sources of materials on the adverse effects of gender stereotypes on girls are the American Association of University Women's *AAUW Report: How Schools Shortchange Girls*,[38] Peggy Orenstein's *School Girls: Young Women, Self-Esteem and the Confidence Gap*,[39] Myra and David Sadker's *Failing at Fairness*,[40] and other publications sponsored by the American Association of University Women.

denied access to the high-paid, influential professions that are based on these disciplines—an outcome that is bad not only for women but for all of society.

Precisely because girls and women are stereotypically socialized to be more concerned about relationships (that is, about other people) and boys and men are stereotypically socialized to be focused on goal achievement abstracted from the social context, efforts to involve more women in science and technology will lead to greater concern for the impacts of science and technology on our lives (see Box 5.7). We have already seen how the involvement of women brings an important new perspective to scientific and technical professions.[42] It brings to science what the sociologist Jessie Bernard calls an "ethos of love-duty" and the educator Nel Noddings calls an "ethos of caring." Both are urgently needed in our high-technology age.

Moreover, as women enter higher-status professions, thereby rising in status themselves, the status of stereotypically feminine values also rises— and men can more easily embrace those values without feeling that they are not being "masculine."

Art and Creativity

Creativity is a quality all of us possess that has been expressed by humans since the dawn of culture.

Art both reflects and affects how we view our world and live in it.

A multicultural and gender-balanced approach to art reveals many traces of partnership spiritual traditions.

Art in partnership and dominator societies emphasizes different themes, illustrating how the historical context of art needs to be understood.

BOX 5.7   Women Scientists and Mathematicians

A fascinating book, noted above, on how both women and stereotypically feminine values such as caring and empathy have been historically excluded from science is David Noble's *A World Without Women*.[43] Its theme is the ironic fact that even though modern science broke with religious dogma, it continued the earlier clerical culture's exclusion and denigration of women and anything connected with them. Also illustrative of this point is Margaret Wertheim's *Pythagoras' Trousers: God, Physics, and the Gender Wars*,[44] which includes stories about women mathematicians and astronomers.

For articles by educators with materials for developing girls' interest and proficiency in math and science, see *New Moon Networker* (July/August 1996), available from New Moon Publishing, P.O. Box 3587, Duluth, MN 55803-3587. A video on this subject titled *Girls and Technology*, produced by the National Coalition of Girls' Schools, is also available from New Moon Publishing. *Math Equals* by Terri Perl is a wonderful resource for teachers about women who have made contributions to math,[45] as is the American Association of University Women, which can provide other excellent suggestions and materials.[46]

A major emphasis of partnership education is to support and inspire creativity, not only through artistic pursuits but in all areas—including so-called ordinary life. As I develop in the section on creativity in *Redefining Destiny* and other writings,[47] from a partnership perspective, the enhancement of our day-to-day lives—for example, by creating an aesthetic home environment—is an important form of artistic creativity.

In the old curriculum, and in many art textbooks, there is a ranking of art into "arts" and "crafts." Artistic media characteristically worked by women, whether as quilters in European cultures or as pottery makers in Native American cultures, have been dismissed as mere crafts rather than real art.[48] Similarly, the art of tribal cultures has generally been described as "primitive" and shown only in ethnographic museums—thus putting it in a less valued category than the art in art museums.

A gender-balanced and multicultural perspective on art, as conveyed by partnership education, does not rank art into these categories. Nor does it sell the idea that only the work of white males is really important.

Partnership education helps students see for themselves how images affect the way we think of our world and how we live in it. It situates art in the context of our human adventure, showing how, from the beginning, art has been an important human expression.

Taught from this perspective, art classes in the early grades will still, as they are now, primarily be designed to help children express their creativity and familiarize them with various creative technologies, from paintbrushes to computer software. But children will be encouraged to create more freely. Moreover, from the beginning, children will learn art in the context of history and in ways that are relevant to their daily lives. Art will therefore be integrated into other classes, and the study of art history—on all levels, from grammar school to university classes—will include archaeological and historical materials from the vertical threads of the partnership curriculum loom.

A good way to engage students' interest is to invite them to be detectives looking for clues to answer questions such as, How and why did art emerge? Why is art meaningful to us? Why does art engage our emotions? What is artistic creativity all about?

If we look at tribal art in its cultural context, it is clear that much of it is what we today would call spiritual or religious. Like the art of the Stone Age and early agricultural era we considered in the last chapter, it deals with yet another set of questions we humans have been asking since time immemorial: What lies behind the cycles of life and nature? Where do we come from before we are born? What is the meaning of our journey here on Earth? What happens to us after death? These are universal, ultimately unanswerable questions that all religious institutions and spiritual traditions address.

Tribal art from non-Western cultures often retains this deep spiritual aspect. This is certainly true of much Native American art. Here we find pottery decoration with the same spiral motifs, symbolic of the continuity and regeneration of life, as those in the more partnership-oriented European Neolithic (see Figure 5.3).

We also find art specifically used for ritual purposes, such as the Navaho sand paintings. Here, Corn-Mother and Grandmother, the givers of life, resonate with these same ancient themes through imagery in which female figures wield great power.

An understanding of these spiritual origins and dimensions of art can be particularly important to adolescents searching for meaning. It can also help students in general see how much of both prehistoric Western

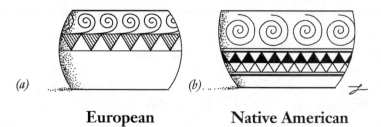

(a)   (b).

European   Native American

FIGURE 5.3   Pottery of Two Cultures

(a) Indigenous Early European. (b) Native American.
CREDIT: John Mason.

art and more recent tribal art bespeaks a partnership-oriented spirituality in which the power to give and nurture life is a major theme.

Despite its frequent dominator overlay, as we saw in the last chapter, the art of India also retains elements from more partnership-oriented spiritual traditions in which women and female deities played important parts. These traditions go back to the earliest known Indian art from the Indus Valley civilizations of Mohenjodaro and Harappa, where archeologists have found female bronze figures dating back long before the Indo-European or Aryan invasions of India. As noted earlier, we can still find traces of these Dravidian traditions in female deities that have survived in the Hindu and Buddhist religions. We can also find such traces in Indian folk art and customs today. For example, we can speculate that the colorful sand paintings rendered by women in the south of India as an act of prayer date back to earlier times, before women lost their property rights and still played leading roles in their community's ritual life.

Indian Mendhi art, whereby women stain henna designs on their hands and feet, undoubtedly has ritual significance going back to a time when decorating a woman's body was done not just to be appealing to men but as a ritual act of self-beautification. It is interesting to note that Mendhi art is popular today among young people in the West, made trendy by musicians and movie stars. This would be a fun activity for students of any age, and could be combined with learning the ancient symbolism and partnership origins of Mendhi—showing students that it's not just a recent fad.

*African artist Loice
Chirubuu, in 1994.*
CREDIT: *Betty LaDuke.*

The "Kilims" or tribal rugs from the Middle East known as Wedding Rugs must also have an interesting early history, as they are a form of partnership art in a number of ways. The women do one part of the weaving and the men do another part. In the first stage of the making of the rug, the women select the wool, spin it into yarn, and dye it in the traditional manner. Then the men weave the basic textile on the looms. The last, and most skilled, stage is the embroidering, which is again done by the women, who wind three or four differently colored yarns into imaginative patterns. Frequent motifs are the sun, the moon, and water—all ancient religious symbols. Also featured are dancers and gazelles, cooking

"Family Planning," by African artist Grace Chigumira.
CREDIT: *Betty LaDuke.*

utensils and cradles, and—demonstrating how far back this artistic tradition goes—the nine-squared rectangle that is the ancient Sumerian symbol.

The art of Africa, which is extraordinarily rich in shapes, patterns, and colors, is like the earlier art of the Neolithic: replete with female figures. Although most museums label these figures simply "woman," many are Goddess figurines, honoring the life-giving and nurturing powers of nature. (See Chapter 4 for more on this subject.) Moreover, as documented in Betty LaDuke's wonderful book, *Africa: Women's Art, Women's Lives*,[49] African women are to this day extremely prolific and creative artists—contradicting the stereotypical assumption that art is, and always has been, a male creation.

"Like the pottery of the Neolithic (which, judging from excavated temple models, was often made by priestesses for use as sacred vessels), the pottery made by African women today is often adorned with beautiful spiral patterns. In Burkina Faso, women paint both the inside and outside mud walls of their houses with extraordinary circular and rectangular patterns that, as LaDuke writes, "seem to echo the rhythmic growth of the surrounding millet" (fields in which women work to feed their families).[50] In Timbuktu, women design and weave beautiful fabrics for clothes. In Cameroon, women bead ritual objects, masks, birds, calabashes, and furniture with intricate patterns. Studying these works helps students appreciate the enormous richness of art formerly dismissed as "primitive"; it also helps them appreciate the enormous richness of the art produced by women worldwide—which is why I am primarily featuring female artists. (For examples, see Figures 5.4 and 5.5.)

Colleen Madamombe of Harare, Zimbabwe, carves magnificent sculptures, including those of lovers and pregnant women reminiscent of similar themes in the more partnership-oriented Neolithic.[51] The work of the Shona women sculptors of Zimbabwe, though diverse in style, also focuses on the female form and on women's lives and experiences. According to Ray Wilkenson, writing in *Newsweek* on September 14, 1987, Shona sculpture is "perhaps the most important new art form to emerge from Africa in this century."[52]

An understanding of this recurrence of similar themes in so many different traditions can help students focus on positive commonalities among world cultures, including early European and American cultures. In this way, multicultural education brings people together rather than, as some fear, causing polarization and strife.

A more gender-balanced curriculum, too, can help students see common threads in the art of contemporary artists who are drawing from ancient traditions. Of particular interest—given that art classes and art history books still focus on art by men with hardly any mention of women artists, much less a fair representation—is the work of women artists who are creating exciting art that combines ancient traditions with themes from women's lives (see Box 5.8).

Judy Chicago incorporates themes from women's contributions throughout the ages into her monumental "The Dinner Party." Her "The Birth Project"—which dramatically demonstrates that weaving, a traditional female artistic expression, is not just craft but art—draws from prehistoric images of the Goddess giving birth.[53] Barbara Schaefer's rich oil paintings are both poetic and mythical. These scroll-like canvases are evocative of ancient magical rites, transforming past and present con-

FIGURE 5.4   "Africa: Sunrise"

Art has ancient spiritual roots.
CREDIT: *Betty LaDuke.*

sciousness into primordial archetypes—as in her multimedia project "The Song of Memory," which contrasts dominator and partnership collective memories. The larger-than-life bronze sculptures of Ann Morris, evoking a holistic union of female and male archetypes, connect us with our most ancient roots through powerful forms that speak to our longing for wholeness and connection.[54]

Mayumi Oda paints full-bodied goddesses from Japanese, Chinese, Indian, and other traditions—playful and strong goddesses who are sometimes compassionate, at other times angry. Yolanda Lopez draws from

FIGURE 5.5   "Millet Rhythms"

Art opens new windows to the world.

CREDIT: *Betty LaDuke.*

Mexican tradition, juxtaposing the pre-Columbian Goddess Coaticu with her hispanicized successor, the Virgin of Guadalupe; at the same time, she incorporates portraits of her mother and grandmother, sacralizing women's day-to-day lives. And Faith Ringgold draws from her African-American heritage, mirroring the social reality of black women's lives in our culture. A powerful example is her "Weeping Women #2," fashioned from beads, raffia, and sewn cloth.

Frieda Kahlo's art, from an earlier period, also powerfully combined her own life struggles with indigenous themes; an example is her oil

---

BOX 5.8   Women Artists

For art featuring prehistoric themes, see Elinor Gadon, *The Once and Future Goddess*,[55] and Gloria Orenstein, *The Reflowering of the Goddess*.[56] *The Power of Feminist Art*, by Norma Broude and Mary Garrard is also a good resource.[57] Betty LaDuke's work draws from many indigenous traditions, particularly those of Africa, Australia, and Latin and North America; the vibrant rhythms of her paintings celebrate women's strengths, joys, and sorrows as well as their struggle to find and create beauty in their daily lives. For examples of her work, see *Multicultural Celebrations: The Paintings of Betty LaDuke*, by Gloria Feman Orenstein,[58] and the videos titled *Betty LaDuke: An Artist's Journey from the Bronx to Timbuktu* and *Africa Between Myth and Reality: The Paintings and Etchings of Betty LaDuke*.[59]

---

painting on sheet metal called "My Nurse and I." Her husband, the Mexican muralist Diego Rivera, also drew from indigenous themes, as did another major Mexican artist, José Clemente Orozsco, in his monumental murals about injustice and liberation.

Artists such as Richard Serra, Othello Anderson, Richard Rosenblum, and Krzysztov Wodiczko address contemporary issues of social justice and environmental balance in ways that bring these issues to life. Wodiczko's "Homeless Vehicle Project," for example, is based on the shopping carts that homeless people use for transport and storage; his depiction of such carts is symbolic of the right of the poor and homeless not to be shunted out of view. As the art critic Suzi Gablik writes, these artists are trying to remythologize consciousness in an attempt to help us shift from the dominator model of culture to a partnership model.[60]

Many other contemporary artists are using art as a way of inviting social critique and imagining a better world. For example, John Mason's visionary art evokes meditations on what the future could become, taking us into colorful scenes of nature and surrealistic fantasy.

Some of these artists are children working in collaborative art projects such as large murals. Through such projects, children are able to express their observations, feelings, and visions, develop their creativity, and work in partnership with others. The muralist Judith Baca, for instance, has organized youth in Los Angeles to create murals depicting their frustrations with society, as well as their hopes and dreams, as a way of helping them learn to channel their energies collectively into constructive expression. At the California State University at Monterey Bay, muralist Patricia Rodriguez has worked with a class of students to design and produce a mural critiquing the use of methyl bromide in strawberry fields and its impact on the health of farm workers—a local hot-button issue. In both cases, the art, the message, and the collaborative process illustrate partnership creativity. (A resource for teachers that presents contemporary U.S. artists and their work, along with lesson plans focusing on issues such as the family, national identity, war, and AIDS, is *Contemporary Art and Multicultural Education*.[61])

Studying art from this larger perspective offers an opportunity to invite students to think about the values that different kinds of works communicate. What messages are conveyed, for instance, by art that shows scenes of rape in a romanticized way, as in Reubens' "Rape of Lucretia," which is often included in art history books as an example of great art. Or by the many paintings of Zeus raping Europa or Leda that hang in the world's museums as examples of beautiful art? Students can contrast this artistic perspective with that of Spanish painter Goya, who was one of the first to show brutality and violence as it is, as well as that of Kaethe Kollwitz, who depicted the real suffering caused by violence and domination. They can also look at male-centered portrayals of women in art—portrayals seen through the "male gaze," as Lynda Nead puts it in her book *The Female Nude*.[62] An example is Edouard Manet's famous "Breakfast on the Grass," showing fully dressed men looking down at nude women. What kind of power relations does this communicate?

Students can also examine whether contemporary artists such as Andy Warhol deepen our understanding, as great art can, or whether his works and those of many other deconstructionists only replicate the inane repetition of the mass media they decry. In one sense, such art highlights the inanity of pop culture. But it fails to take us beyond that level to a probing of more meaningful alternatives.

Such art, including much of the cartoon art in modern museums today, is clearly a reflection of today's pop culture. But is mere reflection really the function of art? What about the role of artists as visionaries? Can art also provide inspiration, without being overly sentimental or sugary, for creating a more equitable and less violent world? How can we all use our creativity to accelerate this process?

Art and Ancient Western History

Art can bring an emotional element to the study of ancient Western cultures.

Art can raise our consciousness of the inhumanity of the dominator model and inspire us to visualize, and work to create, a more peaceful, equitable, and environmentally balanced society.

How can art engage students in learning not only intellectually but emotionally? How can it strengthen the conative element of learning, helping students become more active in shaping their future?

The study of art as an integral part of history classes offers an opportunity to address these kinds of questions. To illustrate, I have chosen an example I have worked with myself: ancient Western history. (I should add that I am here using the term in the traditional sense of the classical Greek and Roman civilizations.)

In Greek and Roman art there are many sculptures and friezes of men killing and maiming one another—scenes that have often been replicated in modern and postmodern art and in movies such as *Ben Hur*, *Caligula*, and *Ulysses*, giving the impression that violence always has been, and always must be, a central part of life. A good way to counter this impression is to contrast such images with those we find in the art of some of the prehistoric European cultures we discussed in Chapter 4. By observing this contrast, young people will be stimulated to ask deeper questions about both violence and art.

As they compare Greek and Roman art with that of more partnership-oriented prehistoric societies, students can see that scenes of men inflicting pain are virtually absent from the art of the Neolithic (about 10,000 years ago) and of Minoan civilization (about 4,000 years ago). They can then explore *why*, as they look in myth and archaeology for clues to a shift from cultures that, although not ideal, were less violent and more equitable than what followed.

Teachers can begin by showing students some of the art from earlier, more partnership-oriented societies—for instance, the beautifully shaped vases produced by the civilization of Minoan Crete. These can then be followed with pictures and slides of later art—in which we see the same beautifully shaped vases, but now covered with scene after scene of warriors killing and maiming one another.

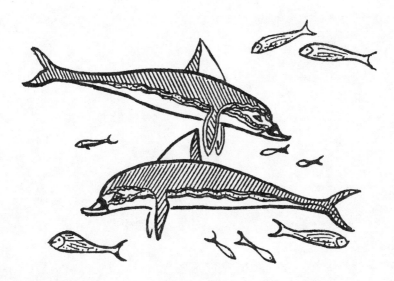

FIGURE 5.6   A Modern Ecology Poster?

What we think of as ecological consciousness is visible in this 3,500-year-old fresco from Minoan Crete.

CREDIT: The Partnership Way: New Tools for Living and Learning, *by Riane Eisler and David Loye. Line drawing from the original: Jim Beeman.*

I have found that strong emotional reactions are elicited when these images are shown in juxtaposition. As Matthew, a 12th-grade student, put it, he felt a terrible pang when he suddenly saw violence for what it is: an act that causes pain and death, rather than something exciting and fun. But the good part, he said, is that seeing these images gave him a different kind of excitement: the excitement of discovering something new.

When we look at how much earlier art celebrates life and nature, we can also experientially reconnect with a worldview in which environmental consciousness seems to have been integral to a more life- and nature-affirming way of life. For example, teachers can show students the beautiful dolphin fresco from the so-called Queen's apartment in the palace of Knossos in Crete—a fresco that looks strikingly like a modern ecology poster (see Figures 5.6 and 5.7). They can then invite students to think about why the partnership-oriented Minoans had the same intense interest in dolphin imagery as we are today seeing as we try to move toward a more partnership-oriented worldview ourselves.

FIGURE 5.7 "Gardens of Thera"

An artist's rendering of a Minoan palace.
CREDIT: *"Gardens of Thera," by John Mason.*

This type of experiential learning, through slides as well as replicas of ancient art objects, has been highly effective with college and high school students, but it can also be used in middle school and even earlier grades. It elicits both emotional responses and lively discussions. It also enables students to see with their own eyes how "reality" is socially constructed—and how different this construction is in partnership- versus dominator-oriented cultures.

In addition, the use of these contrasting artistic images greatly deepens and broadens young people's understanding of Greek and Roman history, periods that are featured in the traditional U.S. high school and college curriculum. As we saw in Chapter 4, most curriculum materials on ancient Greece make no mention of the Minoan civilization. Thus students miss out on learning that the Greek ruling classes, who were descendants of the Indo-European Achaeans, borrowed much of their civilization from the Minoans, who had a rich and technologically advanced civilization that boasted the first paved roads in Europe, the first viaducts, the first indoor plumbing, and an art and architecture that later provided much of the foundation for Greek civilization. The conventional curriculum fails to inform students that this civilization flourished on Crete and other Mediterranean islands until it was finally taken over by Indo-European conquerors and became the Mycenaean civilization we read about in Homer's *Odyssey*. It fails to provide students with the knowledge that the Minoan religion, centering on the worship of a Goddess, greatly influenced the Greeks, who adopted into their later Olympian pantheon many Minoan deities. In short, through the conventional curriculum, students do not learn that the Mycenaeans whom Homer idealized in his epics were Indo-Europeans who adopted much of Minoan culture but still largely oriented to the dominator model. Nor are they given the historical background to understand other stories that reflect the lingering memory of Minoan and other more partnership-oriented civilizations—for example, Hesiod's *Works and Days*, which idealizes a "golden race" who lived "in peaceful ease," before a "lesser race" came in and brought with them Ares, the Greek god of war.[63]

Studying ancient Greece from a perspective that includes this kind of information makes it possible for students to trace the roots of the Greeks' love of art, their democracy, and their humanistic ideals to an earlier more partnership-oriented civilization. But it also enables them to see the dominator elements of Greek culture: the idealization of domination and violence in their art, their limiting of democracy to ruling-class males, and the inhumanity of some of their "humanism" (such as Aristotle's notion that free men are naturally entitled to dominate women and slaves).

Students can also be invited to contrast Roman civilization and art (see Figure 5.8) with that of the Etruscans, from whom the Romans acquired much of their civilization. The Etruscans, too, are rarely included in the study of ancient Italian civilization. It is notable that, as speakers of a pre-Indo-European language (in other words, remnants of the earlier pre-Indo-European population of Europe), the Etruscans, like the Minoans, appear to have preserved many elements from the earlier civilization of Europe before their shift to chronic warfare and ultimate conquest by Rome. Not coincidentally, Etruscan art, in its aliveness, use of evocative colors, and fluidity of line, is reminiscent of the art of the ancient Minoans.

FIGURE 5.8   Roman Hero

Shown here is a Roman frieze that idealizes killing.

CREDIT: The Partnership Way: New Tools for Living and Learning, *by Riane Eisler and David Loye. Line drawing from the original: John Mason.*

Estruscan art depicts scenes of women and men reclining together on couches at banquets, instead of women standing behind men to serve them—"scandalous" scenes, according to certain Roman writers who considered them "immoral" (see Figure 5.9). In Etruria, women were literate and, unlike those in Greece and Italy, bore names of their own. This, too, reflected Etruria's pre-Indo-European heritage, in which, as the Roman writer Theopompus indignantly complained, even "illegitimate" children were raised (rather than being abandoned to slavery or death).[64] In short, before their shift to the dominator model and their conquest by the Romans, the Etruscans preserved many partnership elements in their culture. One such element in Etruscan society was the more equal partnership between the two halves of humanity: women and men.

U.S. History

U.S. history is best understood from a less Eurocentric, more gender-balanced perspective focusing on the point-counterpoint of dominator and partnership elements.

Illustrations of partnership elements can be found in the ideals of democracy expressed in the U.S. Constitution and the Bill of Rights, the abolitionist

FIGURE 5.9   Etruscan Woman and Man on Couch

These Etruscan partners were immortalized in the terra-cotta of their sarcophagus in Cerveteri, Italy, around 520 B.C.E.
CREDIT: The Partnership Way: New Tools for Living and Learning, *by Riane Eisler and David Loye. Line drawing from the original: John Mason.*

and civil rights movements, the feminist and women's rights movements, and the movements for greater economic equity and environmental balance.

Illustrations of dominator elements can be found in the conquest and genocide of native peoples, the enslavement of people of African descent, the denial of political and economic rights to the female half of the U.S. population, and the concentration of economic and political power in the hands of a small percentage of the U.S. population.

An approach that helps students to identify partnership and dominator elements as they have played out historically enables them to understand what is happening in our own time—and to more effectively intervene to strengthen the partnership elements in U.S. culture.

As we have seen, the way in which history is told depends on who and what is considered important enough to be included and on how particular events are interpreted. The old narratives of U.S. history focused almost exclusively on white males, beginning with the first white settlers. A more accurate, and more interesting, story is the multicultural and gender-balanced one, beginning with the people who lived in the Americas thousands of years before whites arrived (see Box 5.9).

I do not mean to suggest that the old curriculum focusing on men such as George Washington and the all-white, all-male "founding fathers" should now be thrown out. If anything, this story about the original ideals of democracy, which made the United States of America the great hope for 18th-century Europeans, needs to be strengthened and placed in the con-

FIGURE 5.10   Discovery
Who "discovered" whom?
CREDIT: *John Mason.*

text of the incremental modern movement to shift from a dominator to a partnership model. In other words, what students need are both a reframing of some of the materials that have traditionally been included in the study of U.S. history *and* an exposure to new materials—a process that is already under way thanks to the work of many dedicated educators.

For example, as Bill Bigelow writes in "Discovering Columbus: Rereading the Past," many teachers are today using phrases other than Columbus's "discovery" of America. Or as a Native American asks Columbus in a skit by comedian Stan Freeberg, "What do you mean you discovered us? We discovered *you* on the beach here."

There are numerous theories about the origins of the people who lived in the Americas long before Columbus arrived. One theory, accepted by many scholars, is that they are the descendants of Ice Age hunters who long ago followed their game over a land bridge across the Bering Strait. Another theory posits their indigenous origins. American Indian oral tradition reflects both.

Among the colorful creation stories that vary from tribe to tribe, many, like the stories found in ancient European mythology, tell of an epic creation by a female. Central to the theology of the Keres Indians of Laguna Pueblo, for example, is the idea of the Creatrix as She Who Thinks. As Paula Gunn Allen writes, the Mother Goddess of the Keres is known as Corn Mother, she who gave the people the gift of corn. An ancestral grandmother also figures into many stories; for example, a Mayan prayer invokes "grandmother of the sun."[65] In Iroquois myth, the world began when Skywoman fell upon an island that grew from sea mud placed on top of a turtle's shell, where she gave birth to a daughter—thus beginning human life.[66] But in addition to such myths about indigenous origins are stories about an epic migration, generally from "the land of the setting sun," although some tribes say they came from the North, South, or even the East.[67]

Most of what has been written about American Indian civilizations has focused on Central and South America: on the Maya, Aztecs, and Incas. But in North America there was also what scholars call a Golden Age of Native American civilization that flourished in both the eastern and western part of North America. This Golden Age lasted for more than two thousand years, from about 1200 B.C.E. to 1250 C.E.[68] The most advanced culture to develop in the Southwest were the Anasazi, who made beautiful pottery and baskets, terraced their highland fields, and trapped water in small reservoirs to irrigate the land. The ruins of their five-story apartment buildings can still be found in Mesa Verde, Colorado. Other Anasazi sites are Canyon de Chelly (Arizona), and Chaco Canyon (New Mexico).[69] On the eastern side of North America lived people who built cities such as Cahokia in southern Illinois, whose population during the Golden Age is estimated to have numbered from 20,000 to 50,000 inhabitants.[70] But whereas the pyramids of Teotihuacan in central Mexico and of Tikal in Guatemala are fairly well known, many people are unfamiliar with the pyramids of Cahokia.

From 1250 to 1500, these North American civilizations underwent a period of decline. In the West, this decline has been traced to a great drought (in approximately 1275–1290) and to invasions by fierce raiders from the North, who began to prey upon the more developed civilizations. By the time the Europeans arrived, around 1500, many smaller tribal units (approximately three hundred tribes) occupied the territory now embraced by the United States.

The true story of what happened to native populations at the hands of their European conquerors is only gradually finding its way into the history curriculum—even though we have long had records of this history of conquest and domination, beginning in the West Indies with the virtual genocide of native populations. For example, in his letter (dated March 14, 1493) to Rafael Sanchez, treasurer of Aragon, Columbus reported being enormously impressed by the indigenous people's generosity and honesty. "They exhibit love to all others in preference to themselves," he wrote. But he also wrote, "Should your Majesties command it, all the inhabitants could be taken away to Castile, or made slaves on the island. With 50 men we could subjugate them all and make them do what we want."[71] And Columbus proceeded to do just that, with horrible cruelty.

Slaves who tried to flee were hunted down with dogs and killed—to set an example for the others. As Hans Koning writes, during just two years of the Columbus brothers' administration "an estimated one-half of the population of Hispaniola were killed or killed themselves. The estimates range from one hundred and twenty-five thousand to one-half million."[72]

In what is today the United States, the carnage did not start until later. It is dramatically portrayed in films such as *Little Big Man* and *Dances with Wolves*.

Another chapter in U.S. history that reflects dominator elements is the history of African-Americans (see Box 5.10). This story, too, has only recently begun to gain entry in the standard curriculum. It starts before the colonization of the United States by Europeans and their import of African slaves—specifically, in the African homeland where many different tribes and nations lived for thousands of years.

Indeed, this story goes back to some of the earliest human fossil remains ever found, which (as we saw in Chapter 3) trace the dawn of our species to East Africa. It tells of African civilizations, such as ancient Egypt, Benin, and Ethiopia (home of the legendary Queen of Sheba that we read about in the Bible), as well as the fact that foreign invasions of Africa began in antiquity (for example, the Greek and Roman invasions of Egypt) and continued for centuries, waged not only by Europeans but also by Arabs.

The history of Africans in America is once again a story of violence and domination. It begins with the slave trade by Arabs and Europeans, as well as by some African tribal chiefs. It includes the unspeakable horrors experienced on the slave ships (where more than half the captured women, children, and men died of hunger, thirst, and disease), continues into the plantation slave system, and culminates with the black struggle for emancipation and civil, political, and economic rights—a struggle that continues to this day.

BOX 5.9   The Native American Perspective

For teaching resources on this phase of American history, see *Rethinking Columbus*,[73] Gary Nash's *Red, White and Black: The Peoples of Early America*,[74] Howard Zinn's *A People's History of the United States*,[75] and *Bury My Heart at Wounded Knee*, edited by Dee Brown.[76] An early book recording the tragic story of the conquest and destruction of Native American peoples and their cultures is John Collier's *Indians of the Americas*, published in 1947.[77] See also *Selu* by Marilou Awiakta,[78] as well as the autobiography of Wilma Mankiller (co-written by Michael Wallis), *Mankiller: A Chief and Her People*.[79] Two other resources, containing lesson plans, handouts, and materials for teaching about American history from Native perspectives, are *Indian Country: A History of Native People in America*, by Karen D. Harvey and Lisa D. Harjo,[80] and *Dangerous Memories: Invasion and Resistance Since 1492*, by R. Golden, M. McConnel, P. Miller, C. Poppin, and M. Turkovich.[81] (The latter book, published by the Chicago Religious Task Force on Central America, also includes information on how Native American people have organized to resist conquest and domination.)

The suffering and hardships of African-American life only a century ago are sometimes hard for students, and adults, to imagine. Many of us are also unaware of how legal constraints deprived blacks of the most basic rights and skills. An example is the fact that laws in the American South made it a crime to teach black slaves to read. It is a testimony to their ingenuity and courage that many slaves nevertheless managed to become literate. A haunting instance is the little-known story of how the boy who later became the abolitionist leader Frederick Douglass devised a plan to teach himself to read: He tricked some white boys to read aloud letters he had carved on pieces of wood—until he was finally able to solve the mystery of the alphabet.

Of course, this struggle for access to equal education has continued well into the 20th century, as evidenced by the battle during the 1960s for school integration. This battle has been dramatically depicted in movies such as *Ruby Bridges*, the story of a six-year-old black student who for one year had to be escorted by federal marshals past an angry mob into her first-grade class in a formerly segregated New Orleans elementary school (shown on ABC in 1998), and the PBS television series *I'll Fly Away*,

BOX 5.10   The African-American Perspective

In their coverage of this chapter of U.S. history, standard textbooks tend
to emphasize dominator relations while at the same time failing to present the full horror of the dehumanization of blacks, Native Americans,
and, later, Chinese and other Asian immigrants. Students can use these
textbooks as a starting point, but for a more comprehensive view, they
should also be directed to sources that emphasize partnership elements
and/or provide the missing perspective of groups that have been dominated, such as W.E.B. Du Bois's early classic *The World and Africa*,[82]
David Loye's award-winning *The Healing of a Nation* (dedicated to Du
Bois),[83] Howard Zinn's *A People's History of the United States*,[84] *The African
American Experience* by Sharon Harley, Stephen Middleton, and Charlotte
Stokes,[85] and the *Historical and Cultural Atlas of African Americans* by
Molefi Asant and Mark Mattson.[86] Additional resources include the famous televisions series *Roots* (and the book by the same name),[87] as well as
the more recent film *Amistad*. A book I found especially moving about
black women and slavery is *More Than Chattel*, edited by David Barry
Gasper and Darlene Clark Hine,[88] which contains many little-known stories about the tragic and often courageous lives of black women who were
slaves.

about the struggle for integration in the South during the 1950s. Both are
good resources for students in the elementary and secondary grades.

Students can also be invited to create stories of their own, perhaps
writing monologues adopting the persona of someone who was an abolitionist or civil rights worker, and present these in oral or written form. In
an 8th-grade project called Quest of Black History, Joe took on the role
of a journalist and wrote an editorial on why we should celebrate the contributions of African-Americans. And in her 12th-grade class, Mary Beth
examined the conditions of slave life for women—from initial capture to,
in some cases, escape through the underground railroad—by reading excerpts from the actual diaries of slaves.

Students often find the works of bell hooks, such as *Sisters of the Yam*,[89]
of great interest because of their insights into the lives of African-American women today. They can read children's books on the underground
railroad, as well as on the later struggle of freed African-Americans
against subsequent Jim Crow laws and lynchings that took place without

any criminal prosecution in the American South until the 1960s. They can delve into inspiring biographies, such as the autobiography of Frederick Douglass who was wrenched from his mother (as many slave children were) and spent most of his adult life fighting for a partnership world, and the inspiring life story of Sojourner Truth, a remarkable black woman who was also forcefully separated from her mother when she was very small. On one occasion, this courageous former slave, who spoke up for the rights of both blacks and women, risked her life by singlehandedly stopping a pack of white ruffians from terrorizing a black revival meeting by calmly talking to them instead of fleeing.

Students can also read inspiring real-life stories about white people, young and old, who have worked together with blacks in their struggle for civil rights. Sometimes they too have risked, even lost, their lives. For example, two young Jewish college students, Andrew Goodman and Michael Schwerner, were killed along with a young black man by the name of James Cheney when they went to Mississippi during the early 1960s as Freedom Riders.[90]

In this era of polarized race relations, teachers need to emphasize that major civil rights organizations, such as the NAACP, were initially developed by white and black American men and women working together—and that the whites were often Jews. This information is particularly important now, at a time when black anti-Semitism is being fomented by some demagogic black leaders.[91]

In short, despite the institutional obstacles faced by blacks in the United States, and despite the fact that American democracy and equality have all too often been mere words rather than living realities, there is also much in U.S. history that we can be proud of. Indeed, as I suggested earlier, at the same time that the old way of teaching tended to sugarcoat U.S. history, it also failed to make young people fully aware of how much there is of value in our nation's past.

We have had extraordinary leaders, such as George Washington, Thomas Jefferson, Abraham Lincoln, Theodore Roosevelt, and Franklin Delano Roosevelt, who made significant positive contributions to U.S. and world history. But significant contributions have also been made by many less well-known leaders of hitherto invisible groups, such as women, blacks, Native Americans, and Hispanics (see Box 5.11). One such individual is the labor leader Emma Goldman, whose autobiography is not only an inspiring portrait of courage, determination, and joy in life, but also provides a dimension to the study of U.S. history that includes

BOX 5.11   Labor Leaders

Power in Our Hands, by William Bigelow and Norman Diamond is a useful source of materials for teaching about the U.S. labor movement and how people have organized to improve their lives.[92] Vicki Ruiz's *Cannery Women: Cannery Lives* is a good resource on the role of Mexican women in the union movement in California. (In addition, *500 Anos del Pueblo Chicano [500 Years of Chicano History and Pictures],* edited by Elizabeth Martinez, is a good resource on hispanic history, including the conquest of what was at the time half of Mexico.)[93]

many of the social reform movements mentioned in Chapter 4. Other examples are the labor leaders Caesar Chavez and Dolores Huerta, the civil rights leaders Martin Luther King and Rosa Parks, and Native American leaders such as Wilma Mankiller and Winona LaDuke.

When teachers place U.S. history in the larger context of the tension between the partnership and dominator models as two underlying human possibilities, young people can better appreciate our history and learn from it lessons that are relevant today. They can recognize the historic role of our nation in the modern movement to shift from a dominator to a partnership social organization. They can see that our Constitution—which, as we saw in Chapter 4, bore the influence of Native American traditions—was a milestone on the path toward world democracy. They can see the enormous contribution of our Bill of Rights (enumerating basic principles such as freedom of speech and the separation of church and state), and that, despite all its problems, U.S. democracy has been an inspiration for peoples' pro-democracy movements worldwide. But they can also see how this movement toward a partnership model has been countered by strong dominator resistance, and how in the United States, as elsewhere, it has been punctuated by periodic regressions.

In sum, the study of U.S. history offers students the opportunity to identify examples of partnership and dominator elements as they have played out in history. In fact, as we saw in Chapter 4, students can best make sense of modern history—and our own postmodern times—by looking at the underlying tension over the last three hundred years between a powerful movement toward the partnership model countered by strong dominator resistance and periodic backlashes or regressions (see Box 5.12).

BOX 5.12   The Point-Counterpoint of History

The Enlightenment philosophies that inspired the U.S. experiment in democracy fueled the partnership movement in the 17th, 18th, and 19th centuries. This movement, as we saw earlier, was facilitated by the technological change, and cultural destabilization, brought by the move from agrarian to industrial society—a time of disequilibrium that, as cultural transformation theory highlights, offered an opportunity for transformational change. Yet at the same time, during the 17th and 18th centuries, witch hunts and other forms of dominator scapegoating, as well as the African slave trade and other barbarities against "inferior" races, continued in Europe and the United States. The 19th century brought the violence of colonial imperialism, the armed suppression of labor organizing, and predatory "robber-baron" capitalism. It also witnessed a resurgence of dominator "masculinity," along with a backlash against the feminist movement and its frontal challenge to the social, economic, religious, and political subordination of women.

The movement toward partnership is not linear. It waxes and wanes as it is countered by resistance and periodic regressions. For example, after the emancipation of black slaves came the backlash of the Jim Crow laws and the violence of the Ku Klux Klan. After the enactment of antitrust laws and social programs such as Social Security that provided basic support for all citizens came the reconcentration of economic power in the hands of huge, often global, corporations designed to accumulate wealth for a few, leading to attempts to rescind the social contract that the New Deal and the War on Poverty tried to create. After the civil rights and women's movement came a backlash that included efforts, successful in some parts of the country, to repeal affirmative action. And after the movement to end violence and abuse in parent-child and intimate man-woman relations came the backlash from the so-called Christian Right, with rallies such as the "Promise Keepers" inciting men to retake control over women as a religious duty, and courses such as parenting "God's Way" inciting parents to violently discipline their children so that once again their word is law—even to the extent of terrorizing eight-month-old babies to quietly sit in their highchairs with hands folded in their laps![94]

This is not to say that no gains have been made in the struggle to shift from a dominator to a partnership form of family, social, and economic organization.

BOX 5.13   History Through a Gender-Balanced Lens

The 19th- and early-20th-century feminist movements freed half the population—women—from many oppressive laws and customs, including the denial to wives of economic rights and even the right to child custody after divorce. They wrested for women the right to higher education, the right to vote, and eventually the right to run for office.

These advances, in turn, greatly humanized society, as they brought more stereotypically feminine values and work from the private sphere of the home (to which women had been generally confined) to the public sphere or "men's world" (from which women had been barred). For example, the work of 19th-century feminists such as Jane Addams and Florence Nightingale led to the creation of whole new professions such as social work and nursing. Dorothea Dix helped bring about reforms in the often barbaric treatment of the mentally retarded and ill. Reporters such as Nelly Bly wrote exposés about sweatshops. Labor leaders such as Emma Goldman worked to bring about labor reforms, including laws requiring safer working conditions. And Margaret Sanger worked for the gradual availability and legalization of contraception, despite persecution and imprisonment. It was also through this important social movement that public education was made possible—as newly educated women provided the womanpower for this essential step toward a more democratic society.

A powerful way of bringing this point home is through a more gender-balanced approach to U.S. history in which the 19th- and 20th-century feminist movements are given the importance they merit. The actual study of these movements—rather than just a mention of them in passing, as in most established texts—dramatically demonstrates that the 19th-century feminist movement played a major role in introducing social reforms that permanently improved the lives of *both* women and men (see Box 5.13).

Teaching students about the contributions of women to history as part of what is considered "important knowledge" leads to a richer and more relevant curriculum (for resources, see Box 5.14). By giving the same importance to the feminist revolution as is given to the American Revolution, teachers can strike a balance between women's *nonviolent* struggles and men's *violent* struggles for freedom from oppression.

BOX 5.14   Resources on Women in U.S. History

Some good sources on women in U.S. history are Linda Kerber and Jane DeHart Matthews, *Women's America: Refocusing the Past;*[95] *Unequal Sisters: A Multicultural U.S. Women's History*, edited by Carol DuBois and Vicki L. Ruiz;[96] and *Feminism in Our Time*, edited by Miriam Schneir.[97] Teachers should also know about a resource for ordering new books as they come out: the National Women's History Project in Windsor, California.[98] And two good videos in this area are Vivienne Verdon-Roe's Oscar-winning *Women—for America, for the World* and the Clarion award-winning *The American Woman: Portraits of Courage.*[99]

If students are to better understand what is happening in our time, it is essential that history classes return again and again to the dynamic of the forward partnership movement and the backward dominator resistance and backlash. By grasping this dynamic, young people can get past the old categories of capitalism versus communism, right versus left, and religious versus secular that have caused so much polarization and ill will (as in the McCarthy hearings of the 1950s and the politics of the so-called Christian Right of the 1990s). These old categories are not useful in equipping young people for the future, because they divert attention from the underlying question of what kind of relations a society supports or inhibits: relations based on partnership or relations based on domination. Worse still, the old ways of thinking engender divisiveness and scapegoating, as we see today in the blaming of the "idle poor" and "welfare mothers" for problems that are actually the result of the dominator aspects of our social organization.

Studying history from this perspective also makes it possible for young people to see that every progressive social movement over the past three hundred years, from abolitionism to environmentalism, has been met by powerful mainstream resistance—which in turn enables them to see that the issue is *not* whether certain social ideas are popular or unpopular.

Historically, it has taken a small minority with progressive, and generally highly unpopular, ideas to make major changes. The social movements that brought lasting improvements in our lives did so because, as the consciousness of a few changed, these people then organized to change even more people's consciousness. In short, every one of us can make a difference—if we avoid becoming discouraged in the face of dominator backlash and work together to attain partnership goals.

Literature

Literature is made more meaningful when students use the templates of the partnership and dominator models as analytical tools.
The study of literature can be used to help students understand how attitudes are unconsciously shaped by stories.
Studying literature using a multicultural and gender-balanced perspective helps students develop more understanding of, and empathy for, members of traditionally marginalized groups.

In the conventional curriculum, literature is seldom studied in a historical and cultural context. Even in high school and university classes, there is almost never a focus on the kinds of relations or social structures that are reflected in the books and plays we study.

For example, Shakespeare's writings are usually discussed as beautifully written works, which they certainly are. But what are the messages some of his plays impart?

The Taming of the Shrew, which is still often performed in high school and college theaters, romanticizes domestic violence. The message is that Kate is an uppity woman who deserves to be beaten, and that these beatings even lead her to love her husband.

In *Hamlet*, we find a self-absorbed hero who first leads Ophelia on, then treats her coldly and denies his romantic interest, and finally so traumatizes her by killing her father that she goes mad. But except for her brother's angry lamentations, there is no real censure of how Prince Hamlet treats this impressionable young girl, or even of his killing of her father, who is portrayed as a long-winded fool. On the contrary, Shakespeare constructed this play in such a way that we are led to empathize much more with Hamlet's suffering than with Ophelia's.

Classics like these reflect the devaluation of women and anything associated with them, and unconsciously condition us to do the same. Precisely because these works are beautifully written and powerful dramas, we learn emotionally as well as intellectually to devalue women and to unconsciously accept, and even romanticize, women's subordination.

I am certainly not suggesting that Shakespeare's works and others taught as classics be removed from the curriculum. These works are not only of great literary interest; they are also important resources for tracing the history of gender assumptions and other values that impact students' lives today. Indeed, looking at Shakespeare's plays through the dominator and partnership lenses makes it possible for students to see how works that present these kinds of relations between women and men as "just the way things are" mirror, and reinforce, a male-dominated social order.

Both *Hamlet* and *The Taming of the Shrew* mirror English society as it was in Shakespeare's time, before equity and democracy became ideals in Western culture. And, to his credit, many of Shakespeare's plays portray strong female characters (such as Portia in *The Merchant of Venice*) as well as empathy for members of vilified, persecuted out-groups (such as the Jewish Shylock).

Inviting students to look at our literary heritage through the analytical lens of the partnership-dominator continuum can lead to a discussion of contemporary stories in which the male characters suffer no adverse consequences for brutalizing and traumatizing women (as in the popular James Bond and Arnold Schwarzenegger movies). This approach can also lead to an exploration of how such stories (which make violence seem sexy) help maintain inequitable and violent relations, whereas stories with more partnership-oriented messages (such as *Fried Green Tomatoes, Alice Doesn't Live Here Anymore*, and *Ground Hog Day*) model relations where there is more respect for women and no idealization of violence.

The inclusion of multicultural perspectives in literature classes also generates greater interest and broader understanding. Toward this end, teachers can introduce their students to a novel, written by a Japanese woman a thousand years ago, that antedates the appearance of the novel in the West by about seven hundred years. This novel, translated into English in the 20th century as *The Tale of Genji*, was written by Mura Saki Shikibu (974–1031). The great-granddaughter of a famous Japanese poet, Shikibu also left a diary and a collection of her poems. In fact, two poems from *The Tale of Genji* are pivotal to the novel, which is today considered by some critics to be the greatest novel ever written, and of a profundity not even approached until the famous early 20th-century French writer Marcel Proust came along.

Teachers can also introduce their students to the poetry of contemporary Japanese women (see Box 5.15). The best known to students will be Yoko Ono, John Lennon's widow. But there are many others as well, including women who have written poetry about the tragedy of Hiroshima and Nagasaki and how it affected their lives. (For a collection, see *White Flash, Black Rain: Women of Japan Relive the Bomb*.)[100]

BOX 5.15   Japanese Women Poets

For a good collection of Japanese women poets with some biographical information, see *Women Poets of Japan.*[101] For a recent anthology of women's poetry, see *Cries of the Spirit*, edited by Marylin Sewell.[102] For an unusual collection of writings by women from the American West, see Susan Butruille's *Women's Voices from the Western Frontier.*[103]

In fact, there is a long and fascinating tradition of Japanese women poets going back to at least the 7th century, to the early Yamato people. (It was from them that the historical royal family of Japan emerged.) These rulers were empresses who may well have been essentially shamanesses or priestesses, the embodiments of the religious values of the clan. One of these empresses, Empress Jito (645–702), was also one of Japan's early poets.

Izumi Shikibu, a poet who lived during the 11th century, is noted for her erotic poetry, although in her later life she also wrote Buddhist poetry. She was married several times, had many lovers, and seems to have led an interesting life.

Following this unbroken tradition of Japanese women poets over the centuries is Yosano Akiko, who wrote more than 17,000 short poems and published 75 books, including translations of classical European literature. Akiko's work was extremely controversial. She had what today we call a feminist consciousness. She was also the first Japanese writer to directly criticize the emperor in a political pamphlet that she wrote when he entered the Russo-Japanese War. In addition, she wrote in defense and memory of socialist and anarchist martyrs in the early 1900s—such as the labor demonstrators who were gunned down in the Chicago Haymarket, and Sacco and Vanzetti, who were executed during the struggle of workers to organize labor unions to change miserable wages and dangerous workplaces.

Educators are beginning to recognize that reading poetry and other writings by women is an important learning experience for both girls and boys. Works by American women from a variety of racial and cultural backgrounds, such as Toni Morrison, Alice Walker, Maya Angelou, Gloria Naylor, Sandra Cisneros, Leslie Marmon Silko, and Amy Tan, are increasingly being recognized as important literary contributions. Such works make it possible for students of African-American, Hispanic, Native American, and Asian backgrounds to find themselves. To students not from those backgrounds, they provide an understanding of both cultural diversity and the underlying humanity we all share. In addition, they offer a perspective that is lacking in much of the "classical" canon: the perspective of the female half of humanity.

For example, Toni Morrison's *Beloved* presents a poignant story of the pain of oppression and the strong bond of love between mother and child. It explores the horrors of slavery, including the moral dilemma faced by a woman who must decide whether to subject her daughter to a life of slavery. At the same time, it affirms love and life, crying out against all forms of brutality.[104]

In the novel *Ceremony*, by Leslie Marmon Silko, a Native American explores what it means to experience balance in a world torn apart by the brutality of discrimination and war. When the novel's main character, Taro, returns home from military service in Vietnam to a country in which whites have marginalized native people, he tries to restore a sense of self and balance through the ancient wisdom of native ceremonies of his people.[105]

In *The House on Mango Street*, Sandra Cisneros tells short stories that celebrate the efforts of women to transform their surroundings and create better spaces for people to inhabit. Through stories of a child called Esperanza (Hope), Cisneros goes back and forth between the reality of living conditions in a poor urban neighborhood and the girl's quest for a place or home in which to grow and create, grounding herself in the neighborhood in which she grew up and building her dreams for a better world.[106]

Another book that tells of the horrors of domination and destruction as well as of the human capacity for caring and hope is *Against Forgetting*, edited by Carolyn Forche. This book is a collection of poems by women and men from around the world who have experienced various forms of violence and repression, ranging from the Jewish Holocaust and World War II to the civil rights struggle in the United States and repression and revolution in Latin America. They write as witnesses, so that we do not forget—and, most important, so that we may create a world in which partnership rather than domination will become the accepted norm.[107]

These kinds of books speak to us with the voices of women whose ideas and feelings have at best been a small addition to conventional literature classes. In addition, they often focus on areas that have been left out of the traditional curriculum, such as the lives of women and children living in poverty, the struggle of workers for better working conditions and a living wage, and the circumstances that beset the vast majority of people in the United States in the early days of "robber-baron" capitalism.

One such work, appropriate in excerpted form for high school students, is the autobiography of a remarkable woman I mentioned earlier: Emma Goldman. For girls, Goldman's extraordinary two-volume *Living My Life* provides a powerful role model of an independent yet caring woman. And for both boys and girls it provides inspiration to work for a better world.[108] Another such work is *Daughter of the Earth*, an autobiographical novel by Agnes Smedley.[109]

A classic of 19th century literature is the aptly titled *The Awakening*, by Kate Chopin,[110] a beautifully written work about a woman's struggle to find her own path. A modern classic is *Wide Saragasso Sea*, by Jean Rhys, which tells the same story as that in Charlotte Bronte's famous *Jane Eyre*—but from the perspective of the "madwoman" in the attic.[111] This slim book is one of the most exquisitely written works in the English language—and it was hailed as such when it first came out at the beginning of the 20th century. But, as is all too often the case with women's works, it has since been dropped from lists of what is taught in our schools as important literature.

In addition, teachers can introduce students to collections of stories about famous women. A beautifully illustrated book in this area is Rebecca Hazell's multicultural *Heroines: Great Women Through the Ages*, which includes women ranging from the French Joan of Arc to the Native American Sacagawea and the Chinese Sun Yat-Sen.[112]

Also of interest are utopias and distopias written by women. Charlotte Perkins Gilman's *Herland* is an early utopia that envisions a society in which caring for children is the paramount social concern—a society governed and organized by women.[113] By contrast, Margaret Atwood's *The Handmaid's Tale* projects a distopia in which women are reduced to male-controlled technologies for reproduction in a nightmare neofundamentalist dominator society of the future. My just published novel, *The Gate*, drawing from my childhood as a refugee growing up in Cuba, is also of interest in that it shows how the will to help build a better future can come out of just a few key experiences.[114] For those who enjoy fantasy-adventure, a story that insightfully contrasts partnership and dominator ways of living is Marie Jakober's *High Kamilan*, which, the author writes, was inspired by her reading of *The Chalice and the Blade*.[115]

BOX 5.16   People with Disabilities

The National Information Center for Children and Youth with Disabilities (NICHCY) offers a Guide to Children's Literature and Disability sorted by age on their website: <http://www.kidsource.com/NICHCY/literature.html>.[116] Another good resource is *Rethinking Our Classrooms: Teaching for Equity and Justice*.[117]

The study of literature also presents teachers with an opportunity to help students develop greater empathy for members of traditionally marginalized groups. Books by or about physically challenged people—such as the remarkable autobiography of Helen Keller, who was born both blind and deaf—are good resources in this area (see Box 5.16).

Particularly useful is the article by Bill Bigelow and Linda Christensen called "Promoting Social Imagination Through Interior Monologues."[118] One activity it suggests is this: First, after watching a film or reading a novel, short story, or essay, students brainstorm particular key moments, turning points, or critical passages that characters confronted. Second, they write about what they have read from the perspective of one of the characters in the piece. Third, they share their writings with the class. During this last phase, they have an opportunity to discuss the social contexts that promote hurtful behaviors versus those that promote helpful and caring ones—yet another way of learning to understand the difference between the partnership and dominator models as human possibilities.

Another tool for engaging students to look at literature (as well as movies and television) through the analytical lens of the partnership-dominator continuum is the exercise from *The Partnership Way* on partnership versus dominator heroes and heroines. An example of how a teacher used this exercise in her high school class, and a paper by a student on how it enabled him to see what kind of roles, relations, and values are modeled in different programs, can be found in Appendix A.

Language

Partnership education enables students to understand how our language can unconsciously reinforce a dominator worldview.

Literature and English classes offer students a direct opportunity to examine how words shape our value systems, but this issue can be addressed in all classes.

Students can actively participate in creating a language of partnership by using—and, where needed, inventing—words and phrases that reinforce partnership.

Language shapes our thoughts, and thus our worldview. It is essential that we become aware that many of the words, phrases, and linguistic constructions we have inherited from times orienting more to the dominator model unconsciously condition us to think in ways that reinforce and perpetuate a dominator, rather than partnership, worldview.

There is growing awareness of how the use of words like *boy* to address a grown man implies white men's superiority over black men and, hence, maintains dominator racial relations. Although such usages are no longer socially accepted, other offensive terms persist. An example is the patronizing *honey* or *dear* custom of addressing women (including perfect strangers).

Indeed, the semantics of gendered power relations are part of the very fabric of most world languages. For example, masculine pronouns—and, in some languages, nouns and adjectives—render the female half of humanity invisible, clearly implying the superiority of male over female.

Some people argue that it makes no difference if words such as *he*, *man*, and *mankind* are used to refer to both men and women. But the alternative, using terms such as *she*, *woman*, and *womankind* to designate both women and men, horrifies such people—even though the terms *woman*, *womankind*, and *she* actually do include *man* and *he*, whereas the opposite is not true.

Young people can be invited to examine this unconscious mindset, which gives more importance to men than to women and, not surprisingly, underlies resistance to a more equitable and inclusive language. They can begin by reading literature that uses *he* and *his*, and then substitute female pronouns, such as *she* and *hers*, for male pronouns. They can observe, and discuss, the feelings this exercise elicits. They can also consider why, even in the face of efforts to make language inclusive, *he* and *his* are still generally placed before *she* and *hers*—much like the traditional custom in Muslim fundamentalist cultures whereby the woman walks a few paces behind the man.

A good entry point into this exploration of how people have been conditioned to equate masculinity with power and privilege is to ask students in an English class to fill in the missing pronouns in the following kinds of sentences. "The judge asked the secretary to type some papers. _____ handed a stack of documents to _____, asking that _____ be specially careful in _____ work." This exercise should be done prior to any discussion of gender or power relations.

Even among college students, most inserted *he* for the judge and *she* for the secretary. And many students have been stunned to find that even those who describe themselves as gender conscious fall into this automatic habit of associating the position of power with men and the subordinate role with women.

Students can be asked to talk about the feelings that are elicited by this kind of experience. They can look at words such as *congressman* and *chairman* and discuss how such terms are part of a language that teaches us to associate only men with positions of power. They can discuss how this practice not only discourages women from even aspiring to leadership, but also conditions both women and men to feel that there is something wrong when women are in positions of authority—thus helping to explain why many of us still find it uncomfortable when women are in leadership positions, whether as bosses in business or as candidates or officeholders in politics.

Students can consider how even calling women *congresswomen* and *chairwomen* poses problems, since in some organizations these terms have traditionally referred to an administrative support rather than executive role. They can see how generic terms such as the gender-neutral *congressperson, chairperson,* or *chair* avoid the diminishing effect of separating these positions by gender.

Students can then be invited to go more deeply into this issue by examining how words such as *emasculate* or *effeminate,* used to express negative meanings, further reinforce the hidden subtext of gender devaluations that ranks men and "masculinity" over women and "femininity." They can talk about how in male peer groups (especially sports and the military) calling boys or men "girls" or "ladies" is a terrible insult.

They can further discuss the ways in which our language traps us into unhealthy modes of thinking and relating. For example, sexuality is given a negative connotation through the use of words describing sexual intercourse or sexual organs as insults. They can also discuss why the term *bitch*, which means simply female dog, is offensive and how this usage relates to our dominator heritage.

Phrases such as "spearheading an effort," "more than one way to skin a cat," or "killing two birds with one stone," in turn, condition us to associate positive meanings with violence. Students can be invited to brainstorm alternatives. "Hatching two birds from one egg," for example, would be a more life-affirming, and more realistic, image.

Young people can also be invited to invent new words. For example, they could brainstorm the use of a single word to replace gendered pronouns—as in Finnish and Hungarian, which use just one pronoun to signify both *she* and *he*. In the same vein, they can look for substitutes for words such as *fellow* for an honorary position and *brotherhood* for friendship.

Since most of our literary and humanities classics are written in sexist (and often racist) language, words are a challenge to both teachers and students. But when this issue is openly discussed, creative approaches can be found. Students can become actively involved in terms of both making others aware of the problem and experimenting with creative solutions.[119]

Because the question of language is so important in shaping our perceptions and interpretations of reality, it should be addressed not just in literature classes but also in English grammar classes, social studies classes, and current events classes, as well as in the study of other languages. (A good resource from *The Partnership Way* is the short section on the language of partnership that I have included in Appendix A.)

The Humanities

The subject of humanities offers an opportunity to engage students in reexamining what are considered major cultural contributions.

From a partnership perspective the subject of humanities is more multicultural, gender balanced, and focused on issues of human rights and responsibilities.

Studying the humanities from a perspective relevant to our time presents teachers with an opportunity to engage students in thinking about basic questions of values and social priorities.

Literature and the humanities are usually taught together in high school, although they are often separated in the university curriculum. I have separated them here to raise the question of what we should properly call "humanities."

As generally taught, the subject of humanities chronicles the thinking of Western philosophers probing universal questions about our cosmos and our species. This approach offers valuable ideas and, at times, some remarkable pyrotechnics of the mind (see Richard Tarnas, *The Passion of the Western Mind*).[120] But it is also limited and problem laden.

To begin with, it is strange to speak of "humanities" when what is taught under this rubric has excluded not only most non-Western cultures but also a full half of humanity: women.

Through the study of humanities from a partnership perspective, students can become aware of the important contributions made by women and nonwhite men. For example, the works of W.E.B. Du Bois, Cornell West, and Darlene Clark Hine provide important African-American perspectives on politics and race relations. Valuable insights into the non-Western perspective can be gained through writings by and about Gandhi as a philosopher and leader in the struggle for social and economic justice—including the fact that when Gandhi began his struggle to free India from British colonial rule, he used nonviolent tactics much like those employed by 19th-century feminists in England and the United States in their struggle to gain civil and political rights for women.

The works of 18th- and 19th-century feminist philosophers such as Mary Wollstonecraft and Elizabeth Cady Stanton, and of 20th-century feminist philosophers such as Charlotte Perkins Gilman, Gloria Steinem, and bell hooks, should be included in the humanities curriculum, rather than limited to women's studies. So, too, should ecofeminist writings, such as those of Vandana Shiva and Susan Griffin, which emphasize a link between the rape of women and the rape of nature.[121]

Beyond this, a humanities curriculum should frontally address the fact that what is all too often included under the description of humanities has contributed to a great deal of *in*humanity. For example, Aristotle's philosophical writings assert that slaves and women "naturally" belong in a subservient place, and even that women are deficient, mutilated males. And the philosopher Nietzsche (whose works are a mainstay of the standard humanities curriculum) asserts that there is a superior master race of men entitled to dominate other men (and all women)—a philosophy that provided inspiration for Hitler's propaganda of Aryan racial superiority, cost many millions of lives, and rationalized the most hideous cruelty and inhumanity.[122]

So what can properly be called "humanities"? If we look at this issue through the lens of the partnership-dominator continuum, we arrive at some basic questions: Which writings in the conventional humanities curriculum help us better understand ourselves and one another, and which writings smuggle inhuman and anti-human messages into our minds? What do we really learn from "classics" such as Homer's *Iliad* and the novels of Hemingway about "nobility" and "heroism"? What do such works teach us about human relations?

The *Iliad* begins with an argument between the hero Achilles and the King Agamemnon about a "prize of war"—a young woman, captured by the Greeks, whom the soldiers have awarded to the hero Achilles but whom Agamemnon covets. Nowhere in this work is there any mention that this young woman, Briseis, is treated not as a human being but as property. Nowhere are her feelings, her needs, her wishes, or for that matter her suffering, even considered. She is no more than an object, a slave, to be sexually used by either Agamemnon or Achilles. The real issue, and dilemma, according to Homer, is which of two men—the king or the hero—is "rightfully" entitled to this "prize."

The study of the humanities from a partnership perspective could begin, as many courses already do, with the *Iliad*. But it would here be used as an invitation to students to think about what can properly be considered "humanities."

Teachers could ask such framing questions as, What cultivates our human capacity for empathy, rather than deadening it? Which writings have contributed to this capacity? Is the *Iliad*, which celebrates killing as heroic, such a contribution? Or should it be studied primarily from a historical perspective as a well-written work that tells of a time when domination and conquest were the most valued of "manly" pursuits?

Using the templates of the partnership and dominator models, students can evaluate the normative messages that "great books," "great philosophers," and "great classics" have taught us to accept as normal and moral. Partnership elements can be found in many of these works, of course. But these beautifully written texts often idealize prejudice and cruelty, conditioning us to emotionally accept such feelings and behaviors. And they rarely offer models for healthy, fulfilling, nonviolent ways of living.

I believe that the study of the humanities should first and foremost inculcate respect for human rights, not just in theory but in practice. Most students have no inkling that over the past half-century there have been major United Nations conventions that blueprint a more humane future. Examples are the 1948 "Universal Declaration of Human Rights," "The Convention on the Elimination of All Forms of Discrimination Against Women," and "The Convention on the Rights of Child." There are also important United Nations conventions on the environment, population, and development.[123] Regardless of conflicting opinions about the United Nations' efficiency, these conventions and documents are important building blocks for a partnership world.

Indeed, the contemporary discourse about values and morality, which so often focuses on punishing and persecuting anyone considered deviant, urgently needs to be reframed in terms of respect for human rights. It also needs to go beyond the abstract perspective of most humanities philosophy texts to our day-to-day responsibilities to others–and even beyond this, to our responsibility to help create a more just and nonviolent society. As demonstrated by Carol Gilligan's research on women's more contextualized, rather than abstract, approach to morality, this discourse would flow naturally from a more gender-balanced approach to the humanities.[124]

In a partnership curriculum, a holistic model of human rights that includes the rights of women and children (the majority of the human population) is highlighted rather than ignored (see Box 5.17). This model enables young people to see a fundamental truth that is still generally overlooked: that it is in our foundational adult-child and man-woman relations that we first learn, and continually practice, either respect for human rights or the acceptance of violations of human rights as "just the way things are."

A more gender-balanced approach to the study of humanities will encourage students of both sexes to more highly value stereotypically feminine traits and behaviors such as nonviolence, empathy, caring, and caregiving. It will also show that, even in periods when women have been generally confined to "helpmate" roles as wives, mothers, domestic servants, or nannies, they have made, and continue to make, essential contributions to human culture—contributions without which none of us would be alive.

This makes it possible for students to look at why work traditionally associated with women—such as caring for the children, the sick, and the elderly in their families and maintaining a clean and aesthetic home environment—has not been valued as a major contribution to human culture. Is this logical? Is this humane? Students could also be asked to think

---

BOX 5.17   Human Rights

For discussions of a truly humanistic model of human rights, see Riane Eisler, "Human Rights: Toward an Integrated Theory for Action," in the *Human Rights Quarterly;*[125] Charlotte Bunch, "Women's Rights Are Human Rights: Toward a Revision of Human Rights," also in the *Human Rights Quarterly;*[126] Charlotte Bunch and Niamh Reilly, *Demanding Accountability: The Global Campaign and Vienna Tribunal for Women's Human Rights;*[127] and Riane Eisler, "Human Rights and Violence: Integrating the Private and Public Spheres," in *The Web of Violence: From Interpersonal to Global.*[128]

---

about whether it seems logical or humane that government-supported funding is available to train men (and, recently, also women) to kill as soldiers, but we have no government-supported funding to help women and men learn how to better take care of children—even though psychological research has long shown that the quality of this care has life-long consequences.

How does this elevation of taking life over giving and nurturing life relate to the frequent idealization of "heroic" violence in the *Iliad* and other works taught in our literature and humanities courses? How does it relate to the fact that in these "classics" there is so little mention of the social contributions made by women who heroically give birth and devote much of their lives to caring for children?

Why is this socially essential work—without which none of us could survive—even today not considered "real work" in national and international measures of productivity, if it is done at home rather than at a childcare center? And why does childcare have such low status and bring such low pay? (See Box 5.18.)

Students can be asked to consider the fact that, because the work of soldiers is considered socially valuable, they receive government pensions, whereas there are no pensions for women and men who do the socially essential and demanding work of caring for children. They can further be invited to consider the fact that plumbers, who are still predominately male, get paid more than childcare workers, who are still predominately female. Is plumbing more important than childcare? Why, despite all the rhetoric about valuing children, do we have such strange

---

BOX 5.18 Women's Work

For materials on this subject, see Marylin Waring, *If Women Counted*; Riane Eisler, David Loye, and Kari Norgaard, *Women, Men, and the Global Quality of Life*; and Riane Eisler, "Changing the Rules of the Game: Work, Values, and Our Future."[129] See also <www.partnershipway.org> for information on the Alliance for a Caring Economy.

---

systems of valuations? What can we do to change this? (The Alliance for a Caring Economy is also a good source here.)[130]

These emotion-laden questions are important if teachers are to include the element of conation, or will to act, in learning. In considering such questions, students will be intellectually stimulated. No doubt they will also be somewhat confused and disturbed. But once young people use the partnership and dominator models as guides to examining values, they can be inspired to actively participate in creating the more humane system of values needed for a better future.

Current Events

Civics and social studies classes can help young people not only to make sounder personal choices but also to understand the importance of social action in ensuring that good choices are available.

Contemporary social, political, and economic issues can be better understood in terms of the tension between a movement toward partnership countered by dominator resistance and regression in both the so-called private and public spheres.

When students understand underlying dynamics that impact our lives, such as dominator gender stereotypes and valuations, they can go beyond conventional polarities, such as right versus left and religious versus secular, to basic issues.

Informing students about organizations working for the environment, equity, and other partnership goals can channel their need for belonging into constructive directions.

In addition to preparing students to become good citizens and assume leadership roles, current events classes can serve as a springboard for community involvement and action.

In 1998, a UCLA survey found that only 27 percent of the nations' 1.6 million first-year college students (less than half the percentage recorded in 1966) believed that keeping up with political affairs is an important life goal, and just 14 percent said that they frequently discuss politics (down from 30 percent in 1968).[131] This indifference to current events does not auger well for a democratic future. But it is also not surprising at a time when so much in our culture encourages passivity, alienation, and apathy, and, at best, emphasizes only personal change, with little attention to the social contexts that shape personal choices.

Especially for members of socially and economically disadvantaged groups, an approach that focuses on personal change without also focusing on social change is both unrealistic and ineffective. It denies the realities of these young people's lives. It fails to acknowledge the real conditions that need to be changed: the poverty and violence of "third world" economic ghettos in the inner cities of affluent countries such as the United States and the inadequate nutrition, poor healthcare, and illiteracy besetting most of the world's people—particularly women, who, with their children, are not only the majority of the world's poor but the poorest of the poor.[132]

Ignoring social and cultural change is also unrealistic and ineffective in relation to issues that affect everyone's life. For example, if we are to be healthy, we need a healthy environment: We need to breathe clean air, drink unpolluted water, and eat food that has not been contaminated by harmful pesticides—all matters that involve social and cultural, not just personal, change.

Not having learned the possibility of working for social change, many young people drop out and escape—sometimes in destructive, even violent, ways. Many simply feel helpless and become alienated and passive.

But it is not enough simply to fault young people for not being more involved, or for making self-destructive choices—as in television spots that tell kids to "just say no" to drugs. I don't mean to minimize the importance of sound personal choices and actions. These are essential components of learning and maturation. But one of the most important lessons to be learned by young people in current events (and other) classes is that their lives are directly impacted by cultural beliefs, social structures, and political and economic policies. A second, related lesson is that it is up to them to ensure that these beliefs, structures, and policies are sound.

How are they to do this? In both our mass media and our schools, even when action for social change is touched upon, it is generally presented in terms of violent struggles between men competing for power. For example, armed rebellions in many world regions, terrorism, and political assassinations get the headlines. When dealing with U.S. politics, the mass media also tend to emphasize who wins or loses—that is, adversarial strategies and tactics rather than substantive issues. This promotes distrust of politicians and a sense of futility about achieving any real cultural and social change.

Civics and current events classes taught from a partnership perspective can help young people learn that there are hundreds of thousands of grassroots groups all over the world working for equity, for human rights, for the environment, for peace—for a better life. In many of these groups, women (for example, Rosa Parks, Betty Friedan, Helen Caldicott, Marian Wright Edelman, Rigoberta Menchu, and Aung San Suu Kyi) have provided important leadership. These groups include organizations working to protect our environment (an area in which a woman, Rachel Carson, provided essential early leadership). They also include organizations that are challenging traditions of domination in intimate relations worldwide. Examples include the women's groups that organized powerful events dramatizing the needs and aspirations of women for the 1985 United Nations Conference on Women in Nairobi, Kenya; established a tribunal on women's rights at the 1993 United Nations Human Rights conference in Vienna; and ensured that violence against women was a key theme at the 1995 UN Conference of Women in Beijing.

The common thread in all these movements is the challenge to entrenched patterns of domination. As we saw in previous chapters, teaching current events in the context of this larger perspective of a strong movement toward partnership helps young people see that social activism can bring—and historically has brought—positive change. It also makes it possible for young people to see something else of critical importance: that the cumulating challenges to domination and violence as normal and even moral are today sparking a strong backlash. One aspect of this backlash is the pressure on schools to avoid issues that may be considered controversial—which of course includes the issues that will most profoundly affect young people's future lives.

Indeed, one of the difficulties teachers of current events face in a time of backlash is how to teach without being accused of being "too liberal." "Is this fair?" they are asked. Isn't fairness the American way? And doesn't it mean that teachers must counterbalance the "case" for all "liberal" views with the "case" for all "conservative" views?

What the partnership educator needs to keep in mind is that, in issue after issue, what is at stake is not liberal or conservative perspectives, but the *human* perspective and the fundamental American perspective of *democracy*. Freedom, peace, and equality are no longer ideological variables to be debated. Rather, they must be the "givens" from which debate is launched—debate as to how they can better be achieved.

We need to keep in mind—and teach our students—the need to broaden our understanding of current events by going beyond conventional political debates about right versus left, religious versus secular, or conservative versus liberal. Once students understand the dynamics of the tension between the partnership and dominator models as two basic human possibilities, they can go beyond these surfaces. They can see the patterns that underlie seemingly unrelated currents and crosscurrents in our world—and thus be better equipped to effectively intervene in shaping their future.

For example, in the United States, at the same time that the injunction to "spare the rod and spoil the child" is increasingly being rejected, some people advocate a return to more corporal punishment in both homes and schools as a requirement for sound childrearing. This issue has nothing to do with being liberal or conservative, religious or secular. It is an aspect of dominator resistance—often unconsciously motivated, as noted in Box 4.3—against the movement toward a less violent and more equitable society. As I touched on earlier, it is through our formative childhood experiences that we first are taught what is normal and moral. Hence challenges to domination and violence in intimate relations are foundational to real freedom, peace, and equality.

At the same time that rape and other forms of violence against women are increasingly being prosecuted (thanks to organized feminist social action), music videos watched by millions of teenagers present the degradation, humiliation, and violent brutalization of girls and women as sexy. Again, these conflicting currents and crosscurrents cannot be understood using the conventional categories of right versus left, liberal versus conservative, or religious versus secular. Some people who think of themselves as conservatives are far more interested in censoring sex than violence. And some people on the secular left and liberal side, even those who advocate peaceful solutions to problems, often see nothing wrong with violent imagery—particularly when it occurs in sexual contexts.

It is only when we look at these images from the perspective of the core configurations of the partnership and dominator models described in Part One that we can see patterns that are obscured by the categories of conservative versus liberal and religious versus secular. Images associating sex with violence communicate the message that male violence is not only normal but sexy. The erotization of domination and violence is a means of unconsciously reinforcing this mindset—a mindset that can be found in many people, regardless of whether they are religious, secular, conservative, or liberal.

As we have seen, how the roles and relations of the female and male halves of humanity are constructed is foundational to either dominator or partnership power structures throughout society. Learning to accept the domination of half of humanity over the other half as normal teaches us that there is nothing wrong with domination and submission in human relations. And presenting violence against women as sexy is yet one more way of making brutality and cruelty seem manly and exciting.

This is why it is critical to help students see the importance of challenges to domination and violence in the so-called private or family sphere of man/woman and parent/child relations. Through such an understanding they will be better able to construct the foundation for a more equitable and less violent world.

Looking at what is happening today from the perspective of the struggle for our future between the dominator and partnership templates for social organization in both the so-called public and private spheres also makes it possible to see how gender stereotypes and gender socialization—which both conservatives and liberals often take for granted—play an important role in maintaining hierarchies of domination in all spheres of life. As an example, consider the subtext of dominator gender stereotypes and valuations that lies behind much of what is happening in contemporary politics.

In the dominator view, the function of government is primarily to maintain control, ultimately based on force. This control is exemplified by the allocation of large sums of tax monies to build prisons (to punish rather than to prevent crime, and to prevent opposition to those who hold power), as well as by the production of ever more technologically complex, and thus increasingly costly, weaponry. In other words, according to this view, government should play only the stereotypical roles assigned to men in dominator societies: the disciplinarian role of the punitive father and the heroic role of the warrior.

By contrast, the emerging partnership view equates power *not* primarily with the blade but with the chalice—and promotes policies allocating tax funds primarily for what are sometimes described as "soft" (stereotyp-ically "feminine") activities: for example, caring for and educating chil-dren (and thus ultimately preventing crime); preserving and protecting the environment; and more equitably distributing wealth (as in the Scan-dinavian nations, where the status of women, and hence, of stereotypi-cally "feminine" values, is higher). According to this partnership view, then, there would still be some funding for weapons, as these are regret-tably necessary in our world today; but weapons would not be vigorously marketed in our country, where they are a major contributor to violent crime. Nor would weapons be exported to other nations, where they can be used to maim and kill neighbors, suppress their own people, or com-mit acts of terrorism—including, as is already happening, terrorism against weapons-exporting nations such as the United States. Nor, for that matter, would weapons be associated with "real masculinity," as they are in much of our toy industry and mass media today.

If students look at how government funding is allocated during periods of dominator regression such as the one we are presently experiencing, they can see how the greater valuation of anything stereotypically associ-ated with men and "masculinity" shapes unsound social policies (see Box 5.19). For instance, the members of Congress who were elected in 1992 severely cut programs to feed children, care for families' health, and maintain a clean and healthy environment—all activities associated with women and stereotypical "women's work" (see Figure 5.11). At the same time, they allocated billions of dollars to build obsolete bombers that the Pentagon did not even want.

Using the analytical lens of the partnership-dominator continuum, students can also see the hidden subtext of gender in the contemporary debate over power and leadership. On the dominator side are those who think a "strong leader" (which is equated with the capacity to control through the threat of pain) will solve all our problems by getting things "under control"—the authoritarian, strong-man dominator formula. On the partnership side are those who see the need for a new kind of leader who inspires and facilitates creative problemsolving, and is less violent as well as more empathic—a conceptualization of leadership that incorpo-rates stereotypically "feminine" traits.

The struggle by women to have equal representation in leadership (and thus in policymaking) in politics, economics, religion, science, education, and the family is an important step toward more humane social policies. This is not to deny that women adopt dominator values. Obviously some

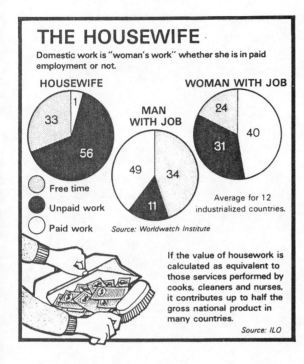

THE HOUSEWIFE

Domestic work is "woman's work" whether she is in paid employment or not.

HOUSEWIFE

WOMAN WITH JOB

MAN WITH JOB

33

1

56

24

40

31

49

34

11

○ Free time

● Unpaid work

Average for 12 industrialized countries.

○ Paid work   *Source: Worldwatch Institute*

If the value of housework is calculated as equivalent to those services performed by cooks, cleaners and nurses, it contributes up to half the gross national product in many countries.

Source: ILO

FIGURE 5.11
Invisible Women

Women the world over are making a vast and unacknowledged contribution to the wealth and welfare of their communities—in unpaid domestic work and in small-scale business and trading activities. Often these women are household heads with sole responsibility for their families.

CREDIT: *United Nations,* The State of the World's Women Report *(1985).*

do. But on the average, as a voting bloc, women legislators tend to favor funding for stereotypical "women's work" such as childcare and healthcare. In any case, real participatory democracy requires more than token representation in policymaking by the female half of humanity.

Nonetheless, there are still people who tell us that only men can be leaders. For example, the leaders of the Christian men's movement that calls itself the "Promise Keepers" tell us that men must again take control of their wives and children. They even claim that men must head their families in the same way that Jesus is head of the Church—in other words, that men's authority in their families should be as absolute as God's!

This battle between autocratic dominator and democratic partnership ways of structuring social institutions—from the family and religion to politics and economics—underlies much of today's struggle over public education. On the one side, we see efforts to dismantle educational programs that teach children to value diversity rather than automatically equating differences of gender or race with inferiority or superiority. We see legislative proposals to reintroduce corporal punishment in schools.

BOX 5.19   Gender Valuations

For a more detailed discussion of how this hidden subtext of gender valuations negatively impacts our lives, see Riane Eisler, Sacred Pleasure, The
Chalice and the Blade, and Redefining Destiny, as well as Women, Men,
and the Global Quality of Life. As noted earlier, this last work, published
by the Center for Partnership Studies, is based on data from eighty-nine
nations showing how a higher status of women correlates with a higher
quality of life for all. This finding helps explain why the Scandinavian
block nations, which are not the richest nations in the world but exhibit
much greater gender equity than most, consistently score high in United
Nations ratings of overall quality of life.

    Another source is my article "Changing the Rules of the Game: Work,
Values, and Our Future," which can be downloaded from the Center for
Partnership Studies website at <www.partnershipway.org>. This article
became the basis for the Alliance for a Caring Economy, co-founded by
the Center for Partnership Studies and the Global Futures Foundation.
The Alliance, composed of a network of organizations, is working for a
change in the economic rules toward recognizing and rewarding the value
of caring and caregiving work—in both the market and nonmarket sec-
tors of the economy.[133]

We even see a push to dismantle the public school system through priva-
tization and vouchers—even though public education is a cornerstone of
modern democracy and private organizations can be extremely inefficient, as evidenced by their high bankruptcy rates.

On the other side, we see efforts by educational leaders to introduce
partnership processes such as cooperative learning, peer teaching, and
criterion-referenced rather than competitive measures of learning. We
see educators working to debureaucratize schools—that is, to shift from
top-down hierarchies of control toward working partnerships between
teachers, students, parents, administrators, and other staff. We also see
educators working to change the primary and secondary curriculum so
that it reflects the teaching of partnership values.

In many standard classrooms, the teacher gives directions and the students follow. In a partnership classroom, the teacher shares power with
the students (at least in some matters) and teaches them partnership competences, such as making responsible, collaborative decisions (see Box
5.20). Current events classes are thus a place for students to practice partnership relations. Here, they can learn that working in partnership still

BOX 5.20   Democracy and Social Action

Following are some resources that teachers can use to help students learn and practice democratic skills, as well as organize politically positive changes: Barbara A. Lewis's *The Kids' Guide to Social Action*;[134] Nancy Schniedewind's and Ellen Davidson's *Open Minds to Equality*;[135] Wendy Schaetzel Lesko's handbook on student civic activism, available through the World Education Center Resources website at <http://www.uvm.edu/~uvmcwe/resources.html>; and The Video Project, which offers an impressive list of award-winning documentaries on issues ranging from the environment and economics to racial and gender equity. Two other excellent sources of videos are the Media Education Foundation and Cambridge Documentary Films.[136]

A film I have personally found moving and inspiring is Margarethe von Trotta's *Rosa Luxemberg*, the life story of the German fighter for peace and economic justice.[137]

means respecting teachers and others who have knowledge to impart, but does not mean blindly following without thinking. Indeed, they can learn to think for themselves, and to form and stand up for their own beliefs.

Current events classes also offer the opportunity to help young people become global citizens. When George and a group of his 12th-grade classmates did a survey of public awareness about events in Africa, they found that most of the people they interviewed had no idea of what was going on, even regarding matters such as food crises that were featured in headlines. They then formed groups to research reasons for these food crises. They found that the problem was related not only to population pressures, soil degradation, and warfare but also to economic and social policies. For example, development programs have given huge subsidies to large enterprises that grow and sell crops for export, rather than to those who, in Africa, do the bulk of the subsistence farming: women. (See Figure 5.12.) From this research, students learned that watching the news on TV or reading the daily paper is not the same as being informed. They also learned a basic lesson in systems thinking: that in trying to solve a problem, one must consider many factors—some of which are hidden by the prevailing paradigm.

Current events classes can also help students who feel alone and isolated in their concerns about the future, by providing a setting in which

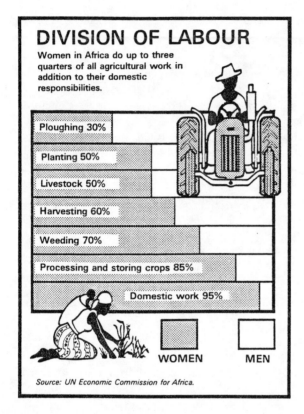

DIVISION OF LABOUR

Women in Africa do up to three quarters of all agricultural work in addition to their domestic responsibilities.

Ploughing 30%

Planting 50%

Livestock 50%

Harvesting 60%

Weeding 70%

Processing and storing crops 85%

Domestic work 95%

WOMEN   MEN

Source: UN Economic Commission for Africa.

FIGURE 5.12   Women in Agriculture

The evidence points to the fact that, given the same kinds of help, encouragement, and incentives as men, women's agricultural productivity at least equals that of men.

CREDIT: *United Nations,* The State of the World's Women Report *(1985).*

they can share their feelings and discover that there are others like them. Students can be encouraged to link with kindred spirits by engaging in activities that help others in their communities and bring about partnership changes in the world at large.

Many local and national organizations offer opportunities for young people to become actively engaged in solving social and environmental problems while at the same time satisfying their need for belonging through positive means rather than by joining gangs or buying the latest teen fashion. But these organizations are, at best, only occasionally featured in the mass media. Schools have a responsibility to help young people become more informed about them. (For a partial listing, see Box 5.21.)

Students can also be encouraged to identify public services in their own and other communities. For instance, Milwaukee, Wisconsin, has

BOX 5.21   Finding Community in Social Action

Thousands of organizations worldwide bring people together on the local, national, and international levels to work for a partnership future. Some offer internships to young people, some have local chapters, and most have conferences and other meetings.

Co-Op America, located at 1612 K Street, NW, Number 600, Washington, D.C. 20006 (phone: 202-872-5307; website: <www.coopamer­ica.org>) has listings of environmental organizations as well as of thousands of products and services from "green" businesses we can support. Other environmental organizations are the Union of Concerned Scientists, Greenpeace, Sierra Club, Rainforest Action Network, and the Earth Island Institute.

The Back to School/Stay in School program of the National Association for the Advancement of Colored People (NAACP) (website: <www.naacp.org>) and the Youth Leaders Program of the National Council of La Raza (website: <nclr.org>) are specifically aimed at young people. The Southern Poverty Law Center, headquartered in Montgomery, Alabama (website: <splcenter.org>), and the Simon Wiesenthal Center, headquartered in Los Angeles, where its Museum of Tolerance is also located (website: <wiesenthal.com>), are leaders in working to end prejudice and hate crimes.

The American Association of University Women, headquartered in Washington D.C., has local chapters and actively supports teachers and students interested in a better educational system. New Moon (Duluth, Minnesota) focuses on the concerns and interests of girls eight to fourteen years of age. National and local chapters of the National Women's Political Caucus, the National Organization for Women (NOW), and the League of Women Voters work for women in the political arena, both as candidates for public office and as educated, active voters. Organizations such as the National Committee on UN/CEDAW (520 North Camden Drive, Beverly Hills, California 90210-3202) work to convince governments, including that of the United States, to ratify the United Nations Convention on the Elimination of All Forms of Discrimination Against Women. As of 1997, 161 countries had ratified this important UN policy statement, but the United States Senate still had not!

Planned Parenthood, which promotes family planning and actively protects women's reproductive health rights, is headquartered in Washington, D.C., and has local chapters. Population Action International (Washington, D.C.) is a leader in work for sustainable population growth.

(continues)

BOX 5.21 *(continued)*

Students for Social Responsibility, Businesses for Social Responsibility, the Social Venture Network, and the World Business Academy provide opportunities to explore environmentally and socially responsible ways of doing business.

The International Partnership Network (IPN) is the membership sister organization of the Center for Partnership Studies (<www.partnershipway.org>). Coordinated by Del Jones, it can be contacted at P.O. Box 323, Tucson, Arizona 85702 (phone: 520-298-6542; fax: 520-298-0639; e-mail: <DelmerAZ@aol.com>) for its Internet listserv. Another CPS sister organization is Alliance for a Caring Economy (ACE), which offers internship opportunities in the Northern California and Boston areas. (Contact Wendy Pratt, Global Futures Foundation, 801 Crocker Road, Sacramento, CA 95864; phone: 916-486-5999; website: <www/globalff. org/ace>).

The Children's Defense Fund (25 E Street NW, Washington, D.C. 20001) and Children Now (1212 Broadway, 5th Floor, Oakland, CA 94612; website:<www.childrennow.org>) are other important organizations. The American Friends Service Committee (1501 Cherry Street, Philadelphia, PA 19102) and the Center for Campus Organizing (P.O. Box 425748, Cambridge, MA 02142) also offer opportunities, and models, for social action. CAPACITAR (23 East Beach St., Suite 206, Watsonville, CA 95076; phone: 831-456-9426; e-mail: <capcitar@igc. apc.org>) works both in the United States and in Latin America to promote personal and social healing through body-mind-spirit practices.

For other organizations, see Barbara A. Lewis, *The Kids' Guide to Social Action* (Minneapolis, Minn.: Free Spirit Publishers, 1998), and chapters 18 and 19 of *Sacred Pleasure*.[138]

one of the best systems of public parks and public swimming pools of any city in the United States—thanks to the working-class citizens of Milwaukee, who could not afford large private spaces for recreation, so they organized to obtain public resources for public use. (An interesting sideline is that the Green Bay Packers football franchise is also owned by the citizens of Green Bay, the only major-league team owned by the public.) These are examples of how partnership benefits all concerned.

Civics and current events classes can also provide young people with an opportunity to become aware that they themselves can form new organizations. For example, Youth for Environmental Sanity, founded by

Ocean Robbins, Sol Solomon, and a group of other concerned high school students in 1990, has held more than forty Action Camps in which young people from twenty-seven countries have participated.[139]

Encouraging students to become actively involved in their communities and the world is particularly important since students today are so immersed in both television and the Internet. As presently programmed, television is essentially a passive activity, another spectator sport. Even the Internet, though more participatory, still tends to focus on the gathering of information, on talking rather than acting.

Nonetheless, the Internet offers the technological opportunity for linking us not only through information but through positive organized action. There is already some progress in this direction, through "zines" or online newsletters produced by environmentally and socially conscious young people. An example is the New Moon website at <http://www.newmoon.org>. Especially now that schools are being equipped with Internet access, educators have a responsibility to nurture and support cyber-activism.

Students can also be encouraged to do peer teaching, not only in their own classrooms but in lower grades, as well as in their communities. They can look at the many studies of contemporary problems available today, but at the same time be made aware that one way of *not* dealing with problems is through endless studies commissioned by governments and corporations—in other words, that merely studying and restudying a problem does not somehow solve it.

In short, current events classes—especially when taught from a partnership perspective—are places where teachers can stimulate students' interest in larger issues by showing their relevance to matters of importance to students' lives right here and now. Most important, these classes are places where students can prepare themselves to assume responsibility and leadership for effecting positive changes not only in their own lives but in their communities and the world at large.

Learning and Living

Interweaving Student
Interests and Concerns

W E ARE BORN CURIOUS. Babies are eager to learn, to explore everything about their world. As children grow up, they ask hundreds of questions. As adolescents, they strive to develop their own ideas and find meaning in life.

But much of this drive to think and explore our inner and outer worlds has been thwarted by pedagogies that suppress independent thought and emphasize rote conformity and obedience to orders. The result is often rebellion. As we see all around us, curiosity and striving for independent identity are all too often diverted into trivial or destructive pursuits.

Schools have a responsibility to help students direct these developmental drives in meaningful and constructive ways. And, as many teachers know, this can be done by starting with matters that interest or concern them.

From early childhood on, young people also have an intrinsic interest in values, in finding out what is rewarded or punished, approved or disapproved. They also seem to have a built-in sense of justice. As Piaget and other scholars investigating moral development in children have found, we can see this sense of justice through simple observation, as when a child passionately exclaims that something is not fair. Its development appears to be related to the evolution of what Darwin called the moral sense and David Loye calls moral sensitivity.[1]

But once again, dominator education has largely been based on a morality of coercion rather than one of caring, on fear of punishment and

205

outside control rather than on empathy, sensitivity, and self-regulation, on extrinsic rather than intrinsic developmentally supported motivations (a subject I deal with later in this chapter). Hence many young people are denied the opportunity to internalize sound values based on positive rather than negative motivations.

Partnership education is designed to offer young people this opportunity. It supports responsible behaviors respectful of human rights and of the intricate and miraculous fabric of life on our Earth—behaviors I describe as "Caring for Life" in a later section of this chapter. It also provides encouragement to young people in their search for sound values as part of growing up, of assuming their adult place in society.

I will here touch on these matters in connection with some issues of immediate interest and concern to students today. What follows can be interwoven into classes ranging from science, health, and literature to history, social science, and current events. Since many of the materials in the sections that follow were sparked by conversations with students in high schools and elementary schools, they can effectively be used as the basis for elementary and high school study projects. Students can also be invited to participate in the development of new curriculum modules that incorporate these materials.

The Mass Media

Schools have a responsibility to provide young people the information and guidance necessary to resist harmful media messages.

The analytical lens of the partnership-dominator continuum is useful in helping sort media messages.

Students can learn how to become actively involved in changing the content of the mass media, both by working with organizations dedicated to this goal and by learning to write and produce partnership media.

Young people today are extremely interested in television, movies, the Internet, and other mass media. The clothes they wear, the foods they eat, the way they talk, walk, hold their bodies, and feel about themselves—all are profoundly influenced by media images, including ads. As noted by Professor George Gerbner, president of the Cultural Environment Movement and former dean of the Annenberg School for Communication, "A child today is born into a home in which television is on an average of more than seven hours a day."[2] And as Diane Levin points out in *Remote Control Childhood? Combating the Hazards of Media Culture*, even before entering kindergarten children in the United States are likely to have spent 4,000 hours in front of TV sets—"more time than they spend doing anything but sleeping, more time even than they will spend in school."[3] So, even before children start school they have already received a massive portion of their education through television.

As part of this education, children will learn what and who is important or not important, good or bad, rewarded or punished. In other words, they will learn values.

For example, children will learn that men are considered more important than women. They will learn this not only because men and boys play far more leading parts than women and girls in both children's cartoons and adult programs, but because it will be subliminally communicated to them through the totally imbalanced ratio of men to women in overall television programming. Rather than reflecting the fact that women constitute more than half the U.S. population, women are cast in only one out of three roles in prime-time television and only one out of four roles in children's programs. They are only one out of five of those included in news reports. They even fall short of majority in daytime serials aimed at stay-at-home women.

Not only is the overall ratio of men to women on television an unrealistic two to one, but women are cast far more frequently than men as victims. Women are still cast primarily in stereotypical feminine roles, with independent women frequently portrayed as evil. In children's cartoons, mature women are barely visible, and almost invariably evil—cast primarily as witches.[4]

By the time they enter school, U.S. children will also have learned from television that white people are more important than other people. Even though people of color constitute the vast majority of humankind, on U.S. television they are less than 11 percent in prime-time shows and 3 percent in children's programs. Poor people also play a negligible role, with the low-income 13 percent of the U.S. population reduced to 1.3 percent or less. Like women, African-Americans, Native Americans, and Latinos, a disproportionate number of characters who are unsuccessful and ill-fated come from the ranks of the poor.[5]

Moreover, because children learn largely by imitation, they also learn what behaviors are "normal" from television. For example, as part of the mass media's education for viewing behaviors associated with a dominator model of human relations as only normal and right is program after program that presents violence—and specifically male violence—as normal, manly, and fun.

By the end of elementary school, the average child will have witnessed 8,000 murders and 100,000 other acts of violence on the TV screen. Most of this violence appears in programs that feature it "for fun"—that is, in cartoons and dramas produced to entertain. And the violence is often perpetrated by characters that are presented as heroic and manly, characters that also have qualities such as good looks and good motives that make them attractive role models for viewers.[6]

Well over 50 percent of video games contain violence, which is often brutal, graphic, and realistic. When playing these games, children are not just watching violence but actively engaged in perpetrating violence—thereby learning the "effectiveness" of violence as a means of dealing with problems. Movies also normalize and glamorize violence, as do many toys that derive from violent television shows and movies—from GI Joe and Teenage Mutant Ninja Turtles to the Mighty Morphin Power Rangers. In 1994, the manufacturer of the latter sold over one billion dollars worth of violent toys and other products. And even before the re-release of the Star Wars trilogy, $4 billion of Star Wars products had been sold. The profits from the violent film *Small Soldiers* and toys corresponding to the most violent aspects of this movie have also been astronomical.

Despite the old theory that violent programs have a healthy cathartic effect, the evidence that they are extremely harmful is overwhelming. For example, the American Medical Associations' *Physician's Guide to Media Violence* points out that study after study shows that media violence leads to increased levels of mean-spiritedness, aggression, fearfulness, mistrust, and self-protective behavior, justifies resorting to violence, and contributes to callousness to others' suffering. These studies verify the obvious: that children (and adults) learn behaviors not only from what is modeled by parents, teachers, and peer groups, but also from characters in books, movies, and television.[7]

In addition, as Gerbner points out, violent images of a mean and dangerous world are instruments of terror in themselves[8]—just as the public tortures and witch burnings of the Middle Ages served to show that what matters above all (in a dominator society) is who has the power to inflict pain and on whom it may be inflicted. (A modern corollary is the disproportionately high ratio of women and minorities as victims on TV.)

In sum, the effects of media violence go far beyond the often-discussed issue of increased real-life violence–such as the growing incidence of random schoolyard shootings by little boys. Media violence also profoundly affects the formation of cultural values, molding them in ways appropriate for dominator rather than partnership relations.

This is a serious situation, particularly because values once acquired are resistant to change. Values are more deeply imbedded in us than beliefs or attitudes precisely because we tend to learn them unconsciously through situations or stories that are emotionally charged—as in TV shows and movies. Moreover, values are important motivators; that is, they have an important conative element that often unconsciously impels us to do or not to do certain things.

However, as the psychologist Milton Rokeach, who studied values over many decades in many countries, and other researchers have shown, values can be changed. One way of doing this is by confronting us with situations, people, or stories that make visible internal contradictions in our value systems, particularly contradictions that conflict with our self-conceptions.[9]

This means that education can help children acquire partnership values if information is presented in such a way as to help them become aware of how certain unconsciously held beliefs acquired through both formal and informal (mass media) education contradict basic American values such as freedom, equality, and democracy, and are maladaptive to their real needs and goals. As we have seen, this is a key theme in partnership education. But because today young people are so immersed in the mass media, it is important for schools to also directly deal with the kinds of messages imparted (see Box 6.1).

We can start teaching media literacy as early as kindergarten. Since young children have a hard time distinguishing between what is pretend and what is real—one reason that "fun" violence is so enormously dangerous—teachers could ask children open-ended questions about real versus pretend in the shows they have watched. In this way adults can provide guidance to help children sort out what they have seen. Teachers could also ask children what they thought about how the hero of a violent show solves problems, and follow that by asking them to think of other ways of solving problems where no one gets hurt.

It is essential to let children say what they think, even if you disagree with them. The important thing is to open channels of communication to help children understand that violence has terrible consequences and to counteract the message that violence is manly and fun.

Children could also be asked to talk about older women they know—for example, their grandmothers—and to compare them to the stereotype

BOX 6.1   Media Literacy

Many materials on media literacy are available to teachers. For example, organizations such as the Center for Media Education (in Washington, D.C.), the Center for Media Literacy (in Los Angeles), Children Now (in Oakland, California), and Teachers for Resisting Unhealthy Children's Entertainment (in West Somerville, Massachusetts) offer kits on topics ranging from media violence to gender bias. They also provide guidelines on how to help children recognize media messages designed to pressure their parents to buy advertised toys and other products.[10] In addition, coalition groups such as the Cultural Environment Movement in Philadelphia (founded by Gerbner) and the Coalition for Quality Children's Media offer opportunities for adults and children to become involved in regaining programming control from commercial interests (many of them media monopolies) that irresponsibly produce programs that pollute the psyches of both children and adults, promote an overconsumption mentality, and contribute to many social problems, including the increase in real-life violence committed by boys and men.[11]

The Media Education Foundation offers a wide range of videos that can make classrooms come alive. These include Sut Jhally's award-winning *Advertising and the End of the World*, which focuses on the connection between environmental degradation and today's consumerist lifestyle; his powerful *Dreamworks* and *Dreamworks II*, which deal with popular music-video images and how they contribute to sexual violence and abuse; Beth Sanders' *Fear and Favor in the Newsroom*, which exposes the internal censorship of news by corporate advertisers and owners; and Jean Kilbourne and Rick Pollay's *A Pack of Lies*, which exposes the tobacco industry's campaign to addict children to nicotine worldwide.[12] Another good source is Media Watch, the producer of *Warning: The Media May Be Hazardous to Your Health*, a documentary about how toys, pornography, beauty pageants, and TV ads affect us, and *Don't Be a TV: Televison Victim*, which won the Silver Apple Award at the National Educational Video and Film Festival.[13]

of old women as witches in children's cartoons and fairy tales. This, too, is important in helping children realize that much of what is on television does not reflect reality—that they need to be more aware and watch more critically.

A good project for creative writing and media classes in grade school and high school is inviting children to analyze some of the violent videos, books, and toys now on the market and brainstorm nonviolent and creative stories and activities that could be developed instead. Children could also be encouraged to participate in boycotts of companies that have profiteered at the expense of our children and our society, making billions from these toxic products—for example, Pizza Hut, Random House, and Nabisco, which profited from publicity, toys, and books deriving from *Teenage Mutant Ninja Turtles* and its sequel, appropriately named *The Secret of the Ooze;* and Burger King, which markets products derived from *Small Soldiers.*

A short, vividly written article for both teachers and older students is Gerbner's "The Turtles Live to Ooze Again," in which the author analyzes *Teenage Mutant Ninja Turtles* and *The Secret of the Ooze.* Each film features an average of 130 acts of mayhem per hour. As Gerbner writes, in these films—aimed expressly at children—"males fight, torture, gorge themselves on pizza (brand names prominently displayed), burn, crush, mutilate and kill" while "one lone mini-miniskirted sex object (intrepid reporter bossed by boorish editor) is assaulted, scared, victimized, and rescued at least three times," until "finally, she too, kills and earns an appreciative, 'you're a natural, sis.'" Ironically, Gerbner notes, the producers of all this choreographed brutality, Mirage Studios, announced that an unspecified percentage from the Turtles II video was to be donated to an obscure environmental organization called Kids for Saving the Earth, at the same time that the environment most vital to our humanity—our cultural environment—is purveying the most toxic messages, polluting children's minds with the brutal notion that barbaric violence is not only manly but fun.[14]

Another excellent project is inviting grade school and high school students to conduct their own television surveys by counting the number of women and men (and girls and boys) they see in each program. This both encourages critical viewing and helps kids see for themselves just how skewed television "reality" is. They can also be asked to count the number of African-American and Latino characters, and, in all cases, to note the kinds of roles such characters are playing. The results of these surveys, along with papers from students telling of their reactions, should be sent to the One-for-One Project of the Cultural Environment Movement. Letters should also be sent to television network executives asking for more representative, fair, and realistic programming.[15]

Since many of the roles assigned to men involve the use of violence, a shift toward gender balance would result in less television violence over the long term. At first, as is already happening, there would be an increase in violent roles for girls and women. But gradually, as the ratio of women and men characters becomes what it should be—reflecting the real-life ratio of one to one—more stereotypically feminine activities, such as caring for children, doing volunteer work, and supporting peace and social reform, would receive more media space.

The templates of the partnership and dominator models are, as we have seen, effective tools for looking at literature and art. In the same way, they are useful for looking at popular culture. For example, Nina Simon has used the partnership and dominator heroes and heroines section in *The Partnership Way* in her middle school and high school classes, and students have found it not only useful but fun, as illustrated by the paper written by one of her students (a boy) in Appendix A.

It is essential that young people become involved in changing media programming—both indirectly, by working with groups dedicated to this goal, and directly, by learning to script and produce their own programs. Here the Internet offers a ready opportunity. Websites are inexpensive, and local servers will sometimes donate a website to a subscriber if it involves a not-for-profit educational activity. Students in art, media, computer, literature, and public affairs classes can work in teams to produce these sites. Some 'zines (webmagazines) have already been produced by young people dedicated to questioning dominator values and propagating sounder ones on the Web. There is room for many more.

Our Bodies

Schools have a responsibility to help students become aware of harmful cultural messages about women's and men's bodies.

Children need information and guidance to understand how their bodies function and change.

The analytical lens of the partnership-dominator continuum is useful in helping young people develop healthier attitudes about their own and others' bodies.

Girls in particular need support during their transition into puberty, and both boys and girls need more accurate information about the influence of hormones, including testosterone, on their feelings and behavior.

Young people need to develop an understanding of how environmental pollution affects their bodies and minds.

Helping young people develop a healthy body awareness will help them develop healthy habits of living.

As we grow up, we become more and more conscious of our bodies—especially of the many changes that happen within them as we move from childhood to adolescence. But our culture, including our school system, offers little help with this important transition.

Our mass media bombard us with commercial messages telling us what our bodies should, and should not, look like. Although some of these media messages are useful (as in stories about the damage caused by cigarettes and junk foods), many are extremely damaging.

For example, the mass media (particularly magazines, stories, and programs aimed at girls and women) tend to present unrealistic images of the female body that make most women feel inadequate, dissatisfied, and even ashamed of their bodies. Many models and actresses have attained these shapes by starving themselves (often becoming bulimic or anorexic) or by undergoing surgical procedures. Clearly, women's bodies are constantly being used as tools to sell everything from cars and vacations to soft drinks and liquor.

Just as damaging is the message conveyed by many women's magazines that girls and women must incessantly make over their bodies, expending all their time, money, and energy on new makeup, clothes, diets, and so on. This message undermines the self-esteem of girls and women. It also robs them of the time, money, and energy they need to plan their lives, develop their talents, and learn useful skills.

Moreover, images of emaciated, sexually available women in the media create unrealistic and damaging expectations in boys, who all too often act on these expectations through their treatment of girls and women. Indeed, as Jean Kilbourne's excellent video *Still Killing Us Softly III* documents, these images—along with ads in fashion magazines of frail, often frightened, helpless-looking young women (sometimes in poses suggesting that they have been struck)—subtly condone violence against women and even glamorize it.[16]

Boys and men, too, are increasingly being subjected to media tyranny. Boys whose bodies to do not fit the "jock" or "hard-body" ideal also suffer from feelings of inadequacy, shame, and sexual self-doubt.

In addition, most of what we are shown in the U.S. media glamorizes light-skinned faces and bodies, idealizing people who are blonde and have thin noses and long shiny hair. By setting up unattainable images of beauty, these valuations communicate to dark-skinned children that their bodies do not measure up, that there is something not quite right about them.

Charmaine, an African-American girl, had for some time been using commercial bleaching creams to lighten her skin, and Wei-Lin had been reading plastic-surgery ads, considering having her eyes unslanted to fit European images of beauty. But when their high school social studies teacher invited the class to look at ads for such products from the perspective of the dominator and partnership models, Charmaine and Wei-Lin had an opportunity to rethink these matters. The class discussed how the real issue is either valuing diversity or looking at difference in terms of superior/inferior rankings. As students in the class began to share their stories, the two young women saw patterns. They saw that what they had believed to be their individual defects were actually cultural defects leading to the internalization of racism—and that, since they would never be white, the road to greater self-liking and self-esteem lies not in creams and surgeries but in learning to accept and take pride in their ethnic identities.

Another area where girls and boys need help and guidance from teachers and other educators has to do with the bodily changes they experience as they approach puberty. (This need is especially acute among girls, who experience dramatic and highly visible bodily changes as they mature.) Even though most states mandate health education, puberty and reproduction are generally addressed superficially, and there is little in the curriculum to adequately prepare girls and boys for these changes. One reason is that many adults are still uncomfortable with such matters and have difficulty discussing them with students. Another reason is that anything to do with the body, particularly in relation to sexuality, is still considered by some people an inappropriate subject for discussion by educators—a peculiar notion, given its implication that ignorance is preferable to education.

Girls and boys are entitled to the best available information about hormonal changes relating not only to puberty but also to childbirth and menopause. This information can be integrated with subjects such as biology and physiology—as it would have been all along if the traditional curriculum had not avoided the vital subjects of sex and reproduction and, on top of this, had not treated the male as the norm.

A gender-balanced curriculum includes books written by and about women and girls, such as *Our Bodies, Ourselves*. This excellent book presents the onset of menstruation and other bodily changes in a natural and positive light. Such books help students examine how, and why, we have been taught to consider the normal onset of menstruation as "the curse"—and how this too has undermined girls' self-esteem and, beyond that, engendered shame about a normal bodily process.

Teachers can begin this topic by discussing the fact that, in some rigidly male-dominant societies, menstruating women are regarded as polluting to anyone who comes into contact with them. To this day, in Islamic as well as orthodox Jewish tradition, women must ritually cleanse themselves after their menses. Islamic women are even forbidden to practice the daily ritualized *nammaz* prayer to Allah during their menstrual period, on the grounds that they cannot appear before God in such an impure, unholy condition.

In this cultural context, girls are made to feel that becoming a woman is a calamity—which, indeed, it often is in rigidly male-dominated societies—to the extent that girls are, even now, in some world regions given less food and healthcare than boys.

Teachers can make students aware that in more partnership-oriented societies, by contrast, there are positive rites of passage marking a girl's first menses. In the more partnership-oriented BaMbuti tribe of the African Congo, as anthropologist Colin Turnbull writes, menstruation is viewed as a blessing: the blessing of the moon.[17] (As we saw in Chapter 5, this association of the moon and menstruation in Western culture seems to go back to the Upper Paleolithic, as suggested by the so-called Venus of Laussel.)

Also in contrast to our mainstream culture's lack of positive images for females going through puberty, some indigenous North American cultures, such as the Mescalero Apache, have a sacred puberty ceremony in which the men of the tribe join young women in celebrating their first menses.[18] During each Apache girl's initiation into womanhood, she is ritually transformed into Changing Woman, the mythological founder of Apache culture, which centers its tradition on the connection to Mother Earth.[19]

Students can be invited to discuss the fact that girls today, with support from parents and teachers, are beginning to create new rites of passage that promote positive self-images. Some of these rites are inspired by ancient traditions from many world cultures where women were priestesses and a Goddess was revered. (Materials on this topic can be adapted from *Sacred Pleasure* and *New Moon*, a magazine edited by girls aged eight to fourteen that features stories written for girls by girls.[20]) By presenting the prehistoric partnership-oriented societies outlined in Chapters 4 and 5 as a springboard, teachers can invite girls and boys to consider how the natural experience of menses is treated differently, depending on whether it occurs in a dominator or partnership context. Girls could imagine what it would be like if their first menstruation was celebrated—as among the BaMbuti, whose entire community celebrates a girl's rite of passage to womanhood with songs and festivities.

At the high school level, teachers can also use the following passage from *Sacred Pleasure*:

> Our Paleolithic and early Neolithic ancestors imaged woman's body as a magical vessel. They must have observed how it bleeds in rhythm with the moon and how it miraculously produces people. They must also have marveled that it provides sustenance by making milk for the young. Add to this . . . the extraordinary capacity of woman's body for sexual pleasure—to experience it and to give it—and it is not surprising that our ancestors should have been awed by woman's sexual power.[21]

This passage can be compared, as Lili Baxter has done in her classes at Emory University, with the following passage from Naomi Wolf's *The Beauty Myth:*

> When they discuss [their bodies], women lean forward, their voices lower. They tell their terrible secret. It's my breasts, they say. My hips. My thighs. I hate my stomach. This is not aesthetic distaste, but deep sexual shame. The parts of the body vary . . . breasts, thighs, buttocks, bellies; the most sexually central parts of women. . . . Those are the parts most often battered by men . . . the parts most often defiled by violent pornography . . . the parts that bear and nurse children and feel sexual. A misogynist culture has succeeded in making women hate what misogynists hate.[22]

What happens when students talk about the feelings that are elicited by this comparison? Baxter reports that young women in her classes feel less shame and dissatisfaction about their bodies, and instead begin to feel pride, and with this, more self-esteem.

Another good exercise for high school students can be obtained from Session Three of *The Partnership Way*, entitled "Free Association on Women's and Men's Bodies." Working in groups, girls discuss what it means to become a woman, focusing on the way they feel about their bodies and how female body images are presented to them by the mass media. Boys, also working in groups, discuss their views about the female body and compare these to their views about their own bodies. They can deal not only with feelings but also with questions such as why so much of what we read places great importance on the advantages of the male body (such as greater height and stronger muscles), whereas the advantages of the female body (such as lesser vulnerability to disease, greater endurance, better-protected genitalia, and the creative capacity of the uterus) tend to be overlooked.[23]

Boys and girls also need more accurate information about male hormones. Particularly important is inviting students to examine beliefs versus research about the relation between testosterone and violence. In fact, scientists have only just begun to adequately investigate the role of testosterone in male behavior, and their findings are inconsistent. For instance, one study found that men with low testosterone become *less* violent when they are given more testosterone (see Appendix A for a report on this study that teachers may want to use to stimulate discussion). *Sacred Pleasure* (ch. 12) contains a summary of another study which shows that hormonal arousal translates into different kinds of behaviors, depending on social cues. Still other studies indicate that, in monkeys, testosterone levels fall, or rise, depending on the social context. Here, too, students can be invited to use the partnership and dominator models to discuss the behaviors taught boys through toys such as swords, guns, and Nintendo games, as well as through stories that glamorize violent male heroes.

Moreover, young people urgently need to understand how dominator attitudes and practices are leading to rampant chemical pollution, which is damaging our health. Indeed, pesticides have been implicated as the cause of permanent brain damage that stunts physical and mental development, altering behaviors and disrupting the ability to do just about everything. A study conducted in a farming area of Sonora, Mexico, found poor hand-eye coordination, memory skills, creativity, and physical stamina, plus a greater tendency toward physical aggression and angry outbursts, among preschool children living in an environment of high pesticide use. Another study in rural western Minnesota found increased birth defects in children conceived during the spring growing season, when pesticide use is high.[24]

As Dr. Wayne Porter of the University of Wisconsin puts it, "Data suggest that we may be raising a generation of children with learning disabilities and hyperaggression."[25] Porter's study, published in March 1999, shows that a common mix of insecticide, herbicide, and fertilizer found in drinking water increases aggressive behavior in mice and suppresses their immune system.[26]

Young people are entitled to know about such studies, as well as about information such as the 1999 Consumers Union report indicating that many fruits and vegetables—the very foods needed for healthy bodily development—contain high concentrations of pesticides.[27] This knowledge will enable them to alert their parents and other adults to the need to shift to more partnership-oriented environmental attitudes and practices, such as organic farming and other ways of radically decreasing pesticide use. It will also enable them to become active in protecting their bodies, and their future—a matter I will return to in the final section of this chapter.

Finally, young people need to develop a self-awareness that does not fall into the trap of viewing our bodies as inferior to our minds and spirits. There is an integral connection among the body, mind, and spirit, as shown by recent studies on how healing is a process that involves all these dimensions.[28]

Our bodies are more than flesh; they hold in them our entire emotional and mental history, from conception to the present moment. Listening to our bodies, to what is today sometimes called our body wisdom, entails relearning how we relate to ourselves. If we become more grounded in our bodies (which is difficult in a dominator system where many of us carry a great deal of pain and hence tend to avoid becoming "conscious"), we can begin to move toward greater physical and mental health. Quietly focusing on our bodies—for example, by breathing slowly and observing our breathing—can help us feel not only more at peace but also more empowered to actualize our plans and realize our potentials. And of course body wisdom is critical for life-long health, as well as for establishing habits that are basic to the larger human task so urgent today: the task of caring for life, both that of humans and of other life forms on our planet.

This honoring of our bodies—as a child might say, being buddies with our bodies—does not mean giving in to every impulse (a subject I will return to in the section on life planning and self-regulation). On the contrary, once we learn to live in greater partnership with our bodies and access their innate vitality, we become more able to relate in partnership to others and to work for a partnership society. (See Appendix A for an article by Patricia Mathes Cane in which the author details some techniques she has successfully used with both children and adults toward these ends.)

Love and Relationships

By becoming aware of their own feelings and the feelings of others, and by understanding how stereotypical gender socialization gets in the way of fulfilling relations, students can enrich their lives.

By using the analytical lens of the partnership-dominator continuum, young people can more effectively sort through conflicting cultural messages about love.

Schools can reinforce healthy and respectful attitudes in young peoples' love relationships.

Like all of us, young people are interested in love—and, particularly after the onset of puberty, in romantic love. But many of the most popular love stories and songs provide a distorted picture of love—for example, by associating "great love" with tragic outcomes, as in the legendary tales of Tristan and Isolde and Romeo and Juliet.

Not only that, the traditional socialization of boys, passed on by peer groups from generation to generation, continues to teach preadolescent boys to look on love as sappy, sissy, something for girls, not boys. It pressures boys to look down on girls as inferior beings to be shunned and excluded until it is time for boys to sally forth and sexually "conquer" them.

The exclusion of girls from preadolescent boys' peer groups—which mirrors the exclusive male clubs that in dominator societies are a way of maintaining economic and political power in the hands of men—perpetuates sexism and gender discrimination. It inhibits boys' natural interest in, and curiosity about, the female half of humanity. It also tends to retard boys' learning of relational skills, which later causes distress to both women and men in relationships.

This is not healthy for either boys or girls, and needs to be brought out into the open. Of course, boys, and girls, should be able to form separate groups. The issue is the culture of these groups.

A related matter is that girls not only tend to reach puberty earlier than boys; they are culturally encouraged to be interested in boys much earlier. Today even little girls are encouraged by ads and media to dress in sexually provocative ways. (Beauty pageants start them on this track at only a few years old.) Not surprisingly, by the time girls reach their early teens, many are intensely preoccupied with being liked by boys, having already internalized the message that this is to be the most important goal of their lives.

Again, there is nothing wrong with focusing on relationships or wanting to please others. But, as Jean Baker Miller highlights in her classic *Toward a New Psychology for Women*,[29] girls are socialized to focus their attention on pleasing others (particularly boys) to the extent that they often have great difficulty even identifying what they want. This damages girls' sense of self-confidence and self-esteem and stunts their developing capacity for independently planning their lives.

By the same token, it is damaging to boys to be taught to devalue relationships (as well as girls), and to expect girls to cater to them and support their goals in unequal relations. When boys learn to devalue love as effeminate, and girls learn to invest themselves completely in relations to the exclusion of pursuing their own independent goals, they enter relations with expectations that are very different from men's—expectations that men cannot understand, much less meet. This has negative repercussions for both women and men, leading to endless misunderstandings and misery.

Students can be invited to look at these problems through the analytical lens of the partnership-dominator continuum. This makes it possible to see that many of the problems girls and boys (and women and men) have in relations are socially constructed through this imbalanced "masculine" and "feminine" socialization—and hence can be avoided.

The fact that this issue is increasingly being recognized shows that positive changes have occurred. But there is still a long way to go. For example, both girls and boys need to learn how to recognize that most of what we read about love between women and men in fairy tales (e.g., Sleeping Beauty and the prince who wakes her) and popular romances (e.g., the "bodice ripper" paperbacks targeted to women in supermarkets) model *in*equality and foster passivity and rescue fantasies (learned helplessness) in girls. Moreover, students need to become more aware that what the mass media teaches about love is at best shallow, and all too often harmful. Consider, for example, the constant modeling of instant love (and, often, instant sex) in movies and television.

How to have good relations is rarely modeled in our mass media. On the contrary, violence is glamorized in "action shows," and most "sitcoms" present hurting and humiliating people as funny. This not only models how to have bad relations, but also desensitizes viewers to the pain of others. Indeed, insensitivity and lack of empathy are often made to seem "cool."

As noted in the last chapter, many of our literary classics do no better. So once again, schools have an obligation to show young people that insensitivity and cruelty are not cool, that caring and empathy are not unmanly, that meanness is not natural, and that we can learn to have healthy and fulfilling relationships.

Talking about relationships also offers an opportunity to explore with students why, when this is an area of such importance in our lives, relationships are not part of the academic curriculum—especially today, when we have access to a great body of literature on the subject of what makes for healthy and fulfilling relations drawing from psychological and sociological research. Why is coursework offering guidelines in family and intimate relations not included in academic work as a discipline equally valid and important as other disciplines?

Other questions, too, can stimulate student thinking and discussion. Given that the relations between parents and children—particularly during the formative early years—so profoundly impact our lives and our society, why are courses on parenting literacy and competency not part of the school curriculum? Why haven't schools taught us to look at the interconnection between the so-called public and private spheres of life? And how can learning skills for partnership relations in the private sphere help us not only lead more satisfying lives but also move toward a partnership world? (See Box 6.2.)

BOX 6.2   Good Relations

Students' enormous interest in relationships is dramatically illustrated in Nancy Ruben's engaging book *Ask Me If I Care: Voices from an American High School*.[30] The author credit on the book cover reads "By Nancy Ruben and a Cast of Hundreds" because the book speaks through the voices of high school girls and boys from all social and economic groups. Full of information for young people, it focuses on such themes as sexuality, racial identity, alcohol, tobacco, and drugs. This book is a resource that teachers and students can use to talk about young people's lives, hopes, fears, and, as Ruben repeatedly emphasizes, the choices before them.

Another excellent resource is Alfonso Montuori and Isabella Conti's *From Power to Partnership: Creating the Future of Love, Work, and Community*,[31] a book that offers a good overview of the application of partnership principles to self, relationships, work, community, and ecology.

Guidelines for the teaching of relational literacy and competency can be found in booklets and other publications from the Center for Research on Women, which provides sound information on subjects ranging from family relationships and self-esteem to sexual harassment, employment,

(continues)

BOX 6.1 *(continued)*

and diversity.[32] Another source that I consider a must for teachers is *Rethinking Our Classrooms: Teaching for Equity and Justice*.[33] Edited by a team of teachers, this book contains provocative, well-written articles such as Linda Christianson's "Unlearning the Myths That Bind Us" (which discusses the need to reexamine our literature and media), Nan Stein and Lisa Sjostron's "Flirting Versus Sexual Harassment: Teaching the Difference," Bill Bigelow and Linda Christianson's "Videos with a Conscience," and Bob Peterson's "Coping with T.V." Two additional resources were noted earlier: the girl's magazine *New Moon* and Jean Kilbourne's video *Still Killing Us Softly III*.[34] Teachers can also consult the books and articles by Nel Noddings that deal with education informed by themes of caring, as well as Ron Miller's *What Are Schools For?*, Jeffrey Kane's *Education, Information, and Transformation*, and, for a vision of a more caring society, Michael Lerner's *The Politics of Meaning*.[35]

Another good resource is *The Partnership Way*, which offers discussion questions dealing with relationships. For example, in Session Two there is a section designed to help students explore their own experiences and feelings, as well as the advantages and disadvantages of partnership and dominator relations.[36] For young children, as well as teenagers, there is a website called "Bearable Times Kids & Teens Club: Kids Helping Kids Through Love, Support, & Understanding," located at <www.bearabletimes.org>. It includes a page on Kids Who Are Different, such as children with disabilities and children suffering from critical illnesses, as well as a listing of opportunities for volunteering, an important experience for children in that it develops not only empathy but habits of caring for others that are essential for good relationships (a subject to which I will return).

Helping children develop their capacity for empathy can be furthered through stories and movies showing how this benefits both those who are helped and those who help. For example, in the *Wizard of Oz*, the Tin Man, the Scarecrow, and the Lion all benefit from helping Dorothy. Children can also learn empathic behaviors by visiting retirement homes, which offer the opportunity not only to forge intergenerational relationships but also to gather oral histories from people whose life experiences can enrich their lives.

I want to include one more resource on relationships: relationships with animals. Monty Roberts's *The Man Who Listens to Horses*[37] is a true story of how partnership relations can apply to other species. Roberts has studied horses almost his whole life. But instead of "breaking" horses, he "starts" them. Astonishingly, working with a wild horse, he can "start" the animal in about thirty minutes, without whips, fear, or violence. By contrast, "breaking" a horse takes weeks—and models dominator rather than partnership relations. Mistreated horses, as Roberts observes, never lose their fear or dislike of humans.

Little girl and boy walking. CREDIT: *John Mason.*

Grandfather and grandson. CREDIT: *David Loye.*

Sexuality

Failure to educate young people about sexuality does not reduce sexual activity, but deprives them of information they need to make informed and responsible sexual decisions.

A sexual ethic of respect for the bodies of others as well as for our own should be part of sex education.

We can counter the vulgarized and depersonalized portrayal of sex in much of popular culture by teaching young people about the evolution of sex and love as part of human spiritual development.

Paradoxically, at a time when sex is a constant theme in popular culture—from morning talk shows to the evening news—the extent of ignorance about sexuality in the United States is staggering. In 1990, the Kinsey Institute published the results of what it termed a "sexual literacy test" given to a large sample of Americans. The majority, as institute director June Reinish put it, flunked. They correctly answered only half or fewer of the questions.

Young adults scored somewhat higher, with 55 percent of women and 52 percent of men correctly answering more than half the questions.[38] But even here, as a Harris Poll of teenagers dramatically illustrates, a large percentage lack even the most rudimentary sexual knowledge. For instance, the Harris Poll found that some teens believe a girl cannot become pregnant the first time she has intercourse. Others believe a woman can get pregnant only if she has intercourse lying flat on her back. Still others are under the impression that to get pregnant a woman has to have an orgasm.[39]

Obviously, such mistaken beliefs play a large part in the high U.S. teen pregnancy rate. Nonetheless, there are still those who would like to forbid schools from teaching young people anything about sex except that they should abstain from it.

Young people certainly need to learn to resist peer and media pressure to have "instant sex." They need to learn to postpone sexual relations and to understand the dangers of sexually transmitted diseases. They need to know about the emotional consequences of casual sex, and about the fact that caring is integral to long-term satisfaction, both physically and emotionally. But young people are also entitled to information about how to prevent the sexual transmission of AIDS—through the proper use of condoms and other forms of contraception as well as through the use of HIV tests before they have sex. (Without support from parents and teachers, young people often have a hard time discussing these subjects with their romantic partners.)

The teen pregnancy rate in the United States is more than twice as high as in other industrialized nations with comparable rates of teen sexual activity. The difference—and it is a dramatic difference—is that in other industrialized countries adults teach young people about contraception and contraceptives are accessible.[40]

It is noteworthy that a 1997 study reported in the *American Journal of Public Health* concluded that, contrary to the fears of some parents and religious groups, programs that make condoms available in public schools do *not* result in teens having more sex. Researchers compared more than 7,000 students from twelve randomly selected New York City schools to approximately 6,000 students from ten comparable schools in Chicago. The only significant difference between the two groups was that condoms are available in New York to students who request them. The study revealed that, although the teens in New York City used condoms more often, their level of sexual activity was nearly identical to that of their peers in Chicago.[41]

American girls are often pressured (by boys, their peer groups, and media messages) to have sex practically on demand. Sometimes a girl will have sex because she wants to please a boy, hoping he really means it if he says he loves her. Other times, girls (and women) are afraid to say no, or even to demand safe sex. A wrenching book on this topic is *Romance to Die For: The Startling Truth About Women, Sex, and AIDS.*[42]

In Linda's health class, this life-and-death issue was brought home when her teacher asked two young women to speak about how they had contracted AIDS. One was a girl from a well-to-do family; the other was a prelaw college student. They both knew better; but their low self-esteem, and their desire to please boys so that they would be loved by them, got in the way. Neither girl wanted to be tested, because of the shame involved, so they did not find out they had been infected by the HIV virus until symptoms such as eczema and weight loss began to appear. Now they are struggling to live, constantly on medication, and committed to helping other girls *not* follow in their path. After this talk, the class discussion became much more honest, as Linda and her classmates realized not only how false the stereotype of AIDS-infected people is but also how close to home the threat of AIDS is. Later, Laura and her friends began talking about sex in a different way, supporting one another either in abstinence or in making sure that their sexual relations were safe and responsible.

All too often girls are devastated by their first sexual experiences. They are left with, at best, a bad start for later sex and, at worst, an unplanned pregnancy or a sexually transmitted disease. Even when girls clearly say "no," their refusals are often disregarded—as evidenced by the prevalence of acquaintance and date rapes.

Again, these are issues that young people need to talk openly about in a safe and supportive environment. Here they can explore the partnership sexual ethic of respect and consideration for the bodies of others as well as their own. And they can contrast this ethic with the dominator morality that is our legacy from cultures in which men were legally entitled to control women, particularly women's sexuality.

Such discussion encourages what social psychologist David Loye calls partnership moral sensitivity, as opposed to dominator moral insensitivity.[43] As an illustration, consider the biblical stories of men who had sex with many women; King Solomon, for example, possessed a large harem, with no hint of censure for this. Not only that, there are stories in the Bible of how fathers give their daughters—probably still children, as girls were sold into marriage very early in those days—to mobs to be raped. But again, there is no hint of censure for this hideously immoral behavior, as in the famous story of how Lot was actually rewarded for doing this to his little daughters when only he was saved when the "sinful" cities of Sodom and Gomorrah were destroyed. (This is discussed in *The Chalice and the Blade* and *Sacred Pleasure*, where I address the need for a new ethic and morality for intimate relations based on partnership rather than domination.)

The partnership ethic of respect for one's own body and the bodies of others can also be applied to the controversial issue of sexual diversity (see Box 6.3). Some people are homosexual or bisexual rather than heterosexual, and this diversity is found in cultures worldwide. The question that students can be invited to discuss is how this diversity should be viewed. Should people be condemned and vilified because they are not heterosexual—or should this difference be accepted as a human variation that deserves respect?

The need for discussing and understanding these issues is urgent, since words like *faggot* or *fag* are often used by children to shame others, reflecting a demonizing cultural climate toward nonheterosexual people. One can only imagine the destructive effects of this humiliation on the developing sexual and relational self-images of boys and girls who do not fit the heterosexual norm.

In some cultures, gays and lesbians were shamans—highly honored members of the community.[44] Other positive lesbian and gay role models include Congressmen Barney Frank and Steve Gunderson; singers k.d. lang, Melissa Ethridge, and Holly Near; comediennes Lily Tomlin and Ellen DeGeneres; and writers Andrea Dworkin and Audre Lorde.

Because partnership is inclusive, it is important not to ignore this issue—as controversial as it may be. After all, the idea of racial equality was once as explosive as homosexuality is now, and gender equality is still controversial. Family planning, too, is still controversial, even though it is integral not only to young peoples' individual futures but to the future of our planet. To avoid or play down the importance of such issues is to perpetuate the divisive tactics of dominator backlash, as Suzanne Pharr makes clear in *Homophobia: A Weapon of Sexism.*[45]

Not only attitudes toward homosexuality but also those toward heterosexuality are culturally molded—and this process is different depending on whether it follows a dominator or partnership model. In periods orienting strongly to the dominator model, sex is for men severed from love and intimacy. (As we saw in Chapter 5, this is illustrated in the *Iliad* by the fight between Achilles and Agamemnon over the young girl Briseis—who is viewed as a mere possession.) Even today, sex is often associated with domination and violence rather than with mutual pleasure. This is true not only in pornography but, more generally, in popular culture—from music videos to some of the brutal rap lyrics that millions of young people are exposed to every day.

Another legacy from earlier, more dominator-oriented times is the sexual double standard, whereby men and boys are expected to "score"—that is, to tally as many sexual "conquests" as possible—yet girls and women are expected to be one man's exclusive sexual property. This double standard was rejected by Jesus when he stopped the stoning of an "immoral" woman. He also preached against divorce, which, in his time, was the exclusive prerogative of men: Not only were they permitted to have several wives, but they could discard a no-longer-wanted wife by simply repeating "I divorce you" three times—as is still legal in some Mideastern Muslim nations today. In other words, what Jesus preached against was not divorce itself but men's immoral treatment of their wives under a double standard that gave men all the power.

The inhumanity of this sexual double standard is something young people need to look at, with adult help.[48] This is particularly important since much in our culture still teaches us that we should accept a sexual

---

BOX 6.3   Attitudes Toward Homosexuality

Chuck Stewart's *Sexually Stigmatized Communities* is a good awareness training manual. Another good resource is *Growing Up Gay/Growing Up Lesbian*, edited by Bennett L. Singer. This literary anthology explores areas such as family, relationships, identity, and facing the rest of the world that can be worthwhile reading for both homosexual and heterosexual young people.[46] Still another resource is Lenore Gordon's "What Do We Say When We Hear 'Faggot'?" which can be found in *Rethinking Our Classrooms*.[47]

There are also websites for organizations such as the Gay, Lesbian, and Straight Education Network at <www.glstn.org> and the P.E.R.S.O.N. (Public Education Regarding Sexual Orientation Nationally) Project at <www.youth.org/loco/personproject/>. And for curriculum materials on gay and lesbian issues, teachers can consult <www.bostonpheonix.com/alt1/archive/1in10/03–96/SCHOOLS_SB.htm>, which features an article by Liza Featherstone titled "Looking for Decent Material."

---

double standard as normal and natural—as rooted in nature—even though it clearly is *not*. Indeed, in most species, *both* males and females either are monogamous or have sex with multiple partners.

Here, too, the partnership-dominator continuum is a useful analytical tool, since a rigid sexual double standard—along with rigid male control over women's sexuality, both individually and collectively—is characteristically seen in cultures that orient closely to the dominator model. For example, the brutally violent and authoritarian Muslim fundamentalist Taliban of Afghanistan have decreed that girls may not go to school and that women may not work outside their homes—ostensibly to prevent them from sexually arousing men by their presence, but in reality to ensure that women cannot escape total dependency on, and control by, men. Among the Taliban, women who do not cover themselves from head to foot are flogged and even killed. Not only that, women have effectively been denied healthcare (even women with severe burns) because female doctors, like other women, are not allowed to work outside their homes. All this on the grounds of "morality"—or as Mr. Qalamuddin, head of the General Department for the Preservation of Virtue and Prevention of Vice (the Taliban religious police), put it in the *New York Times*, because men are deeply vulnerable to sin through unregulated contacts with women.[49] Of course, if this *were* so, boys and men would have to be strictly controlled. But the Taliban, like the Christian witch hunters in the European Middle Ages, blame women for "tempting" and "corrupting" men.

Even now, in much of our culture, women's and men's sexual behaviors are judged very differently, as evidenced by the fact that men's beatings and even murders of women they believe to be having sex with someone else are often presented as crimes of passion or love. These views are deeply embedded. In Shakespeare's famous play *Othello*, the implication is that his strangling of Desdemona would have been justified had she actually been having an affair with another man. And there are still some people today who would justify O. J. Simpson's beatings—and possible murder—of his wife Nicole Brown on the grounds that, as one woman said to me, she was a "slut" (her way of describing a woman who had sexual relations with more than one man). Yet men who have sex with many women are still often admired and even glamorized—as was Wilt Chamberlain, when he bragged to his peers and the general public about his 25,000 "sexual conquests."

Students also need the opportunity to talk openly about the conflicting messages to teenage girls in our culture: that they must be sexually desirable to boys while at the same time they must not have sexual desires themselves. Of course, girls do have sexual desires. Puberty brings a flood of raging hormones to girls as well as boys. It is essential, therefore, that girls be able to acknowledge their sexual feelings rather than pretending that they have none. When girls are able to acknowledge their own sexuality, they are able to make more conscious choices about sex.

Teachers can also invite students to discuss the constant depiction of sexuality on television with hardly ever any conversation about the prevention of pregnancy through contraception or the responsibilities of parenthood if a child is born. Young people, particularly girls, sometimes have romanticized expectations that if they have a baby, they will finally have someone who loves them, with little knowledge of the skills, time, and work entailed in caring for a baby. This is one reason that parenting education needs to be part of the school curriculum, not simply as an optional add-on but as integral to the curriculum.

In addition, sex education should provide young people with information about earlier traditions (discussed in Chapter 4) in which sexuality was considered sacred. For example, teachers can pose the question of why the nude human body and sex are included in the category of the obscene—when we all have bodies and sexual drives. They can also invite students to examine the consequences of the view that sex is "dirty" and explore how we would look at our bodies and those of others as we heal the unhealthy rift between the carnal and the spiritual.

The spiritual component of sexuality is a good springboard to the subject of sexual love. As we saw in Chapter 3, the human need for love is rooted in our biology. Among babies, it is expressed in the profound need for caring touch, as evidenced by the failure to thrive, and even death, of babies in orphanages whose physical needs are met in a rote and depersonalized way.[50] And although adults do not physically die without love, the psychiatric literature shows that lack of love can lead to psychic death, to an inner numbness that masks pain but all too often leads to destructive, even murderous or suicidal acts.

All humans—both male and female—have this deep need for love and intimacy. Human sexuality is thus a means not only of reproducing our species but also of giving and receiving pleasure through intimate touch. When that intimate touch is also caring touch, when it expresses real love (not the sexual possessiveness and control that in dominator cultures is sometimes called love) and the human need to love and be loved is met, our powerful human yearning for connection—for oneness with each other and with what we call the divine—is also met.

This human need for love, for oneness, for deep caring connection, is a universal spiritual need. But it cannot be met when another human being is dehumanized as a mere sexual object, as women are in so many images in our culture. In short, neither men nor women get what they need in dominator relations. (See *Sacred Pleasure* for additional material on these topics.)

Self-Regulation and Life-Planning

Self-regulation entails learning goal-setting and empathy, and understanding that actions have consequences.

Helping children focus on short- and long-term goal-setting rather than on immediate gratification, and on empathy rather than fear, is a more effective and positive pedagogy.

Caring and caregiving are keys to self-regulation.

How do we deal with our impulses? This is an important issue for young people from early childhood on. I prefer the term *self-regulation* over *self-discipline* or *self-control* because the latter terms have so long been associated with fear and obedience to arbitrary rules and orders. Teaching self-regulation is different from teaching children to do what they are told by shaming them and frightening them with the threat that if they don't obey they will be punished.

Of course, children do need to understand that undesirable behaviors have consequences, and they should be taught this as soon as they have the capacity for such understanding (babies and toddlers do not yet connect events in this way). So if a child is hitting another child, she or he needs help in learning more effective ways of expressing feelings. But the aim is not to make the child feel bad; it is to interrupt the undesirable behavior and show the child that it is not acceptable. In the long term, the most effective way of teaching is through positive rather than negative reinforcements that instill in children a sense of pride and well-being for their relational skills, at the same time that they cultivate empathic feelings as well as the skills and habits of self-regulation.

The development of these skills and habits is important for a truly democratic rather than authoritarian society. By focusing on caring for self and others, rather than control of self and others, children learn behaviors that are appropriate for partnership rather than dominator relations—whether intimate or international.

The skills and habits of self-regulation are also essential if young people are to plan their lives in terms of positive, rather than negative, motivations. Consider the area of sexuality, for instance. The conventional approach has been to teach children to associate sex with fear and guilt—by punishing even toddlers for the natural act of touching their genitals or by telling girls they are "sluts" if they "let" a boy touch them. By contrast, helping children postpone instant gratification in favor of short- and long-term goals that they have learned to set for themselves, links sex primarily with positive associations. At the same time, it cultivates habits of thinking and acting that will serve children well in their adult lives.[51]

Goal-oriented self-regulation shifts the learning emphasis from suppression and control to development and actualization. For example, if children are taught that they should not hit other children because if they do they will be hit by a parent or teacher, they are taught that violence inflicted by a "superior" upon an "inferior" is acceptable—and that they need only grow up to be able to get away with it. Not only violence is modeled, but also the suppression of empathy, since causing someone pain requires stunting the human capacity for empathy—a key component of moral sensitivity. There are times when one has to use some force to physically restrain a child, as when a child is about to run into traffic. But new research indicates that violence against children is not only cruel but an ineffective discipline.[52]

Unfortunately, people who, in their families and schools, are taught to rely on external control and fear of punishment (whether on this earth or in a hereafter), rather than on empathy and self-regulation, tend to require a social structure that uses fear or force to control the violent impulses we all sometimes experience. This in turn reinforces rigid rankings of domination, helping to replicate hurtful dominator patterns of relations in all spheres of life.

By contrast, in societies that orient more to the partnership side of the continuum, the emphasis is on motivations for helpful behaviors— through intrinsic reinforcements such as the feelings of well-being and pleasure we experience when we are empathic and care for others.

This is why I am proposing that education in the 21st century include the experiential teaching and learning of caring and caregiving. I call this important curriculum thread "Caring for Life." I believe it should run through all of education: from preschool to graduate school.

We have already seen the importance of curriculum materials that present empathy and caring as "natural"—that is, rooted in our biological evolution—and acknowledge that our species receives physically and psychologically pleasurable biological rewards for caring and caregiving. But the "Caring for Life" curriculum thread I am proposing here goes much further, offering children the opportunity to experience this pleasure for themselves.

I am convinced that peace education can be achieved only if, as Maria Montessori, Nel Noddings, and other educational pioneers have proposed, caring and caregiving are integral to education from early childhood on. As Montessori wrote in *Education for a New World*, during the first years of life the child almost literally absorbs everything in her or his environment. Anticipating the findings of today's neuroscientists, Montessori also argued that any form of violence, in speech or action, does irreparable harm to the child.[53]

Certainly parenting classes for adults are important. But the adults who need them the most are often the least likely to take them. So this schooling has to start much earlier, not only through partnership process (which makes it possible for all children to experience real one-to-one caring from their teachers) but also through the opportunity to experience the giving of caring themselves. This experiential learning of caring and caregiving behaviors as part of the school curriculum is important for all children, but it is essential for neglected and abused children as well as for children who, in their homes, have learned to associate caring with fear, coercion, and violence.

It is of course important not to incite children to blame their parents (who are usually only repeating what they themselves learned as children), much less to imply that children can change their parents' behaviors. But children can—and should—be given the opportunity to experience the joy that comes from caring and caregiving as a way of helping them acquire different attitudes and habits for their own lives.

These experiences are basic to learning to care for self and others. Not only that, they are a springboard for habits leading to life-long pleasurable relationships, both with others and with our natural environment. Equally important, they help us fulfill our human yearning for connection—for deep involvement not only with other forms of life (human and nonhuman) but also with ideas, with work, with art, with music, with all that can give meaning and purpose to our lives.

As Nel Noddings writes in *The Challenge to Care in Schools*, "Education can best be organized around centers of care: care for self, for intimate others, for associates and acquaintances, for distant others, for nonhuman animals, for plants and the physical environment, for the human-made world of objects and instruments, and for ideas."[54] But as she also points out, an education that focuses on caring as well as academic competence is possible only in a gender-balanced educational system.

She writes, "Our society values activities traditionally associated with men above those traditionally associated with women," including the socially essential caring and caregiving activities that are still generally viewed as women's work. As a result, there is much concern about women's participation in mathematics and science, fields long dominated by men; yet people "do not seem to see a problem in men's lack of participation in nursing, elementary school teaching, or full-time parenting."[55]

Since partnership education is gender-balanced, activities that involve competence in caring and caregiving *can* be integrated into the core curriculum. And by integrated I do not mean just an occasional add-on, such as teaching emotional literacy in early grades and the introduction of service learning units. What I am proposing is that caring for self, others, and nature be a primary curriculum thread that is interwoven into the entire educational fabric.

This integration of "Caring for Life" into the educational fabric from preschool to graduate school can begin with something as simple as the opportunity to learn to care for plants and animals, which today is offered children in some elementary schools. Caring for animals not only helps children acquire habits of caregiving; it also helps them develop a healthy sense of self that is both distinct from and connected with others—organically leading to a morality of respect and support for other beings. As Gene Myers writes in *Children & Animals*, "Embodied interaction is at the root of the self, moral feeling, and other mental phenomena." Hence caring interactions with animals can help children develop a morality that is not externally imposed but, to borrow Myers' phrase, "implicit in the sense of connection the children feel to the animals."[56]

In other words, caring and caregiving support and help us develop our innate human capacity for feeling with others. As we saw earlier, studies show that babies are born with this capacity: Newborns cry when they hear the sound of other babies crying. It is on this basis of empathy that self-regulation of hurtful impulses, and even beyond this, real love, can be built.

Practicing caring and caregiving helps meet our human needs for meaning, for spiritual awareness, for larger purpose. The deeply embedded human yearning for connection that is the evolutionary mainspring for love is also the evolutionary mainspring for spirituality—for the sense of awe and wonder that comes from the intuitive understanding that we are not isolated blips on the evolutionary screen, that we are in a mysterious, and truly miraculous, way actively interconnected with all that is, was, and can be.

Most immediately, an education that integrates learning to care for self, others, and nature as a major curriculum thread is basic to emotional, physical, and mental health. It is basic to finding someone to love and be loved by, to caring and fulfilling relations with families and friends, to the construction of supportive communities and a peaceful, just, and environmentally sound world. I consider this kind of education essential for the ethical and spiritual development necessary for a more just, democratic, and peaceful world.

"Caring for Life"—information, insights, and skills young people need to care for self, others, and nature—is integral to the curricula and learning processes being developed by the Center for Partnership Studies' "Weaving the Future" educational programs. For example, the multidisciplinary systems class spanning biological and cultural history that CPS is developing in collaboration with the Nova High School in Seattle, Washington, includes not only information about stages of child development but also a partnership with a preschool where older students can help care for children. This one-year course educates students about essential aspects of human biological development that are not part of the standard biology curriculum, including the critical fact that the human brain's neural pathways are to a large extent laid *after* birth and, hence, largely determined by the quality of a child's care. The course also highlights a matter we looked at in Chapter 3: the evolution of love as rooted in our biology.

And, of course, this and other CPS collaborations with schools and universities help young people learn how to use the analytical lenses of the partnership and dominator models to sort the often contradictory cultural messages about what is moral and ethical. This enables them to make informed and conscious choices that can guide them all their lives. Some of these choices entail nonviolent conflict resolution, which is the subject of Box 6.4.

BOX 6.4 Nonviolent Conflict Resolution

The argument has sometimes been made that the way order is maintained in some species is through rankings of domination in which the "alpha male" uses violence and the threat of violence not only to maintain his position but also to prevent the occurrence of violence among other members of the group. This is the "law and order" argument still made by people who believe that only "strong man" leaders can maintain order—as is appropriate for a dominator society. But a society that integrates into the socialization of both boys and girls the teaching of empathically and goal-oriented self-regulation skills can maintain order through different means. The latter approach avoids, or at least drastically reduces, the constant bloodshed and suffering caused by wars and other forms of violence.

This distinction between a learning emphasis on suppression and control and a learning emphasis on development and actualization lays the groundwork for discussing with students some of the material on biological and cultural evolution contained in Chapters 3 and 4. It also raises the question of whether nonviolent conflict resolution may be a more evolutionarily advanced method of dealing with conflict than the violent tactics of warfare and other kinds of violence (such as "domestic violence") to suppress conflict and control others.

An important component of education for self-regulation is teaching children the literacies and competences detailed in my book *Redefining Destiny*, which include skills for nonviolent conflict resolution. There are many materials for this purpose designed specifically for children (see Box 6.5).

Our Living Planet

Young people need up-to-date information about the web of life that is our natural habitat.

Schools have a responsibility to educate students about the importance of environmental caregiving.

The analytical lens of the partnership-dominator continuum is useful in helping young people see interconnections that are often ignored—such as the relationship among overpopulation, stereotypical dominator gender roles and relations, and our mounting environmental problems.

Students need to learn about organizations they can join to care for our Mother Earth.

Young people today are the first generation who have to worry about acid rain, holes in the ozone layer, and global warming. They carry in their bodies the residues of pesticides and hormones that were once hailed as great boons to humanity but are now recognized as toxic to life. They are the first generation who, during their lifetimes, may witness the disappearance from our Earth of hundreds of thousands of animal, bird, and plant species—species that, as studies by the National Wildlife Federation show, are undergoing catastrophic rates of extinction due to the degradation and loss of their habitats through human activities.[63] They are also the first generation who have to worry about the effects of nuclear and biological warfare or terrorism on their own habitat. In short, they have to worry about the possibility of their own extinction.

These are not happy subjects. But they point up the urgency of integrating environmental education into the entire curriculum. Addressing environmental issues that young people are concerned about is also, as we have seen, a good way to engage students not only in science but in the overarching question of the evolution of our planet, our species, and our responsibility as co-creators of our cultural, and through this, planetary evolution. And of course, it is still another way of integrating "Caring for

---

BOX 6.5 The Children's Television Resource and Education Center (C-TREC) and Other Programs

A veritable treasure trove of resources is the Children's Television Resource and Education Center (C-TREC). C-TREC creates educational services and products that increase children's positive social development skills, including cooperation, empathy, conflict resolution, and critical thinking. Recognizing that one-shot interventions have little chance of long-term success, the designers of C-TREC's projects have produced learning tools and training programs that can become integral parts of the curriculum, rather than mere add-ons. Based on research evidence indicating that social learning can significantly enhance students' motivation, affinity, and achievement in learning, C-TREC creates products and training programs that enable students, teachers, and parents to practice skills and build positive learning communities on a daily basis from preschool to middle school.

For example, C-TREC's Getting Along Interactive project is designed to bring social development learning and computer literacy to low-income preschoolers, their families, and the early childhood educators who work with them. Its read-along bilingual (English/Spanish) books for young children, such as *It's the Only Fair Thing to Do*, feature a delightful menagerie of animals in various situations that raise issues of fairness. (In *P-u-r-r-r-fectly Different*, Andrea Tiger learns to value and respect diversity; in *Roberto Joins In*, Roberto the hippo learns that being nice is better than being mean.[57]) C-TREC audiotapes include stories about girls, such as "The Adventures of Christina Valentine"—an action-oriented adventure series that originally aired on NPR Playhouse.[58]

Two other C-TREC programs are its Getting Along/Thinking Ahead project, which provides guidelines to fifth- and sixth-graders for more ef-

(continues)

Life" into the educational tapestry, this time from an environmental as well as personal and moral perspective.

There are many good sources for environmental literacy teaching. For example, the Rainforest Action Network, headquartered in San Francisco, offers a *Kids Action Guide* for protecting our rainforests that contains colorful and interesting materials appropriate for children in primary school. These materials help children understand that it is possible

BOX 6.5 *(continued)*

fectively dealing with adolescence, and "Bingo and Molly," a television series for preschoolers co-created by C-TREC and The Learning Channel,
which uses both puppet characters and animation to help young viewers
learn to understand and deal with universal growing-up issues such as
teasing, fairness, and respect for others.

Several other programs are also used by schools to train teachers to
help students solve problems creatively. For example, the Resolving Conflicts Creatively Program (RCCP) offers training workshops to show
teachers and parents how to teach children that there is an alternative to
being either aggressive or passive: that they can take active roles in creating a more peaceful world.[59] The Peacebuilders Program is another program that empowers children to be peacemakers. It is designed not only
to reduce aggressive behaviors but also to prevent substance abuse and to
promote pro-social behaviors, both at school and at home. The Peacebuilders program offers staff-training workshops that teach partnership
relational competencies, such as the modeling and positive reinforcement
of supportive and caring behaviors.[60]

Also of particular interest are programs that apply partnership principles offered by the Child Development Project (CDP). These programs
are explicitly designed "to help schools become communities in which
students feel cared for and learn to care in return"—communities in
which they are helped to acquire the practical skills needed "to function
productively in society and in which they are helped to develop the ethical and intellectual understandings needed to function humanely and
wisely."[61] CDP offers workshops for teachers based on empirical findings
indicating that effective (and life-long) learning is a process that cannot
be isolated from the learner's social and cultural context; that children
learn when their search for coherence and making sense of the social and
physical world is met; and that teachers need to help each child become
intrinsically, rather than extrinsically, motivated to understand and practice ethical principles such as fairness and kindness—the goals that partnership education promotes and practices.[62]

to protect both our rainforests, which are the lungs of our planet, and the
human rights of the indigenous peoples living in them, who are increasingly being displaced by large industrial enterprises.[64]

Sut Jhally's powerful video *Advertising and the End of the World*, available from the Media Education Foundation, shows how consumerism has
become a major factor in our environmental crises. Nations of the "devel-

oped" world are disproportionately consuming our Earth's natural resources and, in processing them, polluting our environment. In addition, as "developing" nations increasingly adopt an industrialized consumerist way of life, our global problems will escalate even further—unless we shift toward an environmentally conscious partnership economics.[65]

Students in higher grades can read excerpts from Theo Colburn, Dianne Dumanoski, and John Peterson Myers's *Our Stolen Future,*[66] which details the effects on future generations of pollutants and other toxins produced by industrial processes. Another source is Herbert L. Needleman and Philip Landrigan's *Raising Children Toxic Free,*[67] which proposes measures to halt the damage done by toxins to our environment and health, particularly the health of children.

Young people need to be aware of the interconnection between overpopulation and our environmental problems. For example, the extinction of many animal and plant species in Africa is directly related to human population pressures, as is the loss of arable land and desertification through overcultivation and urbanization.

Environmental literacy entails the awareness that overpopulation can be halted, and that here again dominator gender stereotypes and relations are a major obstacle. Study after study shows that unless women have reproductive freedom, as well as life options other than bearing children as a means of survival and status, there is no way of stemming population growth. Hence the critical need for equal access to education, property ownership, and other basic human rights on the part of billions of girls in the most overpopulated and poorest world regions who are today reaching their reproductive years. But this will only happen if we work for it (see Box 6.6).

Students in the higher grades can be invited to examine the values that guide our social, political, and economic policies—and what each of us can do to influence this. Are our policies really guided by the American ideal of equality? Do they really work for the greater good of our nation and our planet? This kind of discussion will take students back to the need for an economic system that recognizes and rewards the "women's work" of caring and caregiving—as well as to the issue of how this work relates to caring for our planetary home. Good resources here are ecofeminist writings such as *Reweaving the World: The Emergence of Ecofeminism* and, for a lighter touch, two short pieces from the *Utne Reader* titled "A Beginner's Guide to Housework" and "Cooperation."[69]

Environmental literacy also entails an understanding of the urgent need for more realistic economic measures. Current bookkeeping meth-

BOX 6.6   Women and the Population Explosion

Useful resources in this area of study are the annual State of World Population Reports from the United Nations Population Fund (UNFPA), which can be obtained from the United Nations in New York; the report titled "Closing the Gender Gap: Educating Girls," available from Population Action International in Washington, D.C.; and "Population Pressure, Women's Roles, and Peace," an article I wrote for the first *World Encyclopedia of Peace* showing the systemic connections among overpopulation, violence, and dominator gender roles and relations.[68]

ods actually encourage rather than discourage the pollution and degradation of our natural environment. For example, current business profit and loss accountings fail to include in the loss or cost side of the equation the environmental pollution and degradation caused by many business operations. Similarly, measures such as the Gross National Product (GNP) include as valuable the costs of cleaning up the environment *after* it is damaged—but fail to accord any value to preventive measures, to the work of environmental housekeeping.

Another important aspect of environmental education involves informing students about organizations that they can join and/or do volunteer work for—organizations ranging from the Alliance for a Caring Economy, which is working on changing economic rules so that they recognize and reward caring and caregiving,[70] to the Sierra Club, Conservation International, Greenpeace, the National Audubon Society, the Rainforest Action Network, and Earth Island Institute. (Resources are listed in Box 6.7; see also Box 5.21 in Chapter 5.)

Since environmental education needs to start early and be integrated into all aspects of the curriculum, for young children environmental education can tie in with the enormous interest little girls and boys have in animals, trees, flowers, and other aspects of nature. Children are fascinated by animals, in picture books, in zoos, in their homes. Trees, flowers, fruit, and other aspects of nature are also of great interest. For those who live in areas where they can roam in fields and woods, or for children who get to go on camping trips, these experiences provide unending fun along with newly gained knowledge. As children grow older, they generally empathize with animals, not only their beloved pets but animals they see or read about such as dolphins, whales, elephants, and other species

---

BOX 6.7   Environmental Education

Following are some additional resources for environmental education. Conservation International's *Rainforest Imperative* is a 25-minute video and discussion and activity guide focusing on the importance of rainforests.[71] The National Audubon Society's "Living Lightly on the Planet," for grades seven to nine (volume 1) and grades ten to twelve (volume 2), contains activity guides, background information, maps, student role cards, and case studies, emphasizing environmental problemsolving.[72] For upper high school and college undergraduate classes, the Global Tomorrow Coalition's "Global Ecology Handbook Study Guide" provides seventeen units, bibliographic entries, discussion topics, projects, and a list of contact organizations focusing on sustainable development.[73] Another good resource is the Center for Ecoliteracy.[74]

Excellent materials are also available from Population Action International[75] and the World Population Institute. The latter publishes *POPLINE*, which provides information gathered by the World Population News Service.[76] Finally, I recommend that teachers obtain the fact sheets supplied by Zero Population, showing the relationship between overpopulation and air pollution, overcrowded schools, traffic jams, higher rates of teen pregnancy, endangered species, ozone depletion, higher taxes, increasing crime rates, urban sprawl, rainforest destruction, and infrastructure decay.[77]

---

that are today threatened. In these and other ways, young people have a natural interest in, and concern for, nature.

Partnership education, as we have seen, builds on this interest and concern, making environmental consciousness not just an add-on but a core component of the curriculum thread I have called "Caring for Life." It connects students with indigenous contemporary and early European traditions that view nature as part of the sacred, strengthening their sense of spiritual connection to the planet that supports them. It helps students understand empathy as an important evolutionary development, beginning with what some scientists call kinship selection and reciprocal altruism, and gradually progressing to a more evolved empathy with all of humanity and our Mother Earth. And it helps students become actively involved in caring for life, not only individually but collectively, as is urgently needed at this time.

SIX KEYS TO PARTNERSHIP EDUCATION— REVISITED

Tools

Teaching how to use the partnership and dominator models as analytical tools
Showing the interaction between broadening our personal choices and developing a partnership cultural and social organization
Teaching partnership literacies and competencies
Creating a democratic and nurturing learning environment through partnership process

Values

Teaching and modeling values appropriate for partnership living
Teaching appreciation for our natural habitat and the pageantry of the evolution of our universe
Showing the connections between human cultural evolution and the fate of our planet and all life forms on it, including our own
Teaching responsibility for our role in cultural evolution
Helping students understand and overcome the hidden subtext of gender valuations
Teaching the valuing of diversity
Teaching standards of human rights and responsibilities applicable to all cultures

Structures

Helping students understand the configurations of the partnership and dominator models
Showing the connections between different clusters of values and different social structures
Tracing cultural evolution from prehistory to the present in terms of the tension between partnership and domination
Showing the interconnection of the so-called public and private spheres of life
Building schools that model partnership structure

Science

Physical Sciences: Moving beyond Newton's fixed laws to the new physics of possibilities and contingencies

Natural Sciences: Understanding the diversity of animal behaviors and the emergence of our human species, with its enormous flexibility and capacity for creativity and caring

Social Sciences: Understanding the relationship between a partnership social organization and the actualization of our unique human potentials

Integration

Integrating multicultural education into traditional subjects

Balancing information about the female and male halves of humanity throughout the curriculum

Expanding the framework of education to include the larger picture of our human adventure on Earth

Inspiration

Stimulating inquiry

Encouraging sound personal choices

Inspiring active participation in building a more peaceful, equitable, and sustainable future

Epilogue
Our Children's Future

CₕᵢₗDHOOD IS A TIME TO PLAY, to dream, to look forward to exploring the world and all it has to offer. But when the futurist Elenora Masini did a survey of children's visions of the future, she found that many children regard their future with fear rather than hope. A song protesting nuclear weapons written by the children's troubadour Raffi poignantly echoes these feelings. It asks:

> *"Will I ever grow up, Mama?*
> *Do you think that I can, Papa?*
> *Will I ever grow up to be like you,*
> *so big and so strong?"*[1]

This awareness that we face an uncertain future often becomes more conscious, and acute, when children enter their teens. Confused and alienated, with no clear sense of alternatives and feeling powerless to make any difference, teenagers sometimes immerse themselves in trivial or destructive pursuits. Some become disillusioned and cynical. Some live only for the moment, influenced by what they see not only in the mass media but in the consumerist culture all around them. Girls often spend enormous time, energy, and money in futile attempts to look like the models in magazines aimed at teenage girls and women, rather than developing their own interests and potentials. Boys often still equate masculinity with control, domination, and "heroic" or "fun" violence. Some young people turn to drink and drugs, not as an occasional diversion but as an escape from life. Some join gangs. Others succumb to the rhetoric of demagogic religious leaders spreading apocalyptic messages and inciting hate and persecution of socially disempowered groups such as minorities and homosexuals, rather than helping young people find constructive solutions to the enormous environmental, economic, and personal challenges they face.

This is a dangerous situation, both for young people's individual futures and for our future as a society. As we have seen, partnership education offers young people what they sorely need: grounded hope for the future. It provides both a more realistic understanding of our past and present and a clearer picture of our choices for the future. It models partnership, showing that it is a viable and far more satisfying alternative. It encourages young people to take on leadership roles in advancing partnership goals in all aspects of life—and thus to play a leading role in shaping their own future.

I began this book with an invitation. As we approach its end, I want to again ask you to become actively involved in partnership education. If we are to ensure the future of today's and tomorrow's children, we can no longer conform to outdated ideas about education. We must find ways of equipping young people for the challenges they face. We cannot leave this to others. Every one of us needs to take an active role in bringing partnership process, content, and structure into our schools.

Moving Toward Partnership Education

Fortunately, a growing number of educators recognize that fundamental educational changes are needed, not only if we are to change the course that threatens our future but if today's and tomorrow's children are to grow into creative and capable people who can learn throughout their lives, relate well to others and themselves, be environmentally conscious, flexible, venturesome, and capable of empathy not only for their immediate kin but for all of humankind. These educators may not use the terms *dominator* and *partnership;* but due to their efforts various aspects of what I have described as partnership education are gradually beginning to enter our schools.

I have already mentioned the Nova High School in Seattle, Washington, an alternative public school where students are encouraged to work in teams as well as to participate in all school decisions, including the hiring of faculty. As noted earlier, teachers at Nova have introduced partnership curriculum materials into their classrooms; for example, they offer a systems class in which students learn more holistic ways of thinking and learning, utilizing *The Chalice and the Blade* as a text.[2] Another example is La Escuela Fratney (The Fratney School), a democratically run, bilingual

(English and Spanish) public elementary school in Milwaukee, Wisconsin, that sets high academic standards and is the focal point for a multiethnic neighborhood. Here, staff, students, parents, and other members of the community are deeply involved in curriculum development, and students are treated by administrators and teachers as peers.[3] A growing number of other experimental U.S. public schools known as charter schools are also beginning to use more partnership-oriented learning processes and structures.

In Montessori, Sudbury, the School in Rose Valley, and other alternative private schools, children are allowed greater freedom to pursue what interests them, with more emphasis on self-directed learning, personal responsibility, and group relations. Parent involvement is invited, and students often have a direct voice in school decisions. For example, in schools that follow the Sudbury model, students and staff together make such fundamental decisions as who will be the staff each year, how the tuition will be spent, what the school rules will be, and who will be suspended or expelled for violating these rules, thus modeling a democratic, non-autocratic way of relating.[4] Virtual High, an alternative secondary-level learning center in Canada attended by about twenty teenagers, was structured along similar lines. Instead of teachers and students, there were learning consultants and learners. Here, too, young people proceeded at their own pace, experiencing the pleasure of total immersion in their own interests and of choosing from among several mentors with whom to study.

Schools in such diverse places as Australia, Israel, Germany, Greece, South Africa, Hungary, the Philippines, Italy, and Sweden are experimenting with cooperative education methods where teachers act as resource providers and facilitators and students learn to work cooperatively in groups while at the same time building skills for individual responsibility and achievement. Students choose their own group leaders rather than having them assigned by the teacher, every student is encouraged to assume leadership roles, and some of these schools also use cooperative decisionmaking in their administration. Organizations such as the Norwegian-based International Movement Toward Educational Change (IMTEC) and the California-based Children's Television Resource and Education Center (C-TREC) are working to promote partnership process, content, and structure.[5]

In addition, teachers in many schools are introducing partnership curriculum materials into their classes. In Iowa, Sharon Thomas has developed partnership lesson plans for several classes of gifted children. In Canada, Nina Simons has used the partnership and dominator models in her classes, including classes composed of children from diverse ethnic backgrounds ranging from Pakistan and India to Jamaica and Native North American tribal societies. In Monterey, California, Maj-Britt Eagle has for many years assigned *The Chalice and the Blade* to her high school classes. At the college and university level, partnership curricula are being developed in areas ranging from Christine Sleeter's multicultural education classes at California State University at Monterey Bay and Rob Koegel's sociology classes at the University of New York in South Salem to Rosemarie Hoffman's school counselor's program at the University of California at Long Beach and the partnership studies program introduced at Prescott College, Arizona, by the Tucson-based International Partnership Network.

But we need many more such schools and teachers. We need many new partnership lesson plans and curriculum modules. We need websites offering partnership materials, as well as partnership education clearinghouses and other organizations that make resources available to teachers, school administrators, and college and university education departments. We need many partnership teacher development programs, and workshops and conferences on how to develop partnership education in ways that also involve parents and other members of the community.

Moving Toward a Partnership Culture

It is my hope that teachers and other educators will use this book as the basis for developing lesson plans and other materials for partnership education from kindergarten to 12th grade, and that teacher education departments in colleges and universities will design programs for training teachers to effectively work with both partnership educational content and process. The Center for Partnership Studies can be a catalyst and consultant to the creation of these materials and programs through its "Weaving the Future: Partnership Schools" initiative, which is developing partnership education prototypes that can be replicated, adapted, and disseminated worldwide. (See "Becoming a Partner in Weaving the Future" in Appendix A.)

Through a process of cumulation, these materials and programs can gradually transform education. We know that fundamental change *is* possible, sometimes in a relatively short time, when a sufficient number of nodules for change come together as the nucleus—or, in the language of nonlinear dynamics, the attractor—for a new system.

There will of course be opposition, not only from some educators but from entrenched institutions in the larger culture. However, there will also be support for partnership education. In fact, there is already a large reservoir of support from people and groups who recognize that what I have described as partnership values and institutions are urgently needed.

According to a recent study of American values conducted by sociologist Paul Ray, a rapidly growing segment of the U.S. population (he estimates approximately 44 million people) already hold many partnership values. This 24 percent of Americans that Ray called the "cultural creatives" represent the fastest-growing cultural stream. Cultural creatives is an apt term because, even though this is still not recognized in our mass media, this one-quarter of the U.S. population is at the forefront of an emerging new culture.[6]

Ray points out that cultural creatives are not only concerned with self-realization and self-expression, but also with social equity and environmental sustainability. They want to rebuild neighborhoods and communities, see nature as sacred, want to stop corporate polluters, are interested in voluntary simplicity as a less wasteful and destructive lifestyle, love travel, do a good deal of volunteer work, embrace feminism, place great importance on caring relationships and family, are concerned about violence against women and children, are interested in holistic health, spirituality, and nature, and although they emphasize personal development this is often combined with social activism. In sum, in this new, most recently emerging group, we find the strongest preponderance of partnership values and the most conscious rejection of dominator values. Not only that, here we find a strong participation in social movements—from civil rights, peace, and environmentalism to social justice, feminism, and communitarianism.

Equally important is that Ray also found some measure of partnership values in the groups he describes as the other two major cultural streams in U.S. society: the "heartlanders" (29 percent) and the "modernists" (47 percent). Whereas some of the heartlanders' ideals are dominator values, such as strong in-group versus out-group attitudes in matters of race, religion, ethnicity, sexual orientation, and gender, as well as opposition to anything other than "traditional" (and thus largely dominator) gender relations, others are partnership values, such as a strong sense of family responsibility (particularly by women), neighborliness, and community.[7] Although the modernists' values emphasize materialism (and with it, consumerism, and often lack of concern for environmental consequences), personal success (often also without much concern for others), and a belief that science and technology will somehow find cures for all problems (even those it causes)—values that tend to maintain dominator social structures and technological uses—they also reject authoritarian religious and political controls, thus in part espousing partnership values.

This survey is important in that it shows that there are partnership values in all three of the mainstreams of American society. Indeed, the fact that so many grassroots groups worldwide are working to actualize partnership values indicates that these values are spreading globally. But what is most important about this study is that it shows that a significant shift toward partnership values can happen in a relatively short time—since the cultural creatives have most of their roots in the 1960s (that is, only a generation ago).

Other studies reveal similar trends, not only in the United States but in other world regions. For example, in *Modernization and Postmodernization: Cultural, Economic, and Political Change in 43 Societies*,[8] political scientist Ronald Inglehart describes his World Values Survey, which points to partnership trends in most parts of Europe and North America as well as in some nations in South America, Asia, and Africa. Inglehart reports movement away from authoritarianism, from the view that motherhood is the only fulfilling and proper role for women, and from confidence in armed forces and police to solve national and international problems—in other words, a movement away from dominator values. His survey also shows movement toward partnership values such as greater flexibility in sexual norms and gender roles, more consciousness of environmental issues and economic justice, less nationalism, and increased interest in satisfying relations, parent-child ties, meaningful work, and nonviolent solutions to disputes.

Among Inglehart's most interesting findings is an increase in the belief that people in general can be trusted—a belief that reflects some weakening of dominator dogmas and practices. Also of particular interest was a shift from a focus on survival values (which are always predominant in dominator-oriented societies, where artificial scarcities, threats to life, and other survival threats are chronically created by the system) to a focus on what he calls well-being values (the more stereotypically "feminine" values of human welfare congruent with the emphasis on human development of cultures moving toward the partnership side of the partnership-dominator continuum).

The great challenge for partnership education is to broaden and accelerate this cultural movement toward a partnership worldview, which is foundational to a more sustainable, equitable, and peaceful world. Achieving this goal will take courage, perseverance, and endurance. There will be resistance and setbacks. But I am convinced that we can succeed if we keep in mind that the stakes are the future of our children and our planet.

The Partnership School of the Future

In the opening lines of this book, I spoke of possibilities and hopes. I want to end on that note. I would like us together to envision the partnership schools of the future: schools that we can build as we work together to complete the shift to partnership education and culture.

When I think of the school of the future, I see a place of adventure, magic, and excitement, a place that, generation after generation, adults will remember from their youth with pleasure, and continue to participate in to ensure that all children learn to live rich, caring, and fulfilling lives. An atmosphere of celebration will make coming to this school a privilege rather than a chore. It will be a safe place, physically safe, and emotionally safe, a place to express and share feelings and ideas, to create, and to enjoy, a place where the human spirit will be nurtured and grow, where spiritual courage will be modeled and rewarded.

In this partnership school, children will learn about the wonder and mystery of evolution. When they look at the sky, they will know the amazing truth that our stars, which seem so tiny from afar, are not only immense but afire with enormous energy, and that the energy of one of these stars, our sun, made possible the miracle of life here on Earth. They will be awed by how the inanimate became animate and enchanted by the myriad ways life has continued to reinvent itself. When they look at a stone, leaf, or raindrop, they will be aware that the tiniest subatomic particles share properties with the largest constellations of stars, that energy and matter are not really separate, and that all life forms on our planet share elements of the same genetic code and come from a common ancestor. They will understand that this interconnected web of life that we call Nature is both immensely resilient and terribly fragile, that we need to treat our natural habitat with caring and respect, not only because we depend on nature to survive, but also because nature is a thing of wonder and beauty—because, as our Native American and prehistoric European partnership traditions tell us, it is imbued with the Sacred.

In this partnership school, young people will hear many stories of the wonders of life on our Earth. They will learn that cooperation and caring play a major part in the life of many species with whom we share our planet, and that what marks our human emergence is not our capacity to inflict pain but our enormous capacity to give and feel pleasure. They will know about chemicals that, by the grace of evolution, course through our bodies, rewarding us with sensations of sometimes exquisite pleasure when we create and care. And they will understand that this pleasure is ours not only when we are loved but when we love another, not only when we are touched with caring but when we touch another with caring.

Tomorrow's children will know that all of us, no matter what our color or culture, come from a common mother, way back in Africa millions of years ago. They will appreciate diversity—beginning with the differences between the female and male halves of humanity. They will have mental maps that do not lead to the scapegoating and persecution of those who are not quite like them.

Both girls and boys will be aware of the enormous range of their human potentials. They will be equipped to cultivate the positives within themselves and others. They will understand what makes for real political and economic democracy, and be equipped to help create and maintain it. They will have learned to value women's contributions throughout human history, and to give particular value to the caring and caretaking work that was once devalued as "merely women's work." They will also understand that this work is the highest calling for both women and men, that nonviolence and caretaking do not make boys "sissies," and that when girls are assertive leaders they are not being "unfeminine" but expressing part of their human potential.

In this school of the future, children will learn to be just as proficient in using the tools of the partnership and dominator models as in using computer technology. Partnership literacy and competency will be cross-stitched into all aspects of the curriculum. Children will learn to regulate their own impulses, not out of fear of punishment and pain, but in anticipation of the pleasure of responsible and truly satisfying lives and relationships.

"The Great Leap of Faith"

To the partnership world.

CREDIT: *"The Great Leap of Faith," by Jane Evershed.*

Stories will be told of heroic women and men who worked for a safer, more equitable world. There will be tales of inspirational leadership. There will be laboratories for developing partnership social and economic inventions: laboratories not only for learning about the natural sciences, but also about the social sciences and how we may use them to create a partnership world.

Partnership education will be part of everyone's consciousness, as the whole community will recognize that children are our most precious resource—to be nurtured, cultivated, and encouraged to flower in the unique ways each of us can. Partnership schools will be resources of and for the whole community, linked to other schools, communities, and nations through electronic communications fostering a world community.

In partnership schools, tomorrow's children will form visions of what can be and acquire the understandings and skills to make these visions come true. They will learn how to create partnership families and communities worldwide. And they will join together to construct a world where chronic violence, inequality, and insensitivity are no longer "just the way things are" but "the way things once were."

Many of us are already fashioning some of the educational building blocks for constructing the partnership schools of the future. As we saw in these pages, there are many resources for us to use and develop. There is also, as we saw, a great deal that stands in our way. But working together, we can build a new educational system based on the principles of the partnership school. And as we do, we will lay the foundations not only for the new education that young people need for the 21st century but also for a more sustainable, equitable, and caring world.

Additional Resources

Appendix A

Sample Curriculum
Materials and Handouts

Some of the materials listed here can be used as handouts, and permission is hereby given to duplicate them.

"A FORAY INTO THE TEACHING OF PARTNERSHIP STUDIES IN THE ELEMENTARY SCHOOL,"
by Sharon Thomas

Do you recall those days in youth when, once your awareness of something new was raised, you were a collector of any information (or artifacts) related to it for some time to come (and these were suddenly everywhere)? With this in mind, I embarked upon the task of creating "partnership collectors" with three of my Talented and Gifted Service Learning classes, spanning grades 4 to 6. Call it the passion of the gifted child, or natural curiosity of any child. I decided to try channeling this phenomenon in the constructive direction of partnership studies, figuring that a child has a better chance of internalizing its messages for a productive life if it harnesses the fun inherent in collecting.

So began my brief but positive experiences with Partnership Studies. My initial entrance into this area was charted as our new Service Learning project, an area that alos had a positive connotation with my classes because of prior projects undertaken.

Early on came that sense of importance in having special "collectors notebooks" which we personalized by creating class composites of the members' imagined symbols for partnership on their covers. Next came clarification regarding the qualities exhibited in true partnership. Quick to pick up the differences between this model and that of the dominator, these students were now armed with the sensitivities which their antennae would need in order to sniff out partnership examples to share in class.

Interest was keen and ownership of this concept developed quickly. Students read a different book each week with related themes. The books were from a list of titles by Jean Craighead George, Byrd Baylor, and the books in the Value Tales series. Then we worked through articles I had collected about animals partnering with humans in tremendous stories of helping. Then came the social activist stories, about humans serving a cause in some way. The students were dying to try out Cooperative Double Solitaire and Frozen Beanbag, both cooperative, partnership games. In Frozen Solitaire, students help each other keep beanbags on their heads. When the student's beanbag slips off, the student must freeze until a classmate comes over to help.

Next we read a series of readings on Random Acts of Kindness and the students were challenged to see how many caring acts they could report in class in the weeks that followed.

As the semester drew to a close, one of the local banks was to hold a Community Human Relations Conference. My principal suggested it for our class, and it turned out to be the perfect gala celebration/outing to close our exploration of the partnership model. These students listened through the filters (and watched through the lenses) of partnership to each of the diverse speakers from our community that morning. I'm sure that the audience would have been surprised at our debriefing session afterward, to hear how keenly these concepts and messages were understood by the only children in attendance. Their vote for attending again next year matched their enthusiasm for this undertaking known as Partnership Studies!

"LECTURE NOTES FOR HIGH SCHOOL CLASS ON THE PARTNERSHIP AND DOMINATOR MODELS"
(based on Riane Eisler's *The Chalice and the Blade*), by Maj Britt Eagle

The partnership and dominator models present two choices for us: on a personal level, how we live our lives, and on a social level, whether to choose a dominator or a partnership model of society.

The Chalice & The Blade tells a story that is more congruent with the evidence. The book reports a multidisciplinary study examining the problem of how to work to build a sustainable future.

War and the war between the sexes are interrelated. The most important issue in *The Chalice & The Blade* is the issue of alternatives to brutality.

How is *The Chalice & The Blade* different from other studies? "Man" is said to be a generic term, yet few pages in traditional anthropology/archaeology texts cover woman's activities. Eisler takes a gender-holistic approach: her data base includes the whole of humanity. If we look at only part of a picture, we get a distorted view; what we can't see are the patterns.

A holistic approach will call for a reassessment. We humans live by stories. The old stories preclude alternatives for the most part. For example, original sin. We're bad. And we're bad because of woman, which justifies male dominance. This dominance creates unhealthy tension: the woman is forced to manipulate, connive, while the man must continue to suppress.

Another example is the "scientific" story: usually opposed to the religious story, yet the origins of science are shaped by male dominance; e.g. "We all are born with selfish genes," therefore it is inevitable that the stronger will dominate, that there will be a pattern of dominance. "Hey! There are no alternatives!" These are just stories? We live by stories. When we are told there are no alternatives, we can't change. We struggle, and are told "but it can't be done." (We need to remember that the partnership model has been done, and for a much longer time. It is perhaps, the "natural" way for men and women to interact.)

Through a veritable archaeological revolution, a new story of origins is emerging. We are told that war is inevitable, that it is all part of the package, meaning the way things are. But for centuries newly uncovered evidence shows that men and women lived in more peaceful societies.

Archaeology is an interdisciplinary science which draws from folklore, mythology, paleontology; yet it is relatively new. In the 19th century, when archaeology began, excavators were close to grave robbers, looking for treasures for the big European museums. As our perceptions become systems-oriented, they also become more gender-holistic; e.g., "man is a hunter" but what were the other men doing? And the women? Allowing the diversity to become represented restructures the paradigm.

Problem of the paradigm (Khun). "You mean I've lived my life this way for 25 years and now you're telling me it's all wrong?" We balk at change.

Before Sumer, 3200 B.C.E., there were many cradles of civilization. The way they were structured was different than the way we have been taught societies have to be structured.

Neolithic: the first agrarian societies, they were the beginning of civilization with reliable food supplies. In their remains, there is a remarkable absence of signs of destruction through warfare, a paucity of fortification. In art (the stuff dreams are made of), there is an absence of heroic battles between men, an absence of hallowed rulers dragging prisoners in chains, an absence of men raping women (Note: in later stories and art Zeus is depicted raping everybody . . . rape is the "godly" sport). There is no idealization of violence, few signs of warfare. This is first part of the partnership configuration.

There is also a more equitable distribution of wealth, e.g. Catal Huyuk, Minoan Crete. This, and a more democratic, less authoritarian structure are the second part of the partnership configuration.

When we look at complex systems, we do not see simple linear cause–effect dynamics. Rather, there are mutually supportive interactions. For example, when your liver goes out, soon your circulation systems suffers, etc. This is an interactive configuration.

The third part of the partnership configuration is compelling evidence that men did not dominate women in these societies: women are depicted as priestesses, craftspeople, captains of ships. They are not relegated to the private realm of the household as they would have been later in ancient Greece, already a slave society where all women and male slaves (the vast majority of the population) had no voice whatsoever in society despite its fabled "democracy." An authoritarian state has its roots in the authoritarian family (where household is a microcosm of a tyranny).

Fourth: the way the earlier societies imaged the creative powers of the universe was not with a thunderbolt, a weapon, which suggests that the highest power is the power to dominate, the power to destroy. Rather they imaged creation as the chalice, i.e., life sustaining, life illuminating. The power that created the universe is the great mother, from whose womb all life ensues and to whose womb it returns at death.

Denial (by blade mentality): that life emerges from the body of woman. The denial of this extends throughout our mythology. Woman created only as an afterthought, out of Adam's rib.

Even in later iconography, the Goddess always had divine sons and divine daughters. Isis, in Egypt, had the divine son Horus; in Greece, Demeter had the daughter, Persephone. Both men and women were divine.

The hoofed, horned God, the bull god is the male principle which accompanies the Goddess. Goddess figurines are imaged erect with arms held in U, hands upward, facing inward, creating a field of energy.

When evidence of these earlier societies already began to surface in the 19th century, scholars decided if our early societies were not a patriarchy, then we had to have been matriarchal. The primary principle of social organization in the dominator model is ranking: hence this mindset led to erroneous conclusions.

In the dominator model, men are ranked over women, and as with all rankings—be they race over race or nation over nation, this is backed up by violence. It is a model which is inherently dangerous. We must see another alternative when in our day the blade is represented by the nuclear bomb.

The alternative to patriarchy is not matriarchy, but partnership. Here difference (implying diversity) is not a relationship of inferior/superior.

Every society has folk memories of the earlier more partnership-oriented time. The Yin or feminine principle was honored in China. In Eden (the garden planted by Neolithic societies) woman and man lived in harmony. Why would a woman listen to a snake? The snake was one of the epiphanies of the earlier age; (1) it sheds, loses, regains its skin and serves as a symbol of regenerative powers; (2) the oracle of Delphi was a snake (python) and the sibyl or priestess was a woman asking for wisdom from the snake.

Of course, these earlier societies were not ideal, but they were societies structured toward a partnership model. Then followed 5000 years of chaotic shift to the blade, and now we're diverging again.

We're recognizing the process of denial. We are becoming more conscious of alternatives, and of the danger of the dominator model to us all. The dominator model, after a certain period, goes into self-destruct.

The blade: model for totalitarian control, modern version of rigid dominator societies. We see this danger even in the U.S. (e.g., incitement to violence against those who are "different," denial of family planning technologies, etc.).

Signs of change: gender roles changing; nurturing, caring principles more valued; men finding emotions other than anger. Both halves of humanity are saying they want to be fully human. Ecological consciousness is an update of the earlier consciousness, that the earth is our Mother, to be revered. Recognition that there is a strong connection between wife battering and rape and war. We're in a thrust toward a shift from blade to chalice. The last 5000 years were only a dominator detour? Or were they an evolutionary dead end?

Questions: What were men like in earlier more partnership-oriented societies? What did they do? We see images in the art of men and women partnering in bull dancing; men as musicians, fishermen, a prince with butterflies in the garden "being." They had all the roles, the only role which is not idealized is "man the conqueror."

Even science has not "conquered" (see resistance to sprays, immunity of genes). Both women and men need to define their roles as part of the shift to a partnership society.

But this does not mean all will be cooperation. There can be competition in partnership society, but it does not go for the jugular; there can be cooperation in the blade society—take a look at the massive war efforts! Moving toward partnership means, as Eisler documents, not throwing out everything about us and our society; but it is a restructuring of some of our habits and roles in ways that help us realize our potentials.

"HANDOUT ON PARTNERSHIP ETHICS FOR HIGH SCHOOL CLASS,"
by Maj Britt Eagle

Guidelines to Ethics

1. "Everybody else does it." Peer pressure does not justify an action as right.
2. Consider the impact an individual action has on the community.
3. Consider the individual's responsibility vis a vis the community.
4. Consider the impact an individual's action has on her/his character.
5. Does the end justify the means?
6. Consider the long range vision of the kind of world you'd like to live in. Does your action reflect the values of this world?
7. Universalize your action. What kind of world would you live in if everyone acted exactly in the way you have decided to do?
8. Passive versus active good: We may choose not to harm (passive) or we may choose to do good (active).
9. If you should decide that one ought to help one's neighbor, who is your neighbor? How far out does this identification extend?

"GRADE 10 POETRY UNIT USING THE PARTNERSHIP AND DOMINATOR MODELS," by Nina Silver

This pilot was done with 10 students in an inner city school who come from diverse racial and religious backgrounds. The absenteeism for these students is high, and self-esteem is often low due to many unresolved family and community issues. It took about one month, taking 45 minutes out of each 75 minute period for the first 4 lessons, and extending the time spent to an entire period for lessons 5 to 8. This material was covered concurrently with a basic unit of poetry study in which we looked at the role of poetry, imagery, and denotation vs. connotation in print. It was a very successful experiment.

Lesson One

1. Showed the students some artistic images published in *The Partnership Way*, by Riane Eisler and David Loye, that demonstrate domination and partnerships. (Did not use these words to discuss them.)
2. Asked the students to write out their own lists of words that these images connoted.

Lesson Two

1. Split the class into two groups, a partnership group and a dominator group. Each group was given the equations of Partnership means A=B, Domination means A is greater than or less than B.
2. Each group was asked to record a list of words or associations they could make with these two models.
3. Roles were assigned to everyone in a group:
   Reporter
   Secretary
   Limerick writer/Photo researcher
   Concrete poem writer
4. Using the list they generated in #2 above, each person was to produce the product they were assigned based on the group's input.

Lesson Three

1. Student groups presented their work to the class.
2. Marks were given for group reports/projects and marks were given to each individual for her or his role in the group.

3. Extra students were asked to select the key words that came up in the presentations that expressed the partnership and dominator models.

Lesson Four

1. Discuss aspects of partnership behavior and dominator behavior in my personal life, and invite students to identify partnership and dominator behavior in their own lives. Looking at: PARENTS, FAMILY, JOBS, SCHOOL, CHURCH, AND SPORTS. (Entire class of informal chat.)

Lesson Five

1. Asked students to generate lists of ideas that were generated in the previous class discussion. Working in two groups of four at this point. One group created a list of examples of dominator models and partnership models with PARENTS, FAMILY, AND SPORTS. The other dealt with SCHOOL, CHURCH, AND JOBS.

Lesson Six

1. A formal discussion of the Partnership Way theories.
2. Showed the students lists of words and concepts from *The Partnership Way* that identify the two models.
3. Split the class into pairs to brainstorm partnership images that could be used in poetry.

Lesson Seven

1. Gave students a poetry anthology and asked them to analyze the book for poems that discuss partnership philosophy and dominator philosophy. GAVE THEM MARKS FOR POEMS ACCURATELY FOUND.

Lesson Eight

1. Class was split into two groups. The students chose to split along gender lines: girls together, boys together, although the teacher would have preferred a gender mix.
2. Each group was asked to use their previous brainstorming to write two poems each from the group that discussed the value of a partnership model in any aspect of life.

SAMPLE FINAL POEM
(Full marks were given to each student who clearly demonstrated an involvement in the poetry writing.)

Partnership

Members: Jasprit Guraya, Ranjecta N. Barratt, Anita Uditram, and Tania Bryan

Poem

I miss the time
when we first met
you and me
hand in hand
I miss the time
when we walked and talked
about memories of the past
the relationship together
I miss the time
of sharing equally
half and half
I miss the time
of happiness and fun
that came all at once
I miss the time!

"TEST ON PARTNERSHIP AND DOMINATOR ARCHETYPES FOR HIGH SCHOOL MEDIA LITERACY CLASS," by Nina Silver

Review Your Notes on the Partnership and Dominator Models

Observe closely the reproductions of art forms from early humanity in *The Partnership Way*. Remember that pottery and frescos were the mass media in the dawn of early civilization. REMEMBER THAT THE MASS MEDIA OF ANY ERA CAN TELL YOU A GREAT DEAL ABOUT THE PREVAILING IDEOLOGIES OF THE TIME.

You can see that in early history partnership models prevailed. It was not until later history that the media images began to change. (See "Roman Warriors" from an ancient mosaic and "The Murder of Penthesilea" in *The Partnership Way*.)

This historical evidence suggests that violence is not necessarily a natural trait of humankind. But somewhere along the line it became popular to demonstrate violence. There are several theories as to what changed the art forms of civilization. Most of these theories point to a shift in the power structure of society. Once society became a place which was ruled rather than a place where people cooperated, violence was a natural response in behavior. (Violence is a way of maintaining domination, and people without power often resort to violence.)

Today, the dominator model is said to predominate in our society, and therefore our mass media. This is one explanation for the abundance of the violence that we are seeing everywhere.

NOW READ PAGES 9–10, 59–63, 66–67, AND 196 OF *THE PARTNERSHIP WAY*.

    A)   Based on the above reading, give one example of your own from our culture of DOMINATOR heroines and heroes:
    'the scheming heroine'
    'the masochistic heroine'
    'the helpless heroine'
    'the foolish heroine'
    'the deranged heroine'
    'the outstanding hero'
    'the courageous hero'
    'the omniscient hero'

EXPLAIN WHY YOU CHOSE YOUR EXAMPLES.

POPULAR CULTURE = movies, radio, television, magazines, videos, children's toys, music, celebrities, etc.

B) Now give me 5 examples from our popular culture of women and men who could be considered PARTNERSHIP heroines and heroes. Think about adventurous women, wise women, women as counselors, politically active heroines, healing heroes, heroes as mediators, heroes as nurturers, or sensitive heroes.

NOW READ THE PAGE MARKED INTRODUCTION, THE FOLLOWING PAGE ON MEDIA ACTION, AND THE CHART ON THE PARTNERSHIP WAY, THE DOMINATOR WAY, AND ACTION (PAGES 33, 98–102, AND 172–173 OF *THE PARTNERSHIP WAY*).

C) Based on your studies in media over the last two years, your experiences working in groups, your recent experiences helping to solve some important global issues, your documentary on violence, and the above reading, comment on how the media play a part in perpetuating dominator models, and offer a personal solution to how producers and the public can use the media to "heal" the world around us, instead of continuing to destroy it.

Write your comment in the form of a letter to the Canadian Radio and Television Commission (CRTC) that could be published in the editorial section of a daily newspaper. Be persuasive, be creative, use your analytical thinking skills.

(A substantial quantity of information should be present in this letter. Use the points and evidence raised in the readings provided as well as your own ideas.)

"ANSWERS TO MEDIA LITERACY TEST,"
by Vincenzo Ricci

Part A

The Scheming Heroine

For the above I chose Jill Abbott from "The Young and the Restless." She is often punished for asserting herself and seeking self-expression. She tries to be as powerful as the men are on the show but her plans usually backfire making her look stupid.

The Masochistic Heroine

I think for this I would put any movie where there are wives being beaten and raped or also prostitutes. Usually prostitution movies show the prostitutes taking pride in what they do. Often the movies with wife beating imply that it's okay to hit your wife and that men have all the power and can do this. The movie "Paris Trout" shows the most violent abuse against a woman I have ever seen.

The Helpless Heroine

A good example of this is Margot K. in "Superman." She is always being saved by the "Mighty Superman." If it wasn't for the male hero, who knows where she'd be.

The Foolish Heroine

An example of this is Christina Applegate as Kelly Bundy on "Married with Children." She is very ignorant on the show and can't even remember how to spell her name. She definitely exemplifies the "Dumb Blonde."

The Deranged Heroine

I chose Glenn Close in "Fatal Attraction" for this. She is a romantic madwoman who loses her head for a man. This eventually leads to her death.

The Outstanding Hero

For this I chose the movie "The Godfather." He is calm and is in control of everything. He is definitely on top and is a leader.

The Courageous Hero

I chose Jean Claude Van Damme. He beats everybody up in order to save the world and then gets the women in the end.

The Omniscient Hero

For this I've chosen a kids' cartoon, "He-Man." He-Man could always foretell evil, but his friend Teela, who is a women, could never do it, so she would always be caught and He-Man would have to get her out of her mess. This can have great effects on children.

Part B

Adventurous Women: Vikki Keith (Swam Great Lakes, the English Channel, and the Catalina Channel)
Sensitive Heroes: MacGyver
Politically Active Heroines: Audrey MacLauglin (Leader of New Democratic Party [NDP]).
Women as Counselors: Oprah Winfrey

Part C

Dear Canadian Radio and Television Commission (CRTC),

I am writing this letter because I am very annoyed at the programs which are being shown on our television sets. Many people often wonder what went wrong with our world. I say to these people "look no farther than in your own living room." Television mainly, but all forms of media are destroying our world. We get phrases like "Friendly Fire" into our vocabulary from media. What is "Friendly Fire" anyway? Are people not dying just the same?

We get all kinds of negative images put into our heads everyday. We see movies where violence is fun and enjoyable and no one seems to be getting hurt by it. We see sitcoms based on "funny" insensitivity. I was very appalled by a recent show I saw on FOX, it was called "In Living Color." The show showed a skit of a super-hero it made up called "Handicap Man," who acts like he's actually handicapped by stupid gestures. This is not the kind of show I want my kids to be watching.

The media is getting worse and worse every year with the dominator programs it is showing. Producers must learn to show shows of partnership models so that we can try to fix the mess we are in right now. We have to start seeing less insensitivity. We should be seeing more women and men working together instead of the man going to work and the women staying at home to cook for her husband. I do think that there are good partnership shows like MacGyver and Mom P.I. but there should be a lot more. We must heal our world through the media now before it is too late.

Please take heed to what I am saying. I know that I'm just a small voice but a lot of small voices can be real loud and I am willing to start groups against television, radio, magazine, and anyone else who perpetuates dominator models.

Thank You,
Vincenzo Ricci

"STUDENT'S ESSAY FOR HIGH SCHOOL WORLD HISTORY CLASS," by Miszka Evans

In this paper I will be looking at the art of the goddess compared to its contemporary resurgence. A large number of goddess artifacts have been unearthed by archeologists in Eurasia dating back to the Paleolithic and Neolithic ages. These artifacts are mostly figurines, of which hundreds have been found. It is my theory that the goddess symbolized not just nature, but the humans' relationship with nature. This would explain why the goddess was usually represented in the form of a human female or half human-half animal.

To understand the contemporary goddess art, we must first look at its Paleolithic beginnings. Although we lack the written records of that era, we can interpret the art to gauge the Paleolithic humans' societal values. Through this method it is theorized that the prehistoric culture of Eurasia worshipped the earth as a mother, who gave birth to life and renewed it after death. When looked at in this light, the ancient female figurines with swelling stomachs and heavy breasts lose the interpretation of earlier archeologists as "Prehistoric Playboy Centerfolds."

Throughout the Paleolithic era, the human relationship with nature (symbolized as the goddess) was based on a hunter-gatherer relationship, hence symbols associated with the goddess in cave paintings were of life-giving qualities such as, prey (bison, woolly mammoth, mountain goat, wild horse and deer), and depictions of women gathering honey from wild bee hives.

When the human relationship with nature shifted from hunter-gatherer to agriculture, new images for the goddess appeared. The Neolithic (neo – new; lithic – referring to the stone tools used) was an age of change. The drawing back of the glaciers made the climate warmer and wetter.

Women were the main factor in the shift from hunter-gatherer to agriculture. As the primary gatherers, women discovered that the grasses and plants were reproduced by seeds. Perhaps then, the next logical step was to experiment by sowing the seeds of choice plants on their own.

The shift to agriculture changed not only eating habits, but it created new possibilities and stresses in social structure. The Neolithic people had new roles to fulfill. Towns were formed, new inventions such as the sickle were perfected for harvesting grasses. Evidence is that the Neolithic communities continued with the equal based society of the Paleolithic era.

No longer was the goddess a symbol of fertility of the hunt, but a symbol of fertility among the crops. When agriculture came to Eurasia, new images for the goddess evolved, such as grain, bread, the spinning of fibers, and weaving, which are also associated with women. The human female in Neolithic Eurasia continued to be a representation of the goddess.

Reclaiming the Lost Throne

In our era, the feminist movement has given women the self-awareness to rediscover their power. In reimaging the ancient goddess into forms which are relevant to modern experience, women artists are using the ancient female deity as a tool in their art to heal the female psyche of thousands of years of repression. The throne of the goddess which stood empty for centuries is being reclaimed.

A number of ancient and contemporary images (with captions) were included in this paper. A sample follows, but the art is not reproduced here because of copyright issues:

*Throne of the Queen-Priestess, palace of Knossos, ca.1600.

A priestess probably sat on this gypsum throne, the oldest royal seat of authority found in Europe.

The Throne of the Sun Queen, by Suzanne Benton, 1975.

The bond between the warm nurturance of the sun and passionate intensity acknowledged by the sculptor in her monumental throne to the goddess.

*Information of photos taken from *The Once and Future Goddess*. See bibliography.*

❀   ❀   ❀

Nothing has more affected women throughout time as the shared experience of motherhood. The suffering and joy of motherhood are expressed here, in this set of comparative pictures. Tlazolteotl from 15th century Mexico, and the other, "Birth Mother," a contemporary piece.

Tlazolteotl giving Birth, 15th century.

Aplite with garnets, 8in. Aztec, Mexico.

The Great Mother was the creator in the culture of the pre-Colombian new world. Her home was in the west, the place of women and the primeval hole of the earth out of which humankind once crawled, as well as where the sun descends, the archetypal womb.

Birth Mother, by Deborah Kruger, 1985.

Acrylic, oilstick, pastel, 30in. by 22in.

"At the end of her first pregnancy, the artist, apprehensive at the coming birth, dredges up from deep within the supportive image of the somber Earth Mother, herself in labor."

❀   ❀   ❀

The many breasted form of the goddess is an example of the offering of the earth, or the relationship between humans and earth.

Artemis of Ephesus, second century C.E.
Marble, 72in. Roman
Venerated as the goddess of nature throughout the Roman empire.

Louise Bourgeois as Artemis, from performance.

A banquet/Fashion Show of Body Parts, 1980. New York City.

❀   ❀   ❀

The power of woman emerges in these pictures. Symbols of the earth as a provider of food and nurturance.

The Earth Mother, Navaho sand painting.
The cornstalk represents the spinal column of earth as food.

Lakonkwe (Womankind), by John Fadden, 1981.
Acrylic on canvas 30in by 24in.

"The Native American woman whose body encompasses the planet involves the healing powers of nature so that a peaceful world may be born . . . In one hand, a steward of the garden, she holds the sacred corn; in the other, the deer antler and string of wampum representing political power."

❀   ❀   ❀

The goddess of ancient Eurasia (although ancient) is a new positive model for women. Declining are some sexist physical ideals of women, and in their place is the archetypal goddess who symbolizes nurturance. The rise in feminism comes at a time when there is more awareness of our environment. In ancient Eurasia, nature and women were symbolic of each other. Perhaps these two resurgences don't just parallel each other, but are actually interrelated. I believe that the rise in feminism and environmentalism are not new issues but the reemergence of the equalitarian view of the prehistoric era.

Images from prehistory have a message for modern women, and are a reminder of their own sacred identity with the earth. The reemergence of the goddess in contemporary art is often believed to be subconscious, that women artists are tapping into their "long-suppressed imagery," and are again connecting with the earth through their art.

Bibliography

Brian Hayden, *Archeology: The Science of Once and Future Things.* W.H. Freeman and Company, New York, 1993.

Buffie Johnson, *Lady of the Beasts: Ancient Images of the Goddess and Her Sacred Animals.* Harper and Row Publishers, San Francisco, 1981.

Elinor W. Gaden, *The Once and Future Goddess.* Harper & Row, San Francisco, 1989.

Barbara G. Walker, *The Woman's Encyclopedia of Myths and Secrets.* HarperSanFrancisco, 1983.

Joseph Campbell and Bill Moyers, *The Power of Myth.* Doubleday, 1988.

Geofry Parrinder, *World Religions.* Facts on Life Publications, 1971.

Riane Eisler, *The Chalice and the Blade.* HarperSanFrancisco, 1987.

Olga Soffer, Pamela Vandiver, Martin Olivia and Ludik Seitl, "Fiery Venus," *Archeology.* January/February, 1993.

"EXERCISE FOR HIGH SCHOOL UNIT ON CULTURAL TRANSFORMATION THEORY," by Robin D. Andrea

Riane Eisler wrote about her Cultural Transformation Theory in a book entitled *The Chalice and The Blade* (1987). In this book, she describes two possible worldviews, Dominator and Partnership, and the tension between them.

Objective: Students will come to an understanding of Eisler's Cultural Transformation Theory and be able to express this verbally.

Prior Knowledge: Students have demonstrated an understanding of the social construction of belief and value systems.

Opening Exercise: Discuss the implications, as a class, of the results of the following activity.

Fill in the appropriate pronoun:

"The judge asked the secretary to type some papers. ____ handed a stack of documents to ____, asking that ____ be especially careful in ____ work."

"The teacher gave an assignment to the class. ____ explained that it would be due the next day."

Sequence

1. Students will observe two pieces of art from different time periods and discuss what they see in terms of what the art represents, what it seems to say about *what the artists valued*. (Pieces used were Figures 5.8 and 5.9 from *Tomorrow's Children*.) Discuss in group and report back to class.
2. Students and teacher will define *Culture, Transformation*, and *Theory*.
3. The teacher will explain Eisler's thinking with regard to a cultural transformation occurring between the periods from which the pieces of art were created.
4. The teacher will draw a line representing a continuum between the Dominator and the Partnership Worldviews based on the art and the terms she chooses.
5. The class will brainstorm possible characteristics of each of the worldviews, as they relate to relationships between people, and between people and the biosystem.
6. The students will read a short description which Eisler provides enumerating several characteristics of each worldview.
7. The students will write a definition, as they understand it, of *Cultural Transformation Theory*.

8. The teacher will hand out other documents related to this question and assign students the task of reading for preparation of class discussion. Also, after reading, the students will write at home in their journals what they feel the theory says to them.

9. The teacher will display Eisler's work and allow for light discussion of her works which are available. This will give students additions to their list for our future book study groups later in the semester.

Best Practice

Learning

Lesson attempts to spark student interest with opening exercise, then continues through stages of experiential, holistic, authentic, expressive, reflective, social, collaborative, democratic, cognitive, constructivist, and challenging learning. One of the pieces this observation will help determine is if this lesson is appropriate developmentally.

Social Studies

Emphasis on activity that engages students in inquiry and problem solving about significant human issues. Participation in interactive and cooperative classroom study processes. Integration of social studies with other areas of the curriculum.

Student Feedback

The intention of this initial lesson was to demonstrate that a "shift" did occur from a partnership worldview to a dominator worldview. The student responses by way of writing their own definition would indicate that they understood that the shift occurred and that they understood the basic characteristics of each worldview. In their definitions of Cultural Transformation Theory they included cooperation, love, intimacy and egalitarianism in their description of the partnership way, and authoritarianism, rigid male dominance, fear, threats, and power over people in their description of the dominator worldview. Questions at the conclusion of the lesson were about "why" the transformation occurred and "how" it happened. This, of course, is a perfect lead-in to further explanation and discussion of Cultural Transformation Theory. Their interest and enthusiasm was sparked!

Standards/Benchmarks

The lesson relates directly to the Grade 12 CAM Benchmark in the World History category: "Consider patterns of change and continuity in World History in relation to contemporary events, issues, problems, and phenomena."

"PARTNERSHIP WITH OUR BODIES,"
by Patricia Mathes Cane

Our bodies hold our entire history from conception to the present moment. Unfortunately we have been taught to think of a split in body, mind, and spirit, so that the majority of people are alienated from their bodies. The challenge of the schools today is to help children, as well as adults, relearn and recognize who they truly are beyond all the conditioning. This relearning involves empowering ourselves to listen to our body wisdom, to live again in partnership with our bodies.

This relearning is especially important for adolescent girls and boys as they begin to develop their own identity and understanding of sexuality. Parents and teachers can guide and influence young people to value and appreciate the uniqueness of their own bodies, as well as to respect and honor the bodies of others.

CAPACITAR, the international organization I founded ten years ago, is especially committed to working with women who have suffered abuse and with those living in areas of violence and poverty in the U.S. and in Latin America. Practices such as acupressure, Tai Chi, meditation, visualization, breathing exercises, massage, and energy work are extremely important to heal and transform pain, stress, disease and other wounds of body, mind and spirit. Our method is to teach people simple and ancient practices which they can do for themselves, using, in many cases, the one resource they have their bodies.

When women and families begin to recognize the power they have in their own hands to bring healing to their own bodies and to empower the healing of their families and communities, there is a real shift in awareness.

The following are several simple and basic exercises which can be used individually or with groups, with students as well as with parents, to develop a sense of partnership with the body.

Deep Abdominal Breathing to Balance and Renew the Body

Place your hands gently on your abdomen to direct your attention and focus. Exhale fully, releasing all of the air from the lungs, imagining that with the exhalation you are able to release all of the tension, pain, frustration, and negativity stored in the body.

Slowly breathe in deeply, as if to fill your entire abdomen with air. Hold the breath for several moments and imagine the air filling all the cells of your body with light, cleansing, nourishing and renewing your body.

Then breathe out slowly and completely, hold the exhalation for several moments before taking the next deep inhalation.

Continue this deep abdominal breathing for several minutes. If your mind starts to chatter, gently bring your attention back to focus on your breathing, following the air in and out of your body. With your healing breath stay peacefully present in the moment, appreciating the partnership you have with your body.

The Daily Hug: Appreciating and
Being Grateful for Your Body-Mind-Spirit

We all hunger for love and appreciation and look for affirmation from parents, friends, or those around us. Often children have negative self-images because they are frequently told what is wrong with them in school or at home, and are rarely affirmed or supported. We literally embody the images and messages that we get consciously or unconsciously from significant people or authority figures in our lives.

Part of the process of individuation and growth involves coming into partnership with ourselves by developing a healthy sense of self-love and self-acceptance. We also must learn how to realistically recognize and work with the projections of others, listening to what is helpful and fits, and letting go of what does not ring true with our deepest nature.

At first there may be some discomfort in doing this exercise, because we rarely think about loving and giving affection to ourselves. Often we have been raised with a strong message that we are being selfish if we take care of ourselves or admire ourselves. So if negative messages arise, just recognize them, let them go and enjoy the exercise.

Cross your arms and place your hands on your shoulders or upper arms. Give yourself a big loving squeeze, as if you were holding a child with great love and joyful appreciation. If tears or deep emotion come up for you, let the tears flow, just observing any images and letting them go. Continue hugging yourself, thanking yourself for all you do and for all you are. Do this for several moments and when you feel ready breathe deeply and let go.

You can do this as often as you want during the day.

Releasing Emotions Through Your Fingers

I recently facilitated a Spanish CAPACITAR workshop with Latino Head Start parents at our local school. The mothers and fathers arrived from their jobs, very tired, thinking they were attending a regular teacher-parent meeting. Instead of talking very much, we took time for teaching them some simple Tai Chi movements to release and unblock their energy, and for acupressure to relieve the many aches and pains they had. In fifteen minutes the parents were like different people. No one had every done this kind of body work before, but everyone felt amazingly better. One father kept marveling at how good he felt, even though he almost constantly suffered back pain from his job in the cannery.

One of the favorite practices I taught the parents was how to work with emotions by holding your fingers. Often problems develop at home or in school when children or family members are unable to handle or release emotions in a healthy way. Tantrums, blow ups, and even domestic violence result when emotions are discharged without respect for those around us. Emotions are like waves of energy moving through the body. If the energy builds up without a gradual release, like a volcano, there can be a great explosion. Or if the emotion is denied or the person is cut off from their feelings, the emotions are stored in the body. Over time this can lead to pain, ulcers, and other chronic disorders, as our body absorbs and holds the negativity, frustration, and memories of strong emotions which have never been addressed. It is important to recognize emotions when they arise, and then to choose the appropriate way to work with and release the wave of energy, rather than storing it in the body.

This exercise comes from a modality called Jin Shin Jyutsu which predates traditional acupressure. The theory is that through each finger flows a meridian or channel of energy which is connected with different organs and also associated with a corresponding emotion.

Gently wrap your fingers around the finger related to the emotion you wish to release. You can hold the fingers of either hand. Often after several moments you can feel the energy moving through the finger, like a pulse balancing itself. Hold the finger until you feel relaxed and peaceful, letting the finger you are holding go limp.

The Thumb: to release anxiety and worry—think faith
Index Finger: to release fear—think trust
Middle Finger: to release anger—think love
Ring Finger: to release grief and tears—think joy
Small Finger: to release low self-esteem and feelings of victimhood—think self confidence.

Children love to do these finger holds and find them very effective in learning how to work with their emotions. One inner-city mom commented at a workshop that her angry kids were always giving everyone the finger. Now she had something to help them. She was going to teach them how to hold their middle finger, instead of giving it!

For more exercises and practices for parents and teachers, the CAPACITAR Manual can be obtained by contacting: CAPACITAR, Inc. 23 East Beach St. Suite 206, Watsonville, CA 95076 831-465-9426 (fax: 831-722-7703; e-mail: <capacitar@ igc.apc.org>).

"TESTOSTERONE WIMPING OUT?"
by Jeane Seligmann with Bruce Shenitz

Science: The He-Hormone May Not Be So Virile—or Villainous

Why are men hard and hairy, fascinated by end runs and carburetors? Because of testosterone, of course—that he-man, T-bone, chest-expanding sex hormone that makes guys incapable of asking directions. Testosterone. Just saying the word makes a man feel more muscular. But now the thundering hormone—like so much else that men hold dear—is getting an overhaul by the experts. And what they've discovered is unnerving. First of all, when males feel aggressive, it may be because they have too little testosterone, not a hefty supply. Some scientists also now suspect that testosterone's effects on male behavior may occur only after it's converted into the female hormone estrogen. Whew. Don't tell Ah-nold about this. Among the most intriguing findings:

A group of 54 men with abnormally low testosterone reported feeling more irritable and angry *before* their hormone levels were brought to normal. At the University of California, Los Angeles, researchers led by Dr. Christina Wang asked them to rate their mood and well-being before and for two months after treatment. Once their testosterone reached normal levels, the men felt friendlier.

In a study at the Seattle Veterans Affairs Medical Center, researchers artificially reduced the testosterone levels of 48 healthy young men. When the hormone was diminished in this reversible procedure, "there was a trend toward increased irritability and aggression," says Dr. William J. Bremner. "I think guys just feel bad when testosterone is low," he suggests. "They feel frustrated by troubles with sexual functioning. That translates into irritability and aggression on the questionnaire."

Adolescents are always unpredictable—and a group with medically delayed puberty was no exception. At Penn State University, researchers led by pediatrician Dr. Howard Kulin gave each youngster varying doses of sex hormones. For successive three-month periods, each boy got either testosterone or a placebo, and each girl got estrogen or a placebo. Both genders reported more aggressive feelings when they received their respective sex hormones—but the urges were stronger and occurred on lower hormone doses in the girls. Because estrogen had such a marked effect on them, the researchers theorized that testosterone may also be converted to estrogen in the male brain, which has many estrogen receptors.

So far, most of the new finding are more speculation than firm science. But it's a little surprising to realize we don't know as much about testosterone as we thought. After all, the hormone was identified 60 years ago—back when Gloria Steinem was still too young to pronounce its name.

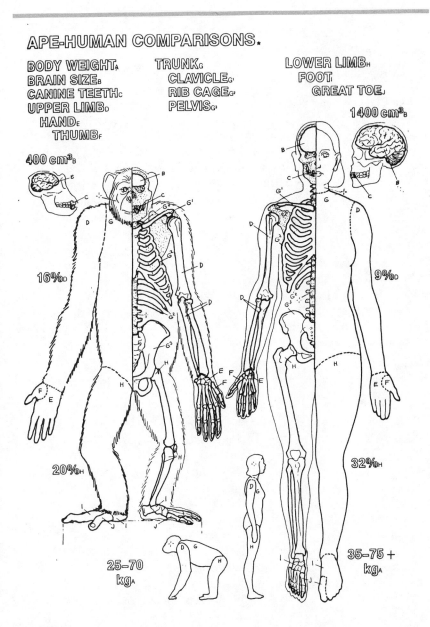

Ape-Human Comparisons

Here's an example of how we can introduce a more gender-balanced view than that found in most textbooks, where male figures are shown as the human norm.

CREDIT: *From* The Human Evolution Coloring Book *by Adrienne Zihlman. Copyright © 1982 by Coloring Concepts, Inc. Reprinted by permission of Harper Collins Publishers, Inc.*

"THE LANGUAGE OF PARTNERSHIP"
from *The Partnership Way,*
by Riane Eisler and David Loye

In trying to shift from a dominator to a partnership way of thinking and living, a major obstacle is our language. How can we think and live as partners if the words in our heads keep reinforcing dominator stereotypes?

Words have a powerful effect on how we think and act. The semantics of power relations are particularly striking in the use of words that serve to define the relationship of women and men. In English, for example, the ostensibly generic use of words like *mankind, man,* and *he* to include both sexes unconsciously conditions both women and men to think in male-centered ways, effectively teaching us that women are secondary or do not count.

Today, as the equal value and equal rights of all people are increasingly asserted, changes in language are also being recognized as important steps toward the creation of a just society. But these changes are not easy to make. Because linguistic habits are established very early in life, it is difficult to break them.

The following terms already in common usage are a few suggestions for those who want to break out of the prison of words that unconsciously force us to think of one half of humanity as less valuable than the other.

Dominator Language	*Partnership Language*
mankind	humanity/humankind
man	human
he	she or he/one/they
chairman	chairperson/chair
congressman	congressperson
man hours	work hours
manpower	work power, work force
to man	to staff
gentlemen	ladies and gentlemen
Dear Sir	Dear Madam and Sir/Dear Sir or Madam/Dear Madam or Sir/Dear Manager
emasculated	weak/nonassertive
effeminate	decadent/weak
statesman	diplomat/leader/policymaker
sissy	sensitive boy
brotherhood	community/kinship/friendship/unity/ partnership
craftsman	artisan/skilled worker
spokesman	speaker/spokesperson/representative
common man	average person

TABLE A.1 Key Words for the Dominator and Partnership Models

Dominator	Partnership
fear	trust
win/lose	win/win orientation
power over	power to and with
male dominance	gender partnership
sadomasochism	mutual pleasure
control	nuture
ranking	linking
one-sided benefit	mutual benefit
manipulation	open communication
destruction	actualization
hoarding	sharing
codependency	interdependency
left-brained thinking	whole-brain thinking
negative conditioning	positive conditioning
train by punishment	train by encouragement
violence against others	empathy with others
taking orders	working in teams
alienation	integration
nuclear arms race	international partnership
war	peace
secrecy	openness/accountability
coercion	participation
indoctrintaion	education
conquest of nature	respect for nature
conformity	creativity

SOURCE: The Partnership Way: New Tools for Living and Learning, *by Riane Eisler and David Loye.*

"MACHIAVELLI AND EISLER: FINAL EXAMINATION QUESTION FOR EDUCATION 700,"

by Michelle Stimac

1. In a maximum of *one and one-half* double-spaced pages, compare and contrast the concepts articulated in Riane Eisler's *The Chalice and the Blade* (the selection read for this class) and concepts and tenets in Machiavelli's *The Prince* (the selection read for this class) (10 points)

"THE CHALICE AND THE SWORD:
ANSWER TO FINAL EXAMINATION QUESTION
FOR EDUCATION 700,"
by Ray Gen

Riane Eisler's book *The Chalice and the Blade* could have easily been entitled *The Chalice and the Prince*. Eisler argues that the blade represents the male-dominated, power position, hierarchical world that history has recorded. Machiavelli's prince is the quintessential representative of the blade because the prince is the master of the "dominator" model. For Eisler, the chalice is the representation of partnership. Eisler's partnership emphasizes the responsibility of both males and females to share in the transformation of human society. The chalice is the power to help all people reach their full potential in a partnership of mutual responsibility and benefit.

Machiavelli emphasized the seizure of power and the maintenance of that power through a combination of force, fear and manipulation. Machiavelli's paradigm includes deception and naked aggression. It operates amorally from an "end justifies the means" conception of the world. Machiavelli wrote, ". . . it is necessary to be able to disguise this character[istic] well, and to be a great feigner and dissembler; and men are so simple and so ready to obey present necessities, that one who deceives will always find those who allow themselves to be deceived" (1940, pp. 64–65). Thus the prince functions in a "domination hierarchy" or in a power position from which he dictates overwhelming authority.

Conversely, the chalice paradigm operates from an "actualization hierarchy" wherein different levels of hierarchies exist because of the different stages of actualization in which people function. The chalice offers a partnership society. People cooperatively and collaboratively work and think together, not in opposition to each other. The chalice does not seek to replace the male dominated world with a female one; it seeks a partnership between the two aspects of humanity. Eisler describes the historical, traditional paradigm as being "androcratic." Eisler suggests an alternative term "gylany" which proffers a paradigm that combines female and male aspects of humanity in a working partnership.

The chalice is morally and ethically centered. The principles of the prince and the blade are decidedly amoral at best, and probably immoral. Machiavelli suggested, "a prince who wishes to maintain the state is often forced to do evil" (1940, p. 71). The chalice offers a social shift from a male "dominator model" to a model that embraces both genders in mutual moral and ethical transcendence.

"EXCERPTS FROM SYLLABUS FOR SOCIOLOGY 307 (Human Sexuality)," by Margret Crowdes

Course Description

"If every tool in your toolbox is a hammer, then everything looks like a nail."
—*Frequent saying among San Diego*
Alternatives to Violence Project participants

This course focuses on the dynamic interconnections among social structure, ideologies, and everyday relations that comprise human sexuality. Persistent questions and debates surrounding beliefs about, and expressions of, human sexuality focus the substance of the course. A central sociological theme that frames the course is: Sexual attitudes, values, experiences, and identities are neither biologically pre-determined nor wholly dictated by society; they are fundamentally shaped and influenced by the dynamic interconnections among interactional, sociocultural and historical factors. Key questions are: What do we mean when we say "human nature"? What is human nature in relation to human sexuality? What meanings do we ascribe to intimacy and human sexuality? Whose meanings are they and from whence do we derive them? What are the implications and ramifications of those meanings for human consciousness and relationships? What difference does it make how we answer these and related questions?

In many cases, theories of sexualities and love have become a part of our popular culture. For example, what would a Woody Allen movie be like if there had never been a Sigmund Freud; or *Rambo* without a prevailing concept of a certain type of masculinity; or *The Crying Game* and *Fried Green Tomatoes* without some degree of dispute about what is "natural" and "real" in sexual love? Increasingly, new thought on human sexualities is reaching public discourse; that thought challenges and counters many definitions of human sexualities that have been institutionalized and assumed "inevitable." In this course, we will take this new thought seriously in the context of historical, symbolic, interactionist, critical, and feminist inquiries into human sexualities: How do people develop sexual identities? In what communities and subcultures? Under what historical circumstances? Whose voices do we listen to and whose do we ignore? Why? And, what are the consequences for the quality and vitality of human relationships?

Course Objectives

1. To acquaint students with sociological, cultural and historical dynamics shaping expressions of human sexualities.

2. To reflect critically on dominant theories, popular myths, and assumptions about human sexuality.
3. To examine alternatives to mainstream theories and perspectives on sexuality, love, and intimacy among humans.

Course Readings

1. Eisler, Riane. 1995. *Sacred Pleasure: Sex, Myth, and The Politics of the Body— New Paths to Power and Love.* HarperSanFrancisco
2. Customized Reader called *Human Sexuality* (In bookstore under professor's name; two on reserve in the library)

Coursework

1. "Who am I sexually and how did it happen?" Anonymous short essay
2. Library assignments
3. Seminar-ing, including reflection papers
4. Four analytic essays
5. Final Project

Attendance and Participation

This course is organized in a discussion format emphasizing interactional communication, reflective-critical thought, and relating readings to everyday life. Lecturettes are designed to introduce core concepts; occasional classroom experiential exercises, guest lecturers, and films are included to stimulate applications and thoughtful discussion.

Part I: Studying Sexuality Sociologically: Methodological and Theoretical Questions

Part II: Body, Society, and Power: What Is "Natural" for Humans?

Part III: Bodies, Identities, and the Politics of Intimacy

Part IV: Gylanic Responses to Androcratic Relationships: Interpersonal Communications and Social Images of Bodies, Minds, and Relationships

Part V: Beyond Androcracy, But Not Beyond Sex and Sensuality

290

Public Symposium: "From Dominator Sex to Partnership Love and Sexuality"

What does it look, sound, and feel like?: polarism, fragmentation, sexual oppression, pain, prejudice and harm COMPARED WITH what it could look, sound, and feel like to embody pleasure, partnership, authentic choice, love, whole-person sexuality, creativity, freedom.

"EXCERPTS FROM ROLE PLAYS AND CREATIVE PROJECTS FOR SOCIOLOGY 305 (Sociology of Women)," by Margret Crowdes

Introductory Remarks

Says C. Wright Mills: We need to see the relationship between individual private lives and the social structure so we can see what the nature of society is, the types of men and women we make ourselves to be, and to see not only what the impact of "the world" is on us, but, as importantly, to recognize the creative impact we have on constructing our social world. Interpersonal interactions, daily relationships are the bricks of the structural building or social organization.

Recall Adrienne Rich's call to women to claim their educations. In this voice she says:

> Responsibility to yourself means refusing to let others do your thinking, talking, and naming for you; it means learning to respect and use your own brains and instincts; hence, grappling with hard work . . . It means that you refuse to sell your talents and aspirations short, simply to avoid conflict and confrontation.

And Eisler reminds us that:

> As individuals with different needs and desires and interests come together and come into contact, conflict is inevitable. The question directly bearing on whether we can transform world [and relationships] from strife to peaceful coexistence is how to make conflict productive rather than destructive . . . Destructive conflict is the equation of conflict with the harshness and violence required to maintain domination . . . Through productive conflict, individuals, organizations, and nations can grow and change (*The Chalice & The Blade*, 1987; 192).

So we need to start asking of, and for ourselves, the concrete behaviors, thoughts, feelings, and language that align with and embody these calls to action. How do we do this? What does it look, sound, and feel like in action?

What you are doing here is a visual and interactive demonstration of the analytic process of: Identify, Name, Describe, Explain, Confront, and Clarify Alternatives, Transform Behavior. So, three points to bear in mind (at least for our purposes here):

A. NAME "HERE" ACCURATELY (i.e., deconstruction). *Identify* the current "dominant paradigm" in action and interaction. *Describe specific* behaviors, words, postures that create "androcracy."

B. NAME THE ALTERNATIVE "THERE." What values, attitudes, specific communications, body postures support "gylany"? Recognize and describe *specifics in action.*

C. REWRITE THE TYPICAL SCRIPT. Which ways of thinking and being do you want to keep doing, which ones do you want to transform? How do you decide? Identify and clarify STEPS that can lead from here to there, i.e., identify concrete behaviors, actions, words, and feelings.

A point of reminder about transformative change compared with a simple changing of the guards: Changing minds always involves changing bodies, hearts and actions. Any one without the other keeps the false dualism in place and disempowers from within . . .

Process

The idea is to demonstrate the process, the direction, the feeling, and the action of movement toward gylanic partnership. So this part means you take the androcratic/dominator language, communication, postures, etc., and show us what gylanic language, communication, and postures would look, sound, and feel like as you transform the typical situation.

1. Pick a "typical situation" that reproduces "androcratic relations." Write a short script complete with language, tones of voice, body gestures, etc. that depict the typical androcratic interchange. Stay real; don't overdo or underdo.

    Ask yourselves and each other: "What's going on here?" Then use course materials to create your "freeze frames." Use freeze frames to stop the action periodically in order to draw particular attentions to significant points in the conflict or interchange, and make analytic commentaries on them.

2. Then: Think and feel through "from here to there" and REWRITE the script. That is, TRANSFORM the situation into an interchange that is expressive of intention and movement toward "gylanic relating." Stay real; don't overdo or underdo.

Freeze Frames

A main goal of freeze frames is to show the audience what you want them to look and listen for as it happens, what it MEANS, how it feels to the actors involved, and what sorts of consequences result. Do exactly the same process for the reconstruction/transformation.

So, you will definitely want to use analyses from Eisler and other course readings to help you do the freeze frames. (You could think of the freeze frames as the "citing your sources" part of writing a good and compelling story.)

What You Should Wind Up With

One act, two scenes. Scene 1 should be a scripted interchange that lasts about 3–5 minutes, complete with several freeze frames pointing out the significant actions that you want to transform. Scene 2 should be a scripted transformation of Scene 1. If you were a gylanic thinking/feeling being, what would you *want* to think, say, and do in this situation? "Doing" gylany involves compassionate and active listening, effective communication (i.e., owning your own feelings and interests, empathy, etc.), intellectual and emotional agreement with linking rather than ranking, a willingness to respond to the other person as a person, not as a stereotypical composite, *and*, a willingness to work creatively with doing something other than the dualistic "either-or" this or that thing. So Scene 2 ought to take between 5–8 minutes; it takes longer because creativity is more involved and depthful in gylanic constructions than in androcratic reactions.

So, altogether your one-act, two-scene role plays should last about 15 minutes. And then the audience gets to ask questions for about 5 minutes; 20 minutes per groups of, say, 6 people.

Final Notes

This is not so much about creating the "perfect" ideal new scene. It's about *showing the process* of getting from here to there.

This is a collaborative effort. Even if every person does not have a speaking part, every person needs to contribute to the analysis and production of the details of the gylanic transformation. Taken together, your projects tell a story.

"BECOMING A PARTNER IN WEAVING THE FUTURE"

We invite you to become a partner in **Weaving the Future: Partnership Education.** **The Center for Partnership Studies**

- offers consulting on **Partnership Education** materials, training, and procedures to lay the educational foundations for a more peaceful, equitable, and sustainable future
- partners with elementary and secondary schools, universities, and other organizations that want to create **Partnership Education** curricula, processes, and structures
- fully includes young people (preschoolers to university students) in this creative process, preparing them to assume leadership
- offers speakers for conferences and other meetings.

We invite you to participate in two exciting educational opportunities:

- Continuing teacher education workshops are offered by the Center for Partnership Studies in collaborations with the University of Kansas Center for Research on Learning, a leader in continuing education, to help teachers use partnership process, content, and structure in classrooms or home schooling. These workshops are held in various regions of the United States and can be taken for continuing education credit. For information, contact Jim Knight at 785-864-0623; email: mjknight@ukans.edu

- A Master of Art in Education degree with a specialty in partnership education is being developed by the Center for Partnership Studies in collaboration with the Institute for Field-Based Teacher Education at California State University, Monterey Bay, a pioneer in education dedicated to diversity, equity, and systemic learning. The program offers a distance learning component so that teachers from all parts of the country and world can participate. For information, contact Professor Christine Sleeter at 831-582-3641; email: christine_sleeter@monterey.edu or go to <www.csumb.edu/academic/graduate/education/partnership>.

For general information, or to send a tax-deductible donation to support Weaving the Future, write Center for Partnership Studies, P.O. Box 51936, Pacific Grove, CA 93950, USA. You can also e-mail us at <center@partnershipway.org> or send a fax to 831-626-3437.

Appendix B
More on Books and Videos

Detailed discussions of the partnership and dominator models, as well as of the cultural transformation theory that informs these guidelines for curriculum development, are accessible for both technical and nontechnical readers in my books *The Chalice and the Blade* (San Francisco: Harper & Row, 1987, 1988), *Sacred Pleasure* (San Francisco: Harper Collins, 1995, 1996), and *Redefining Destiny* (work in progress).

Teachers may want to assign *The Chalice and the Blade*, as Maj-Britt Eagle and other high school teachers have done. For younger students, teachers may want to make copies of the line drawings on prehistory in this book and/or use color reproductions from library books.

The Partnership Way, rev. ed. (Brandon, Vt.: Holistic Education Press, 1998), which I wrote with my partner, social psychologist David Loye, can also be assigned. It includes experiential work, discussion questions, and charts that have been used successfully in university and high school classes as well as in community and church workshops.

The audiotape of *The Chalice and the Blade* (New World Library, 1997), in which I read an abridged version of the book, is another useful learning tool in that it can stimulate discussion when excerpts are played for students.

Articles by several authors concerning applications of the partnership model in areas ranging from education and business to politics and spirituality are also available from the Center for Partnership Studies (P.O. Box 51936, Pacific Grove, CA 93950) and the International Partnership Network (P.O. Box 323, Tucson, AZ 85702). Some of these articles can be downloaded from the Center for Partnership Studies (CPS) website at <http://www.partnershipway.org>.

For teachers who want to learn more about the Neolithic as well as the Minoan civilization of Bronze Age Crete, I recommend the works of Marija Gimbutas, James Mellaart, Nicolas Platon, R. F. Willetts, and Lucy Goodison that are listed in the Bibliography. For an overview of some of their findings and an extended bibliography, I also recommend *Sacred Pleasure* and *The Chalice and the Blade*.

Cristina Biaggi's *Habitations of the Great Goddess* (Manchester, Conn.: Knowledge, Ideas & Trends, Inc., 1994) deals with the fascinating Neolithic civilization on the island of Malta, with its giant Goddess statues and temples. Paula Gunn Allen's *The Sa-*

cred Hoop (Boston: Beacon Press, 1986) is a good source for information about Native American traditions involving the feminine.

Children's books that teach young people how the partnership model can work include Jyotsna Sreenivasan's _The Moon Over Crete_ (St. Louis: Smooth Stone Press, 1996), about time travel back to prehistory; Sreenivasan's _Aruna's Journey_ (St. Louis: Smooth Stone Press, 1997), about an eleven-year-old Indian American girl who visits her relatives in India; Alyssa Chase's _Jomo and Nata_ (Shawnee Mission, Kans.: Marsh Media, 1995), an illustrated book for young children about how elephants learn to cooperate; Patty Sheehan's _Gwendolyn's Gifts_ (Gretna, La.: Pelican Publishing Company, 1991), an illustrated book that is a good antidote to the Cinderella myth; and Douglas Larche's _Father Gander's Nursery Rhymes_ (Santa Barbara, Calif.: Advocacy Press, 1986), which counters some of the gruesome and cruel messages about human relations in the Mother Goose rhymes. A good source for some of these books is Advocacy Press in Santa Barbara, California (phone: 1-800-676-1480). The Advocacy Press also has an excellent series for teenagers called "Making Choices: Life Skills for Adolescents," which addresses issues ranging from career and life planning to adolescent pregnancy prevention.

I can also recommend some novels relevant to the sections in this book on biological and early cultural evolution. One of these is _Circle of Stones_ by Jone Dahr Lambert (New York: Pocketbooks, 1997). Another is Mary Mackey's _The Year the Horses Came_ (San Francisco: Harper, 1993). Already quite well known is _The Mists of Avalon_ (New York: Ballantine, 1982) by Marion Zimmer Bradley. Less well known is Marie Jakober's _High Kamilan_ (Calgary, Canada: Gullveig Books, 1993), a lively historical/fantasy novel that contrasts partnership and dominator ways of relating in a stunning tale of adventure and romance that offers both entertainment and informative reading for high school students. Another lively fantasy tale is Sheri Tepper's _The Gate to Women's Country_ (New York: Doubleday, 1988).

Eva Keuls's _The Reign of the Phallus_ (Berkeley: University of California Press, 1993) is an accessible scholarly book on ancient Greece, and Robert Graves's _I, Claudius_ (New York: Vintage Books, 1989) is a good source on ancient Rome. Teachers who want to learn more about the ancient Sumerian civilization (a hybrid of old partnership and new dominator elements) can look at _The Myths of Enki_ (New York: Oxford University Press, 1989), which Sumerologist Samuel Noah Kramer wrote with John Maier. As noted earlier, this work incorporates cultural transformation theory as its framework.

On the environment, Rachel Carson's classic _The Silent Spring_ (Boston: Houghton Mifflin, 1962) and Carolyn Merchant's _Radical Ecology_ (New York: Routledge, 1992) are excellent background reading. For updates on current developments, newsletters from organizations such as the Earth Island Institute (415-788-3666), Greenpeace (1-800-326-0959), and Coop America (1-800-58-GREEN) are good resources, as is Popline, published by the Population Institute (202-544-3300), which often features articles showing the connection between environmental problems and population growth. An excellent all-purpose source on important social issues is *The Humanist*, published by the American Humanist Association (1-800-743-6646); and for issues of particular importance for women, *WIN News* (published by Women's International Network [fax: 781-862-1734]) is excellent.

There are many works on U.S. history. Examples are *Women's America: Refocusing the Past*, 4th ed., edited by Linda K. Kerber and Jane DeHart (New York: Oxford University Press, 1997); Mary P. Ryan's *Womanhood in America: From Colonial Times to the Present*, 3rd ed. (New York: Franklin Watts, 1983); Sarah M. Evans's *Born for Liberty: A History of Women in America* (New York: Free Press, 1989); *Unequal Sisters: A Multicultural U.S. Women's History*, edited by Carol DuBois and Vicki L. Ruiz (New York: Routledge, 1990); Darlene Clark Hine and Kathleen Thompson's *A Shining Thread of Hope* (New York: Broadway Books, 1998); and Gerda Lerner's *Black Women in White America: A Documentary History* (New York: Random House, 1972).

For transforming the high school English curriculum, *Weaving in the Women* by Liz Whaley and Liz Dodge (Portsmouth, N.H.: Boynton/Cook Publishers, 1993) is easy to use because it provides suggestions by grade level as well as by historical period. Blanche Wiesen Cook's biography of Eleanor Roosevelt, Volume I (New York: Penguin, 1993) and Volume II (New York: Viking, 1999), and the story of Wilma Mankiller's life (New York: St. Martin's Press, 1993), are also good resources.

Focusing on the Enlightenment is Susan Moller Okin's *Women in Western Political Thought* (Princeton, N.J.: Princeton University Press, 1979). For revolutionary movements of the 19th and 20th centuries and the role women played in them, I recommend Sheila Rowbotham's *Women, Resistance, and Revolution* (New York: Vintage Books, 1974). Anthologies of feminist writings are *Feminist Theorists*, edited by Dale Spender (New York: Pantheon Books, 1983), and Miriam Schneir's *Feminism: The Essential Historical Writings* (New York: Vintage Books, 1994) and her *The Vintage Book on Feminism: The Essential Writings of the Contemporary Women's Movement* (New York: Vintage, 1994).

Mathew Callahan's *Sex, Death, and the Angry Young Man* (Ojai, Calif.: Times Change Press, 1991) is an excellent resource for older students. A conversation between the author (a rock musician) and my partner David Loye and me, it asks and suggests answers to provocative questions about masculinity, femininity, art, creativity, and life in general. Raffi's *The Life of a Children's Troubadour* (Vancouver: Homeland Press, 1999) offers a good model of partnership masculinity.

Important African-American perspectives are voiced in bell hooks's *Yearning: Race, Gender, and Cultural Politics* (New York: Vintage Books, 1994) and *Sisters of the Yam* (Boston: South End Press, 1993); Alice Walker's moving novels *The Color Purple* (New York: Harcourt, Brace, Jovanovich, 1982) and *Possessing the Secret of Joy* (New York: Harcourt, Brace, Jovanovich, 1992); Louisah Teish's *Jambalaya* (New York: Harper & Row, 1995); Toni Morrison's *Beloved* (New York: Knopf, 1987); and Audre Lorde's *Sister Outsider* (Freedom, Calif.: Crossing Press, 1984).

Among the materials on Native American and African societies reflecting early partnership roots, I recommend Gregory L. Schaaf's "Queen Coitcheleh and the Women of the Lost Shawnee Nation," in *Views of Women's Lives in Western Tradition*, edited by Frances Richardson Keller (New York: Leviston, 1990), which indicates that in Native American tribal societies that were more democratic, women had higher status; and Daniel McCall's "Mother Earth: The Great Goddess of West Africa," in *Mother Worship*, edited by James J. Preston (Chapel Hill: University of North Carolina Press, 1982), which discusses the traces of greater female power in a number of African tribal societies. (Both articles are cited in *Sacred Pleasure*.)

As noted in the main text, in 1995 at the Chinese Academy of Social Sciences in Beijing, a group of Chinese archaeologists, anthropologists, historians, and other scholars published a book titled *The Chalice and the Blade in Chinese Culture: Gender Relations and Social Models*. This book (available in English and Chinese from the Center for Partnership Studies, P.O. Box 51936, Pacific Grove, CA 93950) tests cultural transformation theory by looking at Chinese prehistory and history. It uncovers in China a similar sequence to what I found in Western cultural evolution: the shift from a more peaceful, mother-centered society in which women and men were equally valued to chronic warfare, rigid male-dominance, extreme oppression, and other characteristics of the dominator configuration.

Good introductions to gender literacy are Mary Pipher's *Reviving Ophelia: Saving the Selves of Adolescent Girls* (New York: Ballantine, 1995); Peggy Orenstein's *Schoolgirls: Young Women, Self-Esteem, and the Confidence Gap* (New York: Anchor, 1995); and Myra Sadker and David Sadker's *Failing at Fairness: How Our Schools Cheat Girls* (New York: Touchstone Books, 1995). The new field of men's studies too has much to contribute here; examples are works such as Harry Brod, editor, *The Making of Masculinities* (Boston: Allen & Unwin, 1987) and Michael Kimmel and Michael Messner, editors, *Men's Lives, Fourth Edition* (Boston: Allen & Unwin, 1998). Another excellent resource is the American Association of University Women's *How Schools Shortchange Girls: A Study of Major Findings on Girls and Education* (New York: Marlowe & Co., 1995).

These and other sources will be useful to educators in designing projects that can be carried out by students in partnership with faculty, mentors, and other resource people. For example, teachers can invite high school and college students to write a simplified version of chapter 3 of *The Chalice and the Blade* (on Minoan civilization). They can use chapter 8 of *The Chalice and the Blade* and chapter 6 of *Sacred Pleasure* as materials on classical Greece in which (in contrast to most available sources on this period) the situation of women and stereotypically feminine values are given due importance.

Such materials can be used in peer teaching in the students' own schools and in the production of additional materials to share with other schools. They can be given wider distribution through the World Wide Web.

Appendix C
More Curriculum Materials and Handouts

These are longer pieces that can be of particular use to teachers and students. They are easily available from books and other publications in print. Items marked with an asterisk (*) can be obtained from the Center for Partnership Studies, and some can be downloaded from the Center website at <www.partnershipway.org>.

Excerpts from Chapter 9 of *Sacred Pleasure*

Excerpt from Chapter 3 of *The Chalice and the Blade*

Excerpt from David Loye's *Darwin's Lost Theory of Love*

Excerpt from "Partnership and Dominator Heroes and Heroines" from *The Partnership Way*

Charts on the partnership and dominator models from *The Partnership Way*

*Herb Martin and Terri Wheeler's multicultural reading list
*Christine Sleeter's multicultural essay
*Takayashi Kano's article on bonobo chimpanzees
*Meg Bowman's tests on *The Chalice and the Blade*

Riane Eisler's "Dominator and Partnership Shifts," in Johan Galtung and Sohail Inayatullah, eds., *Macrohistory and Macrohistorians: Perspectives on Individual, Social and Civilizational Change*

Notes

Prologue

1. For example, the 1993 Parliament of the World's Religions, a convocation of world religious leaders, issued a declaration called "Towards a Global Ethic," in which they admonish us to recognize that "the world is in agony"; condemn "the abuses of the Earth's ecosystems" along with chronic violence, poverty, and hunger; and call for a culture of partnership, including partnership between women and men ("Declaration and Principles," Council for a Parliament of the World's Religions, 1993). In the same year, the Union of Concerned Scientists, an organization of leading international scientists, published a statement by 1,670 scientists from seventy countries, including 102 Nobel laureates, warning that our present course is unsustainable and urging the adoption of a new ethic that can "motivate a great movement, convincing reluctant leaders and reluctant peoples themselves to effect the needed changes" ("World Scientists Warning to Humanity," statement published by the Union of Concerned Scientists, April 1993).

2. Johann Pestalozzi, *Leonard and Gertrude* (New York: Gordon Press Publishers, 1976; originally published in 1781); Maria Montessori, *The Montessori Method* (New York: Schocken Books, 1964; originally published in 1912); John Dewey, *Democracy and Education* (New York: Free Press, 1966; originally published in 1916); and Paolo Freire, *Pedagogy of the Oppressed* (New York: Seabury Press, 1973). These works foreshadowed much that is still today considered progressive education. For example, Pestalozzi, as early as the 18th century, rejected the severe corporeal punishments and rote memorization methods prevalent in his time and, instead, used approaches geared toward children's stages of development.

3. See Riane Eisler, *The Chalice and the Blade: Our History, Our Future* (San Francisco: Harper & Row, 1987, 1988); Riane Eisler, *Sacred Pleasure: Sex, Myth, and the Politics of the Body* (San Francisco: Harper Collins, 1995, 1996); and Riane Eisler and David Loye, *The Partnership Way: New Tools for Living and Learning* (Brandon, Vt.: Holistic Education Press, 1998).

4. The Center for Partnership Studies website is located at <www.partnershipway.org>. For further information about these projects, consult the Partnership Schools page.

301

5. Marian Wright Edelman, *Guide My Feet: Prayers and Meditations on Loving and Working for Children* (New York: Harper Collins, 1996).

Chapter 1

1. Because the structures of the roles and relations of the female and male halves of humanity are important elements in the partnership and dominator configurations, the new terms I came up with, as alternatives to the conventional references to patriarchy and matriarchy, were androcracy and gylany. Androcracy derives from the Greek andros (man) and kratica (rule) and means "ruled by men." Glylany derives from gyne (woman) and andros (man) linked by the letter l for lyen (to resolve) or lyo (to set free). It implies that the female and male halves of humanity are linked rather than ranked.

2. *I Am Your Child: The First Years Last Forever*, hosted by Rob Reiner and produced by the Reiner Foundation in 1997.

3. B. D. Perry, R. A. Pollard, T. L. Blakley, W. L. Baker, and D. Vigilante, "Childhood Trauma, the Neurobiology of Adaptation, and 'Use Dependent' Development of the Brain: How 'States' Become 'Traits,'" *Infant Mental Health Journal* 16 (1996): 271–291.

4. See, for example, Penelope Leach, *Children First* (New York: Alfred A Knopf, 1994); and N. R. Carlson, *Physiology of Behavior* (Boston: Allyn and Bacon, 1994). See also the classic work on touching: Ashley Montagu's *Touching*, 3rd ed. (New York: Harper & Row, 1986).

5. Alice Miller, "Childhood Trauma," lecture at the Lexington YWHA in New York City, October 22, 1998. Miller also writes of "enlightened witnesses" who can help adults uncover abuse in their childhood, so that they can heal instead of repressing and unconsciously replicating this abuse with their own children.

6. Here, I am still using the term Western history in the conventional Eurocentric sense, since this is how it is generally understood. However, as illustrated in what follows, there is also a broader meaning—one that includes, for example, peoples indigenous to the Americas.

7. For an overview of some of this literature, see Riane Eisler, "From Domination to Partnership: The Hidden Subtext for Sustainable Change," *Journal of Organizational Change Management* 7, no. 4 (1994): 32–46; and Riane Eisler, "Women, Men, and Management: Redesigning Our Future," *Futures* 23, no. 1 (January/February 1991): 3–18.

8. Mary Belenky, Blythe Clinchy, Nancy Goldberger, and Jill Tarule, *Women's Ways of Knowing: The Development of Self, Voice, and Mind* (New York: Basic Books, 1986).

9. See, for example, Gina O'Connell Higgins, *Resilient Adults: Overcoming a Cruel Past* (San Francisco: Jossey-Bass Publishers, 1994); and E. James Anthony and B. Colder, eds., *The Invulnerable Child* (New York: Guilford Press, 1987).

10. See, for example, Ira Shor, *Empowering Education: Critical Teaching for Social Change* (Chicago: University of Chicago Press, 1992).

11. See, for example, David W. Johnson, *Cooperative Learning in the Classroom* (Alexandria, Va.: Association for Supervision and Curriculum Development, 1994); David W. Johnson and Roger T. Johnson, *Learning Together and Alone* (Needham Heights, Mass.: Allyn and Bacon, 1994); David W. Johnson and Roger T. Johnson, "Research Shows the Benefits of Adult Cooperation," *Educational Leadership* 45, no. 3 (1987): 27–30; Spencer Kagan, "The Structural Approach to Cooperative Learning," *Educational Leadership* 45 (December 1989–January 1990): 12–15; Robert E. Slavin, "Cooperative Learning and Student Achievement," *Educational Leadership* 46, no. 2 (1988): 31–33; and Robert E. Slavin, "Research on Cooperative Learning: Consensus and Controversy," *Educational Leadership* 47, no. 4 (1989): 52–54. As Slavin writes, cooperative learning is effective when it is designed to balance shared goals and individual accountability; in other words, just asking students to work together is not enough. Slavin also notes that in addition to helping with learning (as it encourages peer teaching and other forms of sharing among students, rather than setting them against each other), cooperative learning can increase friendships, raise self-esteem, and improve race relations, attendance, and liking for school.

12. Marilyn Watson, Victor Battistich, and Daniel Solomon, "Enhancing Students' Social and Ethical Development in Schools: An Intervention Program and Its Effects," *International Journal of Educational Research* 2: no. 7 (1998): 571–586.

13. Robert Gladden, "The Small Schools Movement: A Review of the Literature," in Michelle Fine and Janis I. Somerville, eds., *Small Schools Imaginations: A Creative Look at Urban Public Schools* (Chicago: Cross City Campaign for Urban School Reform, 1998), p. 117. Another good source is Michelle Fine, ed., *Chartering Urban School Reform* (New York: Teacher's College Press, 1994).

14. Quoted in Gladden, "The Small Schools Movement," p. 121.

15. Howard Gardner, *Frames of Mind* (New York: Basic Books, 1983).

16. Jacqueline G. Brooks and Martin G. Brooks, *In Search of Understanding* (Alexandria, Va.: Association for Supervision and Curriculum Development, 1993); Michael Strong, *The Habit of Thought* (Chapel Hill, N.C.: New View Publications, 1997).

17. Pioneering works in this area are Kurt Lewin, *Field Theory in Social Science* (New York: Harper & Row, 1951); and Eric Trist and Fred Emery, *Toward a Social Ecology* (New York: Plenum Press, 1973). Good overviews are also provided in Gareth Morgan, *Images of Organizations* (Newbury Park, Calif.: Sage, 1996); John Naisbitt and Patricia Aburdene, *Reinventing the Corporation* (New York: Warner Books, 1986); Rosabeth Moss Kanter, *When Giants Learn to Dance* (New York: Simon & Schuster, 1989); and Riane Eisler and Alfonso Montuori, *The Partnership Organization* (work in progress).

18. David Bohm, On Dialogue (Ojai, Calif.: David Bohm Seminars, 1990); William Isaacs, "The Power of Collective Thinking," in Kellie T. Wardman, ed., *Reflections on Creating Learning Organizations* (Cambridge, Mass.: Pegasus Communica-

tions, 1994), pp. 83–94; Peter Senge, *The Fifth Discipline: The Art and Practice of the Learning Organization* (New York: Doubleday, 1990).

19. Alfie Kohn, *No Contest: The Case Against Competition* (New York: Houghton Mifflin, 1992).

20. Nancy Schniedewind and Ellen Davidson, *Open Minds to Equality* (Needham Heights, Mass.: Allyn & Bacon, 1997).

21. Jeanne Gibbs, *Tribes: A New Way of Learning Together* (Santa Rosa, Calif.: Center Source Publications, 1994).

22. Richard Vila et al., *Restructuring for Caring and Effective Education* (Baltimore: Brooks Publishing, 1992).

23. See Riane Eisler and Rob Koegel, "The Partnership Model: A Signpost of Hope," *Holistic Education Review* 9, no. 1 (Spring 1996): 5–15.

24. For a moving book about children growing up with violence, see James Gabardino, Nancy Dubrow, Kathleen Kostelny, and Carole Pardo, *Children in Danger: Coping with the Consequences of Community Violence* (San Francisco: Jossey Bass, 1998).

25. Riane Eisler, *Redefining Destiny* (work in progress).

26. Nel Noddings, "A Morally Defensible Mission for Schools in the 21st Century," *Phi Delta Kappan* (January 1995): 366.

27. Thomas Kuhn, *The Structure of Scientific Revolutions* (Chicago: University of Chicago Press, 1970).

28. A good source from the psychoanalytical literature is Calvin Hall and Gardner Lindzey, *Theories of Personality* (New York: Wiley, 1978).

29. See, for example, George Gerbner, Larry Gross, Michael Morgan, and Nancy Signorielli, "Growing Up with Television," in Jennings Bryant and Dolf Zillman, eds., *Media Effects* (Hillsdale, N.J.: Erlbaum, 1994), pp. 17–41; and David Loye, Rod Gorney, and Gary Steele, "Effects of Television: An Experimental Field Study," *Journal of Communication* 27, no. 3 (1977): 206–216.

30. An early classic from anthropology is Ruth Benedict, *Patterns of Culture* (New York: Houghton Mifflin, 1934); and one from sociology is Max Weber, "The Social Psychology of the World's Religions," in Talcott Parsons et al., eds., *Theories of Society* (New York: Free Press, 1961). David Loye, in *The Healing of a Nation* (New York: Norton, 1971; now available from the new Internet publishing house ToExcel <www.iuniverse.com>, 1998), shows the power of racially biased narratives. Feminist writings, including such classics as Dale Spender, ed., *Feminist Theorists* (New York: Pantheon, 1983), demonstrate the attempts by women over many centuries to contradict sexist cultural narratives. And Joseph Campbell, *The Mythic Image* (Princeton, N.J.: Princeton University Press, 1974), is well known in the area of myth.

31. Joan Rockwell, *Fact in Fiction: The Use of Literature in the Systematic Study of Society* (London: Routledge & Kegan Paul, 1974).

32. Milton Rokeach, *The Nature of Human Values* (New York: Free Press, 1973).

33. Riane Eisler, *The Chalice and the Blade* (San Francisco: Harper & Row, 1987, 1995); Riane Eisler, *Sacred Pleasure* (San Francisco: Harper Collins, 1995, 1996).

34. James Banks, "Multicultural Education: Its Effects on Students' Racial and Gender Role Attitudes," in James P. Shaver, ed., *Handbook of Research on Social Studies Teaching and Learning* (New York: Macmillan, 1991), pp. 459–469.

35. Ibid., p. 463.

36. Ibid., p. 467.

37. Ibid., p. 466.

38. See, for example, Eric Trist and Fred Emery, *Toward a Social Ecology* (London and New York: Plenum Press, 1973); and Riane Eisler, "Women, Men and Management," *Futures* 23, no. 1 (January/February 1991): 3–18.

39. Kurt Lewin, widely considered the father of social psychology, conducted some early experiments showing that laissez-faire structures not only are inefficient but end up by leading to the scapegoating and eventual authoritarianism characteristic of dominator structures. See Lewin, *Field Theory in Social Science* (New York: Harper & Row, 1951).

40. Sheila A. Mannix and Mark T. Harris, "Raising Cain: Original Psychic Injury and the Healing of Humanity" (unpublished manuscript, 1997), p. 23.

41. Ibid., p. 26.

Chapter 2

1. Leonard Pitts, "Rebuilding Morality Will Take 'Titanic' Effort," *Miami Herald*, February 26, 1998.

2. Deborah Tannen, *The Argument Culture* (New York: Random House, 1998).

3. Emily Style, "Curriculum as Window and Mirror," *Listening for All Voices* (Summit, N.J.: Oak Knoll School, 1988).

4. Nel Noddings, *The Challenge to Care in Schools* (New York: Teachers College Press, 1992).

5. See Eleanor Maccoby and Carol Nagy Jacklin, *The Psychology of Sex Differences* (Stanford, Calif.: Stanford University Press, 1974). A more recent work on sex differences showing the enormous importance of gender socialization is Anne Fausto-Sterling, *Myths of Gender* (New York: Basic Books, 1985), which, as its title suggests, dispels many false preconceptions about inherent biological differences between women and men.

6. *How Schools Shortchange Girls: A Study of Major Findings on Girls and Education* (New York: Marlowe & Co., 1995).

7. E-mail communication to author from Sharon Thomas of Iowa City on July 20, 1998.

8. Urban Paul Thatcher Edlefsen, "President Clinton's State of the Union Address: A Partnership Analysis," research paper for Nova High School class.

9. The crux of the matter is the ranking of one-half of humanity over the other. This provides a mental map for perceiving relations of domination or submission as normal. It could theoretically be the social ranking of the female half over the male half (i.e., matriarchy)—although there have been no historical instances of this.

10. See Stuart A. Schlegel, *Wisdom from a Rainforest: The Spiritual Journey of an Anthropologist* (Athens: University of Georgia Press, 1998). In my earlier writings I have used the name Tiruray, even though in this book Schlegel has switched to using the name Tiduray rather than Tiruray, as in his earlier writings. It is the same tribe, regardless of the spelling.

11. On the contrary, Jesus challenged the rigid male dominance, hierarchism, and punitiveness of his time—for example, by stopping the stoning of a woman accused of adultery and preaching against men's legal right to throw out no-longer-wanted wives by simply saying "I divorce you" three times (as is still the practice in some Muslim fundamentalist nations today).

12. See Riane Eisler, *Sacred Pleasure: Sex, Myth, and the Politics of the Body* (San Francisco: Harper Collins), ch. 10.

13. The *Kid's Action Guide* can be obtained from the Rainforest Action Network, 450 Sansome Street, Suite 700, San Francisco, California 94111. For more information, check out the network's web page at <www.ran.org/ran/>.

14. Charles Darwin, *The Descent of Man* (Princeton, N.J.: Princeton University Press, reprint of original 1871 edition), pp. 89–90, 404. See also David Loye, *Darwin's Lost Theory of Love* (New York: iUniverse <www.iuniverse.com>, 1999).

15. Frans deWaal, *Good Natured: The Origins of Right and Wrong in Humans and Other Animals* (Cambridge, Mass.: Harvard University Press, 1996), p. 207.

16. Emotions occur when neuropeptides (amino acids strung together like pearls in a necklace) make contact with receptors (complicated molecules found in almost every cell in the body, not just the brain). Although there is still much work to be done to identify the exact nature of these biochemicals, it is clear that different emotions involve different neuropeptides, which are essentially information-carrying molecules. For an accessible account of this phenomenon, see "The Chemical Communicators: Candace Pert," interview with Candace Pert in Bill Moyers, *Healing and the Mind* (New York: Doubleday, 1993), pp. 177–193.

17. Jane Martin, *Schoolhome: Rethinking Schools for Changing Families* (Cambridge, Mass.: Harvard University Press, 1992).

18. See, for example, *AAUW Report: How Schools Shortchange Girls* (Washington, D.C.: American Association of University Women Educational Foundation, 1997). Particularly as girls approach puberty, their sense of self-worth and competence decreases rather than increases—a phenomenon largely due to the fact that girls begin to understand from many social messages (including a school curriculum that basically excludes them) that boys and men are considered more important.

19. United Nations, *The World's Women 1970–1990: Trends and Statistics* (New York: United Nations, 1991), p. 60. For further discussion, see Riane Eisler, David Loye, and Kari Norgaard, *Women, Men, and the Global Quality of Life* (Pacific Grove, Calif.: Center for Partnership Studies, 1995).

20. Eisler, Loye, and Norgaard, *Women, Men, and the Global Quality of Life*.

21. Christine E. Sleeter and Carl A. Grant, "Race, Class, Gender, and Disability in Current Textbooks," in Michael W. Apple and Linda K. Christian-Smith, eds., *The*

Politics of the Textbook (New York: Routledge, Chapman & Hall, 1991), p. 98. The textbooks in question covered the subjects of reading, science, mathematics, and social studies.

22. One such study is reported in Jeane Seligmann, with Bruce Shenitz, "Testosterone Wimping Out?" *Newsweek*, July 3, 1995, p. 61. (This article is included in Appendix A at the end of this book.)

23. Rob Koegel, "Healing the Wounds of Masculinity: A Crucial Role for Educators," *Holistic Education Review* 7 (March 1994): 42–49.

24. Christine E. Sleeter and Carl A. Grant, eds., *Making Choices for Multicultural Education* (Columbus, Ohio: Merrill, 1994).

25. For statistics on dropout rates, see Statistical Abstract of the United States (1998), chart 297, p. 187. This source indicates that the 1996 dropout rate for white students was 9.2 percent, compared to 11 percent for black students and 24.6 percent for Hispanic students (nearly one-fourth of the total). For the Remafede study of young people's suicide rates, see Sandra G. Boodman, "Gay and Teen Boys More Likely to Commit Suicide," *Washington Post*, March 3, 1998, p. Z05.

26. My work has focused primarily on how this shift occurred in the regions surrounding the Mediterranean Sea—regions generally described as the cradles of Western culture. Although the time lines differ, there is strong evidence of the same pattern in other world regions. For example, in Min Jiayin, ed., *The Chalice and the Blade in Chinese Culture* (Beijing: China Social Sciences Publishing House, 1995), which is available in English from the Center for Partnership Studies, scholars at the Chinese Academy of Social Sciences in Beijing have also identified a prehistoric shift to a dominator culture, although it occurred later there than in the West. Cultural transformation theory looks at this shift from the perspective of chaos theory, nonlinear dynamics, and other new approaches to the study of how living systems maintain themselves and change. In particular, it proposes that human societies are living systems that cannot be understood in terms of simple one-way causes and effects. They are self-organizing, self-maintaining, and capable—during periods of great disequilibrium or chaos (such as ours)—of transformational change. See, for example, Riane Eisler, *The Chalice and the Blade: Our History, Our Future* (San Francisco: Harper & Row, 1987, 1988); and David Loye and Riane Eisler, "Chaos and Transformation: Implications of Nonequilibrium Theory for Social Science and Society," *Behavioral Science* 32 (1987): 53–65.

27. For a perspective on Europe, see Marija Gimbutas, *The Civilization of the Goddess* (San Francisco: Harper San Francisco, 1991); on the Middle East, see James Mellaart, *Catal Huyuk* (New York: McGraw-Hill, 1975); on pre-Columbian North America, see Arrell Morgan Gibson, *The American Indian: Prehistory to the Present* (Lexington, Mass.: D. C. Heath, 1980); and on Asia, see Jiayin, ed., *The Chalice and the Blade in Chinese Culture*.

28. See, for example, Ervin Laszlo, *Choice: Evolution or Extinction?* (New York: Tarcher/Putnam, 1994); and Daniela Meadows, *Beyond the Limits* (Post Mills, Vt.: Chelsea Green Publishing, 1992). See also Eisler, *The Chalice and the Blade*, ch. 12.

Chapter 3

1. Maria Montessori, *To Educate the Human Potential* (Adyar, Madras, India: Kalakshetra Publications, 1948), pp. 9–10.

2. Brian Swimme, *The Universe Is a Green Dragon* (Santa Fe, N.M.: Bear & Company, 1984), p. 18.

3. Vatican City, "Faith, Evolution Can Co-exist, Pope Says," *Associated Press*, October 25, 1996.

4. The works of these scientists are cited in Riane Eisler, *Sacred Pleasure: Sex, Myth, and the Politics of the Body* (San Francisco: Harper Collins, 1995, 1996).

5. Bearing out Darwin's own statements to this effect, and contrary to the impression given by prevailing neo-Darwinian accounts of his theory of evolution, psychologist David Loye conducted a computerized search of *The Descent of Man* and found that Darwin wrote ninety-five times about love and ninety times about moral sensitivity. See Loye, *Darwin's Lost Theory of Love* (New York: iUniverse <www.iuniverse.com>, 1999).

6. These universal patterns are discussed in Sally Goerner, *After the Clockwork Universe* (London: Floris Books, 1999). For an excellent summary of the new scientific understanding of living systems as interconnected, see Fritjof Capra, *The Web of Life* (New York: Anchor/Doubleday, 1996).

7. Eric Chaisson, *The Life Era* (New York: Atlantic Monthly Press, 1987).

8. Ibid., p. 15.

9. Ibid., pp. 12, 17.

10. Brian Swimme and Thomas Berry, *The Universe Story* (San Francisco: Harper San Francisco, 1992), p. 8. More recent calculations, based on observations with NASA's Hubble Space Telescope, suggest that the universe is only 12 to 13.4 billion years old.

11. Ibid., p. 8.

12. This exercise, developed by Christine Sleeter, is gratefully acknowledged.

13. *New Columbia Encyclopedia* (New York: Columbia University Press, 1975), p. 61; Elizabeth Gould Davis, *The First Sex* (New York: Penguin Books, 1971), p. 420.

14. Margaret Wertheim, *Pythagoras' Trousers: God, Physics, and the Gender Wars* (New York: Times Books, 1995), pp. 73–77.

15. Ibid., p. 77.

16. "Benjamin Banneker: From Stars to City Planning," *Multiculturalism in Mathematics, Science, and Technology* (Menlo Park, Calif.: Addison-Wesley, 1993), pp. 25–26.

17. Marija Gimbutas, *The Language of the Goddess* (San Francisco: Harper & Row, 1989), p. 311.

18. See, for example, <http://www.pracapp.com/infomine/a217102050/output.html>.

19. Stuart Kauffman, *At Home in the Universe* (New York: Oxford University Press, 1995), p. 18.

20. Brian Swimme and Thomas Berry, *The Universe Story* (San Francisco: Harper, 1992), p. 271.

21. Richard Leakey, *The Origin of Humankind* (New York: Basic Books, 1994), p. 142.

22. Leakey dates human origins to between 2 and 4 millions years ago (ibid., p. 24). But every year the time line gets longer, as scientists discover more fossil remains. The latest find was ardipithecus ramidus, dating back to 4.4 million years ago. There is still some controversy about this find. But it seems clear that australopithecus anamensis, some of whose remains were found in 1988 in Kenya, goes back to between 4.2 and 3.9 million years ago. For a quick scan of various hominid species, see the Hominid Species Introduction at <http://www.talkorigins.org/faqs/homs/species.html>.

23. There is some controversy about this date as well.

24. See Richard Dawkins, *The Selfish Gene* (New York: Oxford University Press, 1976); David Barash, Sociobiology and Behavior (New York: Elsevier, 1977); and Michael Ghiselin, *The Economy of Nature and the Evolution of Sex* (Berkeley: University of California Press, 1974). Ghiselin even asserted that "man" is innately evil: "Given a full chance to act in his own interest, nothing but expediency will restrain him from brutalizing, from maiming, from murdering—his brother, his mate, his parent, or his child. Scratch an 'altruist' and watch a 'hypocrite' bleed. No hint of genuine charity ameliorates our vision of society, once sentimentalism has been laid aside. What passes for cooperation turns out to be a mixture of opportunism and exploitation" (p. 247). For a quick and accessible summary of the views of sociobiologists who present altruistic and caring behaviors as only the result of selfishness and project to humans the same motivations they impute to ants, lions, and other nonhuman species, see Laura Tangley, "Law of the Jungle: Altruism," U.S. News & World Report, February 15, 1999, pp. 53–54. For good critiques, see Ruth Bleier, *Science and Gender* (Elmsford, N.Y.: Pergamon, 1984); and Loye, *Darwin's Lost Theory of Love*.

25. Loye discusses this point in some detail in *Darwin's Lost Theory of Love*.

26. Charles Darwin, *The Descent of Man* (Princeton, N.J.: Princeton University Press, reprint of original 1871 edition), p. 394.

27. Ibid., p. 404.

28. R. C. Lewontin, Steven Rose, and Leon J. Kamin, *Not in Our Genes* (New York: Pantheon, 1984).

29. Allan Combs, ed., *Cooperation* (Philadelphia: Gordon and Breach Science Publishers, 1992).

30. Peter Kropotkin, *Mutual Aid* (Montreal, Canada: Black Rose Books, 1988); Ashley Montagu, *The Nature of Human Aggression* (New York: Oxford University Press, 1976).

31. Lynn Margulis, *Symbiosis in Cell Evolution: Life and Its Environment on the Early Earth* (San Francisco: W. H. Freeman, 1981). See also Margulis, "Early Life," in William Irwin Thompson, ed., *Gaia* (Hudson, N.Y.: Lindesfarne Press, 1987), pp. 98–109.

32. Mae-Wan Ho, "Organism and Psyche in a Participatory Universe," in David Loye, ed., *The Evolutionary Outrider: The Impact of the Human Agent on Evolution* (Twickenham, England: Adamantine Press/Westport, Conn.: Praeger Books, 1998).

33. Glynn Isaac, "The Sharing Hypothesis," *Scientific American* (April 1978): 90–106.

34. Ralph Holloway, "Human Paleontological Evidence Relevant to Language Behavior," *Human Neurobiology* 2 (1983): 105–114.

35. Adrienne Zihlman, "The Paleolithic Glass Ceiling: Women in Human Evolution," in Lori D. Hager, ed., *Women in Human Evolution* (New York: Routledge, 1997), p. 97.

36. Nancy Tanner, *On Becoming Human* (Cambridge, England: Cambridge University Press, 1981).

37. Sally Linton Slocum, "Woman the Gatherer: Male Bias in Anthropology," in Reina Reciter, ed., *Toward an Anthropology of Women* (New York: Monthly Review Press, 1975), pp. 36–50.

38. Adrienne Zihlman, "Women's Bodies, Women's Lives: An Evolutionary Perspective," in Mary Ellen Morbeck, Alison Galloway, and Adrienne L. Zihlman, eds., *The Evolving Female: A Life-History Perspective* (Princeton, N.J.: Princeton University Press, 1997), p. 187.

39. Paul D. MacLean, *The Triune Brain in Evolution* (New York: Plenum Press, 1990). See also Paul D. MacLean, "Women: A More Balanced Brain?" *Zygon* 31, no. 3 (September 1996): 421–439, a fascinating article in which the author contends that evolutionary factors have contributed to a greater balance of function in women's brains, leading to less dualistic and hierarchical thinking.

40. Humberto Maturana and Francisco Varela, *The Tree of Knowledge: The Biological Roots of Human Understanding* (Boston: Shambhala, 1992); Maturana, preface to Riane Eisler, *El Caliz y la Espada* (Santiago, Chile: Editorial Cuatro Vientos, 1990).

41. Humberto R. Maturana and Gerda Verden-Zöller, *Origins of Humanness in the Biology of Love* (Durham, N.C.: Duke University Press, 1998).

42. More recently, mirroring Darwin's earlier projection for the evolutionary development of the moral sense, Paul MacLean's brain research has uncovered evidence of evolutionary development of the "moral brain." David Loye observes that this modern brain research provides support for the long-ignored second half of Darwin's theory. See David Loye, "Charles Darwin, Paul MacLean, and the Lost Origins of 'The Moral Sense,'" *World Futures: The Journal of General Evolution* 40, no. 4 (1994): 187–196.

43. Loye, *Darwin's Lost Theory of Love*. For some of the implications of this refocusing of Darwinian theory, see also David Loye, "Can Science Help Construct a New Global Ethic? The Development and Implications of Moral Transformation Theory," *Zygon* 34, no. 2 (1999): 221–235; and David Loye, *The Glacier and the Flame* (unpublished manuscript).

44. Frans deWaal, *Good Natured: The Origins of Right and Wrong in Humans and Other Animals* (Cambridge, Mass.: Harvard University Press, 1996).

45. Abraham Maslow, *Toward a Psychology of Being* (Princeton, N.J.: Van Nostrand, 1968); Roberto Assagioli, *Psychosynthesis: A Manual of Principles and Techniques* (New York: Viking Press, 1965); Kazimierz Dabrowski, *Positive Disintegration* (Boston: Little, Brown, 1964). See also Elizabeth Maxwell, "Self as Phoenix: A Comparison of Assagioli's and Dabrowski's Developmental Theories," in *Advanced Development* 4 (January 1992): 31–48; and, as an excellent source for information on these theories, Loye's *The Glacier and the Flame*.

46. Robert Ornstein, *The Evolution of Consciousness* (New York: Prentice-Hall, 1991); Allan Combs, *The Radiance of Being* (Edinburgh: Floris Books, 1995).

47. See Eisler, *Sacred Pleasure*; and Eisler, *The Chalice and the Blade: Our History, Our Future* (San Francisco: Harper & Row, 1987, 1988).

48. Jeffrey Moussaieff Masson and Susan McCarthy, *When Elephants Weep: The Emotional Lives of Animals* (New York: Delacorte Press, 1995).

49. Ibid., p. 70.

50. Ibid., p. 71.

51. "Scarlett's Web" can be found at <http://www.nsal.org/scarlett/>. It is run by the North Shore Animal League in Port Washington, Long Island, New York.

52. Masson and McCarthy, *When Elephants Weep*, p. 71.

53. Ibid., p. 71.

54. Ibid., p. 72.

55. Ibid.

56. Ibid., p. 71.

57. This behavior has been shown on various PBS and Discovery Channel documentaries.

58. Ibid., p. 94.

59. Stories detailing the emotional effects suffered by orphaned elephants can be found at <http://www.mck.co.za/bushpilot/txt/baby.html> and <http://web.co.za/mg/news/96mar/1mar-cullfilm.html>.

60. Binti-Jua's extraordinary story can be found at the website for People magazine: <http://www.pathfinder.com/people/sp/intrigue/binti.html> or <http://www.pathfinder.com/people/960902/features/gorilla.html>. In 1996, the magazine named Binti one of the Twenty-Five Most Intriguing "People."

61. Barbara Smuts, *Sex and Friendship in Baboons* (New York: Aldine, 1985).

62. Masson and McCarthy, *When Elephants Weep*, p. 139.

63. Takayoshi Kano, *The Last Ape* (Stanford, Calif.: Stanford University Press, 1992).

64. Paul MacLean, "Women: A More Balanced Brain?" *Zygon* 31, no. 3 (September 1996): 421–439.

65. Sharon Begley, "How to Build a Baby's Brain," *Newsweek*, Special Edition: Your Child (Spring/Summer 1997): 28–32.

66. Adrienne L. Zihlman, *The Human Evolution Coloring Book*, with illustrations by Carla Simmons, Wynn Kapit, Fran Milner, and Cyndie Clark-Huegel (New York: Barnes and Noble Books, 1982); new edition in progress.

67. Linda Marie Fedigan, *Primate Paradigms: Sex Roles and Social Bonds* (Montreal, Canada: Eden Press, 1982).

68. For a more detailed discussion of this multilinear theory of hominid and human origins, see Eisler's *Sacred Pleasure*, ch. 2.

69. Takayoshi Kano, *The Last Ape* (Stanford, Calif.: Stanford University Press, 1992); Takayoshi Kano, "The Bonobos' Peaceable Kingdom," *Natural History* (November 1990): 62–70.

70. See Leakey, *The Origin of Humankind*, chs. 5 and 6.

71. Ibid., p. 24.

72. Zihlman, *The Human Evolution Coloring Book*.

73. Adrienne Zihlman, "The Paleolithic Glass Ceiling: Women in Human Evolution," in Lori D. Hager, ed., *Women in Human Evolution* (New York: Routledge, 1997), p. 91. This article provides a good overview of the struggle against the exclusion of women in narratives of human evolution.

74. Diane Gifford-Gonzales, "You Can Hide, But You Can't Run: Representations of Women's Work in Illustrations of Paleolithic Life," *Visual Anthropology Review* 9 (1993): 23–41.

75. Nancy M. Tanner, *Becoming Human* (Cambridge, England: Cambridge University Press, 1981), p. 274. It is interesting that female chimpanzees seem to be more adept than their male counterparts at using tools such as digging sticks.

76. Ibid.

77. Ibid., pp. 274–275. See also Adrienne Zihlman and Nancy Tanner, "Becoming Human: Putting Women in Evolution," paper presented at the annual meeting of the American Anthropological Society, Mexico City, 1974.

78. Leakey, *The Origin of Humankind*, pp. 44–48.

79. MacLean, *The Triune Brain in Evolution*, p. 544; MacLean, "Women: A More Balanced Brain?" p. 434.

80. Maturana and Verden-Zöller, *Origins of Humanness in the Biology of Love*.

81. Riane Eisler, "Spiritual Courage," *Tikkun* 14, no. 1 (January 1999): 15–20.

82. Dr. Bruce Perry and Dr. Linda Mayes, quoted in Sharon Begley, "How to Build a Baby's Brain," p. 32. Begley's article provides an accessible journalistic summary of some of these findings. For a more technical account of the effects of childhood trauma on the brain, see B. D. Perry, R. A. Pollard, R. L. Blakley, W. L. Baker, and D. Vigilante, "Childhood Trauma, the Neurobiology of Adaptation, and 'Use-Dependent' Development of the Brain: How 'States' Become 'Traits,'" *Infant Mental Health Journal* 16 (1996): 271–291.

83. See Chapter 1 of the present volume for a discussion of this distinction between hierarchies of domination and actualization. See also Riane Eisler and David Loye, *The Partnership Way*, rev. ed. (Brandon, Vt.: Holistic Education Press, 1998).

84. See Perry et al., "Childhood Trauma, the Neurobiology of Adaptation, and 'Use-Dependent' Development of the Brain."

85. See Eisler, *Sacred Pleasure*, especially chs. 9 and 10; and Eisler, *Redefining Destiny* (work in progress), ch. 2.

86. For a collection of articles on this issue, see Loye, ed., *The Evolutionary Outrider: The Impact of the Human Agent on Evolution.* A related discussion can be found in Riane Eisler, "Building a Just and Caring World: Four Cornerstones," *Tikkun* 13, no. 3 (May/June 1998).

87. Ibid. See also Riane Eisler, "Changing the Rules of the Game: Work, Values, and Our Future," on the CPS website at <www.partnershipway.org>.

Chapter 4

1. Sally Strum, cited in Jeffrey Moussaieff Masson and Susan McCarthy, *When Elephants Weep: The Emotional Lives of Animals* (New York: Delacorte Press, 1995), p. 139.

2. Adrienne Zihlman, "Myths of Gender," *Nature* 364, no. 12 (August 1993): 585. Another useful short review is Zihlman's "Looking Back in Anger," Nature 384, no. 7 (November 1996): 35–36, in which the author critiques a book reasserting the old view that violence is built into male genes due to our primate ancestry, citing data about bonobo chimpanzees that contradicts this view.

3. For further discussion of this point, see Adrienne Zihlman, "Women's Bodies, Women's Lives: An Evolutionary Perspective," in Mary Ellen Morbeck, Alison Galaway, and Adrienne Zihlman, eds., *The Evolving Female: A Life-History Perspective* (Princeton, N.J.: Princeton University Press, 1997); and Nancy Tanner, *On Becoming Human* (Cambridge, England: Cambridge University Press, 1981). And for an interesting profile on Zihlman that would make a good handout, as it deals with the entire controversy about the first use of tools (a controversy that is inextricably tied up with gender issues), see Ellen Ruppel Shell, "Flesh and Bone," *Discovery* (December 1991): 37–42.

4. Hierarchies of domination are imposed and maintained by fear of pain. They are held in place by the power that is idealized, and even sanctified, in societies that orient primarily to the dominator model: the power to inflict pain, to hurt and kill. By contrast, hierarchies of actualization are primarily based not on power over but on power to (creative power, the power to help and to nurture others) as well as power with (the collective power to accomplish things together, as in what is today called teamwork).

5. Johan Galtung and Sohail Inayatullah, eds., *Macrohistory and Macrohistorians: Perspectives on Individual, Social and Civilizational Change* (New York: Praeger, 1997). Teachers unacquainted with my work are also referred to *The Chalice and the Blade: Our History, Our Future* (San Francisco: Harper & Row, 1987, 1988) and *Sacred Plea-*

sure: Sex, Myth, and the Politics of the Body (San Francisco: Harper Collins, 1995, 1996), where I discuss cultural transformation theory.

6. Thomas Kuhn, *The Structure of Scientific Revolutions* (Chicago: University of Chicago Press, 1970). For an analysis of the conflict between paradigms in terms of the dominator and partnership models, see David Loye, "Evolutionary Action Theory: A Brief Outline," in David Loye, *The Evolutionary Outrider: The Impact of the Human Agent on Evolution* (Twickenham, England: Adamantine Press/Westport, Conn.: Praeger Books, 1998).

7. Rebecca Cann, Mark Stoneking, and Alan Wilson, "Mitochondrial DNA and Human Evolution," *Nature* 325 (1987): 31–36; reported in "Everyone's Genealogical Mother," *Time*, January 26, 1987, p. 66.

8. Jiao Tianlong, "Gender Relations in Prehistoric Chinese Society: Archeological Discoveries," in Min Jiayin, ed., *The Chalice and the Blade in Chinese Culture* (Beijing: China Social Sciences Publishing House, 1995).

9. Ibid., p. 98.

10. For example, according to R. A. Dart's interpretation of early hominid (australopithecine) finds in the Wankie Game Reserve in Africa, these people had been cannibalistic hunters who killed and collected heads of other tribes, and even those of their own tribe. But when C. K. Brain analyzed this claim, he concluded that rather than being the result of human attacks, the bludgeoned skull remains (some of which turned out to be the remains of animals) were the result of attacks by predatory leopards and other large cats. See C. K. Brain, *The Hunters or the Hunted?* (Chicago: University of Chicago Press, 1981).

11. Alexander Marshack, *The Roots of Civilization* (Mt. Kisko, N.Y.: Moyer Bell, Ltd., 1991).

12. See James Mellaart, Catal Huyuk (New York: McGraw-Hill, 1975), where the author proposes that female goddess figures from the Neolithic are "the missing link" between the Paleolithic culture and that of later Bronze Age civilizations in which a Great Goddess was worshipped. See also Marija Gimbutas, *The Goddesses and Gods of Old Europe* (Berkeley: University of California Press, 1982); and Marshack, *The Roots of Civilization*.

13. See Naama Goren-Inbar, "A Figurine from the Acheulian Site of Berekhat Ram," *Journal of the Israel Prehistoric Society* 19 (1986).

14. Arrell Morgan Gibson, *The American Indian: Prehistory to the Present* (Lexington, Mass.: D. C. Heath, 1980), pp. 16–18.

15. See, for example, Gimbutas, *The Goddesses and Gods of Old Europe*; Mellaart, Catal Huyuk; Gerda Lerner, *The Creation of Patriarchy* (New York: Oxford University Press, 1986); Marija Gimbutas, "The First Wave of Eurasian Steppe Pastoralist into Copper Age Europe," *Journal of Indo-European Studies* 5, no. 4 (Winter 1977); and Riane Eisler, *The Chalice and the Blade* (San Francisco: Harper & Row, 1987, 1988).

16. Edward Westermarck, *A Short History of Marriage* (New York: Macmillan, 1926).

17. J. J. Bachofen, *Das Mutterrecht* (1861); published in English as *Myth, Religion, and Mother-Right*, Ralph Manheim, trans. (Princeton, N.J.: Princeton University Press, 1967); Lewis Henry Morgan, *Ancient Society* (New York: H. Holt and Company, 1877); Friedrich Engels, *The Origin of the Family, Private Property, and the State* (New York: International Publishers, 1884/1972); and Alexander Rustow, *Freedom and Domination* (Princeton, N.J.: Princeton University Press, 1980).

18. James Frazer, *The Golden Bough* (New York: Macmillan, 1922/1969), p. 6.

19. Ibid.

20. Curiously, this view has recently been revived by Ken Wilbur in *A Brief History of Everything* (Boston: Shambhala, 1996). Here, the author talks about harmony prevailing in Goddess cultures, but then, with no supporting evidence, writes "as long as you performed that annual ritual human sacrifice to keep the Great Mother happy and the crops growing, all was well" (p. 49).

21. Gylanic and gylany derive from the Greek *gyne*, referring to "woman," and *andros*, to "man," and they are linked by the letter *l*, which in Greek stands for *lyen*, meaning "to resolve," or *lyo*, meaning "to set free," and which in English represents "linking" (rather than "ranking").

22. Scholars today are increasingly using B.C.E. (Before the Common Era) rather than B.C. (Before Christ).

23. Marija Gimbutas, *The Civilization of the Goddess: The World of Old Europe* (San Francisco: Harper San Francisco, 1991). See also Nikolas Platon, *Crete* (Geneva: Nagel Publishers, 1966).

24. Ibid., p. 324.

25. Ibid., pp. viii–x.

26. R. Brian Ferguson, "Violence and War in Prehistory," in Debra L. Martin and David W. Frayer, eds., *Troubled Times: Violence and Warfare in the Past* (New York: Gordon and Breach Publishers, 1997), p. 322.

27. Ibid.

28. Ibid., p. x.

29. Ibid., p. 324.

30. There is some academic debate about the term Goddess. As I point out in *Sacred Pleasure*, we do not know whether it was used in the Neolithic or Paleolithic, as the first deciphered written records that use the term are already from later Bronze Age civilizations such as those of Sumer and Egypt. But the term Goddess has come into use because it serves as a kind of shorthand to communicate what to us today is a very different way of conceptualizing what we call the divine from what we are accustomed to: a God, Father, Lord, King (in other words, a male image). Clearly, however, the term Goddess should not be interpreted as just a female counterpart of the Judaeo-Christian and Muslim God. For one thing, some of the images we find in excavations have both human and animal aspects, and some have both female and male aspects. For another, we should not project our notions of the powers that govern the universe onto peoples who lived thousands of years ago. What is clear is that what we

have here is a different way of representing the powers that govern the universe—reflecting a different social organization from that of the male-dominated and highly stratified cultures out of which mainstream contemporary religions arose.

31. This point is developed at some length in Riane Eisler, *Sacred Pleasure: Sex, Myth, and the Politics of the Body* (San Francisco: Harper Collins, 1995, 1996).

32. Jiao Tianlong, "Gender Relations in Prehistoric Chinese Society: Archeological Discoveries," in Jiayin, *The Chalice and the Blade in Chinese Culture*, p. 92.

33. Ibid., p. 93.

34. Ibid., p. 65. See also Eisler, *Sacred Pleasure*, ch. 2.

35. T. W. Rolleston, *Celtic Myths and Legends* (New York: Dover Publications, 1990); Anne Ross, *Druids, Gods, and Heroes from Celtic Mythology* (New York: Shocken Books, 1986).

36. Ella Young, *The Wondersmith and His Son* (New York: Longmans, Green and Co., 1927).

37. Robert Lawlor, *Voices of the First Day: Awakening in the Aboriginal Dream Time* (Rochester, Vt.: Inner Traditions International, 1991), pp. 115–116.

38. Ibid., p. 117.

39. Merlin Stone, *When God Was a Woman* (New York: Harcourt Brace Jovanovich, 1976), p. 3. This book is an excellent source of information about ancient female deities. Its only drawback is that it does not make the critical distinction between the female deities' character before the shift to a dominator model and their character afterward, when they were often represented as goddesses of war and sacrifice. For a discussion of this point, see Eisler's *The Chalice and the Blade* and *Sacred Pleasure*.

40. Paula Gunn Allen, *The Sacred Hoop: Recovering the Feminine in American Indian Traditions* (Boston: Beacon Press, 1986).

41. Ibid., p. 14.

42. Ibid.

43. Ibid., p. 15. Here, I want to acknowledge Herb Martin and Terri Wheeler of California State University at Monterey Bay, who contributed material on Goddess myths from Native American traditions.

44. Paula Gunn Allen, *Grandmothers of the Light: A Medicine Woman's Sourcebook* (Boston: Beacon Press, 1991), pp. xiv–xv.

45. See Eisler, *The Chalice and the Blade*; Gimbutas, *The Civilization of the Goddess*; Mellaart, *Catal Huyuk*; Jiayin, ed., *The Chalice and the Blade in Chinese Culture*; and Eisler, *Sacred Pleasure*.

46. Arrell Morgan Gibson, *The American Indian: Prehistory to the Present* (Lexington, Mass.: D. C. Heath, 1980), pp. 30–34.

47. In *Sacred Pleasure* (ch. 5), I explore some of the reasons that the culture of these herding people, who came from arid environments, may have evolved in a dominator direction.

48. Jiayin, ed., *The Chalice and the Blade in Chinese Culture*.

49. Cai Junsheng, "Myth and Reality: The Projection of Gender Relations in Prehistoric China," in Jiayin, *The Chalice and the Blade in Chinese Culture*, p. 44.

50. Ibid., pp. 34–35.

51. Again, I want to acknowledge Herb Martin and Terri Wheeler, who contributed material on Goddess traditions from Africa.

52. See Lawrence Stager and Samuel Wolff, "Child Sacrifice at Carthage: Religious Rite or Population Control?" *Biblical Archaeology Review* (January/February 1984): 31–51. See also Eisler, *Sacred Pleasure*, ch. 7.

53. See, for example, Gimbutas, *The Civilization of the Goddess*. See also Eisler, *Sacred Pleasure*, ch. 7, especially notes 7–15, pp. 428–429.

54. Clear-cut evidence of human sacrifice is found only in association with rigid dominator societies. For example, Aztec art contains image after image of human sacrifice, in sharp contrast with early Neolithic and Minoan art, in which not a single such image can be found. An interesting sidelight is that in the Bible the agricultural Cain (who makes an offering of the fruits of the land) is accused of killing his brother Abel (a herder, whose offering is a killed sacrifice)—when in reality herding peoples were the ones who invaded and killed farming peoples. Also of interest is that when Jeremiah rails against the people for backsliding to the worship of the Queen of Heaven, he is told that when women baked cakes for the Queen of Heaven (rather than making killed offerings), there was peace and prosperity (Jeremiah 44:17).

55. Samuel Noah Kramer and John Maier, *The Myths of Enki: The Crafty God* (New York: Oxford University Press, 1989).

56. See Eisler, *Sacred Pleasure*, ch. 3.

57. Nikolas Platon, *Crete* (Geneva: Nagel Publishers, 1966), p. 178.

58. Ibid., p. 167.

59. Sir Richard Woolley, quoted in Jacquetta Hawkes, *Dawn of the Gods* (New York: Random House, 1968), p. 73.

60. See Eisler, *The Chalice and the Blade*, chs. 3–5; Eisler, *Sacred Pleasure*, ch. 4; and Donna Reed's video *The Goddess Remembered*, produced by the Canadian Film Board.

61. Ruby Rohrlich-Leavitt, "Women in Transition: Crete and Sumer," in Renate Bridenthal and Claudia Koonz, eds., *Becoming Visible* (Boston: Houghton Mifflin, 1977), p. 49.

62. Platon, *Crete*, p. 148.

63. Veronica Ions, *Indian Mythology* (New York: Peter Bedrick Books, 1983), p. 16.

64. John Ranelagh, *Ireland: An Illustrated History* (New York: Oxford University Press, 1981), p. 21. Here, too, I wish to acknowledge Herb Martin and Terri Wheeler, who contributed material on the Celts.

65. Jean Markale, *Women of the Celts* (Rochester, Vt.: Inner Traditions International, 1986), p. 86; James Simon, *The World of the Celts* (New York: Thames and Hudson), p. 93.

318   *Notes*

66. June Nash, "The Aztecs and the Ideology of Male Dominance," *Signs* 4 (Winter 1978): 350.

67. Ibid., pp. 349–362.

68. Louisa Teish, *Jambalay* (San Francisco: Harper & Row, 1985), p. 55.

69. Carolyne Larrington, ed., *The Woman's Companion to Mythology* (London: Harper Collins, 1997); Barbara Walker, *The Women's Encyclopedia of Myths and Secrets* (San Francisco: Harper & Row, 1983).

70. Hawkes, *Dawn of the Gods*, p. 19.

71. A work that does bring out this point is Eva Keuls, *The Reign of the Phallus: Sexual Politics in Ancient Athens* (Berkeley: University of California Press, 1993). See also Eisler, *Sacred Pleasure*, ch. 6.

72. Eisler's *The Chalice and the Blade* (ch. 8) and *Sacred Pleasure* (ch. 6) are good sources for a discussion of ancient Greece.

73. Mario Montuori, *Socrates: An Approach* (Amsterdam, Holland: J. C. Gieben Publishers, 1988).

74. For a discussion of this point, see the essay by the classicist Judith P. Hallett in John Peradotto and J. P. Sullivan, eds., *Women in the Ancient World* (Albany: State University of New York Press, 1984).

75. For resource materials relating to this discussion, see Eisler, *The Chalice and the Blade*, ch. 9; Elaine Pagels, *The Gnostic Gospels* (New York: Random House, 1979); Elizabeth Schussler Fiorenza, *In Memory of Her* (New York: Crossroads, 1983); Carol Christ and Judith Plaskow, eds., *Womanspirit Rising* (San Francisco: Harper & Row, 1979); and Rosemary Radford Ruether, ed., *Religion and Sexism: Images of Women in Jewish and Christian Traditions* (New York: Simon & Schuster, 1974).

76. See Eisler, *The Chalice and the Blade*, chs. 9–10; Eisler, *Sacred Pleasure*, chs. 7–8; and Reed's video *The Burning Times*.

77. Vicki Leon, *Uppity Women of Medieval Times* (Berkeley: Conari Press, 1997). This book also features some excellent line drawings that bring these women, and the times they lived in, to life.

78. Ilya Sandra Perlingieri, *Sofonisba Anguissola* (New York: Rizzoli, 1992). This illustrated book about Anguissola's life includes vivid portraits. See also Judy Chicago, *The Dinner Party* (Garden City, N.Y.: Anchor Press/Doubleday, 1979).

79. John M. Riddle, *Eve's Herbs: A History of Contraception and Abortion in the West* (Cambridge, Mass.: Harvard University Press, 1997).

80. Ibid. See also Anne Llewellyn Barstow, *Witchcraze: A New History of the European Witch Hunts* (London/San Francisco: Pandora, 1994), for one of the best scholarly, yet most accessible, works on this holocaust against women.

81. Riane Eisler, "Dominator and Partnership Shifts," in Johan Galtung and Soheil Inayatullah, eds., *Macrohistory and Macrohistorians* (New York: Praeger, 1997). See also Eisler's *The Chalice and the Blade*, ch. 11, and *Sacred Pleasure*, ch. 10.

82. For examples, see Eisler's *Sacred Pleasure*, chs. 18–19.

83. Women Living Under Muslim Laws, an organization of Muslim women with offices in Pakistan and France, is an excellent source of information in this connection. Its address is Boite Postale 23, 34790 Grables (Montpellier)—France. Another excellent source is the quarterly Women's International Network News; for a subscription, write to 187 Grant Street, Lexington, MA 02173.

84. Some readings that contain materials that could be excerpted are Jerry Mander and Edwin Goldsmith, eds., *The Case Against the Global Economy and For a Turn Toward the Local* (San Francisco: Sierra Club Books, 1996); Hazel Henderson, *Paradigms in Progress: Life Beyond Economics* (Indianapolis: Knowledge Systems, Inc., 1991); David Korten, *When Corporations Rule the World* (San Francisco: Barrett-Koehler, 1995); Spike Peterson and Anne Sisson Runyan, *Global Gender Issues* (Boulder, Colo.: Westview Press, 1993); Riane Eisler, David Loye, and Kari Norgaard, *Women, Men, and the Global Quality of Life* (Pacific Grove, Calif.: Center for Partnership Studies, 1995); Human Development Report 1995, published for the United Nations Development Program (UNDP) by Oxford University Press; and *The World's Women 1995: Trends and Statistics* (New York: United Nations, 1995). A short piece that has some good statistics and could serve as a handout is David Korten, "A Market-Based Approach to Corporate Responsibility," *Perspectives on Business and Global Change* 11, no. 2 (June 1997): 45–55. See also the Center for Partnership Studies' website at <www.partnershipway.org> to download "Changing the Rules of the Game: Work, Values, and Our Future," by Riane Eisler, 1997. And for additional materials, consult David Korten's website at <www.iisd1.iisd.ca/pcdf>.

85. See the Center for Partnership Studies' website at <http://www.partnershipway.org> for information about the Alliance for a Caring Economy, a joint project of the Center for Partnership Studies and the Global Futures Foundation. Additional information is available through Wendy Pratt, Global Futures Foundation, 801 Crocker Road, Sacramento, CA 95864 (phone: 916-486-5999; fax: 916-486-5990; website: <www/globalff.org/ace>).

86. See Riane Eisler, "Changing the Rules of The Game," on the CPS website at <www.partnershipway.org>.

87. These two scenarios are outlined in *The Chalice and the Blade* (chs. 12–13) and detailed in the closing chapters of *Sacred Pleasure*.

88. See especially Eisler, *The Chalice and the Blade*; Eisler, *Sacred Pleasure*; and Eisler and Loye, *The Partnership Way: New Tools for Living and Learning*, rev. ed (Brandon, Vt.: Holistic Education Press, 1998).

89. This point, developed in detail in my forthcoming book on cultural transformation theory, is currently sketched in Riane Eisler, "Conscious Evolution: Cultural Transformation and Human Agency," in David Loye, ed., *The Evolutionary Outrider: The Impact of the Human Agent on Evolution* (Westport, Conn.: Praeger Books/Twickenham, England: Adamantine Press, 1988).

90. See Riane Eisler, "Building a Just and Caring World: Four Cornerstones," *Tikkun* 13, no. 3 (May/June 1998), which can be downloaded from the CPS website at <www.partnershipway.org>.

91. Ibid. See also Eisler, *Sacred Pleasure*; Eisler, "Human Rights and Violence: Integrating the Private and Public Spheres," in Lester Kurtz and Jennifer Turpin, eds., *The Web of Violence* (Urbana: University of Illinois Press, 1996); Riane Eisler, David Loye, and Kari Norgaard, *Women, Men, and the Global Quality of Life* (Pacific Grove, Calif.: Center for Partnership Studies, 1995), available from the Center for Partnership Studies, P.O. Box 51936, Pacific Grove, California 93950; and Eisler, "Changing the Rules of the Game: Work, Values, and Our Future," available on the Center for Partnership Studies' web page at <www.partnershipway.org>.

Chapter 5

1. Charlotte Perkins Gilman, quoted in Ann J. Lane, *The Charlotte Perkins Gilman Reader* (New York: Pantheon, 1980), p. xiv.

2. Candace Pert, "The Chemical Communicators," in Bill Moyers, *Healing and the Mind* (New York: Doubleday, 1993), pp. 177–188. For a summary of the role of these chemicals in human evolution, emotion, and behavior, see Riane Eisler, *Sacred Pleasure: Sex, Myth, and the Politics of the Body* (San Francisco: Harper Collins, 1995, 1996), ch. 9.

3. Evelyn Fox Keller, *Reflections on Gender and Science* (New Haven, Conn.: Yale University Press, 1985).

4. Linda Jean Shepherd, *Lifting the Veil: The Feminine Face of Science* (Boston: Shambhala, 1993).

5. Frans deWaal, *Good Natured: The Origins of Right and Wrong in Humans and Other Animals* (Cambridge, Mass.: Harvard University Press, 1996), pp. 163–164.

6. Adrienne Zihlman, *The Human Evolution Coloring Book* (New York: Barnes and Noble Books, 1982); new edition in progress.

7. See Riane Eisler, *Redefining Destiny* (work in progress), for information about socially responsible businesses and business networks, such as the Social Venture Network and Business for Social Responsibility. See also the Center for Partnership Studies website at <www.partnershipway.org> for links with some of these networks.

8. For information, contact The Video Project, 200 Estates Drive, Ben Lomond, California 95005 (phone: 1-800-4-PLANET; website: <http://www.videoproject.org>).

9. For information about the Alliance for a Caring Economy, contact Wendy Pratt, Global Futures Foundation, 801 Crocker Road, Sacramento, CA 95864 (phone: 916-486-5999; fax: 916-486-5990; website: <www/globalff.org/ace>). Related information can be obtained from the Center for Partnership Studies, P.O. Box 51936, Pacific Grove, CA 93950 (phone: 831-626-1004; fax: 831-626-3734; website: <www.partnershipway.org>).

10. David Noble, *A World Without Women: The Christian Clerical Culture of Western Science* (New York: Knopf, 1992).

11. Margaret Wertheim, *Pythagoras' Trousers: God, Physics, and the Gender Wars* (New York: Times Books, 1995).

12. Ruth Bleier, ed., *Feminist Approaches to Science* (New York: Pergamon Press, 1988).

13. Shepherd, *Lifting the Veil: The Feminine Face of Science*.

14. Keller, *Reflections on Gender and Science*.

15. Michael J. Caduto and Joseph Bruchac, *Keepers of the Earth* (Golden, Colo.: Fulcrum, 1989).

16. Evelyn Fox Keller, *A Feeling for the Organism: The Life and Work of Barbara Mc-Clintock* (San Francisco: W. H. Freeman, 1983). Another good source on feminist approaches to science is Sandra Harding and Merril Hintikka, eds., *Discovering Reality: Feminist Perspectives on Epistemology, Metaphysics, Methodology, and Philosophy of Science* (Boston: D. Reidel Publishing Company, 1983).

17. The groundbreaking theories of David Bohm illustrate this point. See his *Wholeness and the Implicate Order* (London: Ark Paperbacks, 1980).

18. Shepherd, *Lifting the Veil: The Feminine Face of Science*.

19. James A. Banks, "The Canon Debate, Knowledge Construction, and Multicultural Education," *Educational Researcher* 22, no. 5 (June/July 1993): 12.

20. *Multiculturalism in Mathematics, Science, and Technology* (Menlo Park, Calif.: Addison-Wesley, 1993).

21. *Math Across Cultures* (San Francisco: Exploratorium Teacher Activity Series, 1995).

22. Claudia Zaslavsky, *Tic-Tac-Toe and Other Three-in-a-Row Games: From Ancient Egypt to the Modern Computer* (New York: Crowell, 1982).

23. Claudia Zaslavsky, "Bringing the World into the Math Class," in *Rethinking Our Classrooms: Teaching for Equity and Justice, a special issue of Rethinking Schools* (1994), can be ordered for $6.00 from Rethinking Schools, 1001 E. Keefe Ave., Milwaukee, WI 53212 (phone: 414-964-9646; fax: 414-964-7220; website: <http://www.rethinkingschools.org>).

24. Muriel Feelings, *Moja Means One: Swahili Counting Book* (New York: Dial, 1971).

25. D. Nelson, G. Joseph, and J. Williams, *Multicultural Mathematics: Teaching Mathematics from a Global Perspective* (New York: Oxford University Press, 1993).

26. Christine E. Sleeter, "Mathematics, Multicultural Education, and Professional Development," *Journal for Research in Mathematics Education* 28, no. 6 (1997): 630–696.

27. For a discussion of these and other important statistics, see Holly Sklar, "Imagine a Country," in *Teaching Sociology* 22, no. 1 (January 1994); Holly Sklar, *Chaos or Community: Seeking Solutions, Not Scapegoats, for Bad Economics* (Boston: South End

Press, 1995); and Gregory Mantsios, "Class in America: Myths and Realities," in *Teaching Sociology* 22, no. 1 (January 1994).

28. For an analysis of these U.S. Census Bureau figures for 1996, see Mary Dalrymple, "Behind the Income Increase," *Monterey County Herald*, October 9, 1997.

29. Sklar, "Imagine a Country."

30. Mantsios, "Class in America: Myths and Realities."

31. *Too Much* can be ordered from the Council on International and Public Affairs, 777 United Nations Plaza, New York, NY 10017(phone: 1-800-316-2739).

32. Paul Kivel and Ellen Creighton, "Making the Peace: Violence Prevention as Social Justice," *Democracy and Education* 12, no. 1 (Fall 1997).

33. Sklar, *Chaos or Community: Seeking Solutions, Not Scapegoats, for Bad Economics*.

34. M. Frankenstein, *Relearning Mathematics: A Different Third R—Radical Maths* (London: Free Association Books, 1989); Nancy Folbre, *The New Field Guide to the U.S. Economy* (New York: New Press, 1995).

35. Jeff Gates, *The Ownership Solution* (Boulder, Colo.: Perseus Books, 1999).

36. For further discussion of this point, see Eisler, *Sacred Pleasure*, ch. 18.

37. Ethlie Ann Vare and Greg Ptacek, *Mothers of Invention* (New York: William Morrow, 1988), pp. 131–134, 148–152.

38. *AAUW Report: How Schools Shortchange Girls* (Washington, D.C.: American Association of University Women Educational Foundation, 1992).

39. Peggy Orenstein, *School Girls: Young Women, Self-Esteem, and the Confidence Gap* (New York: Anchor, 1995).

40. Myra Sadker and David Sadker, *Failing at Fairness: How Our Schools Cheat Girls* (New York: Touchstone Books, 1995).

41. Jean Baker Miller, *Toward a New Psychology of Women* (Boston: Beacon Press, 1976); Carol Gilligan, *In a Different Voice* (Cambridge, Mass.: Harvard University Press, 1982); David McClelland, *Power: The Inner Experience* (New York: Irvington, 1975).

42. See, for example, Keller, *A Feeling for the Organism: The Life and Work of Barbara McClintock*; and Shepherd, *Lifting the Veil: The Feminine Face of Science*.

43. David Noble, *A World Without Women*.

44. Wertheim, *Pythagoras' Trousers: God, Physics, and the Gender Wars*.

45. Terri Perl, *MathEquals* (Menlo Park, Calif.: Addison-Wesley, 1978).

46. The American Association of University Women can be contacted at 1111 Sixteenth Street, NW, Washington, DC 20036 (website: <http://www.aauw.org>).

47. Riane Eisler, *Redefining Destiny* (work in progress); Riane Eisler and Alfonso Montuori, "Creativity, Society, and the Hidden Subtext of Gender," in Alfonso Montuori and Ronald Purser, eds., *Social Creativity* (Cresskill, N.J.: Hampton Press, in press); Riane Eisler, "Creativity and Social Healing," in Tona Pearce Myers, ed., *The Soul of Creativity* (Novato, Calif.: New World Library, 1999).

48. Unfortunately, this dual terminology is found even in good books such as Jacqueline Herald's *World Crafts: A Celebration of Designs and Skills* (Asheville, N.C.:

Lark Books, 1993)—a work that more accurately (without the implied value judgment) could have been called *Artistic Traditions of the World.*

49. Betty LaDuke, *Africa: Women's Art, Women's Lives* (Lawrenceville, N.J.: Africa World Press, 1997).

50. Ibid., p. 1.

51. Ibid., pp. 94–99.

52. Ray Wilkenson, *Newsweek*, September 14, 1987; quoted in ibid., p. 87.

53. Judy Chicago, "The Dinner Party," photographed in *The Dinner Party* (New York: Anchor Press/Doubleday, 1979); Judy Chicago, "The Birth Project," photographed in *The Birth Project* (Garden City, N.Y.: Doubleday, 1985).

54. Ann Morris, "Figurations of the Human Spirit," works in bronze (1997) exhibited in the Lucia Douglas Gallery, Bellingham, Washington.

55. Elinor Gadon, *The Once and Future Goddess* (San Francisco: Harper & Row, 1989).

56. Gloria Orenstein, *The Reflowering of the Goddess* (New York: Pergemon Press, 1990).

57. Norma Broude and Mary Garrard, *The Power of Feminist Art* (New York: Harry N. Abrams, 1994).

58. Gloria Feman Orenstein, *Multicultural Celebrations: The Paintings of Betty LaDuke* (San Francisco: Pomegranate Artworks, 1993).

59. "Betty LaDuke: An Artist's Journey from the Bronx to Timbuktu" and "Africa Between Myth and Reality: The Paintings and Etchings of Betty LaDuke," available from Media for the Arts (phone: 1-800-554-6008).

60. Suzi Gablik, *The Reenchantment of Art* (New York: Thames & Hudson, 1991).

61. Susan Cahan and Zoya Kocur, eds., *Contemporary Art and Multicultural Education* (New York: Routledge, 1996).

62. Lynda Nead, *The Female Nude* (London: Routledge, 1992).

63. Hesiod, *Works and Days*; quoted in John Mansley Robinson, *An Introduction to Early Greek Philosophy* (Boston: Houghton Mifflin, 1968), p. 4.

64. Larissa Bonfant-Warren, "The Women of Etruria," in John Peradotto and J. P. Sullivan, eds., *Women in the Ancient World* (Albany: State University of New York Press, 1984).

65. Paula Gunn Allen, *The Sacred Hoop: Recovering the Feminine in Native American Tradition* (Boston: Beacon Press, 1986), pp. 17–26.

66. David Hurst Thomas, Jay Miller, Richard White, Peter Nabokov, and Philip J. Deloria, *The Native Americans: An Illustrated History* (Atlanta: Turner Publishing, 1993), p. 37.

67. Arrell Morgan Gibson, *The American Indian* (Lexington, Mass.: D. C. Heath), p. 5.

68. Just as scholars today prefer the term B.C.E. (Before the Common Era) over B.C. (Before Christ), they use C.E. (Common Era) more frequently than A.D. (Anno Domini).

69. Bernyce Barlow, *Sacred Sites of the West* (St. Paul, Minn.: Llewellyn, 1996).

70. Jack Weatherford, *Native Roots: How the Indians Enriched America* (New York: Fawcett Columbine, 1991), ch. 2.

71. Letter from Columbus quoted in Hans Koning, *Columbus: His Enterprise* (New York: Monthly Review Press, 1976), pp. 53–54.

72. Koning, *Columbus: His Enterprise*, pp. 53–54.

73. *Rethinking Columbus* (Milwaukee: Rethinking Schools, 1991).

74. Gary Nash, *Red, White and Black: The Peoples of Early America* (New York: Prentice-Hall, 1970).

75. Howard Zinn, *A People's History of the United States* (New York: Harper & Row, 1981).

76. Dee Brown, ed., *Bury My Heart at Wounded Knee* (New York: Holt, Rinehart & Winston, 1971).

77. John Collier, *Indians of the Americas* (New York: New American Library, 1947).

78. Marilou Awiakta, *Selu: Seeking the Corn-Mother's Wisdom* (Golden, Colo.: Fulcrum, 1993).

79. Wilma Mankiller and Michael Wallis, *Mankiller: A Chief and Her People* (New York: St. Martin's Press, 1993).

80. Karen D. Harvey and Lisa D. Harjo, *Indian Country: A History of Native People in America* (Golden, Colo.: North American Press, 1994).

81. R. Golden, M. McConnel, P. Miller, C. Poppin, and M. Turkovich, *Dangerous Memories: Invasion and Resistance Since 1492* (Chicago: Chicago Religious Task Force on Central America, 1991).

82. W.E.B. Du Bois, *The World and Africa* (New York: International Publishers, 1946).

83. David Loye, *The Healing of a Nation* (New York: Norton, 1971/Delta, 1972). This book is in print again through the Internet publisher ToExcel, <www.iuniverse.com>, as well as through <Amazon.com>. I should add that my own earlier books, *The Equal Rights Handbook* (New York: Avon, 1978) and *Dissolution* (New York: McGraw-Hill, 1977), dealing with important aspects of women's history in the United States, are also now available from both <www.iuniverse.com> and <Amazon.com>.

84. Zinn, *A People's History of the United States*.

85. Sharon Harley, Stephen Middleton, and Charlotte Stokes, *The African American Experience* (Englewood Cliffs, N.J.: Globe, 1992).

86. Molefi K. Asant and Mark T. Mattson, *Historical and Cultural Atlas of African Americans* (New York: MacMillan, 1992).

87. Alex Haley, *Roots* (Garden City, N.Y.: Doubleday, 1976).

88. David Barry Gasper and Darlene Clark Hine, eds., *More Than Chattel* (Indianapolis: University of Indiana Press, 1996).

89. bell hooks, *Sisters of the Yam: Black Women and Self-Discovery* (Boston: South End Press, 1993).

90. This tragic story is told in "Freedom on My Mind" (1994), part of the PBS series *American Experience*.

91. The NAACP website, at <www.naacp.org>, provides some historic information about the development of the organization.

92. William Bigelow and Norman Diamond, *Power in Our Hands* (New York: Monthly Review Press, 1988).

93. Elizabeth Martinez, ed., *500 Anos del Pueblo Chicano* [500 Years of Chicano History and Pictures] (Albuquerque, N.M.: South West Organizing Project, 1991).

94. See, for example, Hanna Rosin, "Critics Question Extreme Childrearing Method," *Washington Post*; reprinted in *Monterey County Herald*, March 1, 1999, p. A10.

95. Linda Kerber and Jane DeHart Matthews, *Women's America: Refocusing the Past*, 4th ed. (New York: Oxford University Press, 1997).

96. Carol DuBois and Vicki L. Ruiz, eds., *Unequal Sisters: A Multicultural U.S. Women's History* (New York: Routledge, 1990).

97. Miriam Schneir, *Feminism in Our Time* (New York: Vintage, 1994).

98. National Women's History Project, 7738 Bell Road, Windsor, California 95492-8518.

99. *Women—for America, for the World* can be ordered from the Video Project (phone: 1-800-4-PLANET), and *The American Woman: Portraits of Courage* is distributed by Goldhil Video in Thousand Oaks, California.

100. Lequita Vance-Watkins and Aratani Marik, eds. and trans., *White Flash, Black Rain: Women of Japan Relive the Bomb* (Minneapolis: Milkweed Editions, 1995).

101. Kenneth Rexroth and Ikuko Atsumi, eds., *Women Poets of Japan* (New York: New Directions Books, 1977).

102. Marylin Sewell, ed., *Cries of the Spirit* (Boston: Beacon Press, 1991).

103. Susan Butruille, *Women's Voices from the Western Frontier* (Boise, Idaho: Tamarack Books, 1995).

104. Toni Morrison, *Beloved* (New York: Knopf, 1987).

105. Leslie Marmon Silko, *Ceremony* (New York: Viking Press, 1977).

106. Sandra Cisneros, *The House on Mango Street* (New York: Random House, 1994).

107. Carolyn Forche, ed., *Against Forgetting* (New York: Norton, 1993).

108. Emma Goldman, *Living My Life*, Vols. 1 and 2 (New York: Dover Books, 1970).

109. Agnes Smedley, *Daughter of the Earth* (New York: Feminist Press, 1973).

110. Kate Chopin, *The Awakening* (New York: Avon, 1973).

111. Jean Rhys, *Wide Sargasso Sea* (New York: Popular Library, 1966).

112. Rebecca Hazell, *Heroines: Women Through the Ages* (New York: Abberville Press, 1996).

113. Charlotte Perkins Gilman, *Herland* (New York: Pantheon Books, 1979). Gilman's book is in one sense a satire of mainstream society, in that it describes a role

reversal in which women do a much better job of organizing society than men have done. It depicts a world without men, until some men discover that it exists.

114. Margaret Atwood, *The Handmaid's Tale* (Boston: Houghton Mifflin, 1986); Riane Eisler, *The Gate* (New York: iUniverse <iuniverse.com>, 1999).

115. Marie Jakober, *High Kamilan* (Calgary, Canada: Jullveig Books, 1993).

116. This is a wonderful website ranging in topics from learning disabilities to cerebral palsy, including a list of picture books for young children that can help them understand, empathize with, and accept children who are different.

117. *Rethinking Our Classrooms: Teaching for Equity and Justice*, a special issue of *Rethinking Schools* (1994). See Note 23 above for information about ordering this resource.

118. Ibid., pp. 110–111.

119. For action projects that can be used by both teachers and students, see Riane Eisler and David Loye, *The Partnership Way: New Tools for Living and Learning*, rev. ed (Brandon, Vt.: Holistic Education Press, 1998).

120. Richard Tarnas, *The Passion of the Western Mind* (New York: Harmony Books, 1991).

121. Vandana Shiva, *Staying Alive* (London: Zed Books, 1988); Susan Griffin, Woman and Nature (New York: Harper & Row, 1978).

122. See, for example, the quotations from Nietzsche's writings in Alburey Castell, *An Introduction to Modern Philosophy* (New York: Macmillan, 1946), pp. 352–353, 358–359. In particular, Nietzsche claimed that the "noble and powerful" are entitled to "act toward persons of lower rank just as they please," that Christian ideals such as neighborly love and charity are a "slave morality," and that men should naturally dominate women, who should naturally submit to men. Yet Nietzsche is still included, and lauded, in many humanities texts to this day.

123. The United Nations' website is located at <http://www.un.org>.

124. Gilligan, *In a Different Voice*.

125. Riane Eisler, "Human Rights: Toward an Integrated Theory for Action," in *Human Rights Quarterly* 9, no. 3 (August 1997): 287–308.

126. Charlotte Bunch, "Women's Rights Are Human Rights: Toward a Revision of Human Rights," *Human Rights Quarterly* 12 (1990): 35–52.

127. Charlotte Bunch and Niamh Reilly, *Demanding Accountability: The Global Campaign and Vienna Tribunal for Women's Human Rights* (New York: Center for Women's Global Leadership and the United Nations Development Fund for Women, 1994).

128. Riane Eisler, "Human Rights and Violence: Integrating the Private and Public Spheres," in Jennifer Turpin and Lester Kurtz, eds., *The Web of Violence: From Interpersonal to Global* (Chicago: University of Illinois Press, 1996), pp. 161–185.

129. Marylin Waring, *If Women Counted* (San Francisco: Harper & Row, 1988); Riane Eisler, David Loye, and Kari Norgaard, *Women, Men, and the Global Quality of Life* (Pacific Grove, Calif.: Center for Partnership Studies, 1995); and Riane Eisler,

"Changing the Rules of the Game: Work, Values, and Our Future," on the CPS website at <www.partnershipway.org>.

130. For information about the Alliance for a Caring Economy, see Note 9 above. For related information, see Eisler, "Changing the Rules of the Game: Work, Values, and Our Future," which can be downloaded from the CPS website at <www.partnershipway.org>.

131. Robert Greene, "College Freshmen Traveling Middle of the Road Politically," Associated Press, January 12, 1998. A student who was quoted in this article summed up the sense of powerlessness that students seem to be feeling: "I don't think our opinion matters in the great scale of things," she said.

132. See Eisler, Loye, and Norgaard, *Women, Men, and the Global Quality of Life*, which provides references to other sources. See also Women's International News Network (WIN) News (published quarterly by Fran Hosken, 187 Grant Street, Lexington, MA 02173–2140), which, as a source of information about women worldwide, should be in every school library.

133. Again, see Note 9 above.

134. Barbara A. Lewis, *The Kids' Guide to Social Action* (Minneapolis: Free Spirit Publishers, 1998).

135. Nancy Schniedewind and Ellen Davidson, *Open Minds to Equality* (Needham Heights, Mass.: Allyn and Bacon, 1997).

136. See Note 8 above for information on the Video Project. The Media Education Foundation is located at 26 Central Street, Northhampton, MA 01060 (phone: 1-800-897-0089; website: <www.mediaed.org>), and Cambridge Documentary Films can be reached at P.O. Box 390386, Cambridge, MA 02139 (phone: 617-484-3993; website: <www.shore.net~cdf>).

137. Margarethe von Trotta's Rosa Luxemburg is distributed on video by New Yorker Video, 16 West 61st Street, New York, NY 10023.

138. Lewis, *The Kids' Guide to Social Action*; Eisler, *Sacred Pleasure*.

139. A good resource for high school students is Ocean Robbins and Sol Solomon, *Choices for Our Future* (Summertown, Tenn.: Book Publishing Company, 1994).

Chapter 6

1. David Loye, *The Glacier and the Flame* (work in progress).

2. George Gerbner, "Casting and Fate: Women and Minorities on Television Drama, Game Shows, and News," in Ed Hollander, Coen van der Linden, and Paul Rutten, eds., *Communication Culture Community* (Bohn: Staflue van Loghum, 1995).

3. Diane E. Levin, *Remote Control Childhood? Combating the Hazards of Media Culture* (Washington, D.C.: National Association for the Education of Young Children, 1998), p. 9.

4. George Gerbner, "Marketing Global Mayhem," *The Public* 2 (1995): 72.

5. Ibid.

6. Levin, *Remote Control Childhood? Combating the Hazards of Media Culture*, p. 9.

7. American Medical Association, *Physician's Guide to Media Violence* (Chicago: American Medical Association, 1997).

8. Gerbner, "Marketing Global Mayhem," p. 73. See also Riane Eisler, *Sacred Pleasure: Sex, Myth, and the Politics of the Body* (San Francisco: Harper Collins, 1995, 1996), ch. 18.

9. Milton Rokeach, *The Nature of Human Values* (New York: Free Press, 1973).

10. Center for Media Education, 2120 L Street, NW, Suite 200, Washington D.C., 20037 (website: <http://www.cme.org>); Center for Media Literacy, 4727 Wilshire Blvd., Suite 403, Los Angeles, CA 90010 (website: <http://www.medialit. org>); Children Now, 1212 Broadway, 5th Floor, Oakland, CA 94612 (website: <http://www.childrennow.org>).

11. Cultural Environment Movement, P.O. Box 19104, Philadelphia, PA 19014 (e-mail: <CEM@libertynet.org>); Coalition for Quality Children's Media, 535 Cordova Rd., Suite 456, Santa Fe, NM 87501 (website: <http://www.cqcm.org>).

12. Media Education Foundation, 26 Center Street, Northampton, MA 01060 (phone: 1-800-897-0089; website: <http://www.mediaed.org>).

13. Media Watch, P.O. Box 618, Santa Cruz, CA 95061-0618 (website: <www.mediawatch.com>).

14. George Gerbner's "The Turtles Live to Ooze Again," *Journal of the Center for the Study of Commercialism* 1, no. 3 (October 1991), can be ordered through the Cultural Environment Movement, P.O. Box 3187, Philadelphia, PA 19104 (e-mail: <CEM@libertynet.org>).

15. See Note 14 above for the Cultural Environment Movement's address.

16. *Still Killing Us Softly III*, the most recent update of *Killing Us Softly*, was released in 2000. It is available from the Media Education Foundation (phone: 1–800–897–0089). The website for this organization is <www.mediaed.org>.

17. Colin M. Turnbull, *The Forest People* (New York: Simon & Schuster, 1961).

18. Louise Mahdi, ed., *Betwixt and Between: Patterns of Masculine and Feminine Initiation* (LaSalle, Ill.: Open Court Press, 1987).

19. Carolyne Larrington, ed., *The Woman's Companion to Mythology* (London: HarperCollins, 1992), p. 337.

20. Eisler, *Sacred Pleasure*; New Moon Publishing, P.O. Box 3587, Duluth, MN 55803-3587 (phone: 1-800-381-4743; website: <http://www.newmoon.org>).

21. Eisler, *Sacred Pleasure*, p. 25.

22. Naomi Wolf, *The Beauty Myth* (New York: W. Morrow, 1991), pp. 149–150.

23. Riane Eisler and David Loye, *The Partnership Way*, rev. ed. (Brandon, Vt.: Holistic Education Press, 1998).

24. Marla Cone, "Studies: Pesticides Stunt Kids, Produce More Aggression," *Los Angeles Times*; reprinted in *Monterey County Herald*, March 15, 1999, p. A5.

25. Dr. Porter, quoted in ibid.

26. Ibid.

27. Joby Warrick, "Pesticide Hazards in Fruit Cited," *Washington Post*; reprinted in the *Monterey County Herald*, February 19, 1999, p. A1.

28. See, for example, Bill Moyers, *Healing and The Mind* (New York: Doubleday, 1993); and Christiane Northrup, *Women's Bodies, Women's Wisdom* (New York: Bantam, 1994).

29. Jean Baker Miller, *Toward a New Psychology for Women*, 2nd ed. (Boston: Beacon Press, 1987).

30. Nancy Ruben, *Ask Me If I Care: Voices from an American High School* (Berkeley: Ten Speed Press, 1994).

31. Alfonso Montuori and Isabella Conti, *From Power to Partnership: Creating the Future of Love, Work, and Community* (San Francisco: Harper Collins, 1993/now available through the Internet publisher ToExcel, at <www.iuniverse.com>).

32. Catalogs and order forms can be obtained from the Center for Research on Women, Publications Department, Wellesley College, 106 Central Street, Wellesley, MA 02181-8259 (fax: 617-283-2504).

33. *Rethinking Our Classrooms: Teaching for Equity and Justice*, a special issue of *Rethinking Schools* (1994) that can be purchased for $6.00 by writing to Rethinking Schools, 1001 E. Keefe Avenue, Milwaukee, WI 53212 (fax: 414-964-7220).

34. New Moon can be ordered from New Moon Publishing (see Note 20); and Jean Kilbourne's video *Still Killing Us Softly III* can be obtained through Cambridge Documentary Films, P.O. Box 39386, Cambridge, MA 02139 (phone: 617-484-3993, website: <www.shore.net~cdf>).

35. Nel Noddings, *The Challenge to Care in Schools* (New York: Teachers College Press, Columbia University, 1992); Nel Noddings, *Philosophy of Education* (Boulder, Colo.: Westview Press, 1998); Ron Miller, *What Are Schools For?* (Brandon, Vt.: Holistic Education Press, 1990); Jeffrey Kane, *Education, Information, and Transformation* (New Jersey: Merrill/Prentice-Hall, 1999); Michael Lerner, *The Politics of Meaning* (Reading, Mass.: Addison-Wesley, 1997).

36. Eisler and Loye, *The Partnership Way*.

37. Monty Roberts, *The Man Who Listens to Horses* (New York: Random House, 1997).

38. June M. Reinisch, with Judy Beasley, *The Kinsey Institute New Report on Sex* (New York: St. Martin's Press, 1990).

39. "American Teens Speak: Sex, Myths, TV, and Birth Control," a poll conducted for the Planned Parenthood Federation of American by Louis Harris and Associates, 1986.

40. For more information, contact the California Wellness Foundation Teenage Pregnancy Prevention Initiative, 466 Green Street, Suite 300, San Francisco, CA 94133.

41. This study was published in the September 1997 issue of the *American Journal of Public Health*, as well as in *Reproductive Freedom News* 6, no. 16 (October 3, 1997): 7.

42. Dr. Fleur Sack, with Anne Streeter, *Romance to Die For: The Startling Truth About Women, Sex, and AIDS* (Deerfield Beach, Fla.: Health Communications, 1992).

43. Loye, *The Glacier and the Flame*.

44. Randy Connor, *Blossoms of Bone* (San Francisco: Harper, 1993).

45. Suzanne Pharr, *Homophobia: A Weapon of Sexism* (Berkeley: Chardon, 1988).

46. Chuck Stewart, *Sexually Stigmatized Communities* (Thousand Oaks, Calif.: Sage, 1999); Bennett L. Singer, ed., *Growing Up Gay/Growing Up Lesbian* (New York: New Press, 1994).

47. See Note 33 above.

48. In some world regions today, this sexual double standard is still the basis for the sexual mutilation of millions of girls every year through barbaric surgeries involving the cutting off of the vaginal labia, the sewing together of the vaginal opening so tightly that it must be cut open for intercourse, and/or the cutting off of the clitoris—to ensure that girls and women have no pleasure in sex and thus will not sexually "stray." Alice Walker's novel about this horrendous human rights violation is ironically titled *Possessing the Secret of Joy* (New York: Harcourt Brace Jovanovich, 1992). Among the many scholarly sources on this subject, one of the best is Fran Hosken's *The Hosken Report: Genital and Sexual Mutilation of Females*, 4th ed. (Lexington, Mass.: Women's International Network News, 1994). Another excellent resource, also available through Women's International Network News, is Fran Hosken's *Universal Childbirth Picture Book*, with illustrations by Marcia L. Williams. This simple teaching guide to reproductive literacy for women, available in English, French, Arabic, and Somali, includes a section on the prevention of sexual mutilation (which women are in some regions taught is necessary if they are to be capable of giving birth!).

49. "Afghanistan: Taliban Use Islam for Violence Against Women," *New York Times*, August 29, 1997. See also "Women's/Girls' Health Care Ignored by Afghan Islamic Rulers," in *Women's International Network News* 23, no. 4 (Autumn 1997).

50. A groundbreaking book on touch is Ashley Montagu's *Touching*, 3rd ed. (New York: Harper & Row, 1986).

51. An interview with me on this subject for New Moon Network (March/April 1996), a publication that provides information and advice for parents of girls, is available from New Moon Publishing (see Note 20 above). It can also be downloaded from the CPS website at <www.partnershipway.org>.

52. For some of this research, see Irwin Hyman, *The Case against Spanking* (San Francisco: Jossey-Bass, 1997).

53. Maria Montessori, *Education for a New World* (Oxford, England: Clio Press, 1989; originally published in 1946.).

54. Nel Noddings, *The Challenge to Care in Schools* (New York: Teachers College Press, Columbia University, 1992), xiii.

55. Ibid., p. 51.

56. Gene Myers, *Children & Animals* (Boulder, Colo.: Westview Press, 1998), pp. 5, 152.

57. These books are published by SRA McGraw-Hill in Columbus, Ohio.

58. C-TREC is located at 444 De Haro Street, Suite 117, San Francisco, California 94107 (phone: 415-864-8424; fax: 415-864-8529; e-mail: <ctrec@aol.com>).

59. "Resolving Conflicts Creatively Program," *Connections* 1, no. 1 (June 1994): 6.

60. Peacebuilders is a program designed by Heartsprings, Inc., P.O. Box 12158, Tucson, Arizona 85732 (phone: 1-800-368-9356).

61. Marilyn Watson, Victor Battistich, and Daniel Solomon, "Enhancing Students' Social and Ethical Development in Schools: An Intervention Program and Its Effects," *International Journal of Educational Research* 2, no. 7 (1998): 571.

62. For information about the Child Development Project, contact the Development Studies Center, 2000 Embarcadero, Oakland, CA 94606-5300.

63. "Wildlife Extinction at All-Time High," *Popline* 20 (January-February 1998): 2.

64. For further information, write the Rainforest Action Network at 450 Sansome Street, Suite 700, San Francisco, California 94111, or check out its website at <www.ran.org/ran/>.

65. Media Education Foundation, 26 Center Street, Northampton, MA 01060 (phone: 1-800-897-0089; website: <http://www.mediaed.org>).

66. Theo Colborn, Dianne Dumanoski, and John Peterson Myers, *Our Stolen Future* (New York: Dutton, 1996).

67. Herbert L. Needleman and Philip Landrigan, *Raising Children Toxic Free* (New York: Ferrar, Straus, and Giroux, 1994).

68. United Nations, 1 UN Plaza, New York, NY 10017; Population Action International, 1120 19th Street, NW, Suite 550, Washington, D.C.; Riane Eisler, "Population Pressure, Women's Roles, and Peace," in Ervin Laszlo and Yong-Youl Yoo, eds., *World Encyclopedia of Peace* (New York: Pergamon Press, 1986).

69. Irene Diamond and Gloria Orenstein, eds., *Reweaving the World: The Emergence of Ecofeminism* (San Francisco: Sierra Club, 1990); Dave Barry, "A Beginner's Guide to Housework," and Riane Eisler, "Cooperation," *Utne Reader* (March/April 1990): 87-90.

70. Alliance for a Caring Economy is a joint project of the Center for Partnership Studies and the Global Futures Foundation. For information, contact Wendy Pratt, Global Futures Foundation, 801 Crocker Road, Sacramento, CA 95864 (phone: 916-486-5999; fax: 916-486-5990; website: <www/globalff.org/ace>). Related information can be obtained from the Center for Partnership Studies, P.O. Box 51936, Pacific Grove, CA 93950 (phone: 831-626-1004; fax: 831-626-3734; website: <www.partnershipway.org>).

71. This video can be obtained from Conservation International, 1015 18th Street, NW, Suite 1000, Washington, DC 20036 (phone: 202-429-5660).

72. Teachers can order these materials by contacting the Schlitz Audubon Center at 111 East Brown Deer Road, Milwaukee, WI 53217.

73. This handbook can be obtained from the Global Tomorrow Coalition, 25422 Trabuco Road, #105-440, El Toro, CA 92630-2792.

74. Center for Ecoliteracy, 2522 San Pablo Avenue, Berkeley, CA 94702 (phone: 510-845-4595).

75. Population Action International, 1120 19th Street, NW, Suite 550, Washington, DC 20036 (website: <www.popact.org>; e-mail: <pai@popact.org>).

76. To order *POPLINE*, teachers can contact the World Population Institute at 107 2nd Street, NE, Washington, DC 20002

77. For example, a July 1998 mailing from Zero Population Growth (1400 Sixteenth Street, NW, Suite 320, Washington, DC 20036) points out that at present rates of growth the world population will double within the next forty-seven years, going from an already crowded 6 billion people to an unbearable 12 billion people—with horrendous implications for our children's and grandchildren's quality of life. Although the highest rates of population growth are occurring in the poorest nations, where diseases (which spread across borders) are already endemic and a powder keg of frustration has led to chronic violence (including international terrorism), the population of the United States is growing at a rate of 2.6 million people per year, largely due to the fact that this country has the highest rate of teen pregnancies of any developed nation—because we do not give our teens the family planning information and access that teens in other developed nations receive. ZPG urges all of us to let our elected officials know the urgency of supporting—rather than, as the 104th Congress did, radically cutting—funding for family planning both in the United States and abroad.

Epilogue

1. From the song "Will I Ever Grow Up?" on the Raffi video *On Broadway* (1993), distributed by Rounder Records, Cambridge, MA.

2. Nova School, 2410 East Cherry Street, Seattle, WA 98122.

3. For more information, contact Rita Tenorio, the program implementer, at La Escuela Fratney, 3255 N. Fratney Street, Milwaukee, WI 53212. The school's website can be accessed through the Center for Applied Linguistics at <www.cal.org/db//2way>.

4. Sudbury Valley School, 2 Winch Street, Framingham, MA 01701 (phone: 508-877-3030; website: <www.sudval.org>).

5. IMTEC, directed by Per Dalin, can be reached through its main office located at Josefines gate 9, N–0351 Oslo, Norway (fax: 47–22–567920). It has built up an international network of people and institutions known as The SCHOOL YEAR 2020 network. C-TREC, directed by Parker Page, is located at 444 De Haro Street, Suite 117, San Francisco, CA 94107 (fax: 415–864–8529; e-mail: <ctrec@aol.com>). Ideas for, and examples of, partnership process, content, and structure are offered in

books such as Nel Noddings, *The Challenge to Care in Schools* (New York: Teachers College Press, 1992); Lisa Goldstein, *Teaching with Love* (New York: Peter Lang, 1997); Paul Cummins, *For Mortal Stakes: Solutions for Schools and Society* (Las Vegas: Bramble, 1998); and Edward T. Clark, Jr., *Designing and Implementing an Integrated Curriculum: A Student-Centered Approach* (Brandon, Vt.: Holistic Education Press, 1997).

6. Paul H. Ray, *The Integral Culture Survey: A Study of the Emergence of Transformational Values in America* (Sausalito, Calif.: Institute of Noetic Sciences, Research Report 96-A, 1996); Paul H. Ray "The Emerging Culture," *American Demographics* (February 1997).

7. Paul H. Ray, "What Might Be the Next Step in Cultural Evolution?" in David Loye, ed., *The Evolutionary Outrider* (Bridgeport, Conn.: Praeger Books/Twickenham, England: Ademantine Press, 1998).

8. Ronald Inglehart, *Modernization and Postmodernization: Cultural, Economic, and Political Change in 43 Societies* (Princeton, N.J.: Princeton University, 1997).

Illustrations

Photos

Bibliography

AAUW Report: How Schools Shortchange Girls. 1992. Washington, D.C.: American Association of University Women Educational Foundation.

Anthony, E. James, and B. Colder, eds. 1987. *The Invulnerable Child*. New York: Guilford Press.

Asant, Molefi K., and Mark T. Mattson. 1992. *Historical and Cultural Atlas of African Americans*. New York: Macmillan.

Assagioli, Roberto. 1965. *Psychosynthesis: A Manual of Principles and Techniques*. New York: Viking Press.

Atwood, Margaret. 1986. *The Handmaid's Tale*. Boston: Houghton Mifflin.

Awiakta, Marilou. 1993. *Selu: Seeking the Corn-Mother's Wisdom*. Golden, Colo.: Fulcrum.

Bachofen, J. J. 1861. *Das Mutterrecht*. Published in English, in 1967, as *Myth, Religion, and Mother-Right*. Ralph Manheim, trans. Princeton, N.J.: Princeton University Press.

Baker Miller, Jean. 1987. *Toward a New Psychology of Women*, 2nd ed. Boston: Beacon Press.

Banks, James A. 1993. "The Canon Debate, Knowledge Construction, and Multicultural Education." *Educational Researcher* 22, no. 5 (June/July): 4–14.

_____. 1991. "Multicultural Education: Its Effects on Students' Racial and Gender Role Attitudes." In James P. Shaver, ed., *Handbook of Research on Social Studies Teaching and Learning*, pp. 459–469. New York: Macmillan.

Banneker, Benjamin. 1993. "From Stars to City Planning." In Thomas Alcoze et al., eds., *Multiculturalism in Mathematics, Science, and Technology*. Menlo Park, Calif.: Addison-Wesley.

Barash, David. 1977. *Sociobiology and Behavior*. New York: Elsevier.

Barlow, Bernyce. 1996. *Sacred Sites of the West*. St. Paul, Minn.: Llewellyn.

Barston, Anne Llewellyn. 1994. *Witchcraze: A New History of the European Witch Hunts*. London/San Francisco: Pandora.

Begley, Sharon. 1997. "How to Build a Baby's Brain." *Newsweek*, Special Edition: Your Child (Spring/Summer).

Belenky, Mary, Blythe Clinchy, Nancy Goldberger, and Jill Tarule. 1986. *Women's Ways of Knowing: The Development of Self, Voice, and Mind*. New York: Basic Books.

Benedict, Ruth. 1934. *Patterns of Culture*. New York: Houghton Mifflin.

Bigelow, William, and Norman Diamond. 1988. *Power in Our Hands*. New York: Monthly Review Press.

Bleier, Ruth. 1984. *Science and Gender*. Elmsford, New York: Pergamon Press.

Bleier, Ruth, ed. 1988. *Feminist Approaches to Science*. New York: Pergamon Press.

Bohm, David. 1980. *Wholeness and the Implicate Order*. London: Ark Paperbacks.

———. 1990. *On Dialogue*. Ojai, Calif.: David Bohm Seminars.

Bonfant-Warren, Larissa. 1984. "The Women of Etruria." In John Peradotto and J. P. Sullivan, eds., *Women in the Ancient World*. Albany: State University of New York Press.

Boodman, Sandra G. 1998. "Gay and Teen Boys More Likely to Commit Suicide." *Washington Post*, March 3, pZ05.

Brain, C. K. 1981. *The Hunters or the Hunted?* Chicago: University of Chicago Press.

Brooks, Jacqueline G., and Martin G. Brooks. 1993. *In Search of Understanding*. Alexandria, Va.: Association for Supervision and Curriculum Development.

Broude, Norma, and Mary Garrard. 1994. *The Power of Feminist Art*. New York: Harry N. Abrams.

Brown, Dee, ed. 1971. *Bury My Heart at Wounded Knee*. New York: Holt, Rinehart & Winston.

Bunch, Charlotte. 1990. "Women's Rights Are Human Rights: Toward a Revision of Human Rights." *Human Rights Quarterly* 12, pp. 35–52.

Bunch, Charlotte, and Niamh Reilly. 1994. *Demanding Accountability: The Global Campaign and Vienna Tribunal for Women's Human Rights*. New York: Center for Women's Global Leadership and the United Nations Development Fund for Women.

Butruille, Susan. 1995. *Women's Voices from the Western Frontier*. Boise, Iowa: Tamarack Books.

Caduto, Michael J., and Joseph Bruchac. 1989. *Keepers of the Earth*. Golden, Colo.: Fulcrum.

Cahan, Susan, and Zoya Kocur, eds. 1996. *Contemporary Art and Multicultural Education*. New York: Routledge.

Callahan, Mathew. 1991. *Sex, Death, and the Angry Young Man*. Ojai, Calif.: Times Change Press.

Campbell, Joseph. 1974. *The Mythic Image*. Princeton, N.J.: Princeton University Press.

Cann, Rebecca, Mark Stoneking, and Alan Wilson. 1987. "Mitrochondrial DNA and Human Evolution." *Nature* 325.

Capra, Fritjof. *The Web of Life*. 1996. New York: Anchor/Doubleday.

Carlson, Neil. R. 1994. *Physiology of Behavior*. Boston: Allyn and Bacon.

Chaisson, Eric. 1987. *The Life Era*. New York: Atlantic Monthly Press.

Chicago, Judy. 1979. *The Dinner Party*. New York: Anchor Press/Doubleday.

———. 1985. *The Birth Project*. Garden City, N.Y.: Doubleday.

Chopin, Kate. 1973. *The Awakening*. New York: Avon.

Christ, Carol, and Judith Plaskow, eds. 1979. *Womanspirit Rising*. San Francisco: Harper & Row.

Cisneros, Sandra. 1994. *The House on Mango Street*. New York: Random House.

Clark, Edward T., Jr. 1997. *Designing and Implementing an Integrated Curriculum: A Student-Centered Approach*. Brandon, Vt.: Holistic Education Press.

Collier, John. 1947. *Indians of the Americas*. New York: New American Library.

Combs, Allan. 1995. *The Radiance of Being*. Edinburgh: Floris Books.

Combs, Allan, ed. 1992. *Cooperation*. Philadelphia: Gordon and Breach Science Publishers.

Cone, Marla. 1999. "Studies: Pesticides Stunt Kids, Produce More Aggression." *Los Angeles Times*; reprinted in *Monterey County Herald*, March 15, p. A5.

Cummins, Paul. 1998. *For Mortal Stakes: Solutions for Schools and Society*. Las Vegas: Bramble.

Dabrowski, Kazimierz. 1964. *Positive Disintegration*. Boston: Little, Brown.

Dalrymple, Mary. 1997. "Behind the Income Increase." *Monterey County Herald*, October 9.

Darwin, Charles. [1871] 1981. *The Descent of Man*. Princeton, N.J.: Princeton University Press.

Dawkins, Richard. 1990. *The Selfish Gene*. New York: Oxford University Press.

"Declaration and Principles." 1993. Council for a Parliament of the World's Religions.

deWaal, Frans. 1996. *Good Natured: The Origins of Right and Wrong in Humans and Other Animals*. Cambridge, Mass.: Harvard University Press.

Dewey, John. 1976. *Democracy and Education*. New York: Free Press.

DuBois, Carol, and Vicki L. Ruiz, eds. 1990. *Unequal Sisters: A Multicultural U.S. Women's History*. New York: Routledge.

Du Bois, W.E.B. 1946. *The World and Africa*. New York: International Publishers.

Edelman, Marian Wright. 1996. *Guide My Feet: Prayers and Meditations on Loving and Working for Children*. New York: Harper Collins.

Edlefsen, Urban Paul Thatcher. 1996. "President Clinton's State of the Union Address: A Partnership Analysis." Paper for Nova High School's class.

Eisler, Riane. *Dissolution*. 1977. New York: McGraw-Hill. Now available through the Internet publisher ToExcel at <www.iuniverse.com>.

_____. 1978. *The Equal Rights Handbook*. New York: Avon. Now available through the Internet publisher ToExcel at <www.iuniverse.com>.

_____. 1987, 1988. *The Chalice and the Blade: Our History, Our Future*. San Francisco: Harper & Row.

_____. 1991. "Women, Men, and Management." *Futures* 23, no. 1 (January/February): 3–18.

_____. 1995, 1996. *Sacred Pleasure: Sex, Myth, and the Politics of the Body*. San Francisco: Harper Collins.

_____. 1996. "Human Rights and Violence: Integrating the Private and Public Spheres." In Lester Kurtz and Jennifer Turpin, eds., *The Web of Violence*. Urbana: University of Illinois Press.

_____. 1997. "Changing the Rules of the Game: Work, Values, and Our Future." Available on the Center for Partnership Studies web page at <www.partnershipway. org>.

_____. 1998. "Building a Just and Caring World: Four Cornerstones." *Tikkun* 13, no. 3 (May/June).

_____. 1998. "Conscious Evolution: Cultural Transformation and Human Agency." In David Loye, ed., *The Evolutionary Outrider*. Westport, Conn.: Praeger Books/Twickenham, England: Adamantine Press.

_____. 1999. "Creativity and Social Healing." In Tona Pearce Myers, ed., *The Soul of Creativity*. Novato, Calif.: New World Library.

_____. 1999. *The Gate*. New York: iUniverse <www.iuniverse.com>.

_____. 1999. "Spiritual Courage." *Tikkun* 14, no. 1 (January): 15–20.

_____. Work in progress. *Redefining Destiny*.

Eisler, Riane, and David Loye. 1998. *The Partnership Way: New Tools for Living and Learning*, rev. ed. Brandon, Vt.: Holistic Education Press.

Eisler, Riane, David Loye, and Kari Norgaard. 1995. *Women, Men, and the Global Quality of Life*. Pacific Grove, Calif.: Center for Partnership Studies.

Eisler, Riane, and Alfonso Montuori, The *Partnership Organization*, work in progress.

_____. 2000. "Creativity, Society, and the Hidden Subtext of Gender." In Alfonso Montuori and Ronald Purser, eds., *Social Creativity*. Cresskill, N.J.: Hampton Press.

Engels, Friedrich. [1884] 1972. *The Origin of the Family, Private Property, and the State*. New York: International Publishers.

"Faith, Evolution Can Co-exist, Pope Says." 1996. *Associated Press*, October 25.

Fausto-Sterling, Anne. 1985. *Myths of Gender*. New York: Basic Books.

Fedigan, Linda Marie. 1982. *Primate Paradigms: Sex Roles and Social Bonds*. Montreal, Canada: Eden Press.

Feelings, Muriel. 1971. *Moja Means One: Swahili Counting Book*. New York: Dial.

Fiorenza, Elizabeth Schussler. 1983. *In Memory of Her*. New York: Crossroads.

Fine, Michelle, ed. 1994. *Chartering Urban School Reform*. New York: Teacher's College Press.

Folbre, Nancy. 1995. *The New Field Guide to the U.S. Economy*. New York: New Press.

Forche, Carolyn, ed. 1993. *Against Forgetting*. New York: Norton.

Frankenstein, M. 1989. *Relearning Mathematics: A Different Third R—Radical Maths*. London: Free Association Books.

Frazer, James. [1922] 1969. *The Golden Bough*. New York: Macmillan.

Freire, Paolo. 1973. *Pedagogy of the Oppressed*. New York: Seabury Press.

Gabardino, James, Nancy Dubrow, Kathleen Kostelny, and Carole Pardo. 1998. *Children in Danger: Coping with the Consequences of Community Violence*. San Francisco: Jossey Bass.

Gablik, Suzi. 1991. *The Reenchantment of Art*. New York: Thames & Hudson.

Gadon, Elinor. 1989. *The Once and Future Goddess*. San Francisco: Harper & Row.

Gardner, Howard. 1983. *Frames of Mind*. New York: Basic Books.

Gasper, David Barry, and Darlene Clark Hine, eds. 1996. *More Than Chattel*. Indianapolis: University of Indiana Press.

Gates, Jeff. 1999. *The Ownership Solution*. Boulder, Colo.: Perseus Books.

Gerbner, George. 1991. "The Turtles Live to Ooze Again." *Journal of the Center for the Study of Commercialism* 1, no. 3 (October).

Gerbner, George, Larry Gross, Michael Morgan, and Nancy Signorielli. 1994. "Growing Up with Television." In Jennings Bryant and Dolf Zillman, eds., *Media Effects*, pp. 17–41. Hillsdale, N.J.: Erlbaum.

Ghiselin, Michael. 1974. *The Economy of Nature and the Evolution of Sex*. Berkeley: University of California Press.

Gibbs, Jeanne. 1994. *Tribes: A New Way of Learning Together*. Santa Rosa, Calif.: Center Source Publications.

Gibson, Arrell Morgan. 1980. *The American Indian: Prehistory to the Present*. Lexington, Mass.: D. C. Heath.

Gifford-Gonzales, Diane. 1993. "You Can Hide, But You Can't Run: Representations of Women's Work in Illustrations of Paleolithic Life." *Visual Anthropology Review* 5, pp. 23–41.

Gilligan, Carol. 1982. *In a Different Voice*. Cambridge, Mass.: Harvard University Press.

Gilman, Charlotte Perkins. 1979. *Herland*. New York: Pantheon Books.

Gimbutas, Marija. 1989. *The Language of the Goddess*. San Francisco: Harper & Row.

———. 1991. *The Civilization of the Goddess*. San Francisco: Harper San Francisco.

———. 1997. "The First Wave of Eurasian Steppe Pastorialist into Copper Age Europe." *Journal of Indo-European Studies* 5, no. 1 (Winter).

Gladden, Robert. 1998. "The Small Schools Movement: A Review of the Literature." In Michelle Fine and Janis I. Somerville, eds., *Small Schools Imaginations: A Creative Look at Urban Public Schools*, pp. 113–137. Chicago: Cross City Campaign for Urban School Reform.

Goerner, Sally. 1999. *After the Clockwork Universe*. London: Floris Books.

Golden, R., M. McConnel, P. Miller, C. Poppin, and M. Turkovich. 1991. *Dangerous Memories: Invasion and Resistance Since 1492*. Chicago: Chicago Religious Task Force on Central America.

Goldman, Emma. 1970. *Living My Life*, vols. 1 and 2. New York: Dover Books.

Goldstein, Lisa. 1997. *Teaching with Love*. New York: Peter Lang.

Goren-Inbar, Naama. 1986. "A Figurine from the Acheulian Site of Berekhat Ram." *Journal of the Israel Prehistoric Society* 19.

Gould Davis, Elizabeth. 1971. *The First Sex*. New York: Penguin Books.

Greene, Robert. 1998. "College Freshmen Traveling Middle of the Road Politically." *Associated Press*, January 12.

Griffin, Susan. 1978. *Woman and Nature*. New York: Harper & Row.

Gunn Allen, Paula. 1986. *The Sacred Hoop: Recovering the Feminine in American Indian Traditions*. Boston: Beacon Press.

_____. 1991. *Grandmothers of the Light: A Medicine Woman's Sourcebook.* Boston: Beacon Press.

Haley, Alex. 1976. *Roots.* Garden City, N.Y.: Doubleday.

Hall, Calvin, and Gardner Lindzey. 1978. *Theories of Personality.* New York: Wiley.

Halloway, Ralph. 1983. "Human Paleolithic Evidence Relevant to Language Behavior." *Human Neurobiology* 2.

Harding, Sandra, and Merril Hintikka, eds. 1983. *Discovering Reality: Feminist Perspectives on Epistemology, Metaphysics, Methodology, and Philosophy of Science.* Boston: D. Reidel Publishing Company.

Harley, Sharon, Stephen Middleton, and Charlotte Stokes. 1992. *The African-American Experience.* Englewood Cliffs, N.J.: Globe.

Harvey, Karen D., and Lisa D. Harjo. 1994. *Indian Country: A History of Native People in America.* Golden, Colo.: North American Press.

Hawkes, Jacquetta. 1968. *Dawn of the Gods.* New York: Random House.

Hazell, Rebecca. 1996. *Heroines: Women Through the Ages.* New York: Abberville Press.

Henderson, Hazel. 1991. *Paradigms in Progress: Life Beyond Economics.* Indianapolis: Knowledge Systems.

Herald, Jacqueline. 1993. *World Crafts: A Celebration of Designs and Skills.* Asheville, N.C.: Lark Books.

Higgins, Gina O'Connell. 1994. *Resilient Adults: Overcoming a Cruel Past.* San Francisco: Jossey-Bass Publishers.

Ho, Mae-Wan. 1998. "Organism and Psyche in a Participatory Universe." In David Loye, ed., *The Evolutionary Outrider: The Impact of the Human Agent on Evolution.* Bridgeport, Conn.: Praeger Books/Twickenham, England: Adamantine Press.

hooks, bell. 1993. *Sisters of the Yam: Black Women and Self-Discovery.* Boston: South End Press.

Hosken, Fran. 1994. *The Hosken Report: Genital and Sexual Mutilation of Females,* 4th ed. Lexington, Mass.: Women's International Network News.

Hosken, Fran, illustrated by Marcia. L. Williams. 1993. *Universal Childbirth Picture Book.* Lexington, Mass.: Women's International Network News.

How Schools Shortchange Girls: A Study of Major Findings on Girls and Education. 1995. New York: Marlowe & Co.

Human Development Report 1995. 1995. United Nations Development Program (UNDP). New York: Oxford University Press.

Hyman, Irvin. 1997. *The Case Against Spanking.* San Francisco: Jossey-Bass.

Inglehart, Ronald. 1997. *Modernization and Postmodernization: Cultural, Economic, and Political Change in 43 Societies.* Princeton, N.J.: Princeton University.

Ions, Veronica. 1983. *Indian Mythology.* New York: Peter Bedrick Books.

Isaac, Glynn. 1978. "The Sharing Hypothesis." *Scientific American* (April).

Isaacs, William. 1994. "The Power of Collective Thinking." In Kellie T. Wardman, ed., *Reflections on Creating Learning Organizations,* pp. 83–94. Cambridge, Mass.: Pegasus Communications.

Jakober, Marie. 1993. *High Kamilan.* Calgary, Canada: Jullveig Books.

James, Simon. 1993. *The World of the Celts.* New York: Thames and Hudson

Jiayin, Min, ed. 1995. *The Chalice and the Blade in Chinese Culture*. Beijing: China Social Sciences Publishing House.

Johnson, David W. 1994. *Cooperative Learning in the Classroom*. Alexandria, Va.: Association for Supervision and Curriculum Development.

Johnson, David W., and Roger T. Johnson. 1987. "Research Shows the Benefits of
Adult Cooperation." *Educational Leadership* 45, no. 3: 27–30.

———. 1994. *Learning Together and Alone*. Needham Heights, Mass.: Allyn and Bacon.

Junsheng Cai. 1995. "Myth and Reality: The Projection of Gender Relations in Pre-
historic China." In Min Jiayin, ed., *The Chalice and the Blade in Chinese Culture:
Gender Relations and Social Models*. Beijing: China Social Sciences Publishing
House.

Kagan, Spencer. December 1989–January 1990. "The Structural Approach to Cooperative Learning." *Educational Leadership*: 12–15.

Kane, Jeffrey. 1999. *Education, Information, and Transformation*. New Jersey:
Merrill/Prentice-Hall.

Kano, Takayoshi. 1990. "The Bonobos' Peaceable Kingdom." *Natural History* (November).

———. 1992. *The Last Ape*. Stanford, Calif: Stanford University Press.

Kanter, Rosabeth Moss. 1989. *When Giants Learn to Dance*. New York: Simon &
Schuster.

Kauffman, Stuart. 1995. *At Home in the Universe*. New York: Oxford University Press.

Keller, Evelyn Fox. 1983. *A Feeling for the Organism: The Life and Work of Barbara Mc-
Clintock*. San Francisco: W. H. Freeman.

———. 1985. *Reflections on Gender and Science*. New Haven, Conn.: Yale University
Press.

Kerber, Linda, and Jane DeHart. 1997. *Women's America: Refocusing the Past*, 4th ed.
New York: Oxford University Press.

Keuls, Eva. 1993. *The Reign of the Phallus: Sexual Politics in Ancient Athens*. Berkeley:
University of California Press.

Kivel, Paul, and Ellen Creighton. 1997. "Making the Peace: Violence Prevention as
Social Justice." *Democracy and Education* 12, no. 1 (Fall).

Koegel, Rob. 1994. "Healing the Wounds of Masculinity: A Crucial Role for Educators," *Holistic Education Review* 7: 42–49.

Kohn, Alfie. 1992. *No Contest: The Case Against Competition*. New York: Houghton
Mifflin.

Koning, Hans. 1976. *Columbus: His Enterprise*. New York: Monthly Review Press.

Korten, David. 1995. *When Corporations Rule the World*. San Francisco: Barrett-
Koehler.

———. 1997. "A Market-Based Approach to Corporate Responsibility." *Perspectives
on Business and Global Change* 11, no. 2 (June): 45–55.

Kramer, Samuel Noah, and John Maier. 1989. *The Myths of Enki, The Crafty God*. New
York: Oxford University Press.

Kropotkin, Peter. 1988. *Mutual Aid*. Montreal, Canada: Black Rose Books.

Kuhn, Thomas. 1970. *The Structure of Scientific Revolutions*. Chicago: University of
Chicago Press.

LaDuke, Betty. 1997. *Africa: Women's Art, Women's Lives.* Lawrenceville, N.J.: Africa World Press.

Lane, Ann J. 1980. *The Charlotte Perkins Gilman Reader.* New York: Pantheon.

Larrington, Carolyne, ed. 1997. *The Woman's Companion to Mythology.* London: Harper Collins.

Laszlo, Ervin. 1994. *Choice: Evolution or Extinction?* New York: Tarcher/Putnam.

Lawlor, Robert. 1991. *Voices of the First Day: Awakening in the Aboriginal Dream Time.* Rochester, Vt.: Inner Traditions International.

Leach, Penelope. 1994. *Children First.* New York: Alfred A. Knopf.

Leakey, Richard. 1994. *The Origin of Humankind.* New York: Basic Books.

Leon, Vicki. 1997. *Uppity Women of Medieval Times.* Berkeley: Conari Press.

Lerner, Gerda. 1986. *The Creation of Patriarchy.* New York: Oxford University Press.

Lerner, Michael. 1997. *The Politics of Meaning.* Reading, Mass.: Addison-Wesley, 1997.

Lewin, Kurt. 1951. *Field Theory in Social Science.* New York: Harper & Row.

Lewis, Barbara A. 1998. *The Kids' Guide to Social Action.* Minneapolis: Free Spirit Publishers.

Lewontin, R. C., Steven Rose, and Leon J. Kamin. 1984. *Not in Our Genes.* New York: Pantheon.

Loye, David. 1972/1998. *The Healing of a Nation.* New York: Norton/New York: Delta. Now available through the Internet publisher ToExcel at <www.iuniverse.com>.

_____. 1994. "Charles Darwin, Paul MacLean, and the Lost Origins of 'The Moral Sense.'" *World Futures: The Journal of General Evolution* 40, no. 4: 187–196.

_____. 1998. "Evolutionary Action Theory: A Brief Outline." In David Loye, ed., *The Evolutionary Outrider: The Impact of the Human Agent on Evolution.* Westport, Conn.: Praeger Books/Twickenham, England: Adamantine Press.

_____. 1999. "Can Science Help Construct a New Global Ethic? The Development and Implications of Moral Transformation Theory." *Zygon* 34, no. 2: 221–235.

_____. 1999. *Darwin's Lost Theory of Love.* New York: iUniverse <www.iuniverse.com>.

_____. 2000. *Making It In the Dream Factory: Creativity, Prediction, and Survival in Hollywood and the Global Marketplace.* Cresskill, N.J.: Hampton Press.

_____. Work in progress. *The Glacier and the Flame.*

Loye, David, ed. 1998. *The Evolutionary Outrider: The Impact of the Human Agent on Evolution.* Westport, Conn.: Praeger Books/Twickenham, England: Adamantine Press.

Loye, David, and Riane Eisler. 1987. "Chaos and Transformation: Implications of Non-equilibrium Theory for Social Science and Society." *Behavioral Science* 32: 53–65.

Loye, David, Rod Gorney, and Gary Steele. 1977. "Effects of Television: An Experimental Field Study." *Journal of Communication* 27, no. 3: 206–216.

Maccoby, Eleanor, and Carol Nagy Jacklin. 1974. *The Psychology of Sex Differences.* Stanford, Calif.: Stanford University Press.

MacLean, Paul D. 1990. *The Triune Brain in Evolution: Role in Paleocerebral Functions.* New York: Plenum Press.

_____. 1996. "Women: A More Balanced Brain?" *Zygon* 31, no. 3 (September).

Mander, Jerry, and Edwin Goldwmith, eds. 1996. *The Case Against the Global Economy and for a Turn Toward the Local.* San Francisco: Sierra Club Books.

Mankiller, Wilma, and Michael Wallis. 1993. *Mankiller: A Chief and Her People.* New York: St. Martin's Press.

Mannix, Sheila A., and Mark T. Harris. 1997. "Raising Cain: Original Psychic Injury and the Healing of Humanity." Unpublished manuscript.

Mantsios, Gregory. 1994. "Class in America: Myths and Realities." *Teaching Sociology* 22, no. 1 (January).

Margulis, Lynn. 1981. *Symbiosis in Cell Evolution: Life and Its Environment on the Early Earth.* San Francisco: W. H. Freeman.

_____. 1987. "Early Life." In William Irwin Thompson, ed., *Gaia.* Hudson, N.Y.: Lindesfarne Press.

Markale, Jean. 1986. *Women of the Celts.* Rochester, Vt.: Inner Traditions International.

Marshack, Alexander. 1991. *The Roots of Civilization.* Mt. Kisko, N.Y.: Moyer Bell, Ltd.

Martin, Jane. 1992. *Schoolhome: Rethinking Schools for Changing Families.* Cambridge, Mass.: Harvard University Press.

Martinez, Elizabeth, ed. 1991. *500 Años del Pueblo Chicano/500 Years of Chicano History and Pictures.* Albuquerque, N.M.: South West Organizing Project.

Maslow, Abraham. 1968. *Toward a Psychology of Being.* Princeton, N.J.: Van Nostrand.

Masson, Jeffrey Moussaieff, and Susan McCarthy. 1995. *When Elephants Weep: The Emotional Lives of Animals.* New York: Delacorte Press.

Math Across Cultures. 1995. San Francisco: Exploratorium Teacher Activity Series.

Maturana, Humberto, and Francisco Varela. 1990. Preface to Riane Eisler, *El Caliz y la Espada.* Santiago, Chile.

_____. 1992. *The Tree of Knowledge: The Biological Roots of Human Understanding.* Boston: Shambhala.

Maturana, Humberto R., and Gerda Verden-Zöller. 1998. *Origins of Humanness in the Biology of Love.* Durham, N.C.: Duke University Press.

Maxwell, Elizabeth. 1992. "Self as Phoenix: A Comparison of Assagioli's and Dabrowski's Developmental Theories." *Advanced Development* 4 (January).

McClelland. 1975. *Power: The Inner Experience.* New York: Irvington.

Meadows, Daniela. 1992. *Beyond the Limits.* Post Mills, Vt.: Chelsea Green Publishing.

Mellaart, James. 1975. *Catal Huyuk.* New York: McGraw-Hill.

Miller, Alice. 1998. "Childhood Trauma." Lecture at the Lexington YWHA in New York City (October 22).

Miller, Ron. 1990. *What Are Schools For?* Brandon, Vt.: Holistic Education Press.

Montagu, Ashley. 1976. *The Nature of Human Aggression.* New York: Oxford University Press.

_____. 1986. *Touching*, 3rd ed. New York: Harper & Row.

Montessori, Maria. [1912] 1964. *The Montessori Method*. New York: Schocken Books.

_____. [1946] 1989. *Education for a New World*. Oxford, England: Clio Press.

_____. 1948. *To Educate the Human Potential*. Adyar, Madras, India: Kalakshetra Publications.

Montuori, Mario. 1988. *Socrates: An Approach*. Amsterdam, Holland: J. C. Gieben Publishers.

Montuori, Alfonso, and Isabella Conti. 1993. *From Power to Partnership: Creating the Future of Love, Work, and Community*. San Francisco: Harper Collins, 1993. Now available through the Internet publisher ToExcel at <www.iuniverse.com>.

Morgan, Gareth. 1996. *Images of Organizations*. Newbury Park, Calif.: Sage.

Morgan, Lewis Henry. 1977. *Ancient Society*. New York: H. Holt and Company.

Morgan Gibson, Arrell. 1980. *The American Indian: Prehistory to the Present*. Lexington, Mass.: D. C. Heath.

Morrison, Toni. 1987. *Beloved*. New York: Knopf.

Multiculturalism in Mathematics, Science, and Technology. 1993. Menlo Park, Calif.: Addison-Wesley.

Myers, Gene. 1998. *Children & Animals*. Boulder, Colo.: Westview Press, 1998.

Naisbitt, John, and Particia Aburdene. 1986. *Reinventing the Corporation*. New York: Warner Books.

Nash, Gary. 1970. *Red, White and Black: The Peoples of Early America*. New York: Prentice-Hall.

Nash, June. 1978. "The Aztecs and the Ideology of Male Dominance." *Signs* 4 (Winter).

Nead, Lynda. 1992. *The Female Nude*. London: Routledge.

Nelson, D. G. Joseph, and J. Williams. 1993. *Multicultural Mathematics: Teaching Mathematics from a Global Perspective*. New York: Oxford University Press.

New Columbia Encyclopedia. 1975. New York: Columbia University Press.

Noble, David. 1992. *A World Without Women: The Christian Clerical Culture of Western Science*. New York: Knopf.

Noddings, Nel. 1992. *The Challenge to Care in Schools*. New York: Teachers College Press, Columbia University.

_____. 1995. "A Morally Defensible Mission for Schools in the 21st Century." *Phi Delta Kappan* (January): 366.

Northrup, Christiane. 1994. *Women's Bodies, Women's Wisdom*. New York: Bantam.

Orenstein, Gloria Feman. 1990. *The Reflowering of the Goddess*. New York: Pergamon Press.

_____. 1993. *Multicultural Celebrations: The Paintings of Betty LaDuke*. San Francisco: Pomegranate Artworks.

Orenstein, Peggy. 1994. *School Girls: Young Women, Self-Esteem and the Confidence Gap*. New York: Doubleday.

Ornstein, Robert. 1991. *The Evolution of Consciousness*. Englewood Cliffs, N.J.: Prentice-Hall.

Pagels, Elaine. 1979. *The Gnostic Gospels*. New York: Random House.

Peradotto, John, and J. P. Sullivan, eds. 1984. *Women in the Ancient World*. Albany: State University of New York Press.

Perl, Terri. 1978. *MathEquals*. Menlo Park, Calif.: Addison-Wesley.

Perlingieri, Ilya Sandra. 1992. *Sofonisba Anguissola*. New York: Rizzoli.

Perry, B. D., R. A. Pollard, T. L. Blakley, W. L. Baker, and D. Vigilante. 1996. "Childhood Trauma, the Neurobiology of Adaptation, and 'Use Dependent' Development of the Brain: How 'States' Become 'Traits.'" *Infant Mental Health Journal* 16: 271–291.

Pert, Candace. 1993. "The Chemical Communicators: Candace Pert" (interview). In Bill Moyers, *Healing and the Mind*, pp. 177–193. New York: Doubleday.

Pestalozzi, Johann. [1781] 1976. *Leonard and Gertrude*. New York: Gordon Press Publishers.

Peterson, Spike, and Anne Sisson Runyan. 1993. *Global Gender Issues*. Boulder, Colo.: Westview Press.

Physician's Guide to Media Violence. 1997. Chicago: American Medical Association.

Pitts, Leonard. 1998. "Rebuilding Morality Will Take 'Titanic' Effort." *Miami Herald*, February 26.

Platon, Nikolas. 1966. *Crete*. Geneva: Nagel Publishers.

Ranelagh, John. 1981. *Ireland: An Illustrated History*. New York: Oxford University Press.

Ray, Paul H. 1996. *The Integral Culture Survey: A Study of the Emergence of Transformational Values in America*. Sausalito, Calif.: Institute of Noetic Sciences, Research Report 96-A.

Reinisch, June M., with Judy Beasley. 1990. *The Kinsey Institute New Report*. New York: St. Martin's Press.

Rethinking Columbus. 1991. Milwaukee: Rethinking Schools.

Rexroth, Kenneth, and Ikuko Atsumi, eds. 1977. *Women Poets of Japan*. New York: New Directions Books.

Rhys, Jean. 1996. *Wide Saragasso Sea*. New York: Popular Library.

Riddle, John M. 1997. *Eve's Herbs: A History of Contraception and Abortion in the West*. Cambridge, Mass.: Harvard University Press.

Robinson, John Mansley. 1968. *An Introduction to Early Greek Philosophy*. Boston: Houghton Mifflin.

Rockwell, Joan. 1974. *Fact in Fiction: The Use of Literature in the Systematic Study of Society*. London: Routledge & Kegan Paul.

Rohrlich-Leavitt, Ruby. 1977. "Women in Transition: Crete and Sumer." In Renate Bridenthal and Claudia Koonz, eds., *Becoming Visible*. Boston: Houghton Mifflin.

Rolleston, T. W. 1990. *Celtic Myths and Legends*. New York: Dover Publications.

Rosin, Hanna. 1999. "Critics Question Extreme Childrearing Method." *Washington Post*; reprinted in *Monterey County Herald*, March 1, p. A10.

Ross, Anne. 1986. *Druids, Gods, and Heroes from Celtic Mythology*. New York: Shocken Books.

Ruether, Rosemary Radford, ed. 1974. *Religion and Sexism: Images of Women in Jewish and Christian Traditions*. New York: Simon & Schuster.

Ruiz, Vicki. 1987. *Cannery Women: Cannery Lives*. Albuquerque: University of New Mexico Press.

Ruppel Shell, Ellen. 1991. "Flesh and Bone." *Discovery* (December): 37–42.

Rustow, Alexander. 1980. *Freedom and Domination*. Princeton, N.J.: Princeton University Press.

Sack, Fleur, with Anne Streeter. 1992. *Romance to Die For: The Startling Truth About Women, Sex, and AIDS*. Deerfield Beach, Fla.: Health Communications.

Sadker, Myra, and David Sadker. 1995. *Failing at Fairness: How Our Schools Cheat Girls*. New York: Touchstone Books.

Schlegel, Stuart A. 1998. *Wisdom from a Rainforest: The Spiritual Journey of an Anthropologist*. Athens: University of Georgia Press.

Schneir, Miriam. 1994. *Feminism in Our Time*. New York: Vintage.

Schniedewind, Nance, and Ellen Davidson. 1997. *Open Minds to Equality*. Needham Heights, Mass.: Allyn and Bacon.

Seligmann, Jeane, with Bruce Shenitz. 1995. "Testosterone Wimping Out?" *Newsweek*, July 3, p. 61.

Senge, Peter. 1990. *The Fifth Discipline: The Art and Practice of the Learning Organization*. New York: Doubleday.

Sewell, Marylin. 1991. *Cries of the Spirit*. Boston: Beacon Press.

Shepherd, Linda Jean. 1993. *Lifting the Veil: The Feminine Face of Science*. Boston: Shambhala.

Shiva, Vandana. 1988. *Staying Alive*. London: Zed Books.

Shor, Ira. 1992. *Empowering Education: Critical Teaching for Social Change*. Chicago: University of Chicago Press.

Silko, Leslie Marmon. 1977. *Ceremony*. New York: Viking Press.

Sklar, Holly. 1994. "Imagine a Country." *Teaching Sociology* 22, no. 1 (January).

———. 1995. *Chaos or Community: Seeking Solutions, Not Scapegoats, for Bad Economics*. Boston: South End Press.

Slavin, Robert E. 1988. "Cooperative Learning and Student Achievement." *Educational Leadership* 46, no. 2: 31–33.

———. 1989. "Research on Cooperative Learning: Consensus and Controversy." *Educational Leadership* 47, no. 4: 52–54.

Sleeter, Christine E. 1997. "Mathematics, Multicultural Education, and Professional Development." *Journal for Research in Mathematics Education* 28, no. 6.

Sleeter, Christine E., and Carl A. Grant. 1991. "Race, Class, Gender, and Disability in Current Textbooks." In Michael W. Apple and Linda K. Christian-Smith, eds., *The Politics of the Textbook*. New York: Routledge, Chapman & Hall.

Sleeter, Christine E., and Carl A. Grant, eds. 1994. *Making Choices for Multicultural Education*. Columbus, Ohio: Merrill.

Slocum, Sally. 1975. "Woman the Gatherer: Male Bias in Anthropology." In Reina Reciter, ed., *Toward an Anthropology of Women*. New York: Monthly Review Press.

Smedley, Agnes. 1973. *Daughter of the Earth*. New York: Feminist Press.

Smuts, Barbara. 1985. *Sex and Friendship in Baboons*. New York: Aldine.

Spender, Dale, ed. 1983. *Feminist Theorists*. New York: Pantheon.

Stager, Lawrence, and Samuel Wolff. 1984. "Child Sacrifice at Carthage—Religious Rite or Population Control?" *Biblical Archaeology Review* (January/February): 31–51.

State of the World's Women Report. 1985. United Nations.

Statistical Abstract of the United States. 1998. Chart 297, p. 187.

Stewart, Chuck. 1999. *Sexually Stigmatized Communities*. Thousand Oaks, Calif.: Sage.

Stone, Merlin. 1976. *When God Was a Woman*. New York: Harcourt Brace Jovanovich.

Strong, Michael. 1998. *The Habit of Thought*. Chapel Hill, N.C.: New View Publications.

Style, Emily. 1988. "Curriculum as Window and Mirror." *Listening for All Voices*. Summit, N.J.: Oak Knoll School.

Swimme, Brian. 1984. *The Universe Is a Green Dragon*. Santa Fe, N.M.: Bear & Company.

Swimme, Brian, and Thomas Berry. 1992. *The Universe Story*. San Francisco: Harper San Francisco.

Tangley, Laura. 1999. "Law of the Jungle: Altruism." *U.S. News & World Report*, February 15, pp. 53–54.

Tannen, Deborah. 1998. *The Argument Culture*. New York: Random House.

Tanner, Nancy. 1981. *On Becoming Human*. Cambridge, England: Cambridge University Press.

Tarnas, Richard. 1991. *The Passsion of the Western Mind*. New York: Harmony Books.

Teish, Louisa. 1985. *Jambalaya*. San Francisco: Harper & Row.

Thomas, David Hurst, Jay Miller, Richard White, Peter Nabokov, and Philip J. Deloria. 1993. *The Native Americans: An Illustrated History*. Atlanta: Turner Publishing.

Tianlong, Jiao. 1995. "Gender Relations in Prehistoric Chinese Society: Archeological Discoveries." In Min Jiayin, ed. *The Chalice and The Blade in Chinese Culture*. Beijing: China Social Sciences Publishing House.

Trist, Eric, and Fred Emery. 1973. *Toward a Social Ecology*. London/New York: Plenum Press.

Turnbull, Colin M. 1961. *The Forest People*. New York: Simon & Schuster.

United Nations. 1991. *The World's Women 1970–1990: Trends and Statistics*. New York: United Nations.

Vance-Watkins, Lequita, and Aratani Mariko, eds. and trans. *White Flash, Black Rain: Women of Japan Relive the Bomb*. 1995. Minneapolis: Milkweed Editions.

Vare, Ethlie Ann, and Greg Ptacek. 1988. *Mothers of Invention*. New York: William Morrow.

Vila, Richard, et al. 1992. *Restructuring for Caring and Effective Education*. Baltimore: Brooks Publishing.

Walker, Alice. 1992. *Possessing the Secret of Joy*. New York: Harcourt Brace Jovanovich.

Walker, Barbara. 1983. *The Women's Encyclopedia of Myths and Secrets*. San Francisco: Harper & Row.

Waring, Marylin. 1988. *If Women Counted*. San Francisco: Harper & Row.

Watson, Marilyn, Victor Battistich, and Daniel Solomon. 1998. "Enhancing Students' Social and Ethical Development in Schools: An Intervention Program and Its Effects." *International Journal of Educational Research* 2, no. 7: 571–586.

Weatherford, Jack. 1991. *Native Roots: How the Indians Enriched America*. New York: Fawcett Columbine.

Weber, Max. 1961. "The Social Psychology of the World's Religions." In Talcott Parsons et al., eds., *Theories of Society*. New York: Free Press.

Wertheim, Margaret. 1995. *Pythagoras' Trousers: God, Physics, and the Gender Wars*. New York: Times Books.

Westermarck, Edward. 1926. *A Short History of Marriage*. New York: Macmillan.

Wilbur, Ken. 1996. *A Brief History of Everything*. Boston: Shambhala.

Wolf, Naomi. 1991. *The Beauty Myth*. New York: W. Morrow.

"World Scientists Warning to Humanity." 1993. Statement published by the Union of Concerned Scientists, April.

Wright Edelman, Marian. 1996. *Guide My Feet: Prayers and Meditations on Loving and Working for Children*. New York: Harper Collins.

Young, Ella. 1927. *The Wondersmith and His Son*. New York: Longmans/Green and Co.

Zaslavsky, Claudia. 1982. *Tic-Tac-Toe and Other Three-in-a-Row Games, From Ancient Egypt to the Modern Computer*. New York: Crowell.

_____. 1994. "Bringing the World into the Math Class." In *Rethinking Our Classrooms*, a special issue of *Rethinking Schools*.

Zilhman, Adrienne. 1982. *The Human Evolution Coloring Book*, with illustrations by Carla Simmons, Wynn Kapit, Fran Milner, and Cyndie Clark-Huegel. New York: Barnes and Noble Books (a division of Harper & Row); new edition in progress.

_____. 1993. "Myths of Gender." *Nature* 364 (August 12): 585.

_____. 1996. "Looking Back in Anger." *Nature* 384 (November 7): 35–36.

_____. 1997. "The Paleolithic Glass Ceiling: Women in Human Evolution." In Lori D. Hager, ed., *Women in Human Evolution*. New York: Routledge.

_____. 1997. "Women's Bodies, Women's Lives: An Evolutionary Perspective." In Mary Ellen Morbeck, Alison Galloway, and Adrienne L. Zihlman, eds., *The Evolving Female: A Life-History Perspective*. Princeton, N.J.: Princeton University Press.

Zihlman, Adrienne L., and Nance Tanner. 1974. "Becoming Human: Putting Women in Evolution." Paper presented at the annual meeting of the American Anthropological Society, Mexico City.

Zinn, Howard. 1981. *A People's History of the United States*. New York: Harper & Row.

Index

353